Lonely Planet

Munich, Bavaria & the Black Forest

Bavaria
p94

Stuttgart & the
Black Forest
p209

Munich
p43

Salzburg
& Around
p178

Marc Di Duca, Kat Barber,
Anthony Ham, Kerry Walker

Meersburg (p253), Lake Constance

CONTENTS

Plan Your Trip

The Journey Begins Here 4

Munich, Bavaria & the Black Forest Map 6

Our Picks 8

Regions & Cities 16

Itineraries 18

When to Go 24

Get Prepared 26

The Food Scene 28

Oktoberfest 31

The Romantic Road 34

The Outdoors 36

The Guide

Munich 43
Find Your Way 44
Plan Your Days 46
The Altstadt 48
Schwabing 60
Maxvorstadt 65
Westend & Theresienwiese 72
Olympiapark & Around 76
Nymphenburg 82
Haidhausen, Lehel & Au 85
Places We Love to Stay 92

Bavaria 94
Find Your Way 96
Plan Your Time 98
Nuremberg 100
Beyond Nuremberg 109
Bamberg 112
Beyond Bamberg 116
Würzburg 118
The Romantic Road 122

Augsburg 134
Füssen 138
Garmisch-Partenkirchen 145
Beyond Garmisch-Partenkirchen 148
Berchtesgaden 152
Chiemsee 157
Regensburg 159
Beyond Regensburg 164
Passau 168
Bavarian Forest 172
Places We Love to Stay 176

Salzburg & Around 178
Find Your Way 180
Plan Your Time 181
Salzburg 182
Beyond Salzburg 201
Places We Love to Stay 207

Stuttgart & the Black Forest 209
Find Your Way 210
Plan Your Time 212
Stuttgart 214
Beyond Stuttgart 221
Freiburg 226
Beyond Freiburg 231
The Black Forest 234
Baden-Baden 241
Beyond Baden-Baden 245
Lake Constance 251
Ulm 258
Beyond Ulm 262
Places We Love to Stay 266

Bayreuth (p117), Bavaria

Christmas market, Munich (p58)

Toolkit

Arriving 270
Money 271
Getting Around 272
Travel by Train 273
Accommodation 274
Family Travel 275
Health & Safe Travel 276
LGBTIQ+ Travellers 277
Food, Drink & Nightlife ... 278
Responsible Travel 280
Accessible Travel 282
Nuts & Bolts 283
Language 284

Storybook

A History of Munich, Bavaria & the Black Forest in 15 Places 288

Ludwig II 292

Germany's Wild South ... 295

Brands & Inventions of Southern Germany 298

Germany's Beer Purity Law 300

Stand up paddling on the Eibsee (p147)

MUNICH, BAVARIA & THE BLACK FOREST
THE JOURNEY BEGINS HERE

For some it's hard to put their finger on why southern Germany, and Bavaria in particular, is unique in central Europe. But for me it's clear – it's that special blend of supermodern and well-established, an intermingling of thigh-slapping tradition with clear-headed modernity like nowhere else on earth. Munich (p43) is the place this juxtaposition of the 21st and all the other centuries comes most into focus. It's a city that keeps all its clichéd promises, with Lederhosen, 1L tankards of frothing lager and *Weisswurst* (traditional sausage) galore. But at dawn, when the dust has settled on the taverns and beer gardens, the locals head off to their high-tech jobs, designing the sustainable future the city so aspires to. And then there are the Alps, a place the denizens of Munich escape to for reassurance that a simpler, more wholesome life is still out there if need be. For me there's no better place in all Germany.

Marc Di Duca

@marcdiduca

Marc has been a travel guide author for two decades and has covered destinations as diverse as Siberia, Switzerland and Brazil for Lonely Planet. He wrote the Munich chapter.

My favourite experience is the view from the Olympiaturm (Olympic Tower) in Munich's Olympiapark, with all Munich and beyond at my feet. Even the Alps can be spotted in the distance when the southern Germany haze lifts.

WHO GOES WHERE

Our writers choose the places which, for them, define Munich, Bavaria and the Black Forest.

For me, Freiburg (p226) has all the best of Germany in one town. Sustainability, snowfields, breweries, half-timbered houses, historic canals, hilltop hikes, Christmas markets and, of course, a stunning old town dominated by a soaring steeple. And with the enchanting Black Forest just a short drive away, it's the perfect base to explore a little further.

Kat Barber

*@katbarber_*

Kat is an Australian writer who spent three years learning German and collecting Glühwein mugs from Christmas markets around the country. Kat wrote the Stuttgart & the Black Forest chapter.

There are many wonderful views in the vicinity of Füssen, from the castles to the Alps and Alpine lakes. But there is one view that I love above all others. Some 5km northeast of town, off route 17 (which connects Füssen with Steingaden), lies the small baroque church of St Coloman (p141). The view from the road between Route 17 and the church is extraordinary – of the church, the Alps, even a distant Neuschwanstein.

Anthony Ham

@anthonyhamwrite

Anthony has been visiting Germany since he was a child, speaks the language, and has travelled the world to research and write nearly 200 guidebooks for Lonely Planet. Anthony wrote the Bavaria chapter.

I fell for the Salzburg region when I first set foot on Austrian snow more than 20 years ago and I've been returning ever since as a Lonely Planet author. Salzburg (p182) gets me every time with its big hit of culture, baroque Altstadt and gripping mountain views, but it's the Alps beyond with their sky-high trails, castles, salt mines and ice caves that are the clincher.

Kerry Walker

@kerryawalker

Kerry has authored scores of Lonely Planet guides. She divides her time between the Alps and home in England. Kerry wrote the Salzburg & Around chapter.

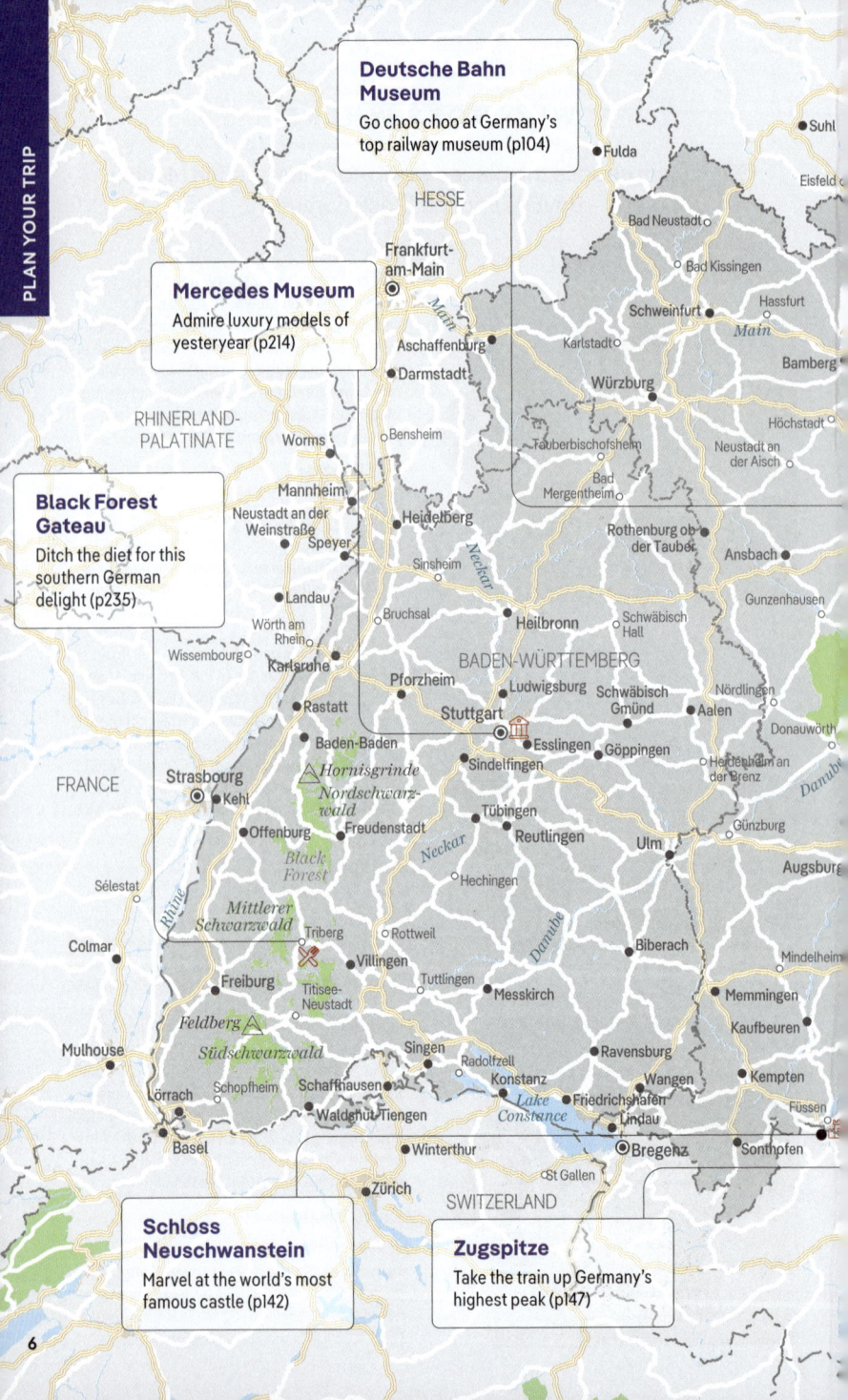

FOR THE LOVE OF LAGER

Those pesky Czechs and Belgians might disagree, but Bavaria really does brew some of the best beer in the world – and locals certainly know how to enjoy the froth better than most. The Free State specialises in beer gardens where you can select from myriad lagers, the vast majority complying with the strict *Reinheitsgebot* (beer purity law). And, of course, Munich puts on the biggest beer bash of them all, the unrivalled Oktoberfest attracting over six million disciples of the hop.

Hoppy Horticulture

In the summer months, southern Germans like to slurp their beer alfresco in pretty, chestnut-shaded gardens that seat thousands under strings of fairy lights.

Mine's a Mass

A half-litre glass simply won't do in these parts – lager-loving locals prefer a *Mass*, a 1L tankard they can bang down with gusto.

Not Just Oktoberfest

Oktoberfest may be the highlight of the drinker's calendar, but there are several other blockbuster beer festivals such as Straubing's Gäubodenfest and Munich's Starkbierzeit.

FROM LEFT: SANDRA ALKADO/GETTY IMAGES, R.CLASSEN/SHUTTERSTOCK, SHULERS/SHUTTERSTOCK

Hofbräuhaus (p49), Munich

BEST BEER EXPERIENCES

Wander ❶ **Forchheimer Kellerwald** (p109), a village in the woods of Franconia where every house is a pub, every yard a beer garden.

Experience the world's most iconic beer hall, the grand ❷ **Hofbräuhaus** (p49) in Munich, with its oompah band and swift-footed waiters.

Order a *Mass* or two at Munich's ❸ **Hirschgarten** (p84), the world's biggest beer garden that seats an incredible 8700 beer lovers.

Taste the unusual beer pulled in Bamberg's brewpubs and traditional taverns, the smokey ❹ **Rauchbier** (p113).

Join millions of drinkers for the planet's greatest celebration of lager, fun and all things Bavarian, the ❺ **Oktoberfest** (p31).

FORTRESS FEVER

If you like castles, you'll love southern Germany. The region is celebrated for producing the sort of fairy tale Schloss that a six-year-old might draw, and even Walt Disney took inspiration for his cartoon fortresses here. Some of the most incredible castles and palaces you'll find in central Europe were purpose built for one King Ludwig II, who transformed his romantic fantasies into real bricks and plaster. One of those is the castle of all castles, Neuschwanstein.

In Today's Money...

To put the amount spent by Ludwig II on Neuschwanstein into today's context, it would cost roughly €70 million to construct now.

Urban Residence

The Munich Residenz, home to the ruling Wittelsbach family for centuries and one of Munich's top attractions, is Germany's largest city centre palace complex.

Schlösser on the Web

Bavaria has an organisation that oversees many of its most important castles and palaces – the website *schloesser.bayern.de* is a mine of information on them all.

FROM LEFT: CANADASTOCK/SHUTTERSTOCK, POSZTOS/SHUTTERSTOCK, TILIALUCIDA/SHUTTERSTOCK - BUILDINGS SHOWN COURTESY OF THE BAVARIAN PALACE ADMINISTRATION, WWW.SCHLOESSER.BAYERN.DE

Schloss Nymphenburg (p82), Munich

BEST CASTLE & PALACE EXPERIENCES

Wonder at the magnificent opulence of Ludwig II's most celebrated Schloss, ❶ **Neuschwanstein** (p142), the world's most fairy tale of fairy tale castles.

Explore Ludwig II's ❷ **Schloss Herrenchiemsee** (p157), an ambitious pile modelled heavily on (and designed in part to outdo) Versailles.

Discover the ❸ **Munich Residenz** (p54), winter retreat for the Bavarian royals and now a major tourist draw slap bang in the Altstadt.

Climb up to medieval ❹ **Festung Hohensalzburg** (p184) high above the city of Salzburg for a tour of its unique interiors.

Take a tour of ❺ **Schloss Nymphenburg** (p82) and its grounds – for most, the best palace experience in Munich.

Eagle's Nest (p155), Berchtesgaden

LOOKING BACK AT WWII

There's no escaping the uncomfortable fact that Bavaria played a major role in the rise of the Nazis, and today dark tourism is big in the region. There are many disturbing locations across the Free State that tell the story of how Hitler rose to power, how WWII affected the region and how Nazi Germany fell in 1945.

Beerhall Putsch

One Nazi-related site you'll no longer find is the Bürgerbräukeller, scene of Hitler's beerhall putsch, demolished in 1979 to make way for a concert hall.

Memorium Nuremberg Trials

The Nuremberg Trials constituted the first ever international war crimes tribunal; you can still visit the **courtroom** where senior Nazi figures were tried. (p106)

BEST WWII HERITAGE EXPERIENCES

Head to Berchtesgaden to make the ascent to Hitler's WWII residence, often called the ❶ **Eagle's Nest** (p155).

Wonder at the sheer scale of Nuremberg's ❷ **Reichsparteitagsgelände** (p104) where the masses once were mesmerised by a ranting Führer.

Pay homage to a rare act of resistance in Nazi Germany at Munich's ❸ **Weisse Rose Memorial** (p63).

Wander the first concentration camp at ❹ **Dachau** (p90), which provided the blueprint for the horrors of the Final Solution.

Marvel at the postwar resurrection of ❺ **Würzburg** (p118), a city almost completely destroyed during a massive air raid in March 1945.

FRESH AIR FEST

Geography may have granted Germany a mere narrow strip of the northern Alps, but the Bavarians certainly know how to use it. Countless ski resorts scour the mountainsides and it would seem locals hike from babyhood. But if you are feeling lazy, simply take the train to the top of Germany's highest peak, the Zugspitze.

BEST OUTDOOR EXPERIENCES

Hike Garmisch-Partenkirchen's dramatic ❶ **Partnachklamm** to the **Königshaus am Schachen** (p145), the least-visited of Ludwig II's projects.

Deutsche Alpenverein

The **German Alpine Club** *(alpenverein.de)* has a lot of information on sporting activities in the Alps and operates some of the mountain huts.

Get Wet!

Southern Germany has its fair share of lakes, making all manner of watersports possible from Bodensee (Lake Constance) windsurfing to Stanberger See swimming.

Let the cable car whisk you up or hike to the top of Germany's tallest mountain, the ❷ **Zugspitze** (p147), where trip-defining, alpine panoramas await.

Grab a paddle and waterproof bag to float down the ❸ **Altmühl River** (p110) in a canoe, Bavaria's most relaxing DIY river trip.

Take the Königssee boat then hit trails of all levels in the ❹ **Berchtesgadener Land** (p154), Bavaria's most spectacular corner of the Alps.

Zugspitze panorama (p147)

Pull on boots for some gentle hiking in the soothing hills and low mountains of the ❺ **Bavarian Forest** (p172).

Deutsches Museum (p85), Munich

TEUTONIC TECH

Four of the world's most respected car brands – BMW, Porsche, Audi and Mercedes – hail from southern Germany and locals are rightly proud of their engineering and technological prowess. Away from the autobahn, Bavaria is a land of railways – Germany's first line ran between Fürth and Nuremberg. Various museums have the lowdown on it all.

Made in Bavaria

Some of the world's most famous brands originated in Bavaria – from Adidas to Levis, BMW to Playmobil, Puma to Stihl.

Climate-Neutral Capital

Munich has ambitious plans to become climate neutral by 2035 and is part of the European Commission's initiative, '100 EU climate-neutral and smart cities'.

BEST SCIENTIFIC & TECH EXPERIENCES

Get behind the wheel of the latest SUVs and admire Beemers of yesteryear at ❶ **BMW Welt** (p80) and the **BMW Museum** (p81) in Munich.

Build up a head of steam at the ❷ **Deutsche Bahn Museum** (p104) in central Nuremberg, one end of Germany's first rail line.

Get a taste for one of the world's most iconic car brands at the ❸ **Mercedes-Benz Museum** (p214) in Stuttgart.

Examine all aspects of the technical world at Munich's excellent ❹ **Deutsches Museum** (p85), also a superb place to take the kids.

Take a break on the Romantic Road to visit the ❺ **Bayerisches Eisenbahnmuseum** (p131) in Nördlingen, a repository of local railway history.

THE BEST WURST

It ain't all about the *Wurst* (sausage) here in Germany's south – the region's cooks plate up much that isn't just about mopping up the beer. Traditional Alpine and sub-Alpine dishes make use of flavour-packed local ingredients, and seasonality is big here with locals going nuts for spring asparagus and autumn apple strudel. But those sausages are nice, though…

BEST FOODIE EXPERIENCES

Breakfast on ❶ **Weisswurst** (p53), a pretzel and a mug of wheat beer, the most traditional of ways to start the day in the capital of Bavaria.

Pop the cork on a bottle of wine, produced using grapes that ripen on the slopes around ❷ **Würzburg** (p121), in a traditional tavern or at a wine festival.

Bavarian Stars

It may come as a surprise to learn that Bavaria can boast 81 Michelin-starred restaurants, 16 of which have two twinklers and a trio even sporting three!

Meat-Free Munich

Munich has become easier to navigate over the years for vegetarians and vegans. Even beer halls and gardens now have a few options on their menus.

Try to pronounce *Schwarzwälder Kirschtorte*, though most waiters will understand this local waist-expander by its English name – ❸ **Black Forest gateau** (p235).

Munch on Franconia's most bizarre Wurst, the 30cm-long ❹ **Coburger sausage** (p117), roasted over pine cones before being inserted into a miniature bun.

Spargelzeit

'Asparagus time' runs from April to June and sees restaurants add this ingredient to their menus, and stalls sprout across Bavaria selling the stuff.

Experience a winter vibe in summer by ordering a ❺ **Rothenburg Schneeball** (snowball; p127), Bavaria's most unusual sweet treat.

REGIONS & CITIES

Find the places that tick all your boxes.

Bavaria

ALPS, CASTLES AND CRAZY KINGS

From the high Alps to the plains around Munich, the cool Bavarian forest to the dark tourism of Nuremberg, Bavaria is an intriguingly action-packed prospect for any traveller. It's also a place that seamlessly combines new and old, oompah with high speed, Lederhosen with e-tech.

Stuttgart & the Black Forest
p209

Stuttgart & the Black Forest

FORESTS, LAKES, SPAS AND AUTOMOBILES

Less well-known than bigger, brasher Bavaria, the state next door is Baden-Württemberg, a place that has given the world much. Black Forest gateau, Mercedes and the cuckoo clock are just some of the instantly recognisable symbols of this castle-dotted landscape with affluent Stuttgart at its heart.

PLAN YOUR TRIP REGIONS & CITIES

Bavaria
p94

Munich
◉ p43

Salzburg & Around
◉ p178

Salzburg & Around

BAROQUE BRILLIANCE AND ALPINE HIGHS

An easy hop from southern Bavaria, the Austrian city of Salzburg has a strong and distinctive brand and always manages to deliver on its clichéd promises. Mozart and Maria, Alpine vistas and Altstadt quaintness, baroque and beer – experience it all in one of the Alps' most engaging cities.

Munich

CITY OF ART AND BEER

Munich is Germany's secret capital as well as the actual capital of Bavaria, and everything that goes with it. Explore the city's many art galleries before heading out into the almost Mediterranean air to kick back with some of the world's best beer in a typical *Biergarten*.

ITINERARIES

The Alps

Allow: 9 days   **Distance**: 300km

The Alps are a definite highlight of Bavaria and almost every visitor should make at least one trip to Europe's premier range. This itinerary includes the best stop-offs and features everything from lakes in the foothills to a train ride to the top of the highest peak.

① STARNBERGER SEE ⏱ 1 DAY

A popular weekend getaway for the nine-to-five folk of Munich, Lake Starnberg (p158) is a sublime body of water that Bavaria's royalty also took a fancy to. But the lake hides a dark secret – it was here that Ludwig II and his doctor were found dead in the water. A sombre cross rises from the water at the spot his body was found.

② OBERAMMERGAU ⏱ 1 DAY

The quintessential Alpine foothill village of Oberammergau (p148) is known for two things: the folksy murals that adorn many of the buildings, and its passion play, a once-a-decade spectacular with a cast of thousands. You can also hike from here to Linderhof, a delightful palace built by Ludwig II against the backdrop of the snowcapped Alps. After that, take a sip of a monkish liquor at nearby Ettal Monastery.

③ GARMISCH-PARTENKIRCHEN ⏱ 2 DAYS

Top billing in the Germany Alps must go to the double-barrelled winter sports resort of Garmisch-Partenkirchen (p145), a short drive or bus ride from Oberammergau. Here you can take the train to the top of Germany's highest peak, the Zugspitze, or set off on a gentle hike along the Partnachklamm Gorge and on into the Alps. Otherwise Ga-Pa is an upmarket ski resort.

④
FÜSSEN & NEUSCHWANSTEIN
⏱ 2 DAYS

The high Alps stand between Ga-Pa and Füssen (p133), but somehow the road manages to burrow its way through. The town itself has some light attractions, but the main reason people come here is to visit Schloss Neuschwanstein, a fairy-tale castle and the brainchild of King Ludwig II. There's also a couple of worthwhile museums and skiing in the area.

⑤
CHIEMSEE ⏱ 1 DAY

It's a good two-hour drive along the foot of the Alps east to Chiemsee (p157), Bavaria's biggest lake. Though many come here to cool down in the sweltering summer of the plains, another Ludwig II castle is the tourist magnet here for most of the rest of the year. Herrenchiemsee on an island in the lake outdoes even Versailles in some vital stats and is a sight to behold.

⑥
BERCHTESGADEN
⏱ 2 DAYS

Another lake beckons – the Königssee near the town of Berchtesgaden (p152). Take an e-boat along this exquisite Alpine to eat trout straight from the depths, or hike in the mountains. There are also popular dark tourism sights including Hitler's Eagle's Nest, now a restaurant.

Detour: *Obtain an Austrian motorway sticker and pop over the border into Austria to enjoy one or two days in Salzburg with its Mozart and* The Sound of Music *connections.*
⏱ 30 minutes

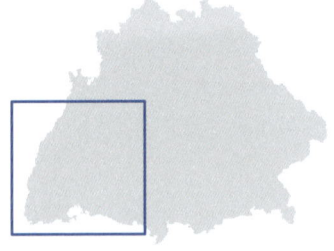

Schlossplatz (p217), Stuttgart

ITINERARIES

Stuttgart & the Black Forest

Allow: 8 days   **Distance**: 420km

This itinerary takes you from the big-city lights of affluent Stuttgart through the Black Forest to the shores of Lake Constance (Bodensee). En route you can take the waters in Baden-Baden, take the cake in Triberg, and take it easy with the students of Freiburg in front of the medieval minster.

❶ STUTTGART ⏱ 2 DAYS

Begin with a couple of days exploring the galleries, stately plazas and vibrant nightlife of the regional capital Stuttgart (p214). High on your agenda should be the city's regal heart, Schlossplatz, the Staatsgalerie's art treasures and evenings spent sampling local Rieslings in a *Weinstube* (wine tavern) or hanging out in Theodor-Heuss-Strasse's lounge bars. Car fans should race to the space-age Mercedes-Benz and Porsche museums.

❷ BADEN-BADEN ⏱ 2 DAYS

A member of Europe's premier league of spa towns, UNESCO-listed Baden-Baden (p241) is a fashionable Art Nouveau spa town picturesquely nestled at the foot of the Black Forest's spruce-cloaked hills. Here you can wallow in thermal waters, saunter through the sculpture-speckled Lichtentaler Allee gardens and try your luck in the casino before heading into the Schwarzwald proper.

❸ TRIBERG ⏱ 1 DAY

Next stop takes you to the Black Forest's most enjoyable and experience-packed town of Triberg (p238). Here, Germany's highest waterfall flows, the world's biggest cuckoo clock calls, and Claus Schäfer bakes the best Black Forest gateau using the original 1915 recipe. Work off all that whipped cream with a walk or cross-country ski in the wooded heights of Martinskapelle or Stöcklewaldturm.

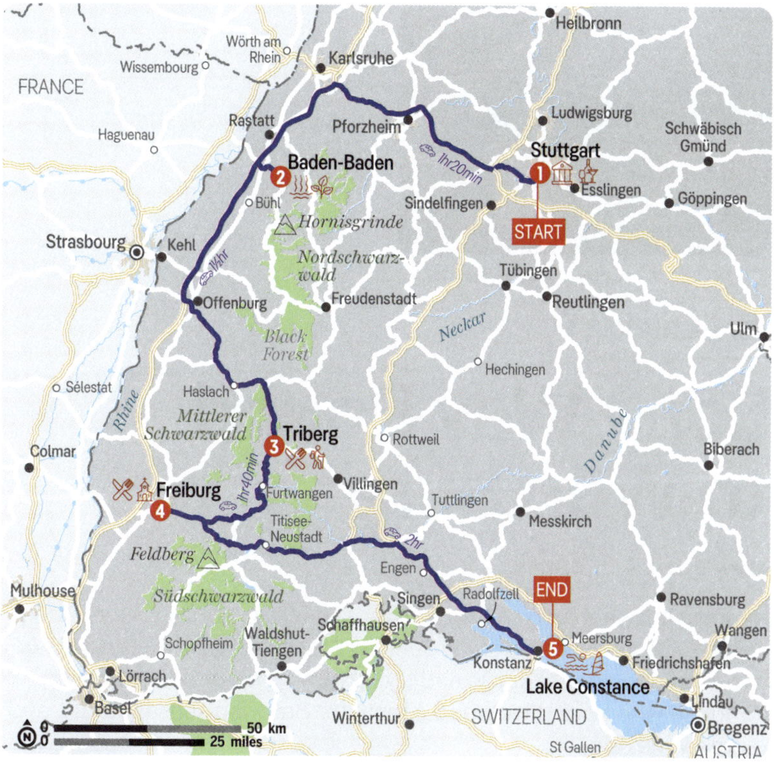

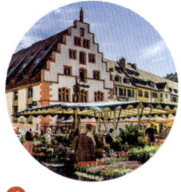

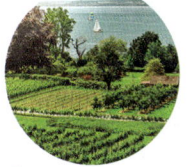

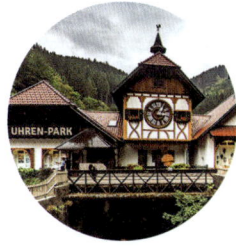

Triberg (p238)

4

FREIBURG ⏱1 DAY

From Triberg it's an easy drive to the sunny and easy-going university city of Freiburg (p226) close to the French border. You can spend the day here absorbing its relaxed flair in the Altstadt's quaint lanes, watched over by a monster of a cathedral, and wander its canals before heading to a tavern to munch on local, French-influenced dishes.

5

LAKE CONSTANCE ⏱2 DAYS

Though shared with Switzerland and Austria, Lake Constance (p251) is Germany's biggest body of water and is known locally as Bodensee. Flanked by quaint villages, vineyards, wetlands and beaches, it's a holiday paradise and major watersports hot spot. The interestingly located Konstanz only just makes it into Germany and is divided into two by a wide channel. It's a great place to hang out at the end of this eclectic itinerary.

FROM LEFT: FOOTTOO/SHUTTERSTOCK, BILDAGENTUR ZOONAR GMBH/SHUTTERSTOCK, FRANCESCO BONINO/SHUTTERSTOCK

Coburger bratwurst (p117)

ITINERARIES

Long Way Round to Würzburg

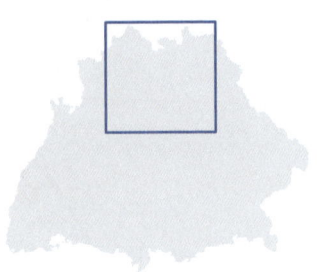

Allow: 8 days   **Distance**: 340km

Running between two of Bavaria's most interesting cities, Nuremberg and Würzburg, this itinerary is definitely for those who like a castle or two, a bit of classical music and trying new types of beer, and also for those who have developed a taste for Bavarian sausages. Oh, and there's wine, too.

❶ NUREMBERG ⏱ 3 DAYS

As far as history goes, Nuremberg (p100) has it all, from the nation's top railway museum to a medieval castle, the Nuremberg trials courtroom to Gothic churches. And when you're done, there's shopping galore, some of the best beer on the planet, and those sausages... There's a danger you won't even get started on the rest of the itinerary, but more delights await.

❷ BAMBERG ⏱ 1 DAY

Some 60km north of Nuremberg, Bamberg (p112) is an architectural highlight where aimless wandering around its old cobbled streets and churches brings the best results. En route, dip into some of the town's taverns where they serve and often even brew the famous Bamberg Rauchbier, a smokey lager like great-great-grandfather used to make, often accompanied by some hefty platters of filling fare.

❸ COBURG ⏱ 1 DAY

If the name Saxe-Coburg means nothing to you, this is the original surname of the British royals (they changed it during WWI) which entered Buckingham Palace via Prince Albert, a native of little Coburg (p116). Tour the palace where Queen Victoria stayed, then head to the main square for one of Bavaria's longest sausages. The whole thing can be tackled in a day between Nuremberg and your next stop, Bayreuth.

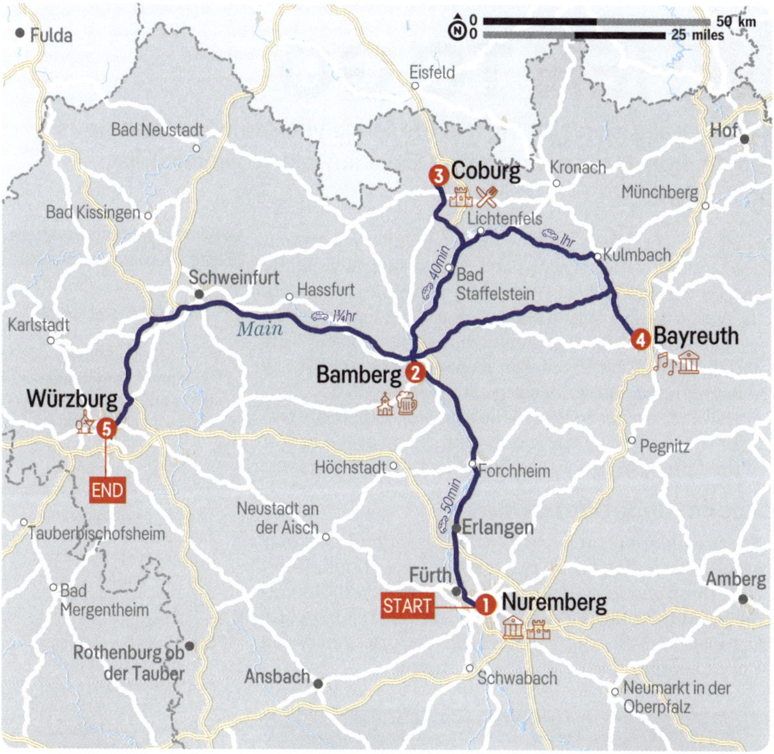

④
BAYREUTH ⏱ 1 DAY

High-brow culture is certainly the name of the game in Bayreuth (p117), 70km to the northwest of Coburg. The composer Richard Wagner pitched up in town in 1871 to build his Festspielhaus and to take up residence in Villa Wahnfried, now the Wagner Museum, behind which the composer is buried. Each August, the town celebrates its classical music associations with the world's top Wagner festival.

⑤
WÜRZBURG ⏱ 2 DAYS

End in Würzburg (p118), a slightly under-visited city which rose from the ashes of WWII in miraculous style. Explore its mix of sights before retiring to a tavern to sample the wine from the surrounding hills. Würzburg is also the start of another famous itinerary, the Romantic Road, Germany's top holiday route. So, if you like, you can just keep going...

Bamberg (p112)

FROM LEFT: ANNE CZICHOS/SHUTTERSTOCK, CANADASTOCK/SHUTTERSTOCK, PETER ADAMS/GETTY IMAGES

WHEN TO GO

There really is something to experience year-round in Germany's south, from lazy summers by a Bavarian lake to winter skiing in the Alps.

Southern Germany's big cities are very much year-round destinations, with November and early spring only slightly quieter times. The best seasons for travelling in most of the region are late spring and autumn when temperatures are pleasant, the days long enough to explore places fully and the crowds largely absent from major sights. We say 'most of the region' as, of course, the seasons differ enormously in Germany's sliver of the Alps where there are two peak times – during the snowy winter and at the height of the European summer holidays in July and August.

Accommodation Lowdown

Accommodation rates vary little throughout the year across the region, with two notable exceptions. Don't even think about trying to book anything in a 100km radius of Munich during Oktoberfest (late September/early October) and the Alps can become very pricey between December and April and again in summer.

⊕ I LIVE HERE

ALPINE SKIING

Sasha Kalinin is a computer programmer from Erding and a keen winter sports enthusiast.

Since I learned alpine skiing 20 years ago, I've visited countless resorts all over the Alps. But my favourite one remains the place where I took my first lesson – Reit im Winkl in Bavaria. Usually not as packed as others as it's not popular among ski tourists who prefer large areas with a massive choice of slopes, it is its cosiness and authenticity that draws me there again and again. For a change and a bit of cardio exercise, there are cross-country trails here, too.

SPRING RAYS

Some of the most pleasant days in southern Bavaria are when the first rays of sun warm the early spring air and you can enjoy your Aperol spritz outdoors for the first time. This usually happens sometime in March and puts a 'spring' in everyone's step.

Reit im Winkl

Weather through the Year: Munich

JANUARY	FEBRUARY	MARCH	APRIL	MAY	JUNE
Avg. daytime max: **3.5°C**	Avg. daytime max: **5°C**	Avg. daytime max: **9°C**	Avg. daytime max: **14°C**	Avg. daytime max: **19°C**	Avg. daytime max: **22°C**
Days of rainfall: **17**	Days of rainfall: **15**	Days of rainfall: **16**	Days of rainfall: **16**	Days of rainfall: **18**	Days of rainfall: **18**

FÖHN WIND

The Föhn is a Bavarian weather phenomenon whereby warm, humid air on the Italian side of the Alps rises, loses moisture and descends onto the Bavarian plains as a dry wind. In these conditions you can see the Alps clearly from Munich.

The Hills Are Alive...

Believe it or not, Europe's largest festival of Afro music, simply called **Africa Festival** (p121), is held in the Bavarian city of Würzburg. It's a wonderfully colourful spectacle attracting artists from all over the continent of Africa. **May**

Germany's oldest Mozart festival (p121), the **Mozart Fest** takes place at Würzburg's Residenz along with several other venues. The innovative programme is about much more than classical music performances. **June**

Bayreuth's **Wagner Festival** (p117) is the top event in the world celebrating this famous German composer. Buy tickets early as it's always a sell-out. **July**

The hot summer months sees the **Salzburger Festspiele** (p197) attract around 200,000 visitors, with Mozart pieces performed by the Vienna Philharmonic playing a huge part. **July and August**

Yuletide Yodelling

Generally regarded as Germany's best Christmas market, Nuremberg's **Christkindlesmarkt** (p100) is worth a special trip. It's mainly held on the central Hauptmarkt and the surrounding medieval streets. **December**

Second in Bavaria only to Nuremberg's Yuletide bash, Munich's **Christkindlmarkt** (p58) occupies the Marienplatz and radiating pedestrianised streets throughout Advent. Things can get very crowded over the weekends. **December**

On the Romantic Road it's Christmas every day! Rothenburg's **Christmas Village** (p127) and the **German Christmas Museum** (p128) mean you can enjoy the most wonderful time of the year, all year.
Year-round

Almost every town and city across Germany's south hosts some kind of Christmas market. Some run every day, others are open only over the four weekends of Advent.
December

⊛ I LIVE HERE

SUMMER LAKES

Maryna Ticha is an office manager from Landshut with a passion for exploring Bavaria's south.

Some years ago I decided to check out the favourite places of the painter Wassily Kandinsky – the nature around Murnau and Staffelsee. I understood why he liked it. Here you find beautiful green hills and meadows with an alpine panorama in the background. Add to this the meditative summer sunset and silence away from crowded towns – it's like a wellness experience on its own.

Sailing on the Staffelsee

WINTER SNOW

Snow is pretty much guaranteed in the Alps and the region's loftier parts such as the Bavarian Forest and Franconia. Even Munich often sees heavy snowfalls but in big cities the flakes soon melt away.

JULY	AUGUST	SEPTEMBER	OCTOBER	NOVEMBER	DECEMBER
Avg. daytime max: **24°C**	Avg. daytime max: **24°C**	Avg. daytime max: **19°C**	Avg. daytime max: **14°C**	Avg. daytime max: **8°C**	Avg. daytime max: **4°C**
Days of rainfall: **15**	Days of rainfall: **16**	Days of rainfall: **10**	Days of rainfall: **10**	Days of rainfall: **15**	Days of rainfall: **16**

A sunny day on the banks of the river Isar, Munich

GET PREPARED FOR MUNICH, BAVARIA & THE BLACK FOREST

Useful things to load in your bag, your ears and your brain.

Clothes

Winter gear Winters are bitterly cold with temperatures below zero so make sure you have a proper winter coat, sturdy boots, a scarf, hat and gloves. If you're heading to the Alps, warm clothes are a good idea year-round, especially if you're planning a trip to altitude.

Summer clothes Summers can be sweltering so the lighter your attire, the better. T-shirts, open shoes and shorts are the way to go. A cap to keep the sun off your head is also advised.

Shoes Trail shoes or trainers are suitable year-round for the footwork cities require. Proper hiking boots are needed for the Alps and possibly the Bavarian Forest.

Swimwear Southern Germany's lakes, rivers and water parks mean taking swimwear along is also a good idea.

Manners

Conversations about WWII should probably be avoided, especially with the older generation.

A degree of reserve is usually maintained towards strangers, and many foreigners wrongly take this as unfriendliness.

Confident greetings *(Grüss Gott/Auf Wiedersehen)* are expected and considered polite, as across central Europe.

Shaking hands is common among both men and women.

Sarcasm, irony and generally inappropriate humour will make you few friends.

READ

Against the Stream: Growing Up Where Hitler Used to Live (Anna Rosmus; 2002) Best-selling Third Reich novel set in Passau, the writer's birthplace.

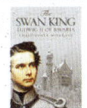

The Swan King: Ludwig II of Bavaria (Christopher McIntosh; 2019) A recent examination of the life and times of Bavaria's most famous monarch.

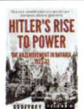

Hitler's Rise to Power: The Nazi Movement in Bavaria 1923–33 (Geoffrey Pridham; 2016) A fascinating look at how Hitler seized power from Bavaria.

The Hofbräuhaus Cookbook (various authors; 2007) The most typical of Bavarian recipes as well as the history of the Hofbräuhaus.

Words

Most Bavarians speak a dialect of German which bears only a passing resemblance to the language spoken elsewhere. However, the vast majority of people can switch between Bairisch (the Bavarian dialect) and Hochdeutsch (standard German) without much problem. Here we list phrases in Hochdeutsch.

Grüss Gott (grüs-got) 'Hello' in southern Germany.
Hallo (ha-lo) Also a common and less formal greeting.
Auf Wiederschauen (owf vee-der-shaw-en) The formal way of saying goodbye. You might hear other variants.
Tschüss (chüs) A common informal way of saying cheerio.
Bitte (bi-te) Means 'please' but can also be used to say 'you are welcome'.
Danke (schön) (dang-ke) Generally used to say thanks in all situations.
Wie geht es? (vee gayt es) A polite ice breaker that simply means 'how are you?'
Es geht mir gut (es gayt meer gut) The answer to the above for you is 'I'm fine', though locals have a tendency to give long and more honest answers.
Ich verstehe nicht (ikh fer-shtay-e nikht) A very useful phrase that means 'I don't understand'.
Prost! (prawst) Not saying cheers before taking your first gulp of beer or wine is deemed the height of bad manners.
Guten Apetit (goo-ten a-peh-teet) Also, as across central Europe, simply tucking into your food without a 'bon apetit' is not the done thing, nor is starting before everyone else without being given permission to do so.
Entschuldigung (ent-shul-di-gung) This long word means 'excuse me' as well as a way of attracting attention, just like in English.
Wie viel? (vee feel) How much? A useful phrase in these days.

WATCH

Sophie Scholl: The Final Days (Marc Rothemund; 2005) A moving cinematic experience telling the story of Sophie Scholl and the *Weisse Rose* resistance movement.

Willy Wonka & the Chocolate Factory (Mel Stuart; 1971; pictured above) This classic was shot entirely in Bavaria.

Die Fischerin vom Bodensee (Harald Reinl; 1956) A typical example of the Heimatfilm genre: a cheap, postwar picture packed with cosy clichés and set in the sticks.

Oktoberfest in Munich – The Wiesn Madness (WELT; 2019) Documentary providing an insight into the organisation of the world's biggest beer festival.

Munich (Steven Spielberg; 2005) Spielberg tells the dramatic story of the terrorist attack on the 1972 summer Olympics.

LISTEN

Lohengrin (Richard Wagner; 2005) This and many other of Wagner's works inspired Ludwig II to build his fairy tale castles.

Hoizhakka Pogo (Hundsbuam; 1996) This track and many others by Hundsbuam blend Bavarian folk music with punk and rock.

BR Heimat (br.de/radio/live/br-heimat) Online radio station from Bavarian Radio with nonstop Bavarian folk and brassband music.

Fichtl's Lied (Die Woodys; 1984) The most famous piece of 1980s Bavarian folk music on the internet. Locals hate it but it will live with you forever.

Michelin-starred dining

THE FOOD SCENE

Southern Germany has it all, from sausage kiosks to Michelin menus, meat loaf to meat-free, veal to vegan.

Sausages at dawn with tankards of cloudy wheat beer in Munich taverns, cricket-ball-sized dumplings with an avalanche of sauerkraut and roast pork in the Alps, Black Forest gateau slathered in chocolate, cream and cherries and plate-hiding schnitzel with a mountain of potato salad – hearty, calorific excess certainly still abounds in southern Germany. But while most menus revel in tradition, there are other options, especially in the cities. Munich can easily switch from pig-trotter-chomping rusticity to the chic flavours of Michelin-starred fine dining. Meanwhile menus in Nuremberg and Freiburg go beyond the obvious, with street food, vegetarian and vegan choices and an increasing appreciation for foreign cuisines.

Seeing it all on its way, Bavaria in particular is perhaps more famous for its beverages, be it Munich or Franconian beer or the wines of Würzburg. Naturally the beer in all its myriad forms takes centre stage for most, especially around Oktoberfest, one of the world's biggest celebrations of things you put in your belly.

Tradition vs Modernity

As with many aspects of life in southern Germany, food is also a blend of alpine and subalpine tradition, more modern trends and influences from beyond Germany. In Munich, omnivores can dine out on wedges of pork one evening, go Afghan the next and try a vegan feast another night. Vegetarians and vegans are well catered for in big cities such as Munich and Stuttgart but in middle-sized towns options may be more limited.

Bavaria has an incredible 81 Michelin-starred restaurants but you'll have to book months in advance to bag a table in any of them.

Best South German Dishes

WEISSWURST
Veal-and-pork-fat sausage served with mustard and a pretzel.

KÄSESPÄTZLE
Al dente southern German noodles baked with gooey cheese.

BLACK FOREST GATEAU
Baden-Württemberg's world-famous chocolate, cream and cherry concoction.

For the Sweet-Toothed

If you're the type of person who's already looking forward to dessert while still munching your starter, southern Germany is a belt-stretching nirvana. By far the most celebrated cake to emerge from the Black Forest is the gateau of the same name, a must-try when in the region. Another lesser-known speciality are the snowballs of Rothenburg, strips of dough rolled into a ball that are fried then dusted with cinnamon and/or sugar.

Bakeries across the south are stacked high with all kinds of pastries, and come autumn, the aroma of apple strudel wafts on the cooling air. *Semmelschmarrn* is bread-and-butter pudding flavoured with cinnamon and served with vanilla sauce, while *Prinzregententorte* is layered cake with a chocolate buttercream filling. Another treat you might find in some restaurants are sweet dumplings, often filled with fruit and swimming in runny vanilla sauce.

Schnell Food

Sausages on the run are the fast food of choice in Bavaria, available almost everywhere. They come in all shapes and sizes, from the 30cm Coburg whopper to the *Weisswurst* of Munich, the tiny bratwurst fingers of Nuremberg to the fat little *Regensburger Wurst*.

Another fast snack is *Leberkäse* which translates as 'liver cheese' but contains no liver and isn't cheese. This is simply Bavarian meatloaf and a thick wedge in a bun with mustard makes for a filling lunch on the go.

Bottles of wheat beer

DRINKS FESTIVALS

Southern Germany, and Bavaria in particular, has given the world some of its best beer and the list below reflects the fact that the region's drinks are far better known than its food.

Oktoberfest (p31) The beer festival of beer festivals and top date in the Bavarian event calendar.

Gäubodenfest (p166) Drinkers arrive by the hundreds of thousands to enjoy Straubing's frothy bash.

Cannstatter Wasen (p219) Stuttgart's answer to Oktoberfest that attracts 4.2 million people.

Wein am Stein (p121) Intimate wine and music festival organised by Würzburg's Weingut am Stein winery.

Hofgarten Wine Festival (p121) Würzburg's top wine event with tastings and finger food to go with the local whites.

Starkbierzeit (p74) Accidental inebriation is common during Munich's 'strong beer time'.

Herbstfest Erding (p74) Erding near Munich is known for its *Weissbier* (wheat beer), celebrated in the town's autumn fair.

Bratwurst stand, Nuremberg

OBATZDA	LEBERKÄSE	SCHWEINSHAXE	SCHWEINEBRATEN	KNÖDEL/KLÖSSE
A blend of camembert, cottage cheese, onion and spices.	Bavarian meatloaf served in a white bun with mustard.	Pork knuckle, marinated then slow roasted and often served with beer.	Bavarian pork roast braised with dark beer available in almost every tavern.	The humble dumpling plays a big part in Bavarian cooking.

Local Specialities

Linked in

Wurstsalat Chopped Regensburger sausage with pickles, onion and dressing.
Nürnberger Bratwurst The little links from Nuremberg are considered the region's finest.
Coburger Bratwurst The 30cm Coburg whopper is grilled over pine cone embers.
Saure Zipfel A Franconian speciality consisting of bratwurst cooked in vinegar.

To Go with a Beer

Breze A pretzel to you and me, often filled with cheese, butter and ham.
Bierrettich Monster radishes are made into a thin spiral with a special knife, then heavily salted.
Roast chicken A firm favourite to go with lager, especially at Oktoberfest.

Sweet Treats

Schneeballen (snowballs) The fried doughballs of Rothenburg dusted with vanilla sugar and cinnamon.
Strudel Normally apple-filled but you might also find cherries, nuts and other ingredients in there.
Dampfnudeln Huge steamed dumpling swimming in vanilla sauce.

Apple Strudel

Prinzregententorte Munich's Prince Regent gateau consists of multi-layered sponge cemented together with buttercream.

Best of the Rest

Kebab The region's large Turkish and Kurdish populations mean kebab here is as good as in Istanbul.
Pizza The Italian *Gastarbeiter* ('guest worker') influx of the 1960s has bequeathed the region's cities with some high-quality pizza-pasta restaurants.
Schnitzel Though strictly a Viennese speciality, thinly pounded, breadcrumbed pork, veal and chicken with a drizzle of freshly squeezed lemon is as good here as anywhere in central Europe.

MEALS OF A LIFETIME

Viktualienmarkt (p56) Put together a gourmet picnic at Munich's central market.
Alois – Dallmayr Fine Dining (p53) The Munich Altstadt's top Michelin dining experience.
Nigrum (p243) Baden-Baden's Michelin-listed restaurant with light, modern tasting menus.
Wirtshaus in der Au (p88) Long-established culinary tavern in Munich's Haidhausen where dumplings take centre stage.
Prinz Myshkin (p58) Still Munich's best vegetarian experience after all these years.
Tantris (p62) Highest quality dining and two Michelin stars to prove it.
Essigbraetlein (p103) Two Michelin stars light up plates at this top Nuremberg restaurant.
Zur Höll (p124) Medieval Rothenburg wine tavern on the Romantic Road.

THE YEAR IN FOOD

SPRING

This time of year across southern Germany sees the locals go cuckoo for asparagus during *Spargelzeit*. This can be bought at special stalls and rare is the restaurant not to offer it.

SUMMER

The hotter months are about alfresco chomping in the region's beer gardens, though summer offers little seasonality. For that you'll need an invite to a Bavarian kitchen table for fresh salads, cherries and mushrooms.

AUTUMN

Central Europeans go crazy for apple strudel in the late autumn. This is also the time for the first, strong new wines from the vineyards around Würzburg. Mushrooming is a major pastime while the weather is still warm.

WINTER

Traditionally in this part of the world winter was about eating the goodies you had preserved and pickled in the autumn. These days its time for retreating to cozy taverns for mulled wine and après-ski.

Marstall beer tent at the Oktoberfest

TRIP PLANNER

OKTOBERFEST

The world's largest drink-a-thon and the traditional highlight of Bavaria's annual events calendar, Oktoberfest is one of the best-known fairs on earth. No other event manages to mix such a level of crimson-faced humour, drunken debauchery and excessive consumption of beer with so much tradition, history...and oompah music.

A BIT OF HISTORY

The world's biggest beer festival has its origins in a simple horse race. In 1810 Bavarian crown prince Ludwig, later King Ludwig I, married Princess Therese of Saxe-Hildburghausen, and following the wedding a horse race was held at the city gates. The six-day celebration was such a galloping success that it became an annual event, and it was extended and moved forward to start in September so that visitors could enjoy warmer weather and lighter nights. The horse race, which quickly became a sideshow to the suds, ended in 1960, but an agricultural show is still part of the Oktoberfest, albeit a minor one.

MASS HYSTERIA

As early as mid-July the brewery crews move in to start erecting the tents which almost fill the **Theresienwiese** (p72), a gravelly open space in the western reaches of Munich city centre known locally as the Wiesn.

Starting at 10.45am on the first day, the brewer's parade – the *Festzug* – travels through the city centre from the River Isar to the fairgrounds. This involves many old, brightly decorated horse-drawn carriages once used to transport kegs from brewery to pub and countless felt-hatted tagalongs. When the procession reaches the Wiesn, focus switches to the Schottenhamel beer tent and the mayor of Munich who, on the

VITAL OKTOBERFEST STATS

Where At the Theresienwiese, to the west of the city centre. Poccistrasse and Theresienwiese are the nearest U-Bahn stations.

When For 16 days up to the first (occasionally second) Sunday in October. 2026: 19 September to 4 October; 2027: 18 September to 3 October; 2028: 16 September to 3 October.

Opening hours Beer is served from 10am to 10.30pm Monday to Friday, 9am to 10.30pm Saturday and Sunday. Other attractions and facilities open longer.

Cost Admission is free.

Price of a 1L Mass of beer Around €15.

Numbers Around six million visitors.

Amount of beer consumed Between six and seven million litres.

Beer tents 35.

stroke of noon, takes a mallet and knocks the tap into the first keg. As the beer flows forth and the thirsty crowds cheer, the mayor exclaims: *'Ozapft ist's!'* (literally 'It's tapped' in Bavarian dialect). If you want to witness this ceremonial opening of the Oktoberfest, be sure to get there as early as 9am to bag a seat.

THE BEER

All the lager pulled at Oktoberfest must have been brewed within Munich's city limits, which restricts the number of breweries permitted to wet your whistle to six: Hofbräu-München (of Hofbräuhaus fame), the world-famous Paulaner, Löwenbräu, Augustiner and the lesser-known Hacker-Pschorr and Spatenbräu.

The famous *Mass* (towering 1L mugs of beer) brought to your table by a Dirndl-trussed waitress contains pretty strong stuff as the breweries cook up special concoctions for the occasion (usually known as Oktoberfestbier). The percentage of alcohol starts at around 5.8% which makes a single Mass the equivalent of almost 3.5 pints of most regular ales in Britain, Australia and the US. Traditionally the most potent brews are piped to the Wiesn by Hofbräu, the weakest by Hacker-Pschorr.

MORE THAN BEER

Oktoberfest is not called the world's biggest fair for nothing, and while the focus of most visitors is on the *Bier*, there's also a lot going on away from the tents. The funfair with its big wheel, ye-olde test-your-strength booths and scarier 21st-century rides are obvious attractions, but magic performances, an agricultural show (more interesting than it sounds) and stalls selling everything from Oktoberfest souvenirs to

Beer serving at the Oktoberfest

TOP TIPS

- No cash changes hands within the beer tents – buy special metal tokens *(Biermarken)* from outside the tents.
- Food at Oktoberfest is as pricey as the beer, so bring your own snacks.
- Beer tents are elbow to elbow all day Saturday and Sunday. For lighter traffic try a weekday afternoon.
- Don't even think of lighting up in any of the beer tents.
- Don't drink excessively – Oktoberfest beer is strong stuff.
- Most beer tents have last call at 10.30pm.
- You can reserve a seat at some of the tents up to a year in advance.
- The Wiesn has a left-luggage office.

waffles constitute other minor diversions. The first Sunday sees an impressive costumed procession wend its way through Munich city centre, a tradition going back to 1835, and the customary religious Oktoberfest mass is held in the Hippodrom beer tent on the first Thursday. A brass band concert huffs and puffs beneath the Bavaria statue on the morning of the second Sunday near the spot from where the gun salute is fired on the last Sunday. These events are mostly attended by locals, but give a more traditional insight into the origins and customs of this blockbuster fair for those with a deeper, less inebriated interest.

FUN OF THE FAIR

During the 16 days of festivities, most travellers dip in for a few days, taking time off from the *Mass* to see Munich's sights and perhaps a castle or two.

Part of the fun at the Wiesn is looking the part: traditional Bavarian Dirndl for the gals, Lederhosen and felt hat for the guys. Dirndl consists of a figure-squeezing bodice, a frilly blouse, a skirt that ends just below the knee and an apron. The real deal costs a fortune but Munich has countless discount *Trachten* (folk costume) shops, some which pop up specially for Oktoberfest, where vastly cheaper versions can be bought or even hired.

The two Tuesdays (to 7pm) are dedicated family days with reduced charges for rides, special family oriented events, and lots of balloons and roasted almonds. Away from these days, the Augustiner Festhalle is regarded as the most family-friendly beer tent, but children are allowed into all the others. Children can stay in the tents after 8pm but must be accompanied by an adult. To find out more about Oktoberfest, log on to *oktoberfest.de*, the definitive Oktoberfest website containing a wealth of facts, figures and maps.

> ### SLEEPING IT OFF
>
> Your chances of scoring a room in Munich once the mayor has driven the tap into the famous first keg are next to nil, and even a bed in the dingiest of dorms will come with an absurd price tag. However, with Munich's excellent transport links to the rest of Bavaria, and the proximity of the Hauptbahnhof to the Theresienwiese, commuting in from Augsburg, Garmisch-Partenkirchen or Ingolstadt, or even Salzburg and Nuremberg, is feasible. This secret got out long ago, though, and accommodation providers across Bavaria hitch up their rates from mid-September, but not as much as in Munich. If possible, book accommodation just as the previous Oktoberfest is finishing. If you decide to stay out of town, make sure you know when the last train back is, or you'll be spending an uncomfortable night at the Hauptbahnhof!
>
> Camping is a fun and relatively inexpensive way to get around the accommodation shortage. **Wies'n Camp** *(munich-oktoberfest.com)* sets up shop every year at the Olympic Equestrian Centre in München-Riem, a 20-minute S-Bahn ride from the Hauptbahnhof.

Dancing in traditional clothes at the Oktoberfest

Rothenburg ob der Tauber (p124)

TRIP PLANNER

THE ROMANTIC ROAD

Germany's oldest tourist route has been attracting romance-seekers since 1950 when someone had the bright idea to link the string of incredibly well-preserved towns on the border between Bavaria and Baden-Württemberg into a single itinerary. Here we give you the lowdown on how to get the most out of the trip.

DOING THE RR

With 29 official stops stretched out along 460km, there are many ways of 'doing' the Romantic Road (RR), or Romantische Strasse in German. If you spend just a day in each place, it would take you a month to complete the route, time most don't have. While tiny Lauda-Königshofen and Hohenfurch are pretty nice places, most stick to the big hitters of Würzburg, Rothenburg ob der Tauber, Dinkelsbühl, Nördlingen, Augsburg and the Wittelsbach castles near Füssen. Even this itinerary takes around 10 days so schedule accordingly. However, that isn't to say you should skip all the small places. Towns such as Tauberbischofsheim, Weikersheim and Donauwörth attract only a smattering of RR pilgrims and can be a relief from the 21st-century tourist excesses of the larger stops.

SLEEPING ON THE ROAD

With so many visitors heading up and down the RR, hotels and guesthouses line the route and you should have no problem bagging a room along its length outside the busier summer months. Accommodation hot spots include Rothenburg and Füssen; the latter of which is the only place where you'll need to book well in advance even in the shoulder seasons.

WHEN TO GO

The RR is great at any time of year but some months are better than others. The height of summer can see some places such as Rothenburg and Neuschwanstein overwhelmed with huge tour groups who pack out the cobbles in the heat. Go in late spring or September for a less crushed experience.

A truly magical time to be in places like Nördlingen and Dinkelsbühl is in mid-winter when the snow falls illuminated by the street lamps onto deserted cobbles and you can retreat to a cosy tavern for something warming. The quietest times are February and November.

There are now few bargains along the RR, but for those on a tight budget there are still youth hostels and campsites, the latter all summer-only affairs. Short-term rentals in some of the RR's historical hot spots provide memorable nights on the road. Several of the better hotels are some of the most characterful places to sleep in southern Germany, though they now come with a hefty room rate.

FOLLOWING THE ROUTE

Ever greater numbers of visitors are using hire cars to tackle the RR. While there is no one single prescribed route, brown tourist signs by the road bearing the words 'Romantische Strasse' indicate you are on the right path. Parking is easy in some places (Nördlingen, Dinkelsbühl), tricky in others (Augsburg, Hohenschwangau), so do a little research. Combinations of bus and train are the only other option (see p122).

Rothenburg snowball (p127)

BEST OF THE BEST ON THE RR

You might want to plan your trip around some of the best places and experiences on the Romantische Strasse.

- **Best single town** The highlight of the Romantic Road for most visitors is Rothenburg ob der Tauber, a town that keeps all its quaint, medieval promises.
- **Best castle** Harburg Castle is a definite highlight, but few could ever compete with Ludwig II's Neuschwanstein at the southern end of the route.
- **Best place to sleep** If we have to name just one place, it would be the Dinkelsbühler Kunst-Stuben where the well-travelled owners really know how to look after their guests.
- **Best place to eat** Ausburg's August has two Michelin stars that illuminate the Romantic Road.
- **Best for medieval history** A toss up between Nördlingen with its intact ring of town walls and Rothenburg with its varied attractions from the Middle Ages.
- **Best non-medieval attraction** Nördlingen's Rieskrater Museum takes a fascinating look at the meteorite that hit the region millions of years ago.
- **Best quirky attraction** Rothenburg's obsession with all things Yuletide manifests itself at the German Christmas Museum and the adjacent Käthe Wohlfahrt Weihnachtsdorf.
- **Best snack** The a snowball, a ball of fried dough dusted with icing sugar and cinnamon.

Eibsee and view of the Zugspitze (p147)

THE OUTDOORS

Southern Germany's mountains, lakes, forests and hills provide ideal conditions for those who like to pull on boots, skis or a cycling helmet.

With its narrow strip of the Alps, countless lakes, thousands of square kilometres of forested hills and kayakable rivers, Bavaria and Baden-Württemberg are two states you'll want to explore with a raised heart rate. But you won't be alone out there – Bavarians are hikers almost from birth, few have never stood on skis and cycling is a leisure activity as well as a serious mode of transport. This means infrastructure such as ski slopes, cycle paths and other facilities are world class.

Hiking & Mountaineering

Whether you want to bag peaks in the high Alps, amble among fragrant spruce and pine or embark on multiday treks through forested hills, this region is superb for exploring on foot.

Trails are usually well signposted, though there's no one unified trail-marking system such as you'll find over the border in Czechia. Most appear on maps, map apps and various websites, but it's worth checking to see if a trail has been hiked recently.

The sky-scraping peaks of the Bavarian Alps are Germany's mountaineering heartland. Here you can pick between day treks and multiday hut-to-hut scrambles, though you'll need to be reasonably fit and equipped with the right gear and topographic maps or GPS. Trails can be steep and narrow, with icy patches lingering well into early summer. Before heading out, seek local advice on routes, equipment and weather. The very informative Deutscher Alpenverein has local branches in practically every town.

Trail, Surf & Snow

RUNNING
The **Munich Marathon** (p83) is Bavaria's top road-running event but there are hundreds more across southern Germany every year.

KAYAKING
Bavaria's top **kayaking trip** (p111) is the relaxing paddle along the Altmühltal.

SPAS
UNESCO-listed **Baden-Baden** (p245) is one of Europe's most illustrious spa towns, with numerous outdoor activities to complement spa procedures.

FAMILY ADVENTURES

Introduce toddlers to hiking
The 2km of boardwalk around the **Triberger Wasserfälle** (p238).

No hills are involved on the short but dramatic hike through the **Partnachklamm** (p275) near Garmisch-Partenkirchen.

An undemanding 6km walking trail called the **Wasserfallsteig** (p225) heads from the spa town of Bad Urach to a wonderful waterfall.

Load the kiddies onto the train for a leg-saving ascent of Germany's highest peak, the **Zugspitze** (p147).

Take your kids to the pools and watery attractions at **Badeparadies Schwarzwald** (p237).

Thrash the locals at cricket or baseball (but maybe not football!) on the lawns of Munich's **English Garden** (p64).

Have a summer snowball fight on the easy(ish) hike to the **Eiskapelle** (p152) ice cave above the Königssee.

Baden-Württemberg also gets in on the hiking act – the Belchensteig has been voted Germany's most attractive hike and there are scores of undemanding walks in the Black Forest to enjoy.

Cycling

Mountain biking is huge in the Black Forest and in the Alpine region, especially around Garmisch-Partenkirchen, Berchtesgaden and Freudenstadt. The Bavarian Forest is another top destination for mountain bikers with more than 450km of challenging routes and climbs. But you'll also find more easy-going rides radiating from every single town in the south, some frequented by early morning commuters. Munich has several high-speed routes linking the suburbs with the city centre.

Southern Germany is criss-crossed by dozens of long-distance trails, making it ideal for *Radwandern* (bike touring). Routes are well signposted and typically are a combination of lightly travelled back roads, forestry tracks and paved highways with dedicated bike lanes.

Skiing

An hour's drive south of Munich, the German Alps offer the best downhill slopes and most reliable snow in the region. The most famous resort is Garmisch-Partenkirchen, a snowball's throw from Germany's highest peak, the 2962m Zugspitze. The resort has 60km of slopes to carve, mostly geared towards intermediates.

For lower-key skiing there's Jenner near Berchtesgaden, with vertical drops up to 600m, and the distracting vistas of the Königssee. The Bavarian Forest and the Black Forest are almost guaranteed snowfalls and there are modest slopes on the Grosser Arber and Feldberg mountains, respectively.

The ski season runs from December to March or April. Every resort worth its salt has a full gear-hire service and ski school.

> **ACTION AREAS**
> For the best outdoor locations, see p38

Skiing, Garmisch-Partenkirchen (p145)

CROSS-COUNTRY SKIING
Tens of kilometres of **cross-country skiing trails** (p237) are prepared each winter in the Bavarian Forest and the Black Forest.

TRAIL RUNNING
The **Zugspitz Ultratrail** (p146) is one of Germany's top trail running events, but if you can't get an entry, the Alps region is one of the world's top places to train.

NEW MOUNTAIN SPORTS
Anyone can try out new, innovative mountain sports at the Garmisch-Partenkirchen's **Alpentestival** (p146).

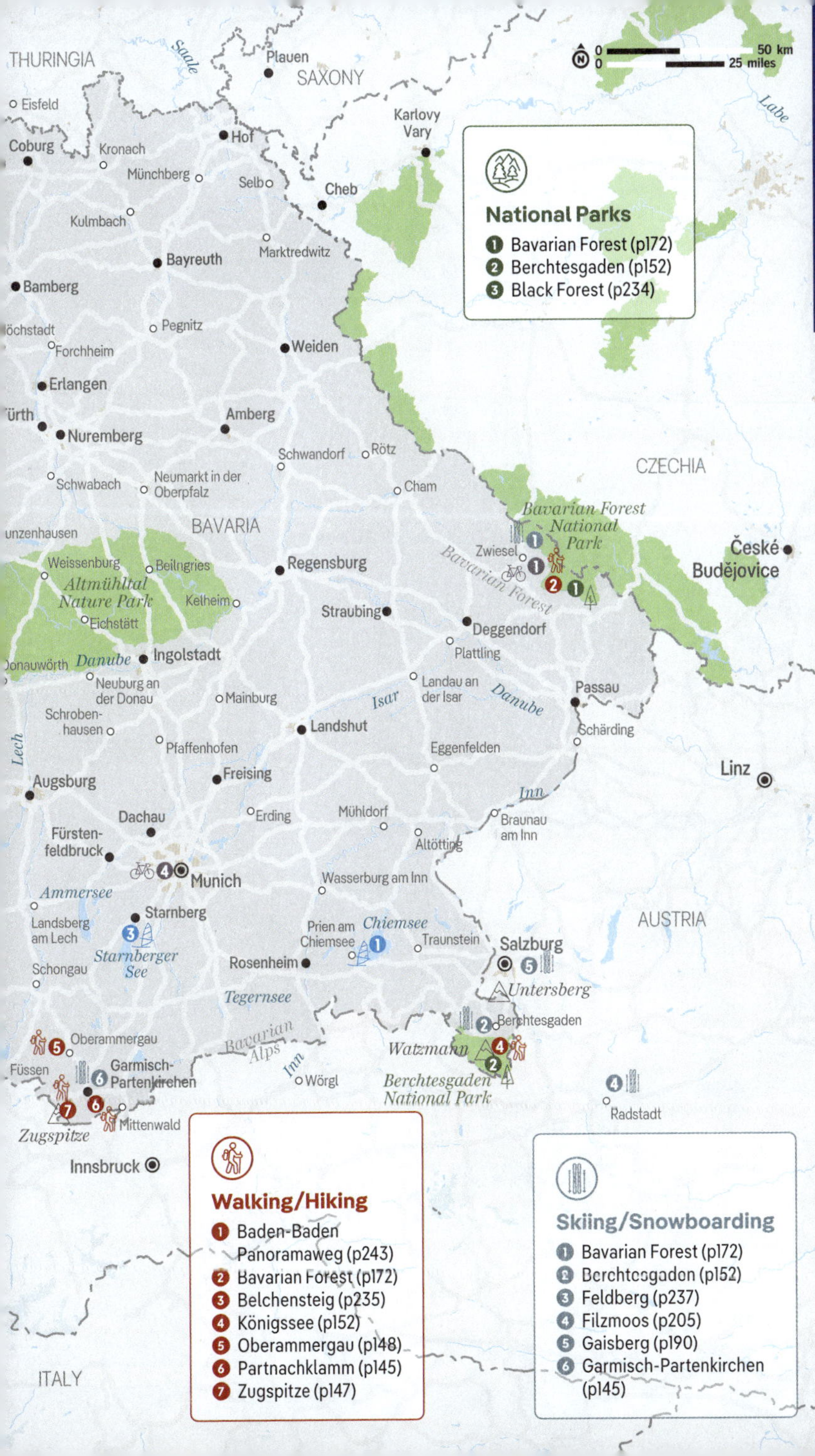

National Parks
1 Bavarian Forest (p172)
2 Berchtesgaden (p152)
3 Black Forest (p234)
Walking/Hiking
1 Baden-Baden Panoramaweg (p243)
2 Bavarian Forest (p172)
3 Belchensteig (p235)
4 Königssee (p152)
5 Oberammergau (p148)
6 Partnachklamm (p145)
7 Zugspitze (p147)
Skiing/Snowboarding
1 Bavarian Forest (p172)
2 Berchtesgaden (p152)
3 Feldberg (p237)
4 Filzmoos (p205)
5 Gaisberg (p190)
6 Garmisch-Partenkirchen (p145)
50 km
25 miles
THURINGIA
SAXONY
BAVARIA
CZECHIA
AUSTRIA
ITALY
Plauen
Eisfeld
Coburg
Kronach
Hof
Münchberg
Selb
Cheb
Karlovy Vary
Kulmbach
Marktredwitz
Bayreuth
Bamberg
Pegnitz
Forchheim
Weiden
Erlangen
Amberg
Nuremberg
Schwandorf
Rötz
Cham
Schwabach
Neumarkt in der Oberpfalz
Weissenburg
Beilngries
Altmühltal Nature Park
Kelheim
Eichstätt
Regensburg
Straubing
Deggendorf
Plattling
Zwiesel
Bavarian Forest National Park
Bavarian Forest
České Budějovice
Ingolstadt
Neuburg an der Donau
Mainburg
Schrobenhausen
Pfaffenhofen
Landshut
Landau an der Isar
Passau
Schärding
Eggenfelden
Linz
Augsburg
Freising
Erding
Mühldorf
Braunau am Inn
Altötting
Dachau
Fürstenfeldbruck
Munich
Ammersee
Starnberg
Landsberg am Lech
Starnberger See
Wasserburg am Inn
Prien am Chiemsee
Chiemsee
Traunstein
Salzburg
Untersberg
Schongau
Rosenheim
Tegernsee
Berchtesgaden
Watzmann
Berchtesgaden National Park
Oberammergau
Füssen
Garmisch-Partenkirchen
Mittenwald
Zugspitze
Bavarian Alps
Wörgl
Radstadt
Innsbruck
Saale
Labe
Danube
Isar
Inn
Lech

MUNICH, BAVARIA & THE BLACK FOREST

THE GUIDE

Bavaria
p94

Stuttgart & the
Black Forest
p209

◉ Munich
p43

Salzburg
& Around
p178
◉

Chapters in this section are organised by hubs and their surrounding areas. We see the hub as your base in the destination, where you'll find unique experiences, local insights, insider tips and expert recommendations. It's also your gateway to the surrounding area, where you'll see what and how much you can do from there.

Marienplatz (p48), Munich
MATTHIAS SCHRÖDER/UNSPLASH

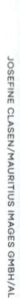

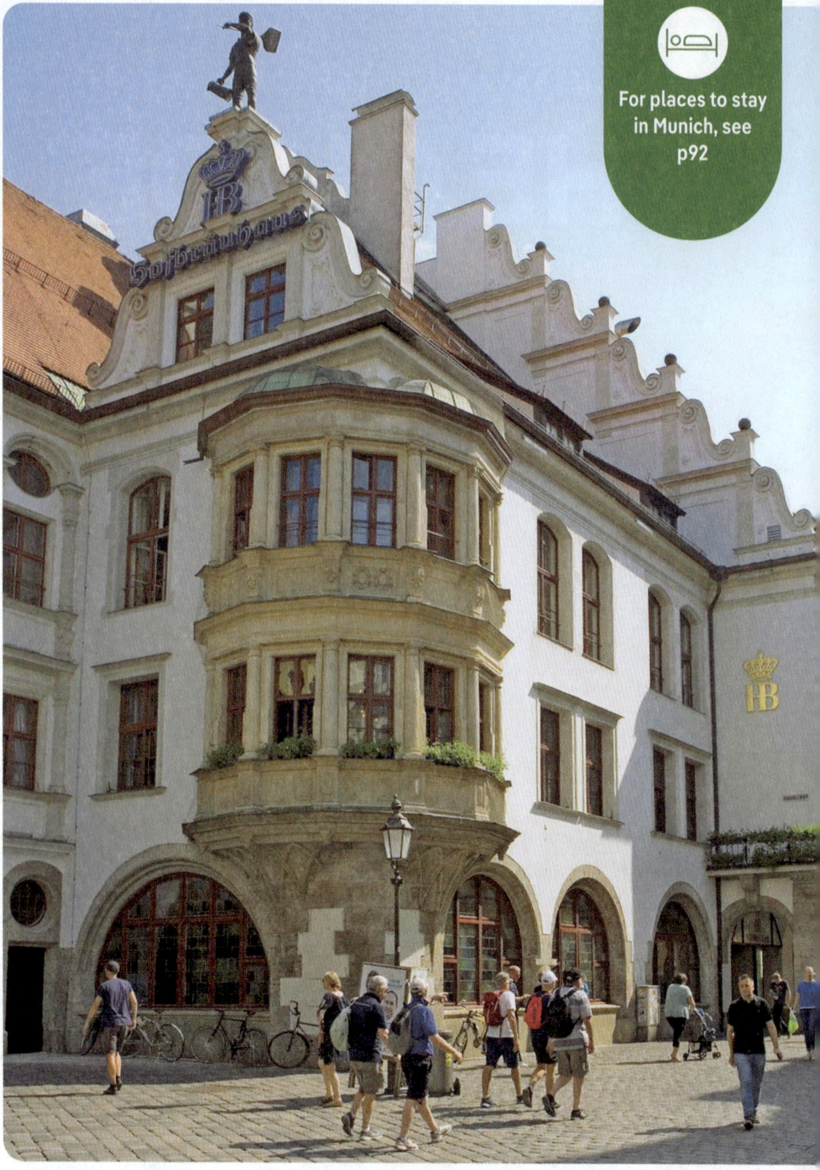

JOSEFINE CLASEN/MAURITIUS IMAGES GMBH/ALAMY

For places to stay in Munich, see p92

Above: Hofbräuhaus (p49); Right: Lenbachhaus (p71)

THE MAIN AREAS

THE ALTSTADT
Munich's medieval core. **p48**

SCHWABING
Relaxed, hip and studenty neighbourhood. **p60**

MAXVORSTADT
The city's arty epicentre. **p65**

WESTEND & THERESIENWIESE
Venue for the famous Oktoberfest. **p72**

Researched by
Marc Di Duca

Munich

CITY OF ART AND BEER

One of the world's most visitable cities, the Bavarian capital has everything from medieval to multicultural, from the Olympics to Oktoberfest.

Munich isn't called Germany's secret capital for nothing. Nowhere else in the Bundesrepublik will you find such a lively blend of past and present, in a city that manages to combine Mediterranean flair with Alpine flavours, traditional oompah culture with the freakishly modern, and horrible history with eco-tech.

Munich (München) is a place where the echoes of the past are loud, where history hollers through the streets of the Altstadt. This is the city that witnessed the Wittelsbachs' pomp, young Sisi's childhood, Hitler's jackboots and the economic miracle of the post-WWII years. Its colourful past is scrutinised in almost 50 museums, not bad for a city of just over one million. Some are big-hitting unmissables like the Residenz, others niche and obscure.

And Munich's nickname isn't the 'City of Art and Beer' for nothing, either. Suffer an art attack at the world-class museums in the Kunstareal, an entire quarter of the city centre given over to galleries and museums. There are also plenty more throughout the city. Then there is the beer, celebrated nightly in countless beer gardens and beer halls including the world's most famous, the Hofbräuhaus. It's so good, the annual Oktoberfest attracts over six million drinkers, and there are other beer festivals, such as the Starkbierzeit, that draw many an elbow-bender to the Bavarian metropolis.

Apart from sipping lager or admiring oils, there is also world-beating sport on offer in Munich. The legacy left behind by the 1972 Games comes in the form of the Olympiapark, as well as a lot of the other infrastructure built in the early 1970s. As every football fan knows, this is also home to Bayern Munich, one of the world's best-known teams.

And as across Western Europe, Munich has become a diverse city, with Turks and Afghans shopping around the Hauptbahnhof, Italian pizza places harking back to the 1960s influx of *Gastarbeiter* (foreign workers), one of Germany's biggest LGBTIQ+ scenes and tourists from across the world milling around the Marienplatz. So come and join the party in one of the most stimulating and engaging cities the world of travel has to offer.

OLYMPIAPARK & AROUND
Olympic heritage and the world of BMW. **p76**

NYMPHENBURG
Munich's finest palace and biggest beer garden. **p82**

HAIDHAUSEN, LEHEL & AU
Neighbourhoods of history, art and architecture. **p85**

Find Your Way

Munich's efficient public-transport system is composed of buses, trams, the U-Bahn and the S-Bahn. It's operated by MVV *(mvv-muenchen.de)*, which operates information offices in the U-Bahn stations at Marienplatz, the Hauptbahnhof and the Ostbahnhof. Tickets can be bought on your phone via the MVV app or at stations from machines.

Dachau Concentrat. Camp (13km)

Olympiapark
Olympiasee

Olympiapark & Around
p7

Schloss Nymphenburg

Schlosspark

Nymphenburg
p82

S-BAHN
Munich's S-Bahn lines typically start out in the sticks, head into the city, rumble along the Stammstrecke between the Hauptbahnhof and the Ostbahnhof then head out back into rural Bavaria on the opposite side. Trains run regularly almost round the clock.

FROM THE AIRPORT
Flughafen München, officially Franz-Josef-Strauss Airport, is located around 30km to the northeast of the city centre. The quickest way to reach the centre is to take the S1 or S8 S-Bahn, which take around 40 minutes to the Hauptbahnhof. An Uber costs around €60-70.

TRAM & BUS
Trams link the centre with the suburbs and are a good way of getting around the centre itself. Buses take over from the end of the S-Bahn and U-Bahn lines but only bus 100 is of any use to tourists.

U-BAHN
The underground railway, the U-Bahn, serves the centre and the inner suburbs. There are eight lines in total and the main interchanges are at the Hauptbahnhof and the Sendlinger Tor. Most visitors will find themselves on the U-Bahn when heading to Olympiapark and the BMW complex.

Plan Your Days

Here we bring you a whirlwind 72-hour itinerary around the Bavarian capital, though seeing the main attractions in three days will leave you gasping for subalpine air.

Chinese Tower, English Garden (p64)

Day 1

Morning
● Start on the **Marienplatz** (p48), one of Germany's most celebrated piazzas. From here it's a short walk to the former royal palace, the **Residenz** (p54).

Afternoon
● After lunch, head along the pedestrianised Kaufingerstrasse to the **Frauenkirche** (p53), Munich's most instantly recognisable landmark. Nearby is **Michaelskirche** (p53), where members of the Bavarian royal family have been laid to rest. Back near Marienplatz, explore **St Peterskirche** (p52) and the **Asamkirche** (p52) to complete the set.

Evening
● In summer, evenings at the **English Garden** (p64) are magic, especially if you can bag a seat in the beer garden at **Chinesischer Turm** (p63).

You'll Also Want to...
After you've seen the big hitters, there are weeks' worth of other attractions to enjoy and experiences to have in Munich.

HAVE A WEISSWURST BREAKFAST
The classic Munich breakfast is a pair of plump *Weisswurst* (literally 'white sausage') with a pretzel, sweet mustard and a tall glass of wheat beer. It's only served until noon, mind.

STOCK UP AT THE VIKTUALIENMARKT
Everyone gravitates to the kiosks, stalls and cafes of the **Viktualienmarkt** (p57) at some point: a market and gourmet (and not so gourmet) foodie experience right in the city centre.

DISCOVER THE DEUTSCHES MUSEUM
Germany's admirable tradition of making things that work is celebrated at this island-based **science museum** (p85). The exhibition is huge and comprehensive.

Day 2

Morning
- After last night's beer, it's time for some art and when you're in search of it, the **Kunstareal** (p68) in Maxvorstadt is the place to go. Realistically a morning is only time enough to see one of the galleries here.

Afternoon
- Refuelled, it's time to stretch your legs at the **Olympiapark** (p77). Explore the venues built for the 1972 Summer Games before taking the superfast lift to the top of the **Olympiaturm** (p78). If time, also call in next door at **BMW Welt** (p80).

Evening
- A night on the lager and pork knuckle at the **Hofbräuhaus** (p49) is a quintessentially Munich experience.

Day 3

Morning
- Straight after breakfast, hop aboard tram 17 to **Schloss Nymphenburg** (p82), one of Bavaria's top palaces and the erstwhile summer residence of the royal Wittelsbach family. Explore the grounds before retreating to the **Schlosscafé im Palmenhaus** (p84) for lunch.

Afternoon
- It's time to hit the cool neighbourhood of Schwabing with its cafes, boutiques and student vibe, perhaps stopping off for a drink at the famous **Alter Simpl** (p63) pub.

Evening
- End your Munich adventure with some heavily loaded platters at the wonderfully atmospheric beer hall **Augustiner Bräustuben** (p74)...and a tankard or two of the city's finest lager. *Prost!*

DRINK AT THE HIRSCHGARTEN

Trust Munich to have the planet's biggest beer garden! The **Hirschgarten** (p84) near Schloss Nymphenburg can accommodate almost 9000 beer fans and the food service is on an industrial scale.

VISIT THE DACHAU CONCENTRATION CAMP

The darkest side of Munich's past can be explored at **Dachau** (p90), the first concentration camp to be built by the Nazis. The surviving structures from the time house a detailed exhibition.

TAKE A DIP AT MÜLLER'SCHES VOLKSBAD

One of the world's most attractive public baths, the Art Nouveau **Müller'sches Volksbad** (p88) in Haidhausen is Munich's most celebrated place to swim. So don't forget to pack your swimwear.

HEAD TO BMW WELT & THE BMW MUSEUM

BMW has its headquarters north of the city centre, where you'll also find the free **BMW Welt** (p80) company showcase and the excellent **BMW Museum** (p81).

The Altstadt

MUNICH'S MEDIEVAL CORE

GETTING AROUND

The streets of the Altstadt are largely pedestrianised so the best way to get around is to walk. The Stammstrecke (the stretch of tracks where almost all of Munich's S-Bahn lines converge and run through the city centre) passes underneath the Altstadt and the main stations are Isartor in the east, central Marienplatz and Karlsplatz/Stachus in the west. There are also U-Bahn stations at Marienplatz and Karlsplatz/Stachus.

☑ TOP TIP

The city's classiest shopping street is **Maximilianstrasse**, a 1km-long ribbon of style where well-heeled shoppers browse. Kaufingerstrasse, running west from Marienplatz, is a more down-to-earth experience. Southeast of the Altstadt, the Gärtnerplatzviertel and Glockenbachviertel's streets teem with local designer boutiques.

Roughly defined by the inner ring road, the Altstadt (Old Town) is more often than not the first slice of Munich most foreign visitors digest. This is where the city began, with Munich and Bavaria's cultural and historical bull's-eye gathered around the energetic Marienplatz, Munich's premier piazza.

North of the Marienplatz a huge chunk of the Altstadt is occupied by the Residenz, the sprawling palace complex that once belonged to Bavaria's erstwhile rulers, the Wittelsbachs. A tour is a must when in town.

In addition to the Altstadt's historical attractions, this is where you can enjoy a smorgasbord of mainstream, luxury and boutique/vintage retail. It's also a neighbourhood of high-brow cultural entertainment, partaken in the company of Bavaria's well-to-do. And when you are done with all the above, just bag a seat at the colourful and fragrant Viktualienmarkt for a gourmet picnic or just a sausage and *Weissbier* stomach-filler.

Meet Munich on the Marienplatz
Munich's most celebrated piazza

The Altstadt's bustling heart and soul, **Marienplatz** heaves from dawn till dusk and beyond with throngs of tourists, revellers and locals. This is where many a tour guide meets their clients and where Munich folk like to rendezvous. It's hemmed with cafes and shops, and there always seems to be something happening here, from Advent markets to political rallies.

Save for the 1638 Mariensäule (St Mary's Column) and the 1950s Fischbrunnen (Fish Fountain) on the eastern side, the inventory of the square is limited. The real interest is in what surrounds it. Completely dominating the northern side of the square, the soot-blackened facade of the neo-Gothic **Neues Rathaus** *(muenchen.travel; tower adult/child €7/3)* is festooned with gargoyles and other statuary. To pinpoint Munich's landmarks without losing your breath, catch the lift up the 85m-tall

Marienplatz

tower. Unfortunately the 'New Town Hall' is the next major building in Munich set for renovation, which could last years.

The Neues Rathaus is an obviously 19th-century creation, so what about its predecessor? You'll find the inconspicuous **Altes Rathaus** on the square's southeastern side – it's a post-WWII rebuild of a 1460 building that now houses a toy museum.

Look up for Performance on the Marienplatz
Bavaria's most famous Glockenspiel

Arrive at the Marienplatz at around 11am and you'll find crowds of tourists craning their necks as they look up at the Neues Rathaus. They are waiting for the famous **Glockenspiel** to spring into action, smartphones at the ready. The jerky, 32-figure automaton performance takes place on a greening bronze stage and depicts the marriage of Duke Wilhelm V to Renate von Lothringen (celebrated in February 1568) and the post-plague Coopers' Dance. The Glockenspiel does its thing every day at 11am and noon, as well as at 5pm from March to October. Sadly, the whole thing is set to fall silent for a few years as the Neues Rathaus takes its turn to be renovated.

Check out the Hofbräuhaus
The world's greatest beer hall

Even committed teetotallers should at least poke their heads around the door of the **Hofbräuhaus** (hofbraeuhaus.de), Munich institution and the world's most celebrated beer hall. For those into Central European lager, a night on the Hofbräu is like the culmination of a hop-scented pilgrimage. The Hofbräuhaus is a beer hall and tourist attraction rolled into one:

continued on p52

BEER GLOSSARY

Alkoholfreies Bier: nonalcoholic beer.
Bockbier/ Doppelbock: strong beer, pale, amber or dark with a bittersweet flavour.
Dampfbier: (steam beer) originating from Bayreuth, top-fermented, fruity.
Dunkles: (dark lager) a reddish-brown, full-bodied lager, malty and lightly hopped.
Helles: (pale lager) a lightly hopped lager with strong malt aromas, sweet taste.
Hofbräu: royal court brewery.
Klosterbräu: monastery brewery.
Malzbier: sweet, aromatic, full-bodied malt beer.
Märzen: full-bodied with strong malt aromas, traditionally brewed in March.
Pils: (pilsener) a bottom-fermented lager with strong hop flavour.
Rauchbier: (smoke beer) dark beer with a fresh, spicy or 'smoky' flavour, found mostly in Bamberg.
Weissbier/Weizen: wheat beer (around 5.4% alcohol) with fruity and spicy flavour.
Radler: mix of Helles Lagerbier and lemonade.

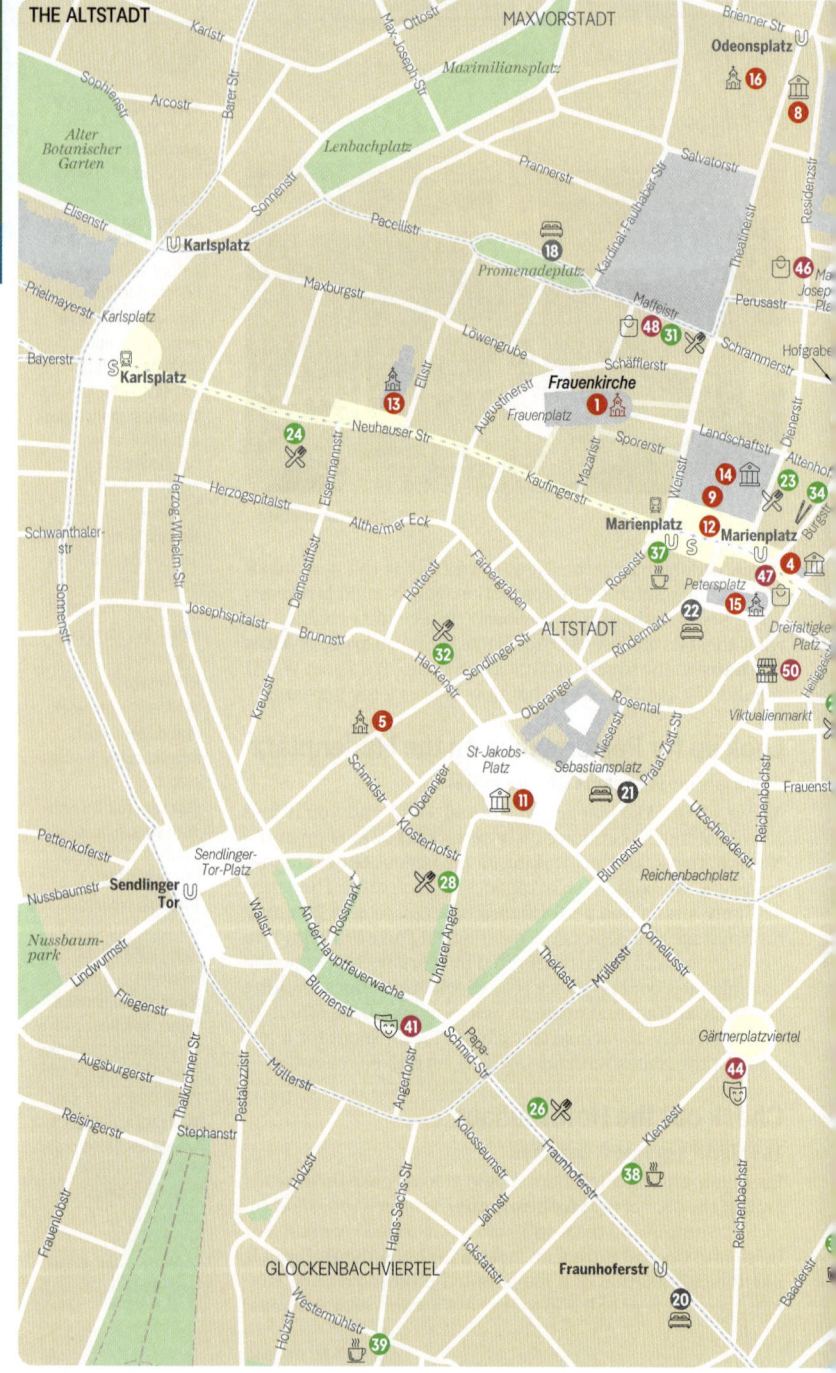

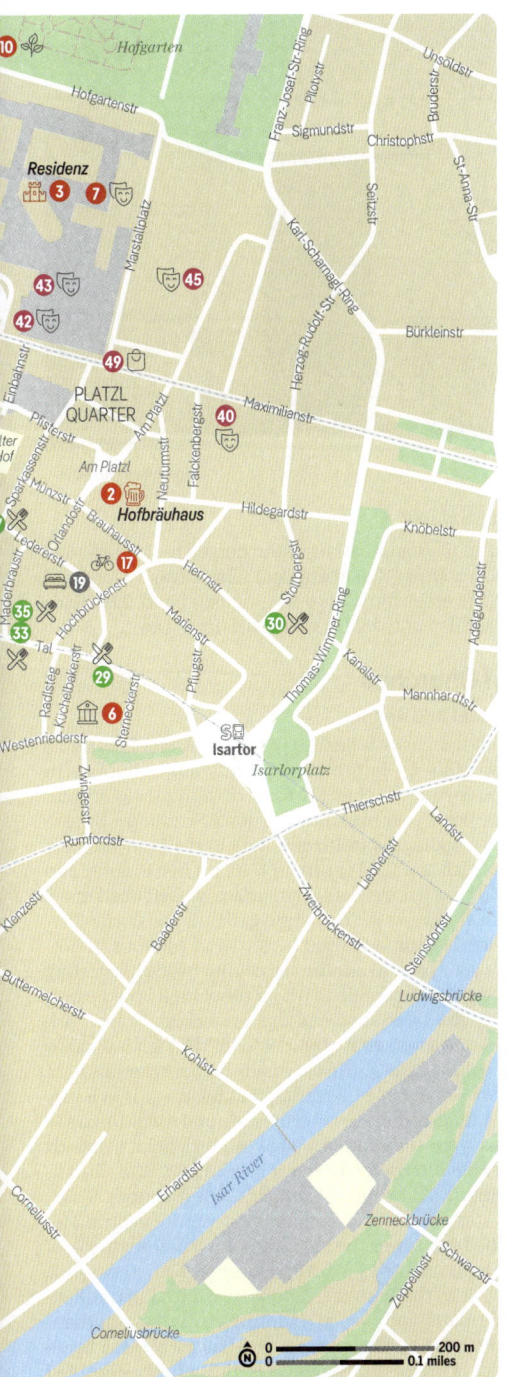

★ HIGHLIGHTS
1. Frauenkirche
2. Hofbräuhaus
3. Residenz

● SIGHTS
4. Altes Rathaus
5. Asamkirche
6. Bier & Oktoberfestmuseum
7. Cuvilliés-Theater
8. Feldherrnhalle
9. Glockenspiel
10. Hofgarten
11. Jüdisches Museum
12. Marienplatz
13. Michaelskirche
14. Neues Rathaus
15. St Peterskirche
16. Theatinerkirche

● ACTIVITIES
17. Mike's Bike Tours

● SLEEPING
18. Bayerischer Hof
19. Cortiina
20. Flushing Meadows
21. Hotel Blauer Bock
22. Louis Hotel

● EATING
23. Alois – Dallmayr Fine Dining
24. Augustiner Stammhaus
25. Bratwurstherzl
26. Fraunhofer
27. Galleria
28. Hewad
29. Indian Love Story
30. Le Stollberg
31. Les Deux
32. Prinz Myshkin
33. Schneider Brauhaus
34. Tohru
35. Weisses Bräuhaus

● DRINKING & NIGHTLIFE
36. Baader Café
37. Café Glockenspiel
38. Cafe Pini
39. Götterspeise

● ENTERTAINMENT
40. Münchner Kammerspiele
41. Münchner Marionettentheater
42. Nationaltheater
43. Residenztheater
44. Staatstheater am Gärtnerplatz
45. Theater im Marstall

● SHOPPING
46. Gössl
47. Inntaler Tractenwelt
48. Loden-Frey
49. Maximilianstrasse
50. Viktualienmarkt

WEISSWURST 101

So what exactly is *Weisswurst*? Traditionally these thick, 12cm-long sausages are made from minced veal and pork fat and flavoured with parsley, lemon, mace, onions, ginger and cardamon. When served in the proper traditional way, a pair of them come with a dollop of sweet, runny, grainy mustard, a freshly baked pretzel and, of course, a large mug of wheat beer (*Weissbier*, to go with the *Weisswurst*).

The reason they are deemed to have such a short shelf life is because as unsmoked and uncured meat products they do actually go off quite quickly, though these days the practice of eating them only until the clock strikes midday is more about tradition than food hygiene. Those occupying supermarket shelves are not the real deal.

Jüdisches Museum

continued from p49

take a seat in the main hall or in the horse-chestnut-shaded garden, order a *Mass* (1L tankard) and some Bavarian food and sway with the other tourists to the oompah band. The place is open every day of the year, even Christmas Day.

A Trio of Churches
Peter, Michael and Asam

The Frauenkirche may take top spot in the Altstadt as far as places of worship go, but there are plenty more churches in the area you should see. Here are three of the most significant.

If baroque floats your boat, head on down Sendlinger Strasse to the mind-boggling **Asamkirche**, built by the Asam brothers Cosmas Damian and Egid Quirin in 1746. It's free to enter, and the first thing you'll notice is that no surface was left unadorned, with the whole nave a rebellion of gilt garlands and docile cherubs, false marble and oversized barley-twist columns. If possible, lie on your back to admire the ceiling fresco illustrating the life of St John Nepomuk, to whom the church is dedicated. The brothers lived next door and this was originally their private chapel; the main altar could be seen through a window from their palace. Egid Quirin is actually buried below his *liabe Kirchl* ('beloved church' in Bavarian) but the crypt is in a very bad state. A fundraising effort is currently underway to save it.

Just steps from the southern edge of Marienplatz rises **St Peterskirche** *(alterpeter.de; tower adult/child €5/2)*, an Altstadt landmark and central Munich's oldest church (1150). Some 306 steps divide you from the best view of central Munich via the 92m tower. Inside awaits a virtual textbook of art through the centuries. Worth a closer peek are the Gothic St-Martin-Altar, the baroque ceiling fresco by Johann Baptist Zimmermann and rococo sculptures by Ignaz Günther.

Largely ignored by shoppers on Neuhauser Strasse heading towards Karlsplatz (Stachus) is the quietly dignified

Michaelskirche *(st-michael-muenchen.de; crypt adult/child €3/1.50),* the largest Renaissance church north of the Alps This huge structure conceals a secret – it is the final resting place of Ludwig II whose humble tomb is down in the crypt.

Have the Weisswurst Experience
The quintessential Munich breakfast
A must-have foodie experience when in the Bavarian capital is a *Weisswurst* breakfast at the Altstadt's **Weisses Bräuhaus** *(weisses-brauhaus-tal.de).* Downing a pair of white veal sausages, a fresh pretzel and a mug of wheat beer at 9am is an essential Munich experience and nowhere does it better. In line with tradition, the tavern only serves *Weisswurst* until noon on the dot. When the bells of the Altstadt chime midday, any Münchner worth their wurst will push a plate of them away, declaring them unfresh.

Munich's Jewish Heritage
Learn about the city's Jewish past
Coming to terms with its Nazi past has not historically been a priority in Munich, which is why the opening of the **Jüdisches Museum** *(juedisches-museum-muenchen.de; adult/child €6/3)* just over two decades ago was hailed as a real milestone. The permanent exhibition entitled *Voices_Places_Times* offers an insight into Jewish history, life, rituals and culture in the city, with the last section using comic strips to bridge the gap between the past and present. For many, the odd thing about the museum is that it shies away from the Holocaust, focusing clearly on contemporary Jewish culture. There are also world-class temporary exhibitions with a Jewish history theme.

The minimalist museum building is part of the Jewish complex on St-Jakobs-Platz, which also includes a community centre with a restaurant and a bunker-like synagogue that's rarely open to the public. Munich has the second-largest Jewish population in Germany after Berlin's: around 10,000 people.

Mother of all Munich Churches
Dominant feature of the Munich skyline
The Altstadt has several churches, but the top temple in all Munich is the **Frauenkirche** *(muenchner-dom.de; South Tower*

continued on p56

BEST PLACES TO BUY LEDERHOSEN & DIRNDL

Holareidulijö: One of the best secondhand Lederhosen and Dirndl resellers in Munich has been around for some years. Call ahead for an appointment.

Loden-Frey: For a better-standard, keep-forever, upmarket Lederhosen and Dirndl outfit, head to this high-priced shop with a tradition going back to 1842.

MOSER Trachtenwelt: The biggest supplier of traditional costumes in Bavaria with seven branches in the Munich area.

Inntaler Trachtenwelt: Just off the Marienplatz, this supplier has trad garb for men, women and Kinder.

Gössl: The Munich branch of an Austrian traditional Alpine clothing seller has a wide variety of colourfully understated traditional dresses that are a joy to own.

 EATING IN THE ALTSTADT: FINE DINING

Alois – Dallmayr Fine Dining: Enjoy the double Michelin-starred menu at this top-drawer Munich stalwart. *7pm-midnight Wed-Sat, 12.30-3pm Thu-Sat* €€€

Les Deux: The modern French cuisine at this restaurant near the Frauenkirche has earned it a Michelin twinkler. *noon-midnight Mon-Sat* €€€

Tohru: Minimalist Michelin Japanese cuisine in a retro dining room prepared by local German-Japanese chef, Tohru Nakamura. *7pm-midnight Tue-Sat* €€€

Le Stollberg: Intimate little restaurant serving Bavarian food with Mediterranean touches. *11.30am-2.30pm & 6pm-midnight Wed-Fri, 4.30-11pm Sat* €€€

TOP EXPERIENCE

Munich Residenz

Munich's most visited sight, the central Residenz was the family home of the ruling Wittelsbach dynasty for over five centuries, from 1508 until WWI. Each generation added to the complex, resulting in a parade of architectural styles from down the ages. Some, but by no means all, of what you see today is a post-WWII reconstruction. Tours are in the company of a rather loquacious audioguide.

DON'T MISS

- Antiquarium
- Reiche Zimmer
- Steine Zimmer
- Royal Palace
- Schatzkammer
- Cuvilliés-Theater

Ancestors' Gallery, Grottenhof & Antiquarium

The tour kicks off in the rococo **Ahnengallery** (Ancestors Gallery), which showcases 121 portraits of Bavarian rulers in chronological order. All of them played their part in creating the piece of heritage you are about to see.

Next comes the **Grottenhof** (Grotto Court), home of the wonderful **Perseusbrunnen** (Perseus Fountain), with its namesake holding the dripping head of Medusa. The decoration here is made entirely of tens of thousands of shells, some large, some no bigger than a fingernail.

Next door is the **Antiquarium**, a barrel-vaulted hall of frescoes created by Duke Albrecht V between 1568 and 1571 to house the vast royal collection of Greek and Roman sculptures. It is the most impressive space in Bavaria and claims the title of the largest Renaissance hall north of the Alps. The

PRACTICALITIES
- residenz-muenchen.de
- adult/concessions €20/16 (all attractions)
- Residenz & Schatzkammer 9am-6pm Apr-mid-Oct, 10am-5pm mid-Oct-Mar
- Cuvilliés-Theater 9am-6pm, Aug-mid-Sep, from 2pm rest of the year

raised platform at one end enables you to get some incredible shots with a widescreen lens.

Royal Living

Generations of big-egoed Bavarian royals shunned their predecessors' living quarters, preferring instead to commission their own, hence the sheer size and scale of the Residenz complex. Some of the most impressive digs in the Residenz are Cuvilliés' **Kurfürstenzimmer** (Electors Rooms) and the wonderful **Reiche Zimmer,** which live up to their name, meaning 'rich'. The **Steine Zimmer** (Stone Rooms) are the finest rococo interiors in southern Germany. Maximilian I's **Kaisersaal** (Imperial Hall) dating from the early 17th century is a huge space for the time it was built, resplendent in gilt stucco and monster Dutch tapestries. The same ruler also commissioned the stuccoed **Hofkapelle** (Court Chapel) where chamber concerts sometimes take place.

All Saints' Church

One stark reminder of the fact that much of the Residenz was destroyed or damaged in WWII Allied bombing raids is Ludwig I's **All Saints' Church**, once a grandly stuccoed and frescoed affair built by Leo von Klenze, but left bare red brick by restorers. It is now used as an occasional concert venue.

Royal Palace

The climax of the Wittelsbachs' deranged grandeur comes in the form of Ludwig I's **Royal Palace**. This no-holds-barred series of neoclassical quarters includes the king's throne room with its entirely gold walls and huge red velvet canopy. Sadly, everything you see here is a reconstruction as this part of the Residenz was reduced to neo-Renaissance landfill in 1944.

Schatzkammer

The **Schatzkammer der Residenz** contains the Wittelsbachs' collections of jewel-encrusted yesteryear bling. The priceless objects they amassed are dramatically illuminated in show cabinets. Highlights include the Bavarian crown insignia, the delicate Gothic crown of Anne of Bohemia (the oldest English crown in existence) and ruby-and-diamond-encrusted jewellery of Queen Therese (1792–1854).

Cuvilliés-Theater

As it is usually closed until around 2pm, most come back later in the day to visit the wonderfully maintained baroque **Cuvilliés-Theater**, the Wittelsbachs' little piece of home entertainment. Take a seat and lift your gaze to the four levels of balconies, each one plastered in gilt and red stucco. When it's illuminated with candles (albeit today with electronic versions for obvious reasons), it's easy to imagine what a magical experience a performance here in the mid-18th century would have been. Cuvilliés' creation is famous for hosting the premiere of Mozart's opera *Idomeneo* and performances still take place here occasionally. Access is limited to the auditorium.

FRANÇOIS DE CUVILLIÉS

Belgium-born François de Cuvilliés (1695-1768) is the architect who had the greatest influence on the appearance of the Wittelsbachs' Munich residence. He was appointed court architect in 1724 by Maximilian II but worked under Charles VII and Maximilian III, for whom he created the baroque theatre that now bears his name. Another of his masterpieces is the Amalienburg at Schloss Nymphenburg.

TOP TIPS

- There's a lot to see here – allow at least three hours to take in everything at a gallop.

- Bring your own (plug-in) headphones for the audioguide.

- No bags are allowed into the Residenz.

- Renovation work is ongoing, so closures are inevitable and you may not see all the highlights.

- Arrive early in the day between Easter and September to avoid the crowds.

- Apart from in the summer, the Cuvilliés-Theater is only open in the afternoons.

- If you are squeezed for time, the tour splits at two points for a shorter route.

Nationaltheater

THE BELLS OF THE ALTSTADT

The Munich carillon is no medieval affair, like Prague's Orloj – the Glockenspiel that performs twice a day for the Marienplatz masses only dates back to 1908 and the construction of the Neues Rathaus. Perhaps unsurprisingly, the bells of the Glockenspiel are solar powered, a typical example of both the Bavarian knack of seamlessly combining the old with the very new as well as the city's commitment to carbon neutral status.

The whole sun-powered performance involving 43 bells and life-size figures takes between 12 and 15 minutes, depending on which tune is played. One similarity to Prague's Orloj is the cockerel that squawks out to tell the gathered onlookers below that it's all over for another day, folks.

continued from p53

adult/child €7.50/5.50), an instantly recognisable symbol on the city's skyline. And why do its twin, onion-dome-topped towers still dominate? Well, the rule is that no building in the Altstadt can stand taller than its 99m, and in typical southern German fashion, this is strictly adhered to.

The Frauenkirche was built between 1468 and 1488, but was severely damaged during WWII. The rebuild created a rather spartan interior, with a low-lit shaft of tall whitewashed columns. Side chapels behind tall iron railings are dedicated to various saints and guilds, and some of the church's impossibly elongated windows disappear up into the haze in a riot of stained glass. The crypt is a strangely modern affair containing the tomb of Ludwig the Bavarian. The highlight (though a rather pricey one) for most visitors here is the opportunity to climb the **south tower** (which measures 98.45m, 12cm shorter than the north tower). A modern lift takes you to the top from where you can peer out of the small windows across the whole of Munich. You can also admire the architectural detail of the north tower standing close by.

Feast at Munich's City-Centre Market

Luxury picnic shopping and beer garden

Looking for a tub of gourmet olives, Brazilian mangoes, bio *Weisswurst*, a wedge of Alpine cheese, a *maracuja* (passion

 EATING IN THE ALTSTADT: TRADITIONAL BAVARIAN PLACES

Augustiner Stammhaus: Monster beer hall with tens of different rooms and a tranquil, old-world courtyard. *10am–midnight* €€

Fraunhofer: Wonderfully characterful, 19th-century Bavarian inn with a tiny theatre at the back. *5pm–1am* €€

Schneider Bräuhaus: One of Munich's classic beer halls, with Alpine whoops accompanying the rabble-rousing oompah band. *9am–10pm* €€

Bratwurstherzl: Sausages are the focus at this old Munich tavern with a Franconian twist. *10am–11pm Mon–Sat* €€

fruit) smoothie bucket or some pickled, well, anything? Just steps from the Marienplatz is Munich's most famous market, the open-air **Viktualienmarkt** *(viktualienmarkt-muenchen.de)*. Originally the city's fruit and veg market, it's been here for over 200 years and occupies 18,000 sq metres of prime city-centre real estate.

However, this is no ordinary farmers market. Over the past two decades the Viktualienmarkt has become a dining hot spot, with countless stalls offering tasty gourmet (and not so gourmet) snacks. It's the best place to put together a (very pricey) picnic or grab a bowl of Asian soup, a plate of sausages or a herring sarnie. And of course, the market has its very own chestnut-shaded beer garden, the Altstadt's best and a Munich institution since 1807. All of Munich's main breweries take turns serving here, so you never know what's on tap. Getting a seat here over summer weekends sometimes involves a long wait.

Take a Tour of Munich's Nationaltheater
Bavaria's grandest stage

Dominating Max-Joseph-Platz and essentially part of the Residenz, the **Nationaltheater** *(staatsoper.de; tours adult/child €10/5)* is one of the city's most spectacular neoclassical facades. Opened in 1818, it's home to the Bavarian State Opera, one of the world's top opera companies, and the lesser-known Bavarian State Ballet. The opera's house band is the Bayerisches Staatsorchester, in business since 1523 and thus Munich's oldest orchestra. Wagner's *Tristan und Isolde* and *Die Walküre* premiered here.

Commissioned by King Maximilian I Joseph and built by architect Karl von Fischer, the theatre has had a troubled history. It was almost completely destroyed by fire in 1823 and had to be rebuilt. It was decimated again in bombing raids during WWII and was slated for demolition. The postwar rebuild increased the size of the stage to 2500 sq metres, making it one of the world's largest opera stages. If you can't get to a performance, tours of the theatre run between 10am and 6pm weekdays.

Admire the Grand Feldherrnhalle
Site of the Beer Hall Putsch

Blocking the southern end of Odeonsplatz is Friedrich von Gärnter's **Feldherrnhalle**, a neoclassical structure with no

MUNICH PRIDE WEEKS

The city's **Pride Weeks** *(csdmuenchen.de)* in May and June are by far Munich's biggest LGBTIQ+ events. Things kick off with myriad exhibitions, parties and demonstrations. These run until the third weekend in June and culminate in the main Munich Pride (Christopher Street Day), which was attended in 2024 by well over half a million people, making it one of the largest annual happenings in the city.

One of the biggest parties during Pride Weeks is the Glockenbach street festival, one of the oldest street festivals in the Bavarian capital. There's a friendly, carnival atmosphere and it's a great time to be in the city even for straight visitors. Many of Munich's attractions take part in some small way.

DRINKING IN THE ALTSTADT: COFFEE

Cafe Pini: Italian cafe recalling the days of the economic miracle when *Gastarbeiter* (foreign workers) streamed into Munich. *9am-11pm Mon-Sat, to 6pm Sun*

Baader Café: Eclectic cafe serving coffee by day and cocktails by night to a very mixed crowd. *10am-1am*

Götterspeise: Twee, choco-centric cafe serving myriad teas, coffees and cakes of the traditional, seasonal and novelty kind. *8am-7pm Mon-Sat*

Café Glockenspiel: This cafe just off Marienplatz is a touristy affair, but has excellent views across the square. *9am-11pm Mon-Sat, 10am-6.30pm Sun*

FOOTTOO/SHUTTERSTOCK

CHRISTKINDLMARKT

Munich's popular Christmas market is held every year throughout Advent on Marienplatz and the adjoining Rindermarkt. Although not as illustrious as more sparkly Yuletide bazaars in Nuremberg and Dresden, the Munich Christkindlmarkt has been running since 1972, and against the backdrop of the Neues Rathaus can still be a magically atmospheric affair.

Locals and visitors gather round the huge Christmas tree as seasonal music rings out from the town hall's balcony. Almost 140 stalls pack the two squares and the streets in between selling the inevitable *Glühwein* (mulled wine), lots of traditional food and countless baubles and trinkets. It's an enjoyable time to be in the city, though be aware that it hardly ever snows in Munich in December.

apparent practical use, the design of which was based on the Loggia dei Lanzi in Florence. The structure pays homage to the Bavarian army including General Johann Tilly, who kicked the Swedes out of Munich during the Thirty Years' War; and Karl Philipp von Wrede, an ally turned foe of Napoleon.

It was here on 9 November 1923 that police stopped the so-called Beer Hall Putsch, Hitler's attempt to bring down the Weimar Republic (Germany's government after WWI). A fierce skirmish left 20 people, including 16 Nazis, dead. A plaque in the pavement on the square's eastern side commemorates the police officers who perished in the incident. Hitler was subsequently tried and sentenced to five years in jail, but he ended up serving a mere nine months in Landsberg am Lech prison, where he penned his hate-filled manifesto *Mein Kampf*.

Explore the Theatinerkirche
Odeonsplatz' main church

The mustard-yellow **Theatinerkirche** on Odeonsplatz' western flank was built to commemorate the 1662 birth of Prince Max Emanuel, and is the work of Swiss architect Enrico

EATING IN THE ALTSTADT: NON-BAVARIAN RESTAURANTS

Hewad: Great little Afghan dinner place in the south of the Altstadt serving salads, spicy rice dishes and grilled meats. *5-11pm* €€

Indian Love Story: Arguably the most authentic Indian dining experience in the Altstadt with spicy street food. *11.30am-2.30pm & 5.30-11.30pm Mon-Fri, noon-11pm Sat & Sun* €€

Prinz Myshkin: Probably still the city's best vegetarian restaurant, with an imaginative menu under whitewashed vaulting. *11am-11pm Tue-Sat* €€

Galleria: Munich has a multitude of Italian eateries, but Galleria is a cut above the rest. *noon-2.30pm & 6.30-11pm* €€€

Feldherrnhalle (left; p57) and Theatinerkirche (right)

Zuccalli. Also known as St Kajetan's, it's a voluptuous design, with massive twin towers flanking a giant cupola. Inside, an ornate dome lords it over the Fürstengruft (royal crypt), the final destination of several Wittelsbach rulers, including King Maximilian II (1811–64).

Kick Back in the Hofgarten
Formal Altstadt gardens

The rectangle of greenery to the north of the Residenz is the **Hofgarten**, a prime city-centre picnic spot. These formal court gardens of the Residenz turned public park are a cool oasis in summer and the perfect place to escape the tourist crowds, though it's a cabbage patch compared to the English Garden. The limestone gravel paths converge at the Dianatempel, a striking octagonal pavilion honouring the Roman goddess of the hunt. If you are into it, this is one of the few places in the Altstadt where you will find a geocache, though you might have to wait for someone to vacate a bench to log it.

Delve into the Hop-Scented Past at the Bier & Oktoberfestmuseum
The story of the Oktoberfest

Head to the popular **Bier & Oktoberfestmuseum** (bier-und-oktoberfestmuseum.de; adult/concession €4/2.50) to learn all about Bavarian suds and the world's most famous booze-up. The four floors heave with old brewing vats, historic photos and some of the earliest Oktoberfest regalia. The 14th-century building has some fine medieval features, including painted ceilings and a kitchen with an open fire. If during your tour you've worked up a thirst, the museum has its very own pub.

BEST PLACES FOR CULTURE IN THE ALTSTADT

The Altstadt is home to many of Munich's top cultural institutions:

Nationaltheater: Home to the world-class Bavarian State Opera, one of Germany's top ensembles.

Staatstheater am Gärtnerplatz: This grand theatre specialises in light opera, musicals and dance.

Residenztheater: The Bayerisches Staatsschauspiel performs here.

Münchner Kammerspiele: Classic plays and new works at an Art Nouveau theatre and in a 21st-century glass cube, the Neues Haus.

Münchner Marionettentheater: This is the city's puppet theatre, located on Blumenstrasse.

Theater im Marstall: Also a venue for the Bayerisches Staatsschauspiel theatre ensemble.

Cuvilliés-Theater: A performance at this original baroque theatre is a time-travel experience.

Schwabing

RELAXED, HIP AND STUDENT NEIGHBOURHOOD

GETTING AROUND

Schwabing is dissected by Leopoldstrasse with two lines of the U-Bahn (U3 and U6) running beneath it. The most central station is Universität. Bus 100 Museenlinie also passes through the neighbourhood. However, the best way to get around Schwabing's busy grid is on foot, though hiring a bike to explore the vastness of the English Garden can save a lot of legwork.

☑ **TOP TIP**

Training for a half-marathon, marathon or other running event? There's no better place to get those runs in than the even, chalky paths of the English Garden. And you certainly won't be alone. For less strenuous physical activity, hire a pedalo on the Kleinhesseloher See in the north of the park.

Though more a place for aimless wandering, people-watching and window shopping, there are some worthwhile sights here. The somewhat rambling Bayerisches Nationalmuseum and the Haus der Kunst are indoor highlights, but running down Schwabing's eastern flank is Munich's green lung, the must-experience English Garden, a place where Münchners go to decompress on the widescreen lawns.

Lose Yourself in the Bayerisches Nationalmuseum

Classic museum experience

Picture the classic 19th-century museum, a palatial neoclassical edifice overflowing with exotic treasure and thought-provoking works of art, a repository for a nation's history, a grand purpose-built display case for royal trinkets, church baubles and state-owned rarities – this is the **Bayerisches Nationalmuseum** (Bavarian National Museum; bayerisches-nationalmuseum.de; adult/child €7/free). It's a good old-fashioned institution for no-nonsense museum lovers, and, as the collection fills 40 rooms over three floors, there's a lot to get through, so be prepared for at least two hours' legwork.

Most visitors start on the 1st floor, where hall after hall is packed with baroque, mannerist and Renaissance sculpture, ecclesiastical treasures (check out all those wobbly dancing Gothic 'S' figures), Renaissance clothing and one-off pieces such as the 1000-year-old St Kunigunde's chest, fashioned in mammoth ivory and gold.

Climb to the 2nd floor to move up in history to the rococo, *Jugendstil* and modern periods, represented by priceless collections of Nymphenburg and Meissen porcelain, Tiffany glass, Augsburg silver and precious items used by the Bavarian royal family. Also up here is a huge circular model of Munich in the first half of the 19th century, shortly after it was transformed into a capital fit for a kingdom.

It's easy to miss, but the building's basement also holds an evocatively displayed collection of *Krippen* (nativity scenes), some with Cecil B DeMille–style casts of thousands. Retold in

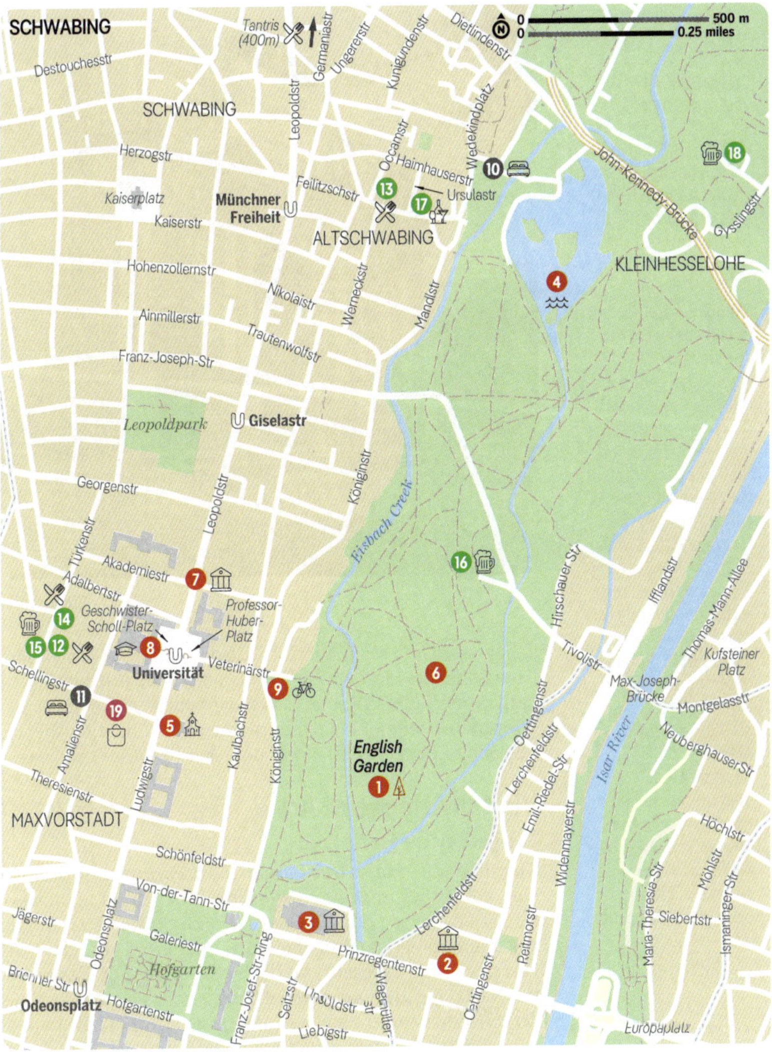

- **HIGHLIGHTS**
  1. English Garden
- **SIGHTS**
  2. Bayerisches Nationalmuseum
  3. Haus der Kunst
  4. Kleinhesseloher See
  5. Ludwigskirche
  6. Monopteros
  7. Siegestor
- **ACTIVITIES**
  8. Ludwig-Maximilians-Universität
  9. MUCbike E-Bike Rent & Tour
- **SLEEPING**
  10. Gästehaus Englischer Garten
  11. Hotel Hauser
- **EATING**
  12. Cafe Zeitgeist
  13. Ruff's Burger
  14. Türkenhof
- **DRINKING & NIGHTLIFE**
  15. Alter Simpl
  16. Chinesischer Turm
  17. Cocktailhouse
  see 3 Goldene Bar
  18. Hirschau
- **SHOPPING**
  19. Words' Worth Books

TRAGEDY AT THE EISBACH

On hot (and even not so hot) days there always used to be a bit of a kerfuffle on the bridge at the southern tip of the English Garden. Onlookers would line the banks of the stream and others would lean over the bridge's balustrade, recording what was happening below on their phones. What they were filming was surfers braving the freezing waters of the Eisbach – taking turns from both sides, they would confidently ride the single wave that surges from under the bridge. However, in April 2025, a 33-year-old surfer died after snagging her board leash on an unidentified object on the stream's bottom. The Eisbachwelle was closed at the time of writing and it's not certain the authorities will ever allow it to reopen.

Siegestor

paper, wood and resin, there are Christmas-story scenes here from Bohemia, Moravia and Tyrol, but the biggest contingent hails from Naples. Also here is the excellent museum shop.

Top-notch temporary exhibitions are also held on themes relating to Bavarian history. The ticket to these costs extra.

Visit the House of Art
The gallery the Nazis built

The infamous **Haus der Kunst** *(hausderkunst.de; admission varies according to exhibition)* sits behind an austere fascist-era edifice that was built in 1937 (Hitler himself laid the foundation stone) to showcase Nazi art. These days the Haus der Kunst presents works by the type of artists whom the Nazis rejected and deemed degenerate. The museum has no collections of its own, acting solely as a venue for temporary shows of contemporary art and design.

EATING IN SCHWABING: OUR PICKS

Türkenhof: This studenty resto-pub is a great stop-off for a no-fuss Bavarian lunch. Hip decor and friendly, non-flustered staff. *11am-midnight* €

Ruff's Burger: When all you want is a filling burger between sights or shops, the 100% Bavarian beef and veggie versions do the trick every time. *noon-10pm* €

Cafe Zeitgeist: Great bistro-cafe serving light lunches to tourists and students. Shady courtyard with people-watching possibilities. *9am-midnight* €€

Tantris: This double-Michelin-starred, psychedelic 1970s retro-resto is one of Germany's best known. Book weeks ahead. *noon-4pm & 6.30pm-midnight Wed-Sat* €€€

The Buzzing Streets of Schwabing
Bookshops, cafes and student life

Schwabing is Munich's university quarter, an erstwhile working-class area that has completely gentrified in the last three decades. The main limestone building of the **Ludwig-Maximilians-Universität** is on arrow-straight Ludwigstrasse. Designed by Friedrich von Gärtner, it has cathedral-like dimensions and is accented with sculpture and other artworks. A flight of stairs leads down to the memorial to Die Weisse Rose, the Nazi resistance group founded by Hans and Sophie Scholl. Nearby is the sombre twin-towered **Ludwigskirche**, which was built by Friedrich von Gärtner between 1829 and 1844 and is a highly decorative, almost Byzantine, affair.

The streets nearby are some of Munich's most vibrant, lined with boutiques, cafes, shops and bars. A highlight is **Alter Simpl** (alter-simpl.com) in Türkenstrasse, one of Munich's most famous historical taverns, where Thomas Mann, Hermann Hesse and many other Schwabing writers, poets and artists once drank. It's a great place to stop off for a drink or a coffee when exploring Schwabing. Cutting across Türkenstrasse is Schellingstrasse, one of Schwabing's busiest streets. By day it funnels students from the nearby university to various watering and feeding spots. In addition to its many cafes, it's also the location of **Words' Worth Books** (wordsworth.de), the city's best English-language bookstore, and the uni bookshop.

Sightsee the Siegestor
Munich's Arc de Triomphe

Splitting Leopoldstrasse in two just north of the university, Munich's massive **Siegestor** was modelled on the Arch of Constantine in Rome and looks like a miniature version of the Arc de Triomphe in Paris. Built to honour the Bavarian army for sending Napoleon packing, it's crowned by a triumphant Bavaria piloting a lion-drawn chariot. Severely damaged in WWII, the arch was turned into a peace memorial. The inscription on the upper section reads: *Dem Sieg geweiht, vom Kriege zerstört, zum Frieden mahnend* (Dedicated to victory, destroyed by war, calling for peace).

WEISSE ROSE MOVEMENT

Munich's main university building stands on Geschwister-Scholl-Platz, a place named after the siblings Sophie and Hans, students who were executed by guillotine along with friend Christoph Probst by the Nazi authorities on 22 February 1943. Their crime was to belong to the Weisse Rose (White Rose) movement that distributed antiwar leaflets in Munich and beyond. Their short-lived activities highlighted the failures on the battlefield, especially at Stalingrad, which the Nazis were not publicly admitting.

Located within the Ludwig-Maximilians-Universität, a memorial exhibit relates this moving story. One of Munich's most heroic, it is told in photographs and items from the period. The 2005 German film *Sophie Scholl – The Final Days* also does an excellent job of telling this tale of valiant, nonviolent resistance.

 DRINKING IN SCHWABING: OUR PICKS

Chinesischer Turm: Around the English Garden's Chinese Tower drinkers wash down Oktoberfest-size portions of food with HB lager. *10am-11pm late-Apr-Oct*

Alter Simpl: This old wood-panelled Schwabing literary pub can still remember the good old days. *11.30am-midnight Mon-Fri, from 10am Sat & Sun*

Goldene Bar: At the Haus der Kunst, this spectacular bar is centred around a huge modernist chandelier. *noon-8pm Mon, to midnight Wed & Thu, to 2am Fri & Sat, 1-8pm Sun*

Cocktailhouse: This Schwabing classic has been mixing drinks for over 30 years and is a great spot to start a night out or for longer lingering. *7pm-late*

TOP EXPERIENCE

English Garden

Strolling through the vast meadows of Munich's sprawling city park is the way the good folk of Munich escape the stresses of the 21st century. The English Garden (Englischer Garten) is one of the world's largest urban parks, Munich's Hyde or Central Park. Dodge the joggers and high-speed cyclists to discover a tranquil world of woodland, birdsong and students swotting up in the sun.

IMAGE BY MATEJ KASTELIC/SHUTTERSTOCK, ENGLISH GARDEN SHOWN COURTESY OF THE BAVARIAN PALACE ADMINISTRATION, WWW.SCHLOESSER.BAYERN.DE

TOP TIPS

- A section of the Berlin Wall lurks hidden between the Haus der Kunst and the US Embassy at the southwest tip of the park.

- High-speed velocommuters rocket along the main paths – take care with small children.

- Some Munich agencies offer English Garden cycle tours.

PRACTICALITIES

- Open 24hr
- Free
- Tram 16 or bus 100 to Nationalmuseum/Haus der KunsEntry adult/youth $40/30, after dark $23, Tactile Dome $16

A Little History

Stretching north from Prinzregentenstrasse for about 5km, the park was commissioned by Elector Karl Theodor in 1789 and designed by Benjamin Thompson, an American-born scientist working as an adviser to the Bavarian government. A prime piece of real estate worth billions, to this day nothing can be built here.

Exotic Follies

Two pieces of folly architecture dominate the park's middle. Rising above the main lawns is the **Monopteros** (1838), a Greek temple with city-centre views. A short walk north brings you to the Chinesischer Turm (p63) (Chinese Tower), the unlikely setting for a classic Munich beer garden.

Boating & Beer

Further north, the English Garden becomes wilder, though there are two spots where nature has been tamed. The **Kleinhesseloher See** is a lovely lake where you can boat around three little islands. Across a footbridge is the **Hirschau** beer garden, one of Munich's best.

Maxvorstadt

THE CITY'S ARTY EPICENTRE

In the 'City of Art and Beer', when you've had the beer and it's time for the art, then it's time for the neighbourhood of Maxvorstadt to the northwest of the Altstadt. Gathered around Ludwig I's Athens-esque Königsplatz and in the parks between Arcisstrasse and Türkenstrasse, in no other area of southern Germany (or perhaps even Central Europe) will you encounter such a high concentration of art museums. The Pinakotheken, the Museum Brandhorst and various other institutions both old and new come together in Maxvorstadt to create the Kunstareal, or 'Art Area'. It's one of Munich's must-sees, even if you can't tell a Rembrandt from a Renoir.

Another, darker side to Maxvorstadt is its role in the Nazi years as the backdrop to parades and rallies. The excellent NS Dokuzentrum does a good job of telling the story of the rise of the Nazis and Munich's part in it.

Learn about the Rise of the Nazis

Hitler and Munich

Located right at the heart of what was once Nazi central in Munich, the aim of the **NS Dokuzentrum** (*National Socialism Documentation Centre; nsdoku.de; free*) is to educate locals and visitors alike about the Nazi period and Munich's oft-misunderstood role in it. The excellent permanent exhibition entitled *Munich and National Socialism* attempts to find the answers to questions about why Hitler came to power, what led to WWII and why democracy failed. Period documents, artefacts, films and multimedia stations help visitors form their own understanding of this history. The NSDAP (National Socialist German Workers' Party) was established in Munich after all, and the city was affected by the early years of Hitler's rise to power like no other in Germany.

In addition to the permanent exhibition there are often superb temporary shows on a Nazi, WWII or general human rights and injustice theme. Shows in the past have focused

GETTING AROUND

The main public transport stop for Maxvorstadt is the Königsplatz U-Bahn station with the U2 and U8 both passing this way. Tram 27 runs up the eastern side of Maxvorstadt, stopping at Karolinenplatz and the Pinakotheken stops. However, many people arrive here aboard bus 100, the so-called Museenlinie, which links the Ostbahnhof and the Hauptbahnhof with Maxvorstadt. The Kunstareal is a relatively compact area so getting around on foot is easy enough.

☑ TOP TIP

Sunday is the day to visit the city's museums. Why? Well, many, including all the major ones, charge only a single euro admission. The downside is that Sunday tends to be the busiest day of all. Note that the Brandhorst is not part of the €1 Sunday tradition.

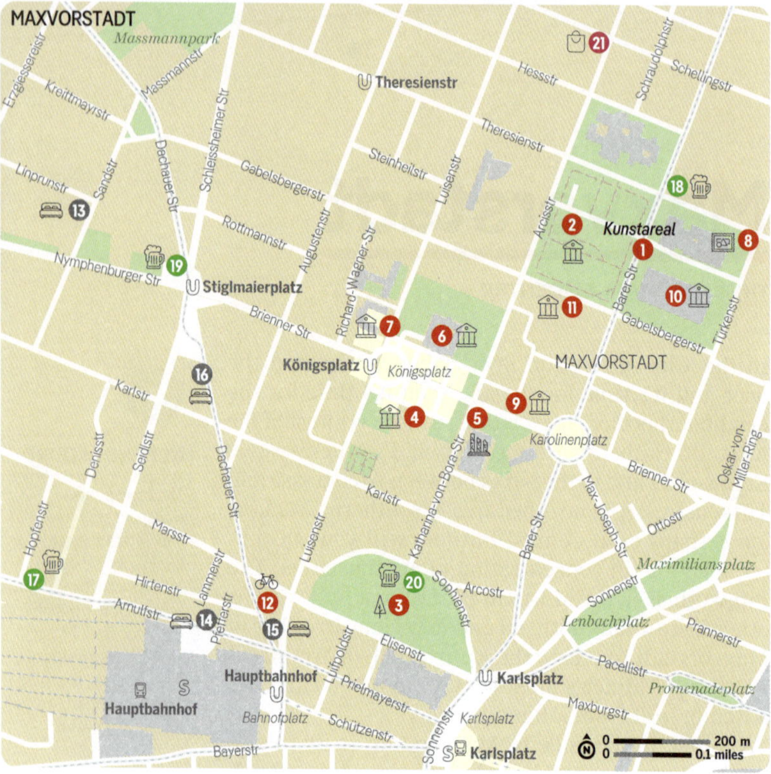

MAXVORSTADT

- ⭐ **HIGHLIGHTS**
  1 Kunstareal
- 🔴 **SIGHTS**
  2 Alte Pinakothek
  3 Alter Botanischer Garten
  4 Antikensammlungen
  5 Ehrentempel
  6 Glyptothek
  7 Lenbachhaus
  8 Museum Brandhorst
  9 NS Dokuzentrum
  10 Pinakothek der Moderne
  11 State Museum of Egyptian Art
- 🔴 **ACTIVITIES**
  12 Radius Tours & Bike Rental
- ⚫ **SLEEPING**
  13 Das Kleine Hotel in München
  14 Eden Hotel Wolff
  15 Pension Locarno
  16 Ruby Lilly Hotel
- 🟢 **DRINKING & NIGHTLIFE**
  17 Augustiner Keller
  18 Die Kneipe 80
  19 Löwenbräukeller
  20 Park Cafe
- 🔴 **SHOPPING**
  21 Holareidulijö

🍸 DRINKING IN MAXVORSTADT: BEER HALLS & GARDENS

Park Cafe: Stylish beer hall and garden at the Alter Botanischer Garten serving Hofbräu and filling southern German food. *11.30am-late*

Augustiner Keller: This 5000-seat beer garden west of the Hauptbahnhof buzzes with fairy-lit thirst-quenching activity. *10am-midnight*

Löwenbräukeller: Beer hall and garden at the Löwenbräu Brewery, one Munich's traditional lager producers. *11am-midnight*

Die Kneipe 80: Next to the Alte Pinakothek, this small pub is strategically located for those who have worked up a thirst (and a hunger) in the nearby galleries. *2pm-late*

Alter Botanischer Garten

MUSEENLINIE 100

By far the most useful bus route in Munich's city centre is the 100, aka Museenlinie, that makes 18 stops between the Ostbahnhof and the Hauptbahnhof, and links over 20 museums and other interesting localities en route. The Königsplatz, Lenbachhaus, the Kunstareal, Haus der Kunst, the English Garden, Eisbachwelle, Villa Stuck and the Bavarian National Museum are all linked by this ordinary *Stadtbus* (city bus).

Leaving every 10 minutes in both directions (every 20 minutes on weekends), the 100 also serves as a kind of budget hop-on-hop-off route, especially if you already have a day pass. The whole route takes around 25 minutes to complete and at both ends there are many connections to other U-Bahn, S-Bahn and tram routes.

on the Warsaw Ghetto, Russia's war in Ukraine and forced labour under the Nazis.

Take a Stroll in the Old Botanical Garden

An oasis of city-centre greenery

The **Alter Botanischer Garten** is a pleasant place to soothe soles and souls after an Altstadt shopping spree or to see out a long wait for a train away from the Hauptbahnhof. Created under King Maximilian in 1814, most of the tender specimens were moved in the early 20th century to the New Botanical Garden behind Schloss Nymphenburg, leaving this verdant city-centre breathing space.

The **Neptunbrunnen** (Neptune Fountain), on the south side, dates from the Nazi period when the garden was turned into a public park. The neoclassical entrance gate is called the **Kleine Propyläen** and is a leftover from the original gardens. The Old Botanical Garden is also home to one of Munich's lower-profile beer gardens, Park Cafe.

Alte Pinakothek

TOP EXPERIENCE

Munich's Kunstareal

The Kunstareal is made up of two areas. The heart and soul of Maxvorstadt is the Königsplatz, north of the Hauptbahnhof. It was commissioned by Ludwig I as part of his 'German Athens' vision for Munich and resembles a city in the ancient world. The addition of the various Pinakotheken, the area's second focus, over the decades expanded the Kunstareal into the attraction it is today.

DON'T MISS

Museum Brandhorst

Alte Pinakothek

Pinakothek der Moderne

Glyptothek

Lenbachhaus

State Museum of Egyptian Art

Alte Pinakothek

With its vast collection of art from the 14th to the 18th centuries, the **Alte Pinakothek** *(pinakothek.de; adult/child €9/free)* is one of the world's top art museums and if you are going to choose just one gallery to visit in the Kunstareal, many would say this should be it. This neoclassical temple to Old European Masters was designed by Leo von Klenze as a purpose-built gallery for the Wittelsbachs' art collections, now administered by a venerable institution called the Bavarian State Painting Collections. The whole thing got a major revamp a decade or

PRACTICALITIES

● kunstareal.de ● admission varies ● each institution has one late opening day

Museum Brandhorst

> **WALK OF ART**
>
> The myriad institutions of the Munich Kunstareal can be a bit overwhelming at first and it's easy to get your Pinakotheken in a twist. However, help is at hand – from the Kunstareal website you can download an interactive stroll through the area with lots of info on the various things to see. You can check it all out from the comfort of your hotel room or before you even arrive in Munich.

so ago, but instead of a 21st-century makeover, the building's austerity and simplicity were preserved, making the whole thing an archetypal European museum experience.

Da Vinci, Cranach the Elder, Dürer, Memling, Bruegel the Elder, Rubens, Botticelli, Rafael, Titian, Velázquez, Raphael…the list of big-name European artists goes on for room after room, every work a recognised, priceless masterpiece. There are too many highlights to mention, though Dürer's bearded self-portrait, Rubens' monster *Great Last Judgement* and Rembrandt's *Passion Cycle* stick in the memory. At the time of writing, some of the Alte Pinakothek was taken up by significant works from the closed Neue Pinakothek, the definite highpoint being one of Van Gogh's *Sunflowers*.

Museum Brandhorst

A bold and aptly abstract building, clad entirely in 36,000 vividly multihued ceramic tubes, the **Museum Brandhorst** (*museum-brandhorst.de; adult/child €9/free*) jostled its way into the Munich Kunstareal in a punkish blaze of colour in 2009. Its walls, floor and occasionally its ceiling provide space for some of the most challenging art in the world. Temporary shows are complimented by changing displays from the Brandhorst's own collections, 1200 pieces of art from the 1960s to the present day. These include many a Warhol, Hirst, Twombly and Katz.

The exhibitions here change every six months to a year, so you never quite know what you are going to get. But whatever is gracing the walls, flung across the floor or draped from the ceiling, it's gonna be world-class, headline-making art. Previous temporary shows have included *Alex Katz: Portraits and Landscapes*, *Warholmania in Munich* and *Five Friends: John Cage, Merce Cunningham, Jasper Johns, Robert Rauschenberg, Cy Twombly*. After your visit, there's a cool cafe in the foyer and one of the best art book shops in the northern hemisphere to peruse.

TOP TIPS

● Some try the Sunday €1 challenge – it is an exhausting slog and at the end of the day you probably won't remember where you saw what.

● The main works from the closed Neue Pinakothek can be seen at the Sammlung Schack and in the Alte Pinakothek.

● Many institutions in the Kunstareal are closed on Mondays.

● You can access the 25,000 works held by the Bavarian State Painting Collections online at pinakothek.de.

● The lawns around the Alte Pinakothek are a lovely place for a picnic lunch between galleries, though you certainly won't be alone.

Pinakothek der Moderne

Germany's largest modern-art museum, the cavernous **Pinakothek der Moderne** *(pinakothek.de; adult/child €10/free)*, brings together four museums under one roof and is therefore an engaging (and often confusing) mixed bag that has something for everyone. The exhibitions would fit into a building 10 times smaller and this is one of Munich's more exhausting museum experiences, but shows are well curated and always thought-provoking.

The State Gallery of Modern Art is the highpoint for most, with works by Picasso, Klee, Dalí, Kandinsky, Warhol, Twombly, Flavin and Beuys. The New Collection is a fascinating parade of applied design with everything from VW Beetles and Eames chairs to early Apple Macs and Czech Tatra cars. The State Graphics Collection has 400,000 pieces of art on paper, including drawings, prints and engravings by such artists as Leonardo da Vinci and Paul Cézanne. Finally, if you make it that far, there's the Architecture Museum, with entire studios of drawings, blueprints, photographs and models by top practitioners like baroque architect Balthasar Neumann and Le Corbusier.

Königsplatz Highlights

The original showcase for royal Wiitelsbach art established by Ludwig I, the Königsplatz features two grand old museum institutions. Both of the structures here, which face off over the lawns and limestone gravel, were designed by Leo von Klenze: the oh-so neoclassical **Glyptothek** *(antike-am-koenigsplatz.*

CLOSING OF THE NEUE PINAKOTHEK

One of Munich's highlights is the Neue Pinakothek. Housing the city's collection of van Goghs, Turners and Monets, it took its turn to close for renovation in 2019 (after the long closure of the Alte Pinakothek) and had been scheduled to reopen in 2025 at the latest. However, in 2022 the authorities dropped a bombshell when they put that date back a full four years to 2029. This means that by the time it reopens, the museum will have been closed for an entire decade. Many claim this is an unacceptable length of time for such a major visitor attraction to be shut.

State Museum of Egyptian Art

mwn.de; adult/child €6/free) is Munich's oldest museum, housing a feast of art and sculpture from ancient Greece and Rome amassed by King Ludwig I between 1806 and 1830, while the **Antikensammlungen** *(antike-am-koenigsplatz.mwn.de; adult/child €6/free)* showcases Greek, Roman and Etruscan antiquities. The collection of Greek vases, each artistically decorated with gods and heroes, wars and weddings, is particularly outstanding. Other galleries present gold and silver jewellery and ornaments, figurines made from terracotta and more precious bronze, and superfragile glass drinking vessels. Both museums are visited on a single ticket. Allow around two hours to do them justice.

The Doric-columned Propyläen is the grand gateway to the square, and on the opposite side the Nazis added the also neoclassical **Ehrentempel** containing the bodies of 16 Nazis killed in the Beer Hall Putsch. The two structures that formed the Ehrentempel were destroyed by the US Army in 1947 as part of denazification efforts and only the foundations remain fenced off at the eastern end of the square, rendered unrecognisable by foliage.

Lenbachhaus

At the northwest corner of the Königsplatz stands the **Lenbachhaus** *(lenbachhaus.de; adult/child €10/free)*, one of Munich's top galleries. The Lenbachhaus is named after Franz von Lenbach, a late-19th-century portrait painter who once had his studio here, a place where Munich's artist community would gather. This celebrated art museum (officially the Munich Municipal Art Gallery) specialises in the vibrant canvases by Wassily Kandinsky, Franz Marc, Paul Klee and other members of groundbreaking modernist group Der Blaue Reiter (The Blue Rider), founded in Munich in 1911. The gallery also puts on shows of contemporary and modern art, and its collections include works by Gerhard Richter, Sigmar Polke, Anselm Kiefer, Andy Warhol, Dan Flavin, Richard Serra and Jenny Holzer.

Tickets are also valid for special exhibits at the nearby **Kunstbau**, a 120m-long tunnel above the Königsplatz U-Bahn station accessible directly from it. This was added a decade ago to a design by British architect Norman Foster, but some regard it as one vanity gallery too far in the Kunstareal.

State Museum of Egyptian Art

If you fancy a change of tack from all the tortured artistic souls of 19th- and 20th-century art, the **State Museum of Egyptian Art** *(smaek.de; adult/child €7/free)* is located on the Königplatz. Completely rebuilt a decade ago, this well-curated, atmospherically illuminated concrete slab of a museum traces 5000 years of Egyptian and Sudanese history and has one of the finest collections in Europe. Descending into the bowels of the building is like delving into an Egyptian tomb beneath a pyramid, one packed with mummies, sarcophagi, ancient jewellery, sculpture and everyday items. It's a great place to bring the kids (who get in free) if they happen to be going through an Ancient Egypt phase.

> **EXPLORING FURTHER**
>
> Here we have listed the biggest attractions in the Kunstareal, but the show goes on in 26 other galleries, museums and venerable institutions. If you visited one a day, you'd need over a month to see everything from 5000-year-old Egyptian art to contemporary installations created while you were on the plane to Germany. For the full list, see the Kunstareal website: *kunstareal.de*.

Westend & Theresienwiese

VENUE FOR THE FAMOUS OKTOBERFEST

GETTING AROUND

The Theresienwiese is a short walk from the Hauptbahnhof (served by all S-Bahn lines and numerous trams and buses) but also has its own eponymous U-Bahn station (U4 and U5 lines) located on its northern edge. The Schwanthalerhöhe U-Bahn station is nearer to the Deutsches Museum Transport branch and the Bavaria statue. The only way to explore the actual Theresienwiese is on foot, unless you have a bike.

☑ TOP TIP

The Hauptbahnhof area has one of the highest concentrations of accommodation options in Munich. This is a good location that puts you within walking distance of many sights. However, don't even think about trying to stay here during Oktoberfest – bagging a room anywhere in Munich is almost impossible unless you book a year ahead.

If you've ever wondered where Munich's famous Oktoberfest actually takes place (some assume it's a city square, but believe us, there ain't one big enough!), it's here in Westend. The massive empty space that is the Theresienwiese fills to the brim with six million visitors over two weeks in late September and early October for the world's most celebrated booze-up and fun fair.

The Theresienwiese may dominate the neighbourhood but there's a bit more to the area than 'the meadow'. The main year-round draw is the second branch of the Deutsches Museum, which focuses on transport, plus there's the Augustiner Bräustuben, one of the Bavarian metropolis' most authentic beer halls. When not in use, the Theresienwiese is great for cycling, skateboarding, scootering and flying kites. It also has two interesting, year-round visitable attractions added by Ludwig I, who kicked off the whole Oktoberfest thing in 1810.

Meet the Meadow
Venue for the Oktoberfest

The vast, ear-shaped **Theresienwiese**, better known as the Wies'n (meadow), is the venue for Munich's world-famous Oktoberfest. Measuring 420,000 sq metres, for most of the year this is a big, vacant, gravelly space (it's not a meadow!), but for around two months in the European autumn it comes alive with one of the biggest annual knees-up anywhere on Earth. The name, meaning 'Theresa's Meadow', comes from Therese of Saxe-Hildburghausen, who married Crown Prince Ludwig I hereabouts in 1810. That launched what was the forerunner to the Oktoberfest we know today.

Oktoberfest isn't the only event that fills the Wies'n. In April, Bavaria's largest flea market occupies a substantial part of the venue and the Frühlingsfest beer festival also takes place here in the same month.

- **SIGHTS**
  1. Bavariastatue
  2. Deutsches Museum – Verkehrszentrum
  3. Ruhmeshalle
  4. Theresienwiese
  5. Umschreibung

- **SLEEPING**
  6. Hotel Königshof
  7. Hotel Krone München
  8. Hotel Mariandl
  9. Sofitel Munich Bayerpost
  10. Wombat's City Hostel Munich Hauptbahnhof

- **EATING**
  11. Kuchentratsch
  12. La Vecchia Masseria
  13. Marais

- **DRINKING & NIGHTLIFE**
  14. Augustiner Bräustuben

- **ENTERTAINMENT**
  see 8 Café am Beethovenplatz

At the western end of the 'meadow' stands Leo von Klenze's 1853 **Ruhmeshalle**, guarding solemn statues of Bavarian leaders, as well as the **Bavaria statue**, an 18m-high Amazon in the Statue of Liberty tradition, with an oak wreath in her hand and a lion at her feet. This iron lady has a cunning design that makes her seem solid, but actually you can climb via the knee joint up to the head for a great view of the Oktoberfest.

Munich's Best Beer Hall?

A true Munich beer experience

A few streets north of the Theresienwiese is another lager-related attraction, the Augustiner brewery, the oldest and second-largest of Munich's big six. Munich beer connoisseurs

MUNICH'S OTHER BEER FESTIVALS

In this city forever associated with world-class lager, Oktoberfest isn't the only hop-infused festival to take place in and around the Bavarian capital:

Starkbierzeit: Literally the 'Strong Beer Festival', this booze-up takes place over Lent in Munich beer halls, though the main action is focused around the Nockherberg.

Frühlingsfest: Simply a smaller version of Oktoberfest, the Spring Festival takes place on the Theresienwiese.

Herbstfest Erding: At the end of the S2 S-Bahn line, Erding is famous for its *Weissbier*, which is consumed by the gigalitre at the town's autumn fair.

Dachau Folk Festival: In mid-August, 300,000 drinkers gather on the town's main square to enjoy some of the most reasonably priced beer of any festival in the region.

LESTERTAIR/SHUTTERSTOCK

will know that Augustiner's unique flavour comes from the fact that this is the only remaining brewery in Munich to store its lager in oak barrels.

Come and experience the flavour for yourself at the **Augustiner Bräustuben** (at Landsberger Strasse 19 – near the Hauptbahnhof) – for many this is Munich's best beer hall. Due to the location, the atmosphere in the evenings is slightly more authentic than that of its city-centre cousins, with fewer tourists at the long tables, plus they do a mean *Schweinshaxe* (pork knuckle) to go with (arguably) Munich's best suds.

Transport Yourself into the Past
Planes and trains and Lastkraftwagen

The Deutsches Museum's 'other branch' is the **Deutsches Museum – Verkehrszentrum** (Transport Museum; deutsches-museum.de/verkehrszentrum; adult/child €8/5), located on a piece of raised land above the Theresienwiese. An ode to the Bavarian obsession with getting around, this museum explores the ingenious ways humans have devised to transport things and themselves. From the earliest automobiles to famous race cars and high-speed ICE trains, the collection is a virtual trip through transport history. The exhibition is spread over three historic trade-fair halls, each with its own theme – Public Transport, Travel, and Mobility & Technology. It's a fun place even if you don't know the difference between

Deutsches Museum – Verkehrszentrum

a piston and a carburettor. Classic cars abound, vintage bikes fill an entire wall and there's even a yesteryear petrol station.

Try to Work out the Umschreibung
Ponder an infinite staircase

Hidden away in the courtyard of a modern office block belonging to the KPMG building, **Umschreibung** is a mind-bending piece of public art created by Danish artist Olafur Eliasson in 2004. This intriguing sculpture consists of a spiralling double helix staircase made entirely of steel. With no beginning or end, the stairs loop infinitely in mid-air. Sadly, climbing the stairs is not allowed (you might be there forever!), but it makes a great selfie spot. This pretty unique piece of sculpture can be accessed at any time.

BEST MUNICH TOURS

Many agencies, companies and individuals run insightful tours around Munich. Here are some of the most enjoyable and worthwhile:

Radius Tours: Themed tours of Munich and beyond (Neuschwanstein, Salzburg). Its Third Reich tour is a longstanding classic.

Dark History Tours: Themed walks led by professional local-expert guides specialising in the Third Reich, WWII and medieval gore.

Munich Walk Tours: All kinds of walking tours in English including beer tours, the English Garden and cycling trips.

OzTour Munich: Award-winning city tours, Dachau trips and days out at Schloss Neuschwanstein.

Heart of Munich: Family-run agency offering city walking tours as well as interesting Third Reich and Munich Suburbs tours.

 EATING AROUND THE THERESIENWIESE: OUR PICKS

Kuchentratsch: This much-celebrated cafe gives local pensioners the chance to earn some cash by baking cakes. *10am-6pm Mon-Fri, 11am-5.30pm Sat & Sun* €

La Vecchia Masseria: This is one of Munich's longest-established Italian *osterie*. Choose between the beer garden out front or the earthy dining room. *11.30am-11.30pm* €€

Marais: Is it a junk shop, a cafe or a sewing shop? Well, Westend's oddest coffeehouse, is in fact all three, and everything is for sale. *8am-8pm Tue-Sat, 10am-6pm Sun* €€

Café am Beethovenplatz: At the Hotel Mariandl, this is one of Munich's last surviving music cafes, with heath-conscious mains and jazz in the evenings. *10am-1am* €€

Olympiapark & Around

OLYMPIC HERITAGE AND THE WORLD OF BMW

GETTING AROUND

U-Bahn is the quickest way to reach the Olympiapark and the BMW complex. The most convenient stop is Olympiazentrum which is near both. Trams 20 and 21 stop at Olympiapark West. Bus 144 cuts through the middle of the Olympiapark from Scheidplatz U-Bahn station. Once in the park, the your own legs are the best way of getting around. Otherwise a shared bike can be a good idea but e-scooters are banned for safety reasons. If arriving by car, there's a huge car park on the western side of the Olympic complex.

☑ TOP TIP

A good first stop is the Info Pavilion at the Olympic Ice Sports Centre, which has information, maps, tour tickets, audioguides and a model of the complex. Note that the Olympiapark went almost entirely cashless in 2025.

A fascinating part of Munich and something of an antidote to all that medieval madness in the Altstadt is the Olympiapark and adjacent BMW headquarters. Laid out for the 1972 Summer Olympic Games, the relatively modest Olympic site still sports its original structures and attractions, and is the venue for countless contemporary concerts and sports events. It's also just a pleasant place to stroll, enjoy a picnic, wander its eclectic sights and learn about the events of 1972, good and bad. Across a busy road is the BMW complex, which has three major attractions for disciples of Bavaria's luxury car brand, one of which is free to enter.

There really is a lot to see and do here, and you could spend a good two days in the neighbourhood if you decided to see everything. Getting here is as easy as jumping on the U-Bahn or a tram.

TOP EXPERIENCE

Munich's Olympiapark

Awarded in 1966, the 1972 Summer Olympics were significant for Munich as they gave the city a chance to make a historic break with the past. It was the first time the country had hosted the Games since the Berlin Olympics in 1936 with Hitler looking on. Under the motto the 'Happy Games', the Olympiapark was begun in the late 1960s.

Olympiastadion

With its contorted steel and plexiglass tent roof, the **Olympiastadion** was the centrepiece for the Munich Olympics and remains an instantly recognisable structure, especially for football fans – Bayern Munich played here until 2006 and West Germany famously won the 1974 FIFA World Cup on this hallowed turf. Still a phenomenal stadium today, it must have seemed like the work of alien beings in 1972. Daredevil tours of the roof run daily and the stadium is still regularly used for sports and live music events.

Ost-West Friedenskirche

One of the most intriguing sights at the Olympiapark has nothing to do with the 1972 Games and predates the complex by two decades. Built illegally after WWII by Russian hermit Father Timofey and his wife using debris from what would become the Olympiaberg, the delightfully rural Orthodox **Ost-West Friedenskirche** (East-West Peace Church) was to have been demolished for the 1972 Olympic Games but protests led to the repositioning of some of the venues further north. When Timofey died in 2004 his adjacent house was made into a museum.

In June 2023 the church burnt down. It's thought the authorities are likely to have it rebuilt as a symbol of peace in

DON'T MISS

Olympiastadion

Olympiaturm

Olympiaberg

Ost-West Friedenskirche site

Erinnerungsort Olympia-Attentat

Sea Life

PRACTICALITIES
- olympiapark.de
- Free admission to the park
- Grounds open 24hr

OLYMPICS RECYCLED?

Bavarians are passionate about recycling but in 2025 Munich's authorities came up with an idea that perfectly combines the locals' passion for sport and reusing stuff – Munich plans to bid for the 2036, 2040 or 2044 summer Games, recycling the 1972 venue for the event, an Olympic first.

'THE GAMES MUST GO ON'

These are the famous words of Avery Brundage, president of the International Olympic Committee during the 1972 Games. A Palestinian terrorist group known as Black September killed two Israeli athletes and took nine others hostage at the Olympic village, demanding the release of political prisoners and an escape aircraft. During a failed rescue attempt by German security forces at Fürstenfeldbruck military base, all of the hostages and most of the terrorists were killed. But the Games went on.

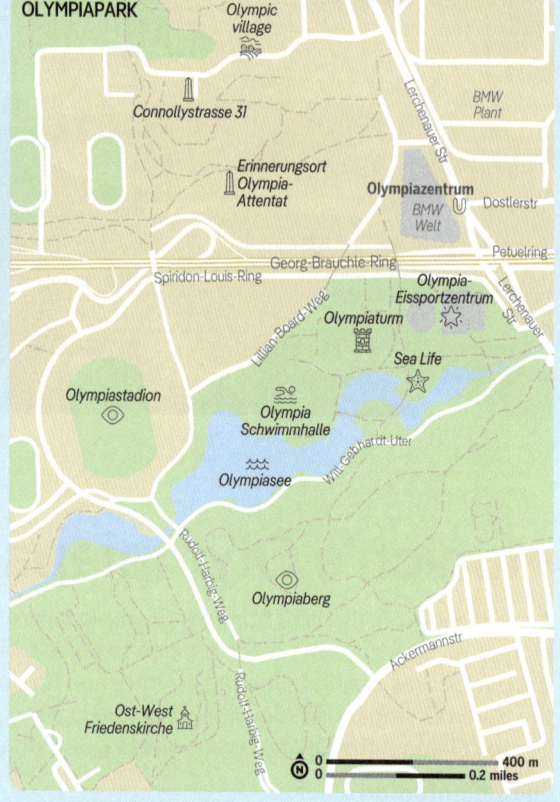

the city, though no definite plans exist as yet. Although the site of the church is now just an empty plot, the small piece of woodland still contains the wonderful museum dedicated to Father Timofey's life and work, and is like a little tranquil corner of rural Eastern Europe stranded in big city Bavaria.

Olympiaturm

The top visitor attraction at the Olympiapark is the 290m-tall **Olympiaturm** *(adult/child €13/10)*. The tower's lift to the three-level viewing platform 190m above ground is so fast that your stomach arrives several seconds after you do! Having recovered digestive composure you'll be rewarded with the best views of Munich bar none. The Alps are clearly visible when climatic conditions play ball. There's a cafe here and Munich's highest geocache as well as various exhibitions on the future of the Olympiapark.

Olympiaberg

A short walk to the south of the tower on the other side of the Olympiasee lake, the **Olympiaberg** (Olympic Mountain) rises 60m into the air and affords views of the park, much of the city and sometimes the Alps in the far distance. Incredibly, the 'mountain' was created from the WWII rubble from the city centre in the late 1940s and predates even the idea of holding the Olympics here. Its slopes have witnessed winter sports championships including snowboarding and slalom events.

1972 Sports Venues

Renovated a couple of times since the 1972 Games, the indoor **Olympia Schwimmhalle** (Olympic Swimming Hall) is the most modern and well-equipped swimming complex in Munich. When there isn't an event on it operates as a public swimming pool. The **Olympia-Eissportzentrum** (Olympic Ice Sports Centre) was actually the first sports facility to open here in 1967. It hosted boxing during the Games but has served as an ice rink and ice-hockey stadium ever since.

Other Attractions

There are many attractions in the Olympiapark, but one that was added decades after the Games ended is **Sea Life** *(visit sealife.com; adult/child €22/17.50)*. Reef sharks, moray eels and seahorses are among the thousands of creatures on display in monster aquariums which are divided into geographical locations, including Munich's own River Isar. The **Olympiasee** is a hive of activity in the summer months. You can even get out onto the water here by hiring a boat *(March to October)*.

Top Tours

The Olympiapark runs fascinating tours, some of which require a certain measure of audacity. The **Stadium Roof Tour** takes you onto the famous tent roof of the Olympiastadion for a vertigo-inducing view of the Olympiapark, while the **Flying Fox** involves a 200m-long zip-line flight 35m above the famous stadium pitch for an Olympian adrenaline rush. The two-hour **Architek-Tour** examines how the Olympic venues were built, but if you just want to go at your own pace, the **Olympiapark audioguide** does a superb job of handholding you round the complex.

Tragedy at the Games

The 1972 Olympics are unfortunately known for the attack carried out by Palestinian terrorists during which Israeli athletes were kidnapped and killed. Obviously not part of the plans for the Olympic complex, the surprisingly recent (2017) memorial **Erinnerungsort Olympia-Attentat**, just to the south of the Olympic village, remembers the victims. Housed beneath a striking wedge of concrete, a 10-minute video plays on a constant loop, relating the events of those terrible days with period footage. The life stories of the victims are posted opposite – some survived Nazi concentration camps only to die at the hands of terrorists in Germany. The hostages were taken within the Olympic village at **Connollystrasse 31**, a five-minute walk from the memorial, where there is a plaque in German and Hebrew. Continue along Connollystrasse to see the rest of the **Olympic village**, where some parts remain in a 1970s time warp.

TOP TIPS

- Take a picnic – surprisingly there aren't too many places to eat at the Olympiapark.

- This is an outdoor attraction – check the weather forecast before you go.

- In typical Munich fashion, the Olympiastadion was set to close for renovation in late 2025.

- Check out Munich's very own walk of fame on the north side of the Olympiasee with handprints left by some of the biggest names in pop and rock.

- The various facilities at the Olympiapark are major events venues – see the website for what's on.

- Leave a small donation to the fundraising effort to rebuild the Ost-West Friedenskirche.

BMW Welt (left) and BMW Museum

TOP EXPERIENCE

The BMW Experience

Munich is the home of BMW (Bayerische Motoren Werke), possibly the biggest brand name ever to emerge from the Free State. The company's headquarters are located right next door to the Olympiapark on the thundering Petuelring and this is where you'll also find BMW Welt and the excellent BMW Museum. Beyond extends the production plant where M3s and X6s are bolted and welded together.

DON'T MISS

BMW Welt

BMW Museum

BMW Plant Tours

Elvis' BMW 507

1950s Isetta models

BMW Welt

Even if you aren't into tomorrow's e-mobiles or spoiler design for the latest M3, the complex is still well worth a look, if only to enviously admire southern Germany's engineering prowess. Most start at **BMW Welt** (BMW World), a free exhibition-showroom-experience all rolled into one.

PRACTICALITIES
● bmw-welt.de ● BMW Welt: 7.30am-midnight Mon-Sat, from 9am Sun; free ● BMW Museum: 10am-6pm Tues-Sun; adult/child €14/8

The first thing you notice when emerging from the Olympiazentrum U-Bahn station is the building's striking, statement architecture, especially the double-cone (the work of Coop Himmelb(l)au Architects) like a tornado spiralling down from a dark cloud the size of an aircraft carrier. Inside, the exhibitions showcase the best of BMW's current output as well as acting as a big branding exercise and as a facility for handing over the keys to proud new owners (for a hefty fee).

Straddle powerful motorbikes, marvel at technology-packed e-saloons and estates (no tyre kicking, please) or learn more about the technology that goes into BMW's cars. There are guided tours, a couple of cafes and robots roam the floor providing information (there are strategically located humans, too).

And if your budget doesn't stretch to a new Rolls Royce Ghost (yes, BMW make those, too), you might at least be in a financial position to buy a branded pencil in the astronomically expensive BMW Welt Lifestyle & Accessory Shop. Otherwise leave via the double cone to reach the museum.

BMW Museum

Linked to BMW Welt by a special space-age footbridge, the **BMW Museum** is another piece of striking architecture, this time a gigantic silver bowl. Inside, the exhibition is divided up into 22 themed spaces, all brightly illuminated and multi-levelled, that take you through the BMW story as well as highlighting certain vehicles, technologies and company-related activities. High points to look forward to include a monster wall of BMW motorbikes down the ages, a room of old adverts and TV commercials in a tiny cinema, an exhibition dedicated to the iconic **1950s Isetta** (which most people erroneously assume only had three wheels), a showroom's worth of M series and **Elvis' 507**, the car he bought while serving in the US Army in Germany in the late 1950s.

More thought-provoking parts deal openly with BMW's use of slave labour during the Nazi period and the company's commitment to sustainable motoring – the section on hydrogen-powered vehicles will certainly grow in future years – watch this space. All in all, it's a fascinating journey, even for those who can't tell a telescopic fork from their axle load distribution. Allow at least two hours to see everything.

BMW Plant Tours

With a bit of forward planning, you can also have a guided tour of the **BMW Plant** *(adult/child €20/18)* which extends beyond the museum. Perhaps only for die-hard BMW fans, this two-hour, 3km stroll takes you behind the scenes of the truly state-of-the-art BMW production facility here, and runs in English and German. It is hugely popular with locals and tourists, and should be booked in advance through *bmw-welt.com*.

BMW & THE OLYMPICS

The BMW Tower, with its four cylinders rising into the blue Bavarian sky, was completed to coincide with the start of the 1972 Olympics, a sly bit of stealth advertising! That said, the company did supply vehicles to the organising committee – believe it or not an electric car with a whopping 30km range. You'll see it in the museum.

TOP TIPS

● Tickets for the BMW Museum can only be paid for by card or purchased online beforehand.

● There are three eateries at BMW Welt, though one of them is a fine dining spot.

● As BMW Welt opens early, it's a good idea to go there first and then to the museum before the crowds arrive.

● Plant tours only run from Monday to Friday.

● Photography on the plant tour is strictly prohibited.

● Many visitors combine the indoor pleasures of BMW with lawn time across at the Olympiapark in a single day out.

Nymphenburg

MUNICH'S FINEST PALACE AND BIGGEST BEER GARDEN

GETTING AROUND

There are two ways to reach the Nymphenburg area. The first is to take tram 17 from the Hauptbahnhof (and several other stops in the city centre) to the Schloss Nymphenburg stop. Laim S-Bahn station is 1.8km south of the palace but only a short walk from the Hirschgarten beer garden.

☑ TOP TIP

Porzellan Manufaktur Nymphenburg is the royal porcelain manufacturer, based near the palace. Its delicate pieces, often bearing traditional Bavarian motifs, are of the highest quality. If you're in the market for a pricey but beautiful souvenir, head for the company's flagship store on the Nördliches Schlossrondell by the lake as you enter the complex.

Jump aboard tram 17 heading west from the Hauptbahnhof and within 15 minutes you'll find yourself at the gates of Schloss Nymphenburg, for many Munich's most illustrious palace. The Wittelsbach dynasty's summer residence (they overwintered at the Residenz) is an opulent, highly decorative baroque and rococo affair with folly-dotted grounds to explore. When you're done with the tour, a couple of worthwhile museums occupy the north and south wings, one a youngsters' favourite.

The neighbourhood is also celebrated for two other things. Nymphenburg porcelain is a Munich phenomenon – the place to admire it is the Marstallmuseum in the south wing. Suitably inspired, you can then proceed to the company's flagship store nearby. As every local lager lover knows, the Nymphenburg neighbourhood prides itself on a world record – planet Earth's largest beer garden, where an entire small town could sit together to enjoy the capital's exceptional Augustiner.

Summer with the Wittelsbachs at Schloss Nymphenburg

Bavarian royal family's warm-weather residence

Set among generous gardens and placid water features, imperious **Schloss Nymphenburg** (*schloss-nymphenburg.de; adult/ concession €10/9*) lies around 5km northwest of the Altstadt. Begun in 1664 as a villa for Electress Adelaide of Savoy, this royal palace was extended over the next century to become the Wittelsbach family's opulent summer abode we see today. Franz, Duke of Bavaria, head of the Wittelsbach family, still occupies an apartment here.

The main palace building consists of a large villa and two wings of squeaking parquet floors and sumptuous period rooms. The self-guided tour kicks off in the highly decorative, rococo **Festsaal** (Grosser or Steinerner Saal), which dominates

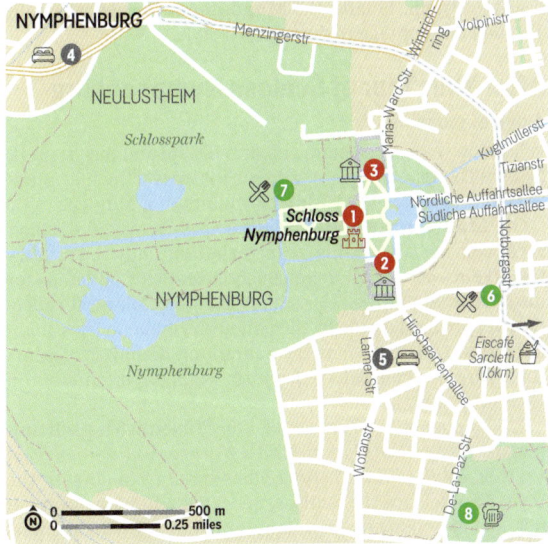

HIGHLIGHTS
1. Schloss Nymphenburg

SIGHTS
2. Marstallmuseum
3. Museum Mensch und Natur

SLEEPING
4. Hotel Amalienburg
5. Hotel Laimer Hof

EATING
6. Café Romanplatz
7. Schlosscafé im Palmenhaus

DRINKING & NIGHTLIFE
8. Hirschgarten

MUNICH MARATHON

Every October the capital of Bavaria puts on its running shoes and turns out for the Munich Marathon. It's one of Germany's 'Big Four' marathons and a World Athletics Federation official race. The start and finish are at the Olympiastadion, as you might expect, but the course is like a sightseeing tour of the capital, visiting the Königsplatz, the Marienplatz, the Residenz and Schwabing en route.

The half-marathon also now begins at the Olympiapark ending 2km later back where it kicked off on the track at the stadium. Sadly the 3km-long Trachtenlauf, a fun run around the Olympiapark in traditional Lederhosen and Dirndl, was not held in 2024 or 2025 but may be reinstated at some point in the future by popular demand.

---

the central section of the building. Soon comes the most famous room in the whole Schloss, the **Schönheitengalerie** (Gallery of the Beauties), housed in the former apartments of Queen Caroline. Some 38 portraits of females chosen by an 'admiring' King Ludwig I peer from the walls. The most famous image is of Helene Sedlmayr, the daughter of a shoemaker, wearing a lavish frock the king gave her for the sitting. You'll also find Ludwig's lover Lola Montez, as well as 19th-century gossip-column celebrity Lady Jane Ellenborough and English Lady Jane Erskin.

The tour route then visits the **Queen's Bedroom**, which still contains the sleigh bed on which Ludwig II was born, and the **King's Chamber**, resplendent with three-dimensional ceiling frescoes. Other notable rooms include Cuvilliés' **Chinese Lacquer Room** and the baroque **chapel**. Allow at least 90 minutes to see everything.

After the tour of the main palace, you can continue your day at Nymphenburg with a wander around the extensive grounds which contain several follies and minipalaces.

The park is at its most magical without the masses, early in the morning and an hour before closing. But even in the daytime, you can usually commune in solitude with water lilies and singing frogs at the **Kugelweiher pond** in the far northern corner.

The park's chief folly is the Amalienburg, a small hunting lodge dripping with crystal and gilt decoration and the work of the Wittelsbachs' favourite architect, Cuvilliés. Inside don't miss the amazing **Spiegelsaal** (Hall of Mirrors). The two-storey **Pagodenburg** was built in the early 18th century as a Chinese teahouse and is swathed in ceramic tiles depicting landscapes, figures and floral ornamentation. The **Badenburg** is a sauna and bathing house that still has its original heating system. Finally, the **Magdalenenklause** was built as a mock hermitage in faux-ruined style.

After Your Tour of Schloss Nymphenburg
A duo of museums

When you've seen the main palace building and the grounds, Schloss Nymphenburg is also home to two worthwhile museums, one of which is a children's highlight of Munich.

The **Marstallmuseum** *(adult/concession €8/7)* displays royal coaches and riding gear, including Ludwig II's fairy tale-like rococo sleigh, ingeniously fitted with oil lamps for his nocturnal outings. Upstairs is the world's largest collection of porcelain, made by the famous Nymphenburger manufacturer. Also known as the Sammlung Bäuml, it presents the entire product palette from the company's founding in 1747 until 1930.

In Nymphenburg's north wing, the **Museum Mensch und Natur** *(Museum of Humankind & Nature; mmn-muenchen. snsb.de; adult/child €3.50/free)* has nothing to do with the royal grandeur of the Schloss, and kids will have plenty of ooh and aah moments here. Anything but old school, it puts a premium on interactive displays, models and audiovisual presentations on themes such as food, the Earth and the human body. It's mostly in German, but few language skills are needed to appreciate the visuals.

Take a Seat at the World's Largest Beer Garden
Another unique Munich beer experience

The gargantuan **Hirschgarten** *(hirschgarten.de)* can hold up to 8700 drinkers, making it the world's largest beer garden. After a thirst-inducing tour of Schloss Nymphenburg, Augustiner beer lovers should steer southeast along Hirschgartenallee to reach the former deer enclosure turned public park (Hirschgarten means 'deer garden'). Let the kids run free on the playgrounds and skateparks as you sip a *Mass* of Munich's best lager and tuck into monster portions of Bavarian fare. The self-service area operates on an industrial scale when busy, a sight to behold, and the whole thing is a quintessentially Bavarian experience.

DUKE OF BAVARIA

Franz von Bayern, head of the Wittelsbach family, resides at Schloss Nymphenburg. Aged in his 90s, he's the grandson of Ludwig III, Bavaria's last monarch. He and his family fled to Hungary when the Nazis seized power in 1933, and by the end of WWII they were in the Dachau concentration camp.

After the death of his father, Albrecht, in 1996, Franz became pretender to the throne. The wealthy Wittelsbachs have an annual income of 14 million euros, though they now have no official say in state affairs. Interestingly, were it not for the Act of Settlement in 1701 that ensured a Protestant succession to the English throne, Franz von Bayern would be the current king of England! He has never pursued the matter...

EATING AROUND NYMPHENBURG: OUR PICKS

Sarcletti: This ice-cream cafe has been around since 1879, making it Munich's oldest. *9am-9pm mid-Feb-mid-Nov* €

Café Romanplatz: Much-lauded neighbourhood cafe with big breakfasts, cakes stacked high and some of Munich's best ice cream. *9am-6pm Sun-Fri* €

Hirschgarten (p84): It certainly isn't all about the beer at the planet's largest *Biergarten* with metric tons of Bavarian fare consumed daily. *11am-10pm* €

Schlosscafé im Palmenhaus: Behind the palace, this elegant lunch spot can be found in the early-19th-century royal hothouse. *10am-6pm Thu-Sun* €€

Haidhausen, Lehel & Au

NEIGHBOURHOODS OF HISTORY, ART AND ARCHITECTURE

Adjoining the Altstadt to the east and straddling the River Isar, the trio of districts called Haidhausen, Lehel and Au form a laid-back and quite eclectic area that's great for aimless wandering. While Haidhausen is mostly residential and relatively light on sights, chirpy Lehel has the second-highest concentration of museums after Maxvorstadt, and Au has a decidedly bucolic, small-town feel. Haidhausen is home to a mixed bag of attractions ranging from Art Nouveau swimming baths to the Bavarian Parliament. Wedged between Haidhausen and Lehel on an island in the Isar is one of Munich biggest must-sees, the Deutsches Museum, essential viewing especially for those in need of entertainment for the youngest of travellers. When hunger strikes, there are some excellent eating options in these parts, mostly without the tourist crush of the Altstadt and offering heaps of neighbourhood flavour. So bag up your swimming trunks and get your walking shoes on for a day in Munich's gentler inner suburbs.

GETTING AROUND

This area of Munich has many public transport stops. The S-Bahn makes a halt at the Ostbahnhof and Rosenheimer Platz while there are U-Bahn stations at Max-Weber-Platz and Lehel. To reach the Deutches Museum, take tram 17 to the Deutsches Museum stop or walk from Isartor. Tram 18 stops at Mariahilfplatz in the south of Au. Most people explore the area on foot, though with a day ticket you can hop on and off trams to save your legs.

Thinking Caps on for the Deutsches Museum

Bavaria's top technical museum

The **Deutsches Museum** (*deutsches-museum.de; adult/child €15/8*) fills the Isar's Museumsinsel (Museum Island) almost to capacity, with its task to persuade you that those unfathomable turn-off subjects you may have disliked at school (physics, geology, engineering, you get the picture) are, after all, quite interesting. Spending a few hours in this temple to technology is an eye-opening journey of discovery, and the exhibitions and demonstrations will certainly be a hit with young, sponge-like minds.

This is a huge museum by any standards, its permanent and temporary exhibitions taking up an overwhelming 20,000 sq metres of Munich real estate. A great way to tackle the place is to download the museum app, which will guide you through the highlights in around two hours. There are 20 permanent

☑ TOP TIP

The Auer Mühlbach stream is an idyllic place to stroll on a warm evening, especially the Klein Venedig (Little Venice) area around Mondstrasse. It's a surprisingly rustic area so close to the city centre. You can end your stroll at the Nockherberg for a tankard of Paulaner.

HAIDHAUSEN, LEHEL & AU

HIGHLIGHTS
1. Deutsches Museum
2. Müller'sches Volksbad

SIGHTS
3. Museum Fünf Kontinente
4. Museum Villa Stuck
5. Prinzregententheater
6. Sudetendeutsches Museum

SLEEPING
7. Hotel Opéra
8. Hotel Ritzi

EATING
9. Ayinger in der Au
10. Biergarten Muffatwerk
11. Cafe Exponat
12. Fischhäusl
13. Hofbräukeller
14. Swagat
15. Wirtshaus in der Au

exhibitions here examining everything from robotics and aviation to healthcare and agriculture to energy, photography...the list goes on. However, some of the most memorable exhibits are the entire planes hanging from the ceiling, the V2 rocket that extends for several floors through the building and the gaze-in-wonder space exhibition.

The place to entertain children aged three to eight is the fabulous **Kinderreich**, where 1000 activities await, from a kid-sized mouse wheel to interactive water fun. Get the kids to climb all over a fire engine, build things with giant Lego, construct a waterway with canals and locks, or bang on a drum all day in a – thankfully – soundproof instrument room. This is one of Munich's top children's attractions, but so popular that a new one-in-one-out system has had to be installed.

The Deutsches Museum is madly popular and you are advised to get there early even in low season. By lunchtime the queue for tickets snakes right around the building.

Visit Five Continents in Two Hours
Munich's fascinating ethnographical museum

One of Munich's least-visited collections (despite the attractive €1 Sunday admission) must be the **Museum Fünf Kontinente** *(Five Continents Museum; museum-fuenf-kontinente.de; adult/child €5/free, Sun €1)*, which is housed in a palace located on thundering Maximilianstrasse. The collections are made up of art and artefacts brought from across the globe by various expeditions. The initial rooms focus heavily on Myanmar before moving on to Thai Buddhas, buildings of the Islamic world, masks from Oceania, Peruvian costumes, North American headdresses and much more. As ethnographical collections go, it's pretty good, but the museum lacks a bit of oomph and innovation. And in case you were wondering, the two missing continents are Europe and Antarctica.

Delve into the Sudetendeutsches Museum
Reveal a lost European Culture

One of Munich's least-visited but best-curated museums must be the excellent **Sudetendeutsches Museum** *(sudeten deutsches-museum.de; adult/child €5/free)* dedicated to the three million Germans ousted from Bohemia and Moravia at the end of WWII. Surprisingly large and modern, the four floors of exhibits trace the history of the Sudeten Germans, from their arrival in Bohemia as miners and glassmakers to their radicalisation under Henlein and Hitler to their mass expulsion from their homes in 1945, and what became of their culture in Bavaria where the vast majority ended up, some of them making a significant contribution to the economic miracle decades. Some of the exhibition examines the traditional industries the Sudeten Germans developed – glass, wood crafts, jewellery, lace, porcelain, beads, etc – many of which the Czechs now call their own. The most moving section is a tumble of actual objects individuals took with them on the transports out of Bohemia and Moravia in 1945. The last floor looks at the life of the one million Sudeten Germans in Bavaria after WWII. Many of them kept the keys to their houses in the hope of a swift return...

TOP PLACES TO TAKE THE KIDS IN MUNICH

Munich is a surprisingly good place for a break with children. Here are our top picks when travelling to the Bavarian capital with kids:

English Garden: Let the kids enjoy the playground and grass as you kick back in the beer garden.

Deutsches Museum: The Kinderreich at Munich's science museum is great hands-on fun.

Münchner Marionettentheater: Children will love Bavaria's top puppet theatre.

BMW Welt: Little ones can grip the wheel of BMW's latest models and wish they were old enough to have a driver's licence.

Sea Life: Budding marine biologists will not want to leave Bavaria's top aquarium.

 EATING IN HAIDHAUSEN, LEHEL & AU: LOCAL LUNCH SPOTS

Cafe Exponat: A solid option within the Deutsches Museum complex if you're after a sandwich and coffee between museums. *10am-4pm* €

Fischhäusl: This Wienerplatz kiosk with a few seats is one of the best spots in Munich to lunch on fish. *9.30am-6pm Tue-Fri, 9am-2.30pm Sat* €€

Hofbräukeller: A Munich original beer hall with a wood-panelled dining room and reputedly Munich's first beer garden out back. *10am-midnight* €€

Swagat: An intimate cellar space with curry is as hot as Bavarians can take it, and plenty to please non-carnivores. *11.30am-2.30pm & 5.30pm-1am* €€

Admire the Grand Prinzregententheater
A Munich theatre for Wagner

One of the area's main architectural landmarks is the **Prinzregententheater**, a typically grand piece of 19th-century public architecture. Its dramatic mix of Art Nouveau and neoclassical styles was conceived under Prince Regent Luitpold as a festival house for Richard Wagner operas. The theatre opened in 1901 with a performance of Wagner's *Die Meistersinger von Nürnberg*. Today it is home to the Bavarian Theatre Academy, which celebrated its 30th birthday in 2023. Performances here range from Beethoven and chamber orchestras to farces and musicals. Wagner is nowhere to be seen on the programme.

Make a Splash at the Art Nouveau Müller'sches Volksbad
Swimming in style

Munich's most celebrated swimming complex, the **Müller'sches Volksbad** *(swm.de; adult/child €5.80/4)* is a real treat for those who like to pack their swimming gear when they head off on a city break or business trip. Built in the Art Nouveau style in 1901, this is one of Europe's most attractive swimming baths that's open to the general public. It was the city's first purpose-built pool and the largest in the world at the time. Today it comprises two pools, one cooler for swimming, the other warmer for relaxation. There's also a sauna, a steam bath and a worthwhile cafe.

Art Nouveau at Villa Stuck
Visit an artist's *Jugendstil* home

The **Museum Villa Stuck** *(villastuck.de; free)* is a must for disciples of the Art Nouveau style. In Germany, this period of art and design is called *Jugendstil*, and you won't find a better example of a home in this style than the house that once belonged to Franz von Stuck, a leading light in Munich's art scene at the turn of the 20th century and co-founder of the Munich Secession. The exterior of the building sports neoclassical lines, but inside von Stuck went to town using the motifs and materials of the day. The artist even won a gold medal at the legendary 1900 Paris World Exposition, making him one of the most celebrated exponents of the Art Nouveau style in all of Europe. Today this exquisite space is an attraction in itself but also functions as a gallery that hosts changing exhibitions. At the time of writing the whole thing was closed for renovation, but the museum has reopened in late 2025.

CYCLING MUNICH

Munich is one of the best cities in the world for those who want to see the sights with feet on pedals. And the good news is you don't have to haul your two-wheeler to Bavaria, nor know where you are going – there are plenty of pedalling enthusiasts here to help you with both.

Radius Tours *(radiustours.com)* is a Munich original that's been around for years, hiring bikes and running tours for tens of thousands of visitors since the 1980s. Its Munich Bike Tour is still the best. Another reliable and longstanding operator is **Mike's Bike Tours** *(mikesbiketours.com)*, which runs organised bike tours of Munich and offers bike rental. **MUCbike E-Bike Rent & Tour** *(mucbike.de)* has e-bike hire near the English Garden.

EATING IN HAIDHAUSEN, LEHEL & AU: OUR PICKS

Paulaner am Nockherberg: The modern restaurant at the Paulaner brewery comes into its own during Starkbierzeit, but is lively year-round. *noon-midnight* €€

Wirtshaus in der Au: Haidhausen's best resto-pub, with a beer-and-dumpling philosophy and cookery courses. *5-11pm Mon-Fri, from 10am Sat & Sun* €€

Biergarten Muffatwerk: An alternative beer garden at the Muffatwerk Arts Centre, with organic menu options. Only open in good weather. *noon-late* €€

Ayinger in der Au: Staunchly traditional, largely tourist-free restaurant serving a seasonal menu. *5-11.30pm Wed & Thu, 10.30am-midnight Fri-Sun* €€

AN ECLECTIC NEIGHBOURHOOD STROLL

Take a stroll across the Isar, passing some iconic sights as well as little-visited locations along the way.

START	END	LENGTH
St-Anna-Platz	St Nikolaikirche	3.1km 1.5 hrs

Start in the heart of Lehel, at the St-Anna-Platz, where the ❶ **Klosterkirche St Anna im Lehel** stands as one of Munich's finest rococo churches. From the square, follow the tramlines north until you hit busy Prinzregentenstrasse. Turn east and walk for 400m towards the river to visit the ❷ **Sammlung Schack**, home to Count Adolf Friedrich von Schack's collections of 19th-century Romantic paintings.

Crossing the River Isar, the Luitpoldbrücke lies at the foot of the ❸ **Friedensengel**, the Angel of Peace. The statue was erected atop a 23m-tall column to mark 25 years of peace after the Franco-German War of 1870–71.

From the Angel, stroll south through the park until you reach the ❹ **Maximilianeum**, an 1874 edifice that since 1949 has been home to the Bavarian Parliament. From the grandeur of the Maximilianeum, it's a short walk to the more down-to-earth attractions of the bustling ❺ **Wiener Platz**. This has become a mini gastro hot spot, with food trucks cooking up artisan takeaway. The large building on the western side is the ❻ **Hofbräukeller** (p87), said to have Munich's oldest beer garden. Head southwest along Innere Wiener Strasse to ❼ **St Nikolaikirche**. Built in 1315 in Gothic style, it was given a complete baroque restyling three centuries later.

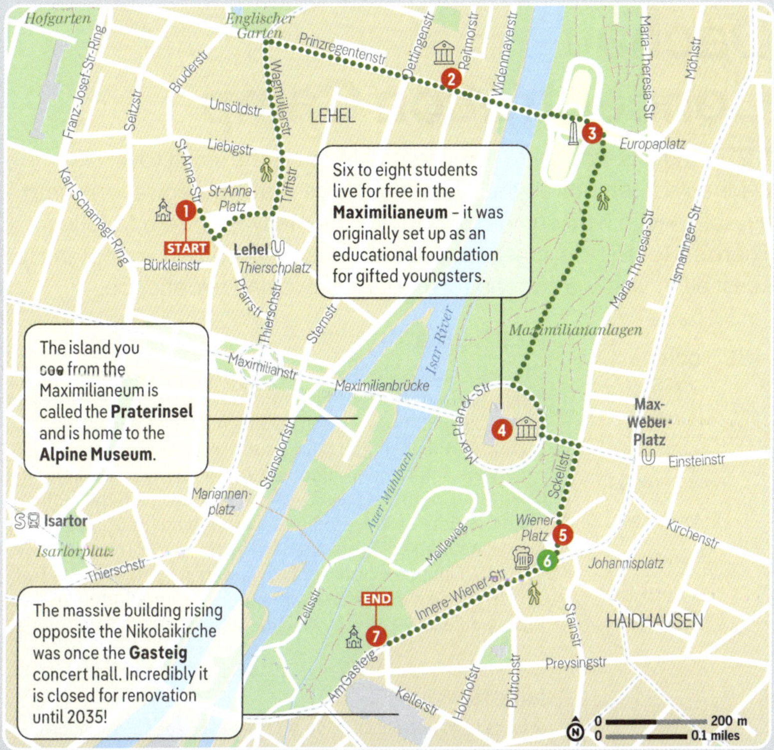

Six to eight students live for free in the **Maximilianeum** – it was originally set up as an educational foundation for gifted youngsters.

The island you see from the Maximilianeum is called the **Praterinsel** and is home to the **Alpine Museum**.

The massive building rising opposite the Nikolaikirche was once the **Gasteig** concert hall. Incredibly it is closed for renovation until 2035!

Barrack foundations

TOP EXPERIENCE

Dachau Concentration Camp

A 22-minute S-Bahn ride from central Munich, the small town of Dachau is infamous as the site of the Nazis' first concentration camp, established in 1933 and a blueprint for the many that were to follow. There's a lot to take in here so leave at least half a day in your plans to see it all. A visit is a soberingly thought-provoking experience.

DON'T MISS

Museum

Film on the camp's history

Crematorium

Barracks

International Monument

A Little History

Officially called the KZ-Gedenkstätte Dachau, this was the Nazis' first concentration camp, built by Heinrich Himmler in March 1933 to house pretty much anyone whom the Nazi regime found uncomfortable. Later, inmates from all over Europe were imprisoned here and in the many subcamps that were set up across Bavaria. As WWII continued, the majority of the inmates were used as forced labour in ammunitions plants, for bunker digging and in the plane construction effort. The main camp became a place largely for the sick and frail. All in all, Dachau 'processed' more than 200,000 inmates, killing at least 41,500. It was liberated by the US Army on 29

PRACTICALITIES
● kz-gedenkstaette-dachau.de ● Free, audioguide €5 ● 9am-5pm

April 1945. Surprisingly, the camp was used for another two decades as 'temporary' accommodation for Sudeten Germans forced out of Czechoslovakia at the end of WWII. It only became a memorial site in the mid-1960s.

The Museum

The main exhibition at the Dachau camp is housed in the former prison, kitchens, SS mess rooms and administrative blocks. Head straight for the cinema where a 38-minute **film** tells the story of the camp through eyewitness accounts. After that you are free to explore the six sections spread out over 13 spaces that examine different aspects of camp life. This includes medical experiments that were carried out here, punishments that were inflicted on inmates, the fates of individual prisoners, the different nationalities that found their way here and the forced labour for which the Nazis used them in their war effort. The last space is a memorial room dedicated to groups, nationalities and individuals who suffered and died here. There are countless information panels throughout the exhibition and it would take several hours to read them all.

The Barracks

Most of the camp grounds were made up of the **barracks** lined up in two rows (only their concrete foundations remain). Although the these were inhabited until the mid-1960s, only two were spared from demolition when the camp was turned into a memorial. You can walk through the building to see the sleeping quarters, washrooms and locker rooms, although everything you see is a mid-1960s reconstruction. The site does little to convey the cramped and sordid conditions the Americans found at the end of WWII. Built for 6000, there were 30,000 crammed into the 34 barracks in April 1945.

The Crematorium

In the far northwest corner of the memorial and actually outside the camp perimeter fence is one of the most chilling buildings in Dachau – the **crematorium**. The huge furnaces are still in place, as are the ceiling hooks from which prisoners were executed by hanging. You can also pass through the gas chamber, possibly the most disturbing space of all here, though mercifully it was never used.

Other Locations

The camp grounds contain many religious sites, churches and monuments. The main memorial site is the **International Monument** dating from 1968, a black metal, angular structure like a jumble of bodies, barbed wire, weapons and bones. At the far north end of the camp is a **Carmelite convent** established in 1964. Some of the **watchtowers** have been recreated along the perimeter fence.

THE DACHAU TRIALS

As in Nuremberg, trials of those responsible for Nazi crimes, some 1900 individuals, were held at Dachau after WWII. Some 28 death sentences were passed down, but some were commuted to life sentences and all those convicted of crimes against humanity were freed by 1958. A new exhibition at the Dachau camp examines this hitherto untold story.

TOP TIPS

- To reach the Dachau camp, take the S-Bahn to Dachau then change to bus 726 to the KZ-Gedenkstätte stop. You'll need a M+1 ticket.

- Dachau really isn't suitable for children or even teenagers who might find the exhibitions too disturbing.

- Time your visit to coincide with the excellent film about the camp shown in English at 10.15am, 11.45am and 2pm.

- There's a self-service cafeteria within the visitors centre serving reasonably priced meals and drinks.

- Visits here involve a lot of walking – in summer take water and sunscreen.

- Always behave with respect when visiting the camp.

Places We Love to Stay

€ Budget €€ Midrange €€€ Top End

The Altstadt MAP p51

Hotel Blauer Bock €€ Near the Viktualienmarkt, this simple hotel is a great deal for the location. Go for the economy rooms as there's little difference in standards and facilities. Also has a cool, '70s retro restaurant where you can end the day or begin the evening.

Flushing Meadows €€ Up-to-the-minute minimalist design on the top two floors of an industrial building in the hip Glockenbachviertel. There are views, designer styling and a restaurant to enjoy.

Louis Hotel €€€ This sophisticated hotel puts you right by the Viktualienmarkt and has elegant rooms, some with balconies affording city-centre views. Rooftop bar and restaurant.

Bayerischer Hof €€€ In an epicentral location since 1841, this is one of the grandes dames of the Munich hotel world. Elegant rooms, impeccably regimented staff, antique-dotted public spaces and five fabulous restaurants.

Cortiina €€€ Trend-setting, cool-minded hotel with feng shui–inspired rooms packed with design elements and funky fabrics. Has a wine bar on the premises.

Schwabing MAP p61

Gästehaus Englischer Garten €€ Occupying a 200-year-old ivy-clad mill, this small guesthouse on the edge of the English Garden offers an intimate, pre-millennium experience in individually done-out, antique-speckled rooms.

Hotel Hauser €€ The small rooms at this been-here-forever hotel in the heart of the uni quarter have a slight student residence feel but put you in an unassailable position at the thick of the city-centre action.

Maxvorstadt MAP p66

Pension Locarno € Absolutely no-frills guesthouse almost at the doors of the Hauptbahnhof with shared bathrooms and basic furnishings. Breakfast may or may not be included depending on how you book.

Das Kleine Hotel in München €€ There's a dearth of accommodation in Maxvorstadt so this 'little hotel in Munich' with its parquet floors, slightly dated fabrics and art sprinkled throughout is a well-used but welcome place to unpack.

Ruby Lilly Hotel €€ Industrial-style design hotel with striking communal areas and rooms, a rooftop bar, distracting views from the upper floors and pleasantly surprising rates.

Eden Hotel Wolff €€€ Looking out over the Hauptbahnhof, this first-rate hotel has been around for over 130 years and is still an exquisitely understated place to stay. There's a bar and restaurant on the premises.

Westend & Theresienwiese MAP p73

Wombat's City Hostel Munich Hauptbahnhof € Around for as long as there have been backpackers, this professionally run hostel comprises en-suite privates and dorms, a coffee shop, bar, clued-up staff and a great location a short walk from the main train station.

Hotel Krone München €€ Right by the Oktoberfest meadow, this boutique hotel has no two rooms the same, each one funkily done out in a fresh, young style. Breakfast is a rich spread and staff are welcoming.

Hotel Mariandl €€ Character-packed, old-tourism hotel with *Jugendstil* period rooms, hand-selected antiques throughout and a Vienna-style downstairs cafe, which also hosts frequent live jazz and classical-music nights.

Sofitel Munich Bayerpost €€€ The restored Renaissance facade of a former post office hides elegant rooms, a dramatically luxurious spa and a French restaurant. Supercentral location almost within the Hauptbahnhof.

Hotel Königshof €€€ Over-the-top luxury and obsessive attention to detail make the 'King's Court' a real treat if you like that sort of thing. Rooms range from better-than-average business standard to sumptuous belle époque–style quarters.

Olympiapark & Around MAP p76

Meininger Hotel Munich Olympiapark €€ This hostel-hotel on the southwest side of the Olympiapark has colourfully basic facilities, spotlessly clean rooms and breakfast for all who book.

Art Hotel Ana €€ This reasonably priced hotel has one distinguishing feature from all similar mid-range hotels in town and that is that it is situated within the Olympic village.

Rooms are inoffensive business standard.

Nymphenburg   MAP p83

Hotel Laimer Hof €€ Five minutes' walk from Schloss Nymphenburg, this hotel in a mini-chateau is a commendably tranquil refuge away from the city-centre crush. No two of the 23 character-packed rooms are alike.

Hotel Amalienburg €€ On the western edge of the Nymphenburg Palace grounds, this large business hotel has rooms of recent vintage that are a good deal when compared with similar in the city centre. Lots of facilities and good Bavarian breakfasts.

Haidhausen, Lehel & Au   MAP p86

Hotel Ritzi €€€ The rooms at this charming art hotel next to a little park teleport you to the Caribbean, Africa, Morocco and other exotic lands. But it's the *Jugendstil* features of the building that really impress.

Hotel Opéra €€€ A smart, petite cocoon of quiet sophistication with peaches-and-cream marble floors, uniquely decorated rooms and a tranquil Italianate courtyard where you can start and end your Munich days over breakfast and cocktails.

Outside the City Centre

Munich Central Camping € Actually located in Thalkirchen around 7km south of the city centre, this campsite offers pitches as well as pre-erected tents with sleeping mats. Facilities are generally clean, but there's no wi-fi. Bring your own bedding.

Apart Hotel Messe Munich € These tiny apartments out at the trade fair grounds in Riem are cheap, clean and suffice if all you need to do is sleep, shower and cook the odd meal. Messestadt West U-Bahn station is a short walk away.

H2 Hotel München Messe €€ Staying at the trade fair grounds can save a lot of euros, especially at weekends and around national holidays. The H2 with its basic rooms and no frills services is as good a place as any.

Schlosshotel Grünwald €€ In Munich's far southern outskirts, this quietly opulent mini-chateau hotel is where the cast of *Willy Wonka and the Chocolate Factory* stayed during the famous 1970 shoot. A real treat by the Isar near the terminus of tram 25.

Bayerischer Hof

Researched by Anthony Ham

Bavaria

ALPS, CASTLES AND CRAZY KINGS

Bavaria packs a lot into its 70,000 sq km, from the glorious Alps and fertile Danube plain to the moody Bavarian Forest and the toytown-medieval Romantic Road.

THE MAIN AREAS

NUREMBERG Explore Bavaria's second city. p100

BAMBERG Tour this architectural gem. p112

WÜRZBURG Wander this historical wine town. p118

THE ROMANTIC ROAD Journey along Germany's most popular holiday route. p122

AUGSBURG Discover this vibrant student city. p134

FÜSSEN Jump off here for Neuschwanstein. p138

GARMISCH-PARTENKIRCHEN Ascend Germany's highest peak – by train. p145

BERCHTESGADEN Take a boat trip on the Königssee. p152

CHIEMSEE Boat or cycle around the lake to a Ludwig II treasure. p157

REGENSBURG Gaze across the Danube at a UNESCO-listed cityscape. p159

PASSAU Marvel at the multihued confluence of three rivers. p168

BAVARIAN FOREST Hike these mysterious border forests. p172

Devouring a vast chunk of Germany's south, Bavaria is like a country unto itself (many locals nostalgically dream it still is), with multilayered diversity and sophistication to match. If you came to Germany to hear the slap of hand on Lederhosen and the tinkle of cowbells, to see storybook castles and half-timbered towns, to witness frothy steins slammed down on oak tables and the crunch of heart-shaped pretzels, then the Free State keeps its clichéd promises, and its millions of visitors happy. But incredibly varied Bavaria offers much more than the chocolate-box, felt-hat idyll. Descend from the Alps to learn about the rise and fall of the Nazis in Nuremberg, to follow the Wagner trail in Bayreuth, to discover Eastern Bavaria's glass-making traditions on the little-known Glass Road, or to sample a different local wine in every tavern in Würzburg. Paddle the River Altmühl, hike the Bavarian Forest or enjoy a smoked beer in Bamberg. Destinations are often described as possessing 'something for everyone', but in Bavaria's case it just happens to be true.

And the other good news is that Bavaria is easy! Munich Airport has a global schedule, a highly developed transport system will get you around, and accommodation and dining are at a high level even by Western European benchmarks. The Free State is no bargain, but is worth every cent to see.

For places to stay in Bavaria, see p176

Kaiserburg (p102), Nuremberg

Find Your Way

Bavaria has a well-developed system of roads and rail links, meaning getting around is simple, if now slightly more expensive than it once was. Note that there are no domestic flights within Bavaria.

Nuremberg, p100
Bavaria's second city, with a medieval Altstadt (old town), high-perched castle, Nazi heritage, lots of local beer, a studenty atmosphere and myriad kids' attractions.

Bamberg, p112
Enjoy a smoky beer before heading out on a stroll to see this pretty town's many attractions.

Würzburg, p118
Encircled by vineyards, this northern city is the best place in the Free State to sample German wine; then you can explore its rebuilt historical centre.

Regensburg, p159
A UNESCO-listed town straddling the Danube with a tightly packed historical centre.

Bavarian Forest, p172
These mysterious wooded hills form the border with Czechia and are known for their outdoor activities and glass-making traditions.

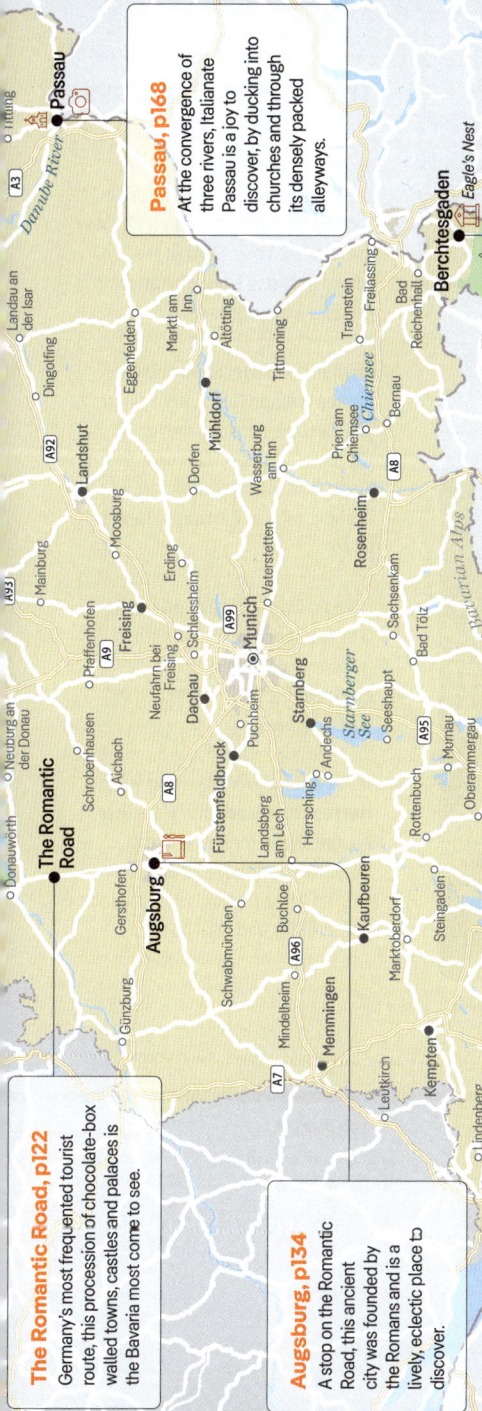

The Romantic Road, p122

Germany's most frequented tourist route, this procession of chocolate-box walled towns, castles and palaces is the Bavaria most come to see.

Augsburg, p134

A stop on the Romantic Road, this ancient city was founded by the Romans and is a lively, eclectic place to discover.

Passau, p168

At the convergence of three rivers, Italianate Passau is a joy to discover, by ducking into churches and through its densely packed alleyways.

Berchtesgaden, p152

A boat ride along the exquisite Königssee is an experience that will live long in the memory, as will the area's Nazi connections.

TRAIN

The vast majority of medium to large population centres in Bavaria are linked to each other and the remainder of Germany by rail. The Bayern Ticket (aka Bayern Regional Day Pass) gives 24-hour access to all of Bavaria's rail system (except high-speec services).

CAR

With its smooth, fast and laudably toll-free autobahn (highway) system, Bavaria is best explored by car. That is, until you reach the big cities, where parking can be a costly adventure and some 'eco' rules apply.

BUS

You'll only find yourself on a Bavarian bus in the Alps, in the Bavarian Forest and possibly if travelling by public transport along the Romantic Road. Larger cities have city-bus systems but you won't need to negotiate these much.

Plan Your Time

It would take at least a month to tick off just the major sights Bavaria has to offer – and that's without visiting its capital, Munich.

Augsburg (p134)

The Alps in Five Days

● Germany has only a sliver of the Alps, but most of these are in Bavaria, and it sure packs a lot into its modest share. Start in Füssen, where **Schloss Neuschwanstein** (p142) is a major draw.

● Then head east to **Garmisch-Partenkirchen** (p145), from where you can take a train to the top of Germany's highest mountain, the **Zugspitze** (p147), and hike along the spectacular **Partnachklamm** (p145).

● From Ga-Pa it's a short hop to **Oberammergau** (p148), with its frescoed buildings and nearby **Linderhof** (p150), one of Ludwig II's crazy castles.

● Travelling ever eastward via the **Herrenchiemsee** (p157) (another castle!), head for the magical **Berchtesgadener Land** (p152), with its amazing Königssee, hiking possibilities and Nazi past.

Seasonal Highlights

Bavarians are world champions at throwing a bash, normally trussed up in Lederhosen and Dirndl and with a *Mass* (1L beer) in hand. And this is no stereotype either.

JANUARY

Head to Garmisch-Partenkirchen on the sixth of the month for the **Hornschlittenrennen** (p146), a traditional sledge race.

FEBRUARY

The skiing season in the Alps reaches its climax with clogged pistes and queues at the ski lifts.

MAY

The summer hiking season slowly gets under way in the Alps, the Bavarian Forest and Franconia.

The Romantic Road in 10 Days

● The Romantic Road is one of Germany's grand epics, a real-life fairy tale of a multiday drive that stretches from **Würzburg** (p118) in the north to **Schloss Neuschwanstein** (p142) in the south.

● Major stops heading north to south include **Rothenburg ob der Tauber** (p124), with its half-timbered houses and walls, charming **Dinkelsbühl** (p128), down-to-earth **Nördlingen** (p130), big-city **Augsburg** (p134), and **Füssen** (p138) at the foot of the Alps, near the famous Wittelsbach castles at **Hohenschwangau** (p143).

● There are also many minor halts in between, each as enchanted as the one before. A road trip visiting two places a day would take around two weeks. You could do the main stop-offs in around a week, even by public transport.

A Two-Week Bavarian Odyssey

● For a whirlwind tour of Bavaria's high points, start in **Würzburg** (p118), with its vineyards and baroque Residenz, before heading south to **Nuremberg** (p100) for a couple of days exploring the Free State's second city; if you have more time, add a few extra days here. Next up is UNESCO-listed **Regensburg** (p159), for a day by the Danube.

● Follow the river to **Passau** (p168) to scramble around its tightly packed centre surrounded by water, before a long journey west to Munich to enjoy the attractions of the capital. With perhaps a stop at **Lake Starnberg** (p158), end your Bavarian odyssey at the base of the Alps at **Schloss Neuschwanstein** (p142), the state's most popular sight.

THE GUIDE

BAVARIA

JULY
Bayreuth's illustrious **Wagner Festival** (p117) starts in late July and continues for the rest of the summer.

AUGUST
Gäubodenfest (p166) is Bavaria's second-largest beer festival and draws over one million people to Straubing in mid-August.

SEPTEMBER
Autumn is the best month for gentle **hiking** (p172) in the Bavarian Forest, when the temperatures are still pleasant but the trails are empty.

DECEMBER
Nuremberg's **Christmas market** (p100) is reckoned to be Europe's prettiest, but almost every other town has a version of the event.

Nuremberg

CHRISTMAS MAGIC | SOULFUL HISTORY | FOOD & WINE

☑ TOP TIP

Available to those staying overnight in either city, the **Nürnberg Card** *(tourismus. nuernberg.de; adult/child €38/12)* is good for two days of public transport and admission to all museums and attractions. It can only be purchased from tourist offices or online from Nuremberg's official tourism website.

A city of half a million people, Nuremburg (Nürnberg) is Bavaria's second city, the thriving capital of Franconia and a place that wears its history for all to see. The Altstadt (old town) is packed with architectural reminders of the city's days as a medieval powerhouse within the Holy Roman Empire, as well as its decades as the centre of Renaissance art, when Albrecht Dürer plied his trade here. More recently it was one of the heartlands of both Nazi power and its demise, in the shape of the Nazi Rally Grounds and the courtroom that witnessed the Nuremberg Trials after WWII.

But away from the weighty medieval and horrific Nazi past, the city does have a lighter side. This is by far Bavaria's best place to bring kids, with more attractions aimed primarily at little ones than any other Bavarian city. A large student population also guarantees there's always a touch of hedonism in the air, much of it fuelled by Landbier, the myriad lagers shipped in from the Franconian countryside.

Christmas in Nuremberg
Germany's best Christmas market?

Of all Germany's Christmas markets, many agree that Nuremberg's is the best (though these days it gets a run for its money from the former GDR atheists of Dresden).

The event takes place on the Hauptmarkt against the backdrop of the city's medieval splendour. Fairy-lit stalls proffer

GETTING AROUND

The Altstadt is Europe's oldest and largest pedestrianised area, which makes getting around the centre a breeze. The only time you will need to jump aboard public transport is to visit some of the outlying sights, such as the Playmobil FunPark (take the S4 train then bus 151) and the Reichsparteitags-gelände (tram 8 from the main train station). Nuremberg Airport is conveniently linked to the city centre by the U3 metro line. For tickets, live info and travel planning, download the NürnbergMOBIL public transport app.

HIGHLIGHTS
1 Albrecht-Dürer-Haus
2 Deutsche Bahn Museum
3 Kaiserburg

SIGHTS
4 Albrecht Dürer Monument
5 Germanisches Nationalmuseum
6 Spielzeugmuseum
7 Way of Human Rights

SLEEPING
8 Agneshof
9 Art & Business Hotel
10 DJH Hostel
11 Five Reasons
12 Hotel Deutscher Kaiser
13 Hotel Drei Raben
14 Hotel Elch
15 Leonardo Royal Hotel
16 Probst-Garni Hotel

EATING
17 Albrecht Dürer Stube
18 Bratwursthäusle
19 Burgwächter
20 Café am Trödelmarkt
21 Essigbraetlein
22 Goldenes Posthorn
23 Heilig-Geist-Spital
24 Metzgerai Ludwig Walk

DRINKING & NIGHTLIFE
25 Barfüsser Brauhaus
26 Bierwerk
27 Café Katz

28 Die Blume von Hawaii
29 Harlem Bar
30 Hexenhäusle
see 26 Kloster

ENTERTAINMENT
31 Bavarian-American Hotel
32 Mata Hari Bar

SHOPPING
33 Käthe Wohlfahrt Christmas Shop

everything from Yuletide baubles and roast chestnuts to toffee and bottles of mead, as Nuremberg's own bratwurst and *Glühwein* (mulled wine) scent the chilly air. And, of course, it wouldn't be complete without a nativity scene. The market opens 1 December (or sometimes a couple of days earlier in late November) and runs until Christmas Eve. Weekends get busy with locals, tourists and Czechs who travel across the border – head here on a weekday for a less crowded experience. For more information on the event, visit *christkindlesmarkt.de*.

WHO WAS ALBRECHT DÜRER?

Nuremberg-born Albrecht Dürer (1471–1528) holds a special place in German hearts, not least because he was the first German artist to seriously compete with the Italian masters. He first established his reputation in the final decade of the 15th century when his woodcuts garnered international acclaim, and he went on to become the heavyweight of German Renaissance art. You'll find his work in museums all across Europe, but German galleries still hold many of his works. Munich's **Alte Pinakothek** is one place showing several famous works, while his Nuremberg **house** is now a museum. He is also credited with inspiring an entire generation of German masters, among them court painter Lucas Cranach the Elder.

Albrecht-Dürer-Haus

There's a slightly less storied Easter version that takes over the same space in the weeks leading up to Easter.

Make the Climb to Nuremberg's Imperial Fortress
Strongbox for the imperial crown jewels

Sitting high above the Altstadt, the Kaiserburg is one of Nuremberg's top attractions and one that reflects the city's erstwhile medieval status and power. Originally dating to the 12th century, this castle was deemed secure enough to be used as a safe location for the Holy Roman Empire's crown jewels (the crown, sceptre, orb etc), which are now kept at the Schatzkammer within the Hofburg palace in Vienna.

The **Kaiserburg** *(kaiserburg-nuernberg.de; adult/child incl Sinwell Tower €9/free, Palas & Museum €7/free, gardens free)* also played a key role in the drawing up of Emperor Charles IV's revolutionary Golden Bull, a document that changed the way Holy Roman Emperors were elected. The exhibition here includes an original statue taken from Prague's Charles Bridge of Charles IV, who spent a lot of time in both Bohemia and Franconia during his reign (he stayed at the castle 52 times). The link with Bohemia is a strong one, as an important trade route once ran directly between the two cities.

EATING IN NUREMBERG: CHEAP EATS

Café am Trödelmarkt: Lovely, peaceful lunch spot on Trödelmarkt Island with great blackboard specials. *10am-7pm Tue-Sun* €

Metzgerai Ludwig Walk: Find a deli and a street-facing counter that serves bratwurst, schnitzel and *Leberkäse* (meatloaf) in rolls. *8am-6pm Mon-Fri, to 4pm Sat* €

Bratwursthäusle: The bratwurst grilled at this rustic little inn next to the Sebalduskirche set the standard for the world to follow. *11am-10pm Mon-Sat, to 8pm Sun* €€

Goldenes Posthorn: Some of the city's best local bratwurst, served in a restaurant setting. *11am-11pm Tue-Sun* €€

At the end of WWII the castle was reduced to landfill. Most of what you see today is a postwar rebuild and a good one, too.

A visit to the Kaiserburg begins with the main attraction, the renovated residential wing (Palas) where you'll find the lavish **Knights' and Imperial Hall**, a Romanesque double chapel and an exhibit on the inner workings of the Holy Roman Empire. This segues to the **Kaiserburg Museum**, which focuses on the castle's military and building history. Elsewhere, enjoy panoramic views of the Altstadt from the **Sinwell Tower** or peer 48m down into the **Deep Well**.

Follow the Footsteps of a German Master
Discover Dürer's Nuremberg

Albrecht Dürer was born in Nuremberg in 1471, and he remained in the city for most of his working life. To begin your immersion in the world of Germany's most revered master artist, set aside at least a couple of hours for **Albrecht-Dürer-Haus** *(museums.nuernberg.de/albrecht-duerer-house; adult/child €7.50/2.50, audioguide €4/2)*. This is where the great man lived and worked for the final two decades of his life, from 1509 to 1528. The multimedia show may be a little OTT, but the audioguide guides you through the four-storey house, as narrated by 'Agnes', Dürer's wife; the tour offers a fascinating insight into Dürer's life and work. Highlights include the hands-on demonstrations (and opportunities to draw) in the recreated studio and print shop on the 3rd floor and, in the attic, a gallery featuring copies and originals of Dürer's work. The museum gift shop across the street is excellent. In addition to the self-guided tour, there's an English-language guided tour on Saturday at 2pm, and a special children's version with guides in period dress most Sundays from May to September at 3pm; both have additional costs.

One of the prettiest squares in Nuremberg's Altstadt, Albrecht-Dürer-Platz has the **Albrecht Dürer Monument**, a finely rendered statue of the painter surveying his city. Nearby, close to Pilatushaus, there's a glassy-eyed hare dedicated to one of Dürer's most famous watercolours, *Young Hare* (1502).

And while most visitors to Nuremberg are aware that Dürer lived and worked in the city, even some locals don't know that he's buried in crowded, medieval **St-Johannis Cemetery**. Surely one of Germany's most beautiful cemeteries, it's northwest of the Altstadt. Signs indicate the location of Dürer's grave.

THE NUREMBERG TRIALS

After WWII the Allied forces put prominent members of the Nazi regime on trial for their part in invasions and crimes against humanity. Some of the Nazi top brass, including Göring, von Ribbentrop and Hess, were made to answer for their roles in WWII. A total of 24 individuals (all of whom pleaded not guilty) were tried, the court handing down eight death sentences, which were carried out in October 1946. Apart from looking backwards at Nazi crimes, the trials also set up the next century of international legal jurisprudence, with crimes against humanity and war crimes entering the legal lexicon: despite arising as a concept earlier in the 20th century, these crimes were officially defined and prosecuted for the first time at Nuremberg.

 EATING IN NUREMBERG: OUR PICKS

Burgwächter: A convenient spot to refuel on Franconian dishes after visiting the Kaiserburg. *4-10pm Tue-Thu, 11am-10pm Fri & Sat, 11am-7pm Sun* €€

Albrecht Dürer Stube: Intimate Dürer-inspired restaurant serving venison, Nuremberg bratwurst and *Spätzle*. *5.30pm-midnight Mon-Sat, also noon-3pm Fri* €€

Heilig-Geist-Spital: This traditional Franconian restaurant is a candlelit affair with a carved-wood dining room and a pretty courtyard. *11.30am-11pm* €€

Essigbraetlein: Even gritty Nuremberg now has a double-Michelin-starred restaurant, serving nouvelle Central European dishes. *noon-3pm & 7pm-midnight Wed-Sat* €€€

A Trip Through the Deutsche Bahn Museum
Germany's top railway museum

Strip away Nuremberg's medieval pomp and you'll discover a gritty old railway town below the surface. In fact, Nuremberg was at one end of Germany's very first railway, which ran between here and neighbouring Fürth all of 6km away. Today the large main train station on the southern edge of the Altstadt is a major stop and junction on the German railway system, and the city's railway heritage and significance is reflected by the fact that German Railways decided to locate its national railway museum, the **Deutsche Bahn Museum** *(dbmuseum.de; adult/child/family €9/5/18)*, here. The large, nostalgia-inducing repository of its railway past is one of Nuremberg's unmissable attractions, especially if you're travelling with children.

Chuffing through almost two centuries of railway history, the main exhibition starts on the ground floor and continues with more recent exhibits upstairs. It passes quickly through the historically inaccurate beginning (as every rail buff knows, the world's first railway was the Stockton & Darlington, not the Liverpool–Manchester), with highlights including Germany's oldest railway carriage dating from 1835 and lots of interesting Deutsche Reichsbahn paraphernalia from the former East Germany.

However, the real stars of the show are the two halls of locos and rolling stock. The first contains Ludwig II's incredible rococo rail carriage, dubbed the 'Versailles of the rails', as well as Bismarck's considerably less ostentatious means of transport. There's also Germany's most famous steam loco, the Adler, built by the Stephensons in Newcastle-upon-Tyne for the Nuremberg–Fürth line. The second hall across the road from the main building houses some mammoth engines, some with their Nazi and Deutsche Reichsbahn insignia still in place.

KIBALA (Kinder-Bahnland – Children's Railway World) is the section of the museum where lots of hands-on, interactive choo-choo-themed attractions await kids. In addition to the permanent exhibitions, the museum also puts on interesting temporary shows with a railway theme.

Learn about Nuremberg & the Rise of the Nazis
Nazi rally grounds

Ever wondered where that B&W footage of Nazi rallies, with Hitler foaming at the mouth and marching masses bearing swastika banners, was shot? Well, some of it was in Nuremberg,

---

FRANCONIAN CUISINE

Franconia takes up much of northern Bavaria, and has its own culture, traditions and, most accessibly, cuisine. Franconian cooking shares many dishes and attributes with surrounding regions of Bavaria. Highlights include *Nürnberger Rostbratwurst* (p107); the *Coburger* (p117), Bavaria's longest sausage; *Klössen* (Franconian dumplings); *Maultaschen* (pork-and-spinach ravioli); and other hearty, more recognisably Bavarian dishes best enjoyed in a medieval, wooden-beamed cellar in winter, such as schnitzel, wild boar and snails. The dishes are not just paired with the region's world-class wines, but also cooked with them: bratwurst in wine, for example, or *Mostsuppe* (wine soup).

 DRINKING IN NUREMBERG: BEER BARS

Kloster: Superbly atmospheric *Landbier* drinking den dressed up as a monastery for those with a holy thirst. *5pm-1am*

Barfüsser Brauhaus: Down in the cellar below street level, this bar brews beer on-site and serves it up in a cavernous vaulted interior. *11am-1am*

Hexenhäusle: Half-timbered inn at the foot of the Kaiserburg serving local Tucher beer and beloved by locals. *11am-10pm Tue-Sat, to 9pm Sun*

Bierwerk: Popular Altstadt perch for beer lovers. Features 12 beers (including its own) and bottles from across the country. *6pm-midnight Mon-Thu, to 2am Fri & Sat*

THE ALTSTADT ON FOOT

This walk through the heart of Nuremberg's historic centre takes in most of the main attractions in an historic city that's ideal for exploring on foot.

START	END	LENGTH
Hauptmarkt	Lorenzkirche	2km 1-1.5 hours

Start on the ❶ **Hauptmarkt**, Nuremberg's epicentral square. At the eastern end rises the ornate Gothic ❷ **Pfarrkirche Unsere Liebe Frau**, also called the Frauenkirche. In the northwest corner, the 19m-tall ❸ **Schöner Brunnen** rises up from the square like a buried cathedral.

Leaving the square from the north, your next stop is the ❹ **Altes Rathaus** (Old Town Hall), below which is the ❺ **Mittelalterliche Lochgefängnisse** (medieval dungeons) with their 12-cell death row and torture chamber. Opposite stands ❻ **St Sebalduskirche**, Nuremberg's oldest church. Still heading north along Burgstrasse, you'll arrive at the ❼ **Stadtmuseum Fembohaus**, which documents the highs and lows of Nuremberg's past.

From here, head west then southwest to Albrecht-Dürer-Platz, with its dignified statue of the great painter, the ❽ **Albrecht Dürer Monument** (p102). Moving up Bergstrasse, you'll reach the massive ❾ **Tiergärtnertor**, a 16th-century tower. Nearby is the half-timbered ❿ **Pilatushaus**. A few steps east is the ⓫ **Historischer Kunstbunker**. By now, the medieval castle ⓬ **Kaiserburg** (p102) looms overhead. Across from the base of the castle stands the ⓭ **Albrecht-Dürer-Haus** (p103), where the Renaissance genius lived. From the castle area, turn back south and continue along Albrecht-Dürer Strasse and Karlstrasse, before crossing the bridge onto the ⓮ **Trödelmarktinsel**, an island in the River Pegnitz. From here, head further south until you reach the large ⓯ **Lorenzkirche**.

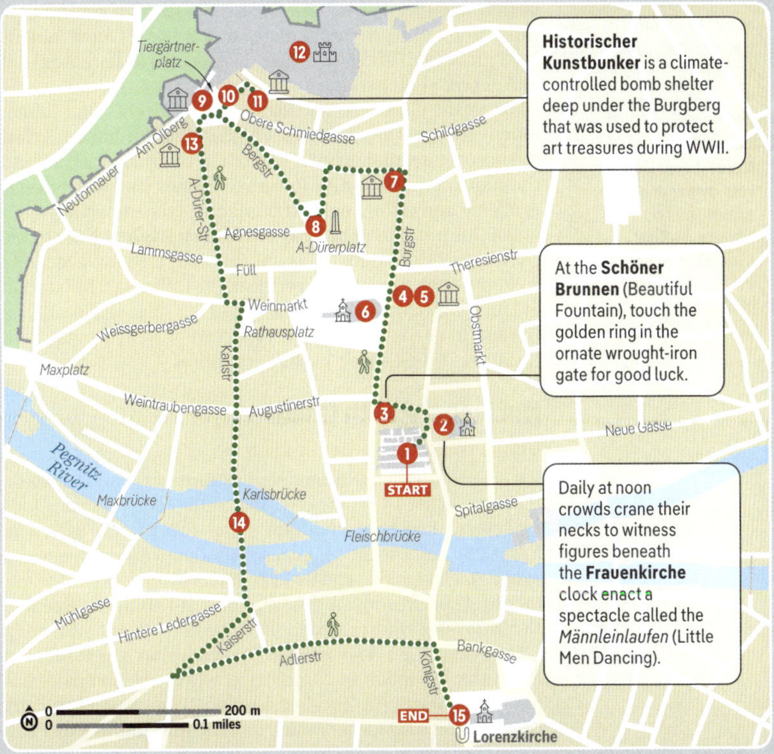

Historischer Kunstbunker is a climate-controlled bomb shelter deep under the Burgberg that was used to protect art treasures during WWII.

At the **Schöner Brunnen** (Beautiful Fountain), touch the golden ring in the ornate wrought-iron gate for good luck.

Daily at noon crowds crane their necks to witness figures beneath the **Frauenkirche** clock enact a spectacle called the *Männleinlaufen* (Little Men Dancing).

NUREMBERG TOURS

Geschichte für Alle: History-themed walking tours of Nuremberg run by real-live historians from the local history institute. *(geschichte-fuer-alle.de)*

Nuremberg: City of Empires Tours: Historical walking tours covering every aspect of the city's history, including group and private tours of the Altstadt and Dachau. *(nurembergtours.com)*

Nürnburg Tours: The local guides association runs walking tours of the old town in English and/or German. *(nuernberg-tours.de)*

Rent a Bike Nuremberg: Design your own tour and explore on two wheels; it's just over 500m south of the Hauptbahnhof. *(rentabike-nuernberg.de)*

at the **Reichsparteitagsgelände** *(grounds free, Documentation Centre adult/child incl audioguide €7.50/2.50)*, around 3.5km southeast of the Hauptbahnhof. It was undergoing major renovation works when we last visited.

Much of the grounds here were destroyed during Allied bombing raids, but enough remains to get a sense of the megalomania behind it, especially after visiting the excellent **Dokumentationszentrum** (Documentation Centre), which examines various historical aspects, including the rise of the NSDAP, the Hitler cult, the party rallies and the Nuremberg Trials.

To the east extends the **Zeppelinfeld**, where most of the big Nazi rallies took place. You can stand on the balcony from which the Führer whipped up the crowds. From the grounds the 2km-long, 40m-wide **Grosse Strasse** (Great Road) runs off to the southeast. This was planned as a military parade road.

To reach the parade grounds, take tram 8 from the Hauptbahnhof.

Revisit the Nuremberg Trials
Return to 1946 Germany

You can visit the courtroom used for the famous trials, now the **Memorium Nuremberg Trials** *(memorium-nuremberg.de; adult/child €7.50/2.50)*. Courtroom No 600 has been left pretty much as it was back then, and there's a multimedia exhibition telling the story of one of the world's most famous legal processes. To get here, take the U1 towards Bärenschanze and get off at Sielstrasse.

For all the darkness that surrounds the events that immediately followed Germany's surrender, the Nuremberg Trials did become a template for a new era in international law and the bid to end impunity for grave crimes like war crimes, genocide and crimes against humanity. One important symbol of this process is the **Way of Human Rights**. Next to the Germanisches Nationalmuseum, 30 austere, 8m-tall concrete columns, each bearing one article of the Universal Declaration of Human Rights in a different language (plus German), run the length of Kartäusergasse. Designed by Israeli artist Dani Karavan, it took shape in the early 1990s.

Nuremberg with Children
Germany's top kids' destination

It's safe to say that Nuremberg has more for children to do than any other Germany city. You could entertain your kids for several days here, and there's something for all ages, too. Every two months the region even produces a comprehensive 'what's on' magazine entitled *Frankenkids (frankenkids.de)*, focusing specifically on things to do with children. Keeping the little ones entertained in these parts really is child's play.

The popular toy Playmobil is known across the world, but few know it's made in Nuremberg, where the company has its headquarters (in Zirndorf, around 12km west of the city centre). That's also where you'll find the **Playmobil FunPark** (*playmobil-funpark.de; admission €22.90*), a large amusement park with rides, fast food, giant Playmobil figures and the inevitable factory shop. At Nuremberg's tourist office look out for Playmobil figures of Dürer, a nice educational souvenir.

The Playmobil FunPark is a pretty active place, but to get kids moving while in the city itself, head for the **Playground of the Senses** (*nuernberg.de; adult/child €9.50/8*). It's located 10 minutes' walk northeast of the Hauptbahnhof and has some 80 hands-on 'stations' designed to educate children about the laws of nature, physics and the human body. Walk or take the U2 or U3 to Wöhrder Wiese.

Celebrate Christmas all year-round with your kids at the **Käthe Wohlfahrt Christmas Shop** (*wohlfahrt.com; 10am-6pm Mon-Sat, 11am-5pm Sun*) in Plobenhofstrasse, just off the Hauptmarkt. It'll also be of interest to grown-ups. The shop sells Christmas decorations made of 10 different materials as well as countless other Yuletide bits and bobs.

Another obvious lure for children visiting the Franconian capital is the **Spielzeugmuseum** (*Toy Museum; museen.nuernberg.de/spielzeugmuseum; adult/child €7.50/2.50*). Nuremberg has long been a centre of toy manufacturing (it hosts the world's largest annual toy and games trade fair), and this large museum presents toys in their infinite variety – from innocent hoops and historical wooden and tin toys to Barbie and more. Kids along with kids at heart will delight in the imaginatively designed play area.

Other museums kids love include the Deutsche Bahn Museum (p104), where the KIBALA play area is superb fun; the small **School Museum** (*museums.nuernberg.de; adult/child €7.50/2.50*) in the suburbs (take tram 8 to the Tafelhalle stop), with mock-ups of period classrooms plus school-related exhibits from the 17th century to the Third Reich; and the **Children & Young People's Museum** (*kindermuseum-nuernberg.de; per person €8*), where heaps of educational exhibitions and hands-on fun for children and their parents await.

Away from the museums and playgrounds, there are other possibly unexpected attractions. Pre-teens can get excited about the city's driverless metro trains, in which you can sit at the front and pretend you are in control. When it comes to feeding time, bratwurst (possibly without the bed of sauerkraut) is always a winner, as is *Kloss*, a simple sweet dumpling with sauce. Or go to a soccer game at **Max-Morlock-Stadion**, the home stadium of **FC Nürnberg** (*fcn.de*), who were last seen languishing in the second tier of the Bundesliga.

NUREMBERG BRATWURST

Although a bratwurst will always be a bratwurst, there are almost as many different kinds of Germany's most famous sausage as there are towns and cities in the country. The Nuremberg version *(Nürnberger rostbratwurst)* is a smaller, slightly thinner affair, so much so that it's sometimes two to a roll. Like all bratwurst, the basic ingredients are ground pork along with salt and pepper, but delicate spices – marjoram is the mainstay, but lemon, ginger and cardamom are also sometimes used – are more often included here than they are elsewhere. Nuremberg bratwurst are sold all over the city from food stalls (especially during the Christmas and Easter markets) or from delis and butcher shops like Metzgerei Ludwig Walk (p102).

 DRINKING IN NUREMBERG: BEST CLUBS & BARS

Café Katz: Retro furnishings, great daytime coffee and a cool after-dark atmosphere when it becomes a wine bar. *11am-1am Sun-Thu, to 2am Fri & Sat*

Mata Hari Bar: Nuremberg institution that shows no signs of fading, with live acts and DJ nights. *3pm-2am Sun-Thu, to 5am Fri & Sat*

Die Blume von Hawaii: Arguably Nuremberg's best cocktail bar, the Flowers of Hawaii is one of Germany's best tiki bars. *6pm-1am Wed-Sat*

Harlem Bar: This low-lit, packed-out American bar concealed in the Altstadt has a long drinks list and DJs. *8pm-1am Thu, to 2am Fri & Sat*

THE BEERS OF FRANCONIA

Franconia shares much with Bohemia across the border to the east: landscape, history, food and, of course, beer. From Nuremberg's red-tinted Rotbier and Bamberg's smoky Rauchbier to wheat beers from tiny village breweries and dark, syrupy Doppelbock, you could try a different lager every day for several months in these parts. Widely known as Landbier, there are many for disciples of the hop to discover in the Franconian countryside, and the vast majority of output is produced adhering to the *Reinheitsgebot* (p300). You can try many of Franconia's obscure beers at an incredible shop appropriately called **Landbierparadies** at Galgenhofstrasse 60 (behind the train station), which stocks well over 50 types of locally micro-brewed lager.

Germanisches Nationalmuseum

Delve into Teutonic History at the Germanisches Nationalmuseum

Repository of the Teutonic past

Founded in 1852 and spanning prehistory to the early 20th century with 1.3 million objects (22,000 of which are actually exhibited), this Bavarian institution is the German-speaking world's biggest and most important museum of Teutonic culture. Note that the area covered includes the territories where German was spoken in the mid-19th century.

The extensive collections at the **Germanisches Nationalmuseum** *(gnm.de; adult/child €10/6)* feature works by German painters and sculptors, an archaeological collection, arms and armour, toys and musical and scientific instruments. Highlights to look out for include the UNESCO-listed Behaim Globe (the oldest in the world and made in Nuremberg), Dürer's anatomically detailed *Hercules Slaying the Stymphalian Birds*, some 20th-century design classics (chairs, kitchens, utensils), a large exhibition tracing the development of clothes since 1700 and a 16th-century pocket watch. When you're done, there's also a cafe and a superb museum shop.

Beyond Nuremberg

Joined at the hip with Nuremberg, Fürth has the region's top Jewish museum. Beyond lies a peaceful area of forested hills, valleys, streams and rock formations.

Nuremberg seamlessly runs into its neighbouring city Fürth, a settlement of over 130,000 people. Though of far less interest than Nuremberg, Fürth does boast the Jüdisches Museum Franken, a top-notch repository of the region's Jewish past.

Nuremberg's hinterland is a sensational place to explore for those who appreciate two things – fresh air and beer. Very similar to neighbouring Bohemia, Franconia is a dappled landscape of thick forests, out of which rise hilltop castles and some climbable rock formations. Also like their Slavic neighbours, Franconians like a lager, and the Forchheim Kellerwald boasts a greater gathering of breweries in one place than anywhere else on the planet. And Eichstätt is one of Bavaria's most underrated cities.

Fürth
TIME FROM NUREMBERG: **20 MINS** U

Explore Franconia's Jewish past

A quick U-Bahn ride away in the adjoining town of **Fürth**, the **Jüdisches Museum Franken** *(Franconian Jewish Museum; juedisches-museum.org; adult/concession/child €6/3/free)* is a must for anyone with an interest in the erstwhile Jewish community of northern Bavaria and its fate. Fürth once had the largest Jewish congregation of any city in southern Germany, and this museum chronicles the history of Jewish life in the region from the Middle Ages to today. It also stages excellent temporary shows with a Jewish theme. To reach the museum, take the U1 to the Rathaus stop in Fürth.

Forchheim
TIME FROM NUREMBERG: **30 MINS**

Oktoberforest on demand at Forchheim Kellerwald

It's often claimed that the area of Germany called Franconian Switzerland has the highest concentration of breweries in the world. And what better place to sample their output than at **Forchheim**'s amazing **Kellerwald**, literally a 'cellar forest'. There are 24 beer cellars, essentially creating the world's largest beer garden, though it's actually more like a village where every house is a pub! There are maps at the entrances showing drinkers where the individual cellars are located – most have a garden where you can sit as well as a

Places

Fürth p109
Forchheim p109
Eichstätt p110

GETTING AROUND

Two railway lines burrow their way north and east from Nuremberg into the wider area. From the main stations in Forchheim and Ebermannstadt local buses will (eventually) bring you to more remote areas, but having a hire car makes life a lot easier. From Eichstätt, regular trains run to Ingolstadt (25 minutes) and Nuremberg (1½ hours).

FRANCONIAN SWITZERLAND

Apart from Switzerland itself, Central Europe has many Switzerlands: places locals at least think look like the land of chocolate and enigmatic banking. Franconia's Switzerland (Fränkische Schweiz) is an area of low hills, rock formations and general tranquillity to the north of Nuremberg – a fine place for pulling on hiking boots and packing a picnic for a circuit through the forest. Very similar to western regions of neighbouring Czechia, this is also a landscape of castles, caves, canoeing and rock climbing. It's also a land of beer and you could spend several weeks exploring tiny village breweries and taverns. For more details and ideas, check the area's official website *(fraenkische-schweiz.com)*.

street kiosk for strolling imbibers. The challenge is to have a beer at every cellar in the forest within a day, but few make it to the end. For a more sober experience, there are also tours of the Kellerwald – check out *forchheim-erleben.de* for a range of options.

Forchheim is a stop on the railway heading north out of Nuremberg. The Kellerwald begins within walking distance of the station, to the northwest.

Eichstätt

TIME FROM NUREMBERG: 1½ HRS

Explore Eichstätt's Christian past

Hugging a strategic S-bend on the meandering River Altmühl, **Eichstätt** radiates a tranquil Mediterranean-style feel, with cobbled streets, elegantly Italianate buildings and leafy piazzas. That southern European look is no accident – it was Italian architects, notably Gabriel de Gabrieli and Maurizio Pedetti, who resurrected the town after the Swedes trashed it during the Thirty Years' War. Throughout Eichstätt's history, it was the power of the Catholic Church that drove its architectural grandeur. Later, WWII spared this small town, leaving its pretty streets and squares unblemished, allowing yet another happy Eichstätt marriage between religion and architecture: since 1980 many of its baroque facades have hosted faculties belonging to Germany's sole Catholic university.

Eichstätt's most impressive structure is its richly decorated **Dom** *(eichstaetter-dom.de; free)*, or Dome St Mariä Himmelfahrt und St Willibald, to give it its full name. This church dates back to the 11th century; the highlights inside include a huge, magnificent 16th-century stained-glass window by Hans Holbein the Elder, and a carved sandstone altar from the late 15th century depicting a pilgrimage from Pappenheim (a small town northwest of Eichstätt) to Jerusalem. Note also the tomb of English-born St Willibald, the town's first bishop.

Adjoining the cathedral on Residenzplatz is the **Domschatzmuseum** *(dioezesanmuseum-eichstaett.de; adult/concession/family €4/2/6)*, which is worth a look to see the robes of St Willibald and the baroque Gobelin tapestries illustrating scenes from the life of St Walburga. As in all cathedral museums, the cabinets filled with ornate silver and gold reliquary can be both dazzling and a little overwhelming.

Directly in front of the museum stands the baroque **Fürstbischöfliche Residenz** *(tour €2)*, where Eichstätt's bishops lived a lavish lifestyle. Entrance is by tour only; check in at the town's **tourist office** *(eichstaett.de)* for opening hours.

Also nearby – across Marktplatz, along Westernstrasse, and right at Walburgiberg – is the **Kloster St Walburga** *(abtei-st-walburg.de)*, a Benedictine convent. The final resting place of St Willibald's sister, the Kloster St Walburga is a popular local pilgrimage destination. Between mid-October and late February water oozes from Walburga's relics in the underground chapel and drips down into a catchment. The nuns then bottle

Willibaldsburg

NATURE PARK VS NATIONAL PARK

Close to Nuremberg and southwest of Regensburg, Altmühltal Nature Park *(naturpark-altmuehltal.de)* is one of Germany's largest nature parks (2900 sq km). It protects a swath of the Altmühl River and its riverbank, meandering through valleys and hills before joining the Rhine-Main Canal and eventually emptying into the Danube. But why is this is a nature park and not a national park? The difference lies in the degree of protection afforded to the landscape and what activities are permitted there. In a German national park, activities are usually restricted to hiking, whereas in a nature park the rules are more relaxed. In other words, the natural world is protected only up to a point in a nature park, and recreation activities are central to the park's existence. Scan this QR code for park info.

diluted versions of the so-called *Walburgaöl* (Walburga oil) and give it away to the faithful.

Don't forget to take the ascending staircase from the lower chapel; although the upper chapel is off-limits, look through the grill at the exquisite tablets and offerings left for the saint. Pause for a while also in the main church, known for its extravagant rococo interior.

Visit the Town Castle

If religion was at the heart of daily life in medieval Eichstätt, so too was the need to keep an eye out for invading armies. The castle of **Willibaldsburg** *(schloesser.bayern.de; adult/concession/child €5/4/free)* is what kept the town safe. Built in 1355, it can be reached on foot via the bridge across the river and passing the train station. The views are what impress the most, and there's a welcome beer garden and a couple of museums up here too. Of these, we especially like the **Jura-Museum** with its local fossils that include a locally found archaeopteryx (the oldest-known fossil bird).

Bamberg

HISTORIC ARCHITECTURE | UNESCO OLD TOWN | CITY LIFE

☑ TOP TIP

The **BAMBERGcard** *(bamberg.info; per person €22)* covers entry to most museums, a two-hour city tour and free local public transport. It's at its best value in summer when all the attractions are open. You can buy it online or from the **tourist office**.

The epicentre of Bavaria's north and a simple day trip from anywhere in Franconia, Bamberg is a disarmingly beautiful architectural masterpiece that the last two centuries seem to have overlooked. It's a place that well deserves its UNESCO listing and is generally regarded as one of Germany's most attractive towns. All of this praise has led to it becoming a popular destination for Bavarians and just about everyone else, and it can become a little overwhelmed with visitors, especially in summer. Most visitors come to stroll the streets and view the cathedral and prince-bishop's residence. Others find a pew in the city's temples to the smoky local lager – Rauchbier – to quench their thirst. The town can be tackled as an excursion from Nuremberg, but to do it justice and to experience the romantically lit streets once the crowds have evaporated, consider an overnight stay.

Admire an Architectural Treasure

Photograph the famous Altes Rathaus

If you've seen any images of Bavaria, chances are that you've seen Bamberg's **Altes Rathaus** *(adult/child €6/5)*. Built to span an artificial island in the Regnitz River in 1462, it's a classic, multistorey half-timbered structure given magical properties by its position overhanging the river. The interior boasts a remarkable collection of porcelain pieces and an opulent rococo

---

GETTING AROUND

Getting to Bamberg is easy, as it has frequent rail connections to Berlin (2¾ hours), Munich (two hours), Nuremberg (40 minutes) and Würzburg (one hour) among others.

Once you're in town, you can only really explore Bamberg's Altstadt on foot, but city buses link the train station with the central bus terminus, and bus 910 connects the terminus to the Domplatz. If you're driving, the old town's tangle of one-way and pedestrian streets can be confusing. Find your hotel, drop off your bags and leave the car in an overnight parking garage (€18 to €20 per 24 hours).

HIGHLIGHTS
1 Altes Rathaus
2 Fränkisches Brauereimuseum

SIGHTS
3 Klein Venedig

ACTIVITIES
4 Klosterbräu

SLEEPING
5 Hotel Residenzschloss
6 Hotel Sankt Nepomuk

EATING
see 4 Klosterbräu
7 Schlenkerla

SHOPPING
8 Käthe Wohlfahrt

INFORMATION
9 Tourist Office

---

hall, but the highlight has always been the view from the pedestrian-only **Greyerswörthbrücke**, south of the structure. Tip for photographers: zoom in all you like, but a wide-angle lens that takes in both banks of the river is the money shot.

According to local legend, the unusual location for the town hall happened because the powerful local bishop at the time refused to give Bamberg's residents and secular authorities any land. Undeterred, they came up with the ingenious solution of building an island in the river. The Rathaus is also known for its gloriously frescoed facades; note the cherub's leg cheekily protruding from the east-facing wall.

And while tourists are busy snapping away, locals often come to the island to relax and chill with a bottle of wine as the day turns the corner into evening.

Follow Bamberg's Beer Trail
Discover the pleasures of Rauchbier

In a region known for its high-quality beers, it takes a lot for a town to stand out as a destination for beer lovers. But Bamberg has cred, thanks to its long history of producing excellent beers, a tradition that very much continues today.

To learn about that history, and to dive deeply into the world of Franconian brewing, a visit to the **Fränkisches Brauereimuseum** *(Franconian Brewery Museum; brauereimuseum.de; adult/*

BAMBERG HISTORY

Bamberg was founded in the 9th century. It was briefly the centre of what remained of the Holy Roman Empire, a key strategic trading centre between Germanic and Slavic spheres, and its own centre of largely independent power. Infamous for its 17th-century witch trials (nearly 1000 were condemned to death), Bamberg lost much of its power when it was folded into Bavaria at the start of the 19th century. The city's antiquity lives on through its architecture.

A STROLL THROUGH BAMBERG

There's no finer way to explore this UNESCO World Heritage–listed marvel than by walking Bamberg's twisting lanes and cobblestones.

START	END	LENGTH
Obstmarkt	Klein Venedig	2.5km; 2 hrs

Start your explorations at the ❶ **Obstmarkt** from where it's a short amble to your first stop, Bamberg's ❷ **Altes Rathaus** (p112), one of Bavaria's most recognisable structures.

From the island, follow Dominikanerstrasse, passing some of the town's Rauchbier breweries as you go, and hang left up to the large Domplatz. There are three attractions here – first up is the ❸ **Bamberger Dom**, a cathedral boasting more than its fair share of artistic treasures. Topping the list is the *Bamberger Reiter* (Bamberg Horseman); the Virgin Mary altar is by Veit Stoss.

The ❹ **Neue Residenz** was the home of the prince-bishops between 1703 and 1802 – guided tours show you around its lavish apartments. Also here is the ❺ **Historisches Museum** in the Alte Hofhaltung, which presents the area's history in a mixed bag of exhibits.

Leaving Domplatz at the northwestern corner, it's a 600m uphill walk to ❻ **Kloster St Michael**, once a Benedictine monastery. The interestingly decorated church is essential Bamberg viewing and the panoramas from the gardens (formerly vineyards) are worth the climb.

Head down from the monastery via the Erthalweg and Elisabthenstrasse back to the river. On the opposite bank, ❼ **Klein Venedig** (Little Venice; p115) is a row of half-timbered cottages that balance on poles set right into the water, hence the nickname.

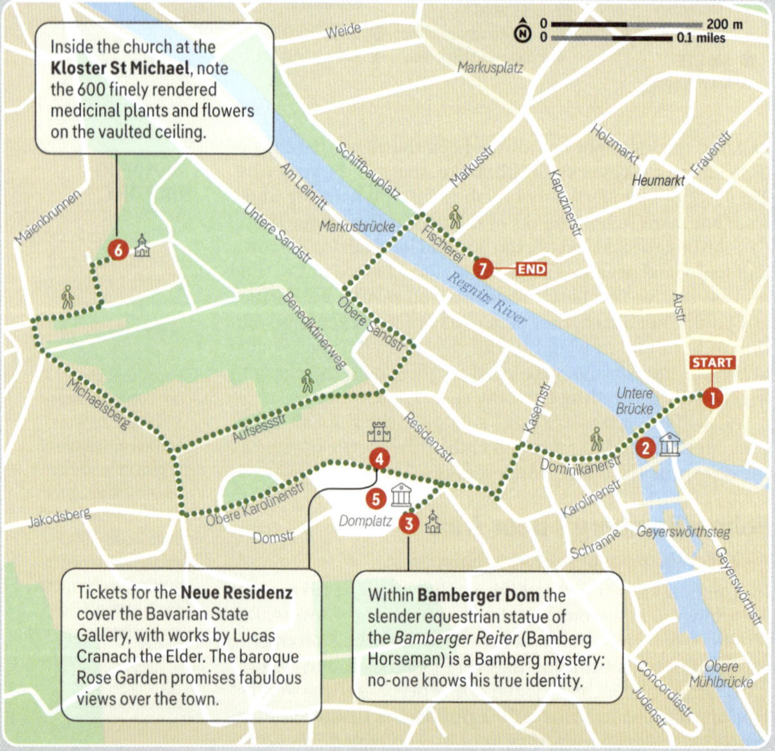

Inside the church at the **Kloster St Michael**, note the 600 finely rendered medicinal plants and flowers on the vaulted ceiling.

Tickets for the **Neue Residenz** cover the Bavarian State Gallery, with works by Lucas Cranach the Elder. The baroque Rose Garden promises fabulous views over the town.

Within **Bamberger Dom** the slender equestrian statue of the *Bamberger Reiter* (Bamberg Horseman) is a Bamberg mystery: no-one knows his true identity.

concession €4/3.50; 1-5pm Wed-Fri, 11am-5pm Sat & Sun Apr-Oct, shorter hours rest of year) is for beer lovers akin to a pilgrimage.

Reinforcing the historical connection in Germany between monasteries and the brewing of beer, the museum occupies the Kloster St Michael, and it's a pretty comprehensive collection of all things brewing. The museum even nods to the importance of the pleasures of temptation, offering a small pub where you can sate your curiosity and quench your thirst.

Having learned about the history and the theory of local beers, it's time to zero in on the Bamberg beer story, and gain some practical experience. No fewer than 10 breweries in Bamberg cook up the town's famous Rauchbier, literally 'smoke beer'. The smoky bouquet comes from the malt being smoked over beechwood, a common practice elsewhere until a couple of centuries ago that still holds sway in Bamberg. **Klosterbräu** *(klosterbraeu.de; tour per person €18)* is Bamberg's oldest brewery, having begun operations in 1533. It's a fine place to start, with a restaurant, a bar and a brewery where you can sample the end product; the brewery tour (advance reservations required) lasts for 45 minutes to an hour.

To broaden your beer horizons, the Bamberg tourist office (p113) has put together a self-guided **BierSchmecker tour** *(bamberg.info; per person €29.50)*, which includes a tankard of the local brew at four of the breweries (you can choose from the Fässla, Sternla, Keesmann, Schlenkerla, Spezial, Greifenklau, Ambräusianum or Klosterbräu breweries), plus entry to the Fränkisches Brauereimuseum and some souvenirs of your boozy stroll. Naturally all of Bamberg's pubs and bars offer Rauchbier to wash down the very filling, meat-heavy local food.

Enjoy the View of Bamberg's Little Venice
Photograph Kleine Venedig

On the east bank of the Regnitz between Markusbrücke and Untere Brücke, you'll find an enchanted collection of small, half-timbered cottages known as **Klein Venedig** (Little Venice). Once fisherfolk homes, they perch atop poles anchored in the river's rushing waters; some have tiny gardens and terraces, while red geraniums cascade from flowerboxes during the summer months. Most of the cottages have small boats moored outside, and they're still used by the inhabitants to move up and down the river.

Any resemblance to the real Venice is, of course, tenuous at best, but no-one seems to mind. Although you can wander along Fischerei, on the land-side of the homes, the best views are from Untere Brücke near the Altes Rathaus, and Am Leinritt on the opposite bank.

CHRISTMAS IN BAMBERG

Apart from the region's Christmas markets, which take over Bavarian towns in the weeks leading up to Christmas, nothing captures the spirit of a German Christmas quite like **Käthe Wohlfahrt** *(kaethe-wohlfahrt.com)*. Arguably the world's most-famous Christmas shop and a German institution, it made its name in Rothenburg ob der Tauber, which is still home to the **flagship store and workshop**. But you can also find smaller versions of the store selling the traditional wooden decorations here in Bamberg, as well as in Nuremberg (p107), Oberammergau and elsewhere around Germany. And, of course, Bamberg has its own **Weihnachtsmarkt** (Christmas Market), which takes place during Advent (late November until just before Christmas) in Maximiliansplatz, a few blocks northeast of the Altes Rathaus.

 EATING IN BAMBERG: OUR PICKS

Spezial-Keller: Malty Rauchbier, food from a wood-fired stove and sweeping views of Bamberg's old town. *3-10pm Tue-Fri, 2-11pm Sat, 11am-3pm Sun* €€

Klosterbräu: The town's oldest brewery serves Franconian dumplings and meat dishes, washed down by local brews. *2-11pm Wed-Fri, 11am-11pm Sat & Sun* €€

Schlenkerla: Rauchbier poured straight from oak barrels and superb Franconian cooking served beneath heavy wooden beams. *10am-11.30pm* €€

Zum Sternla: Bamberg's oldest *Wirtshaus* (inn; established 1380) serves pork dishes, steaks, dumplings and sauerkraut. *11am-11pm Tue-Sun to 9pm Mon* €€

Beyond Bamberg

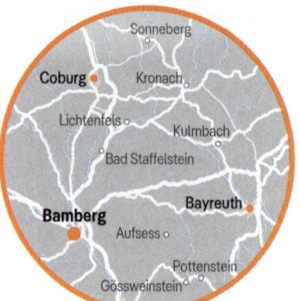

Get to know a double act of fascinating towns with famous former inhabitants.

Places
Coburg p116
Bayreuth p117

Two engaging towns within easy reach of Bamberg merit particular attention, though for quite different reasons. To the north, and once almost encircled by East Germany (and hence the Iron Curtain), Coburg is the birthplace of one of the most famous members of the British royal family. Bayreuth to the east, on the other hand, is celebrated for its Wagner connections, including the world's most popular Wagner festival. Both towns bear the legacy of their erstwhile overlords, the Saxe-Coburgs and Wilhelmine, sister of King Frederick the Great of Prussia. Away from these lofty themes, sample the local Coburg sausages, admire the architecture and don't miss Europe's largest Samba Festival in Coburg in July.

GETTING AROUND

Coburg and Bayreuth have rail connections to Bamberg, Nuremberg and to each other. If you want to visit both by train in one day from Bamberg, you'll need to plan carefully and get started early; depending on the hour, you may need to change at Lichtenfels or Nuremberg in between. If time is of the essence, having your own vehicle makes it a lot easier.

Coburg
TIME FROM BAMBERG: **30 MINS**

Follow in Queen Victoria's footsteps

Coburg was the birthplace of Albert of Saxe-Coburg-Gotha, later Prince Consort to Queen Victoria of England. Albert was born at nearby Schloss Rosenau but spent his childhood at **Schloss Ehrenburg** *(schloesser-coburg.de; adult/child €5/free)* in Coburg.

Queen Victoria made several visits as a young woman, staying in a room with Germany's first flushing toilet. The bed she slept in is still here, as are several depictions of one of Britain's most famous monarchs.

So why is the British Royal Family called Windsor and not Saxe-Coburg? In 1917, with Great Britain at war with Germany, the name was quietly changed to Windsor, after Windsor Castle.

A greening **bronze statue of Prince Albert** occupies the main square called the **Marktplatz**, with its fabulous Renaissance facades.

Visit a castle art gallery

Built in 1225, **Veste Coburg** *(kunstsammlungen-coburg.de; adult/senior/child/family €9/7/2/18)* is a fortress with three rings of fortified walls. It's a visual feast towering over Coburg's centre. Inside the castle, the **Kunstsammlungen** is a world-class art collection with works by Rembrandt, Dürer and Cranach the Elder.

Try the local specialities

Coburg is a terrific place to try local Franconian culinary traditions. Coburg's best-known contribution to world gastronomy is Bavaria's longest sausage, the 30cm *Coburger*, which is grilled over pine cones and inserted into a tiny bun. Food trucks sell it all over town.

For something a little more refined, **Goldenes Kreuz**, just off Marktplatz, is known for serving Franconian food, including the sausages, as well as *Klössen* (dumplings) served with roast meats.

Bayreuth
TIME FROM BAMBERG: 1 HR

On the Wagner trail

For music lovers, **Bayreuth** means one thing: Wagner. The city is known as the venue for the most famous Wagner festival in the world. With the backing of King Ludwig II, Richard Wagner (1813–83) turned Bayreuth into an epicentre of opera and high-minded excess.

Wagner actually designed his own festival hall in Bayreuth, the **Festspielhaus** *(bayreuth-tourismus.de; adult/concession incl tour €10/7)*. North of the train station, it's the main venue for the **Wagner Festival** *(bayreuther-festspiele.de)*. The structure was specially designed to accommodate Wagner's huge and elaborate theatrical sets, with three storeys of mechanical works hidden below stage. It's still one of the largest opera venues in the world. To see inside, you will have to join a daily tour.

The other big Wagner attraction in town is the **Richard Wagner Museum** *(wagnermuseum.de; adult/student €10/8)*, housed in a mini-mansion the composer built with money given to him by Ludwig II, his biggest fan. Exhibitions within the Haus Wahnfried examine Wagner's life and work as well as the history of Bayreuth's Wagner Festival. Behind the house, hidden behind a ring of rhododendron bushes, lies the completely unmarked, ivy-covered tomb of Wagner and his wife Cosima. The sandstone grave of Russ, his loving canine companion, is nearby.

Surprisingly, Wagner shunned the **Markgräfliches Opernhaus** *(schloesser.bayern.de; adult/concession €10/9)*, Bayreuth's UNESCO-listed baroque opera house. Renovated a decade ago, this is one of Europe's most opulent baroque theatres.

BAYREUTH'S WAGNER FESTIVAL

Bayreuth has been holding its **Wagner Festival** *(bayreuther-festspiele.de)* for over 140 years, the event generally regarded as the top Wagner fest anywhere on Earth. The festival lasts for 30 days (from late July to late August), with each performance attended by an audience of just over 1900. Demand far outstrips supply, with perhaps millions competing for around 60,000 tickets.

The vast majority of tickets go onto the open market in an online free-for-all, and every ticket is snapped up in seconds. Alternatively, it's still possible to lay siege to the box office two hours before performances begin in the hope of obtaining cheap returned tickets, but there's no guarantee you'll get in. Scan this QR code festival info

Würzburg

CITY LIFE | LOCAL WINES | BEAUTIFUL ARCHITECTURE

GETTING AROUND

Getting to and from Würzberg is easy. Regular train connections include Bamberg (one hour), Frankfurt (one hour), Munich (two hours) and Nuremberg (one hour). For Rothenburg ob der Tauber (one hour), change in Steinach.

The train station lies north of the city centre and is linked to it by tram. Once you're in the Altstadt, almost all the sights are best tackled on foot. The exception is the Festung Marienberg – to get here you might want to take a taxi or hire an e-scooter.

☑ TOP TIP

The **Würzburg Wine Pass** *(Würzburger Weinkarte; €9.90)* allows you to enjoy three glasses of local wine in any of the participating wine restaurants around town (one per restaurant). These include Juliusspital, the Bürgerspital and the Staatlicher Hofkeller at the Residenz. See *wuerzburg.de* for more details.

On a bend in the River Main, the northern terminus of the Romantic Road is a busy city known for wines, architecture and a miraculous rise from the ashes of WWII. Würzburg was infamously annihilated in an air raid by the British Royal Air Force in March 1945, but the postwar decades witnessed a revival like no other across what was then West Germany. Today this lively city hums with students and tourists, the latter arriving to tour the Residenz, one of Germany's finest baroque buildings, and to sip the delicate wines fermented in local wineries that harvest grapes from the surrounding slopes. The Bürgerspital, Juliusspital and Staatlicher Hofkeller are the three big producers, their wines readily available across town. Würzburg's large student population also keeps things lively. With excellent road and rail connections to the rest of Germany, Würzburg is easy to reach, but hard to leave.

Visit Würzburg's Residenz
Unrivalled baroque masterpiece

The vast UNESCO World Heritage–listed **Würzburg Residenz** *(residenz-wuerzburg.de; adult/child €10/free)*, built by 18th-century architect Balthasar Neumann as the home of local prince-bishops, is one of Germany's most beautiful baroque palaces.

The structure was commissioned in 1720 by prince-bishop Johann Philipp Franz von Schönborn, who was unhappy with his old-fashioned digs up in Festung Marienberg (p121), and took almost 60 years to complete. Today the 360 rooms are home to government institutions, university faculties and a museum, but the grandest 40 have been restored for visitors to admire.

Top billing goes to the zigzagging **Treppenhaus** (staircase), topped by the world's largest fresco, a masterpiece by Giovanni Battista Tiepolo depicting allegories of the four then-known continents (Europe, Africa, America and Asia). After that, feast your eyes on the ice-white stucco-adorned **Weisser Saal** (White Hall) before entering the **Kaisersaal** (Imperial Hall), canopied by yet another impressive Tiepolo

HIGHLIGHTS
1 Festung Marienberg
2 Würzburg Residenz

SLEEPING
3 Babelfish
4 Hotel Rebstock
5 Hotel Zum Winzermännle

EATING
6 Alte Mainmühle
7 Backöfele
8 Bürgerspital Weinstube
9 Capri & Blaue Grotto

DRINKING & NIGHTLIFE
10 Heinrich
11 Juliusspital
12 Wohlsein Weine Würzburg

THE DESTRUCTION OF WÜRZBURG

In March 1945, an air raid carried out by British RAF bombers flattened 90% of Würzburg's city centre. Over 1200 tonnes of explosives were dropped by Lancaster bombers in just 20 minutes, creating a firestorm in which 5000 people died. The historical core was reduced to landfill. The scale of the destruction remains controversial to this day, as is the case with Dresden, which met a similar fate.

fresco. Another memorable interior is the gilt **Spiegelkabinett** (Mirror Hall), covered with mirror-like glass painted with figural, floral and animal motifs.

In the residence's south wing, the **Hofkirche** (Court Church) is another Neumann and Tiepolo co-production. Its marble columns, gold leaf and profusion of angels match the Residenz in splendour and proportions.

Entered via wrought-iron gates, the **Hofgarten** (Court Garden) is a blend of French- and English-style landscaping teeming with whimsical sculptures of children, mostly by court sculptor Peter Wagner.

 EATING IN WÜRZBURG: OUR PICKS

Capri & Blaue Grotto: Around since 1952, this is more than your average pizza and pasta place. *5-11pm Mon-Fri, noon-midnight Sat, noon-10pm Sun* €

Backöfele: Franconian cooking including schnitzel, snails, bratwurst in wine and boar. *5-11pm Mon-Fri, noon-midnight Sat, noon-11pm Sun* €€

Alte Mainmühle: Franconian classics (including river fish) served in a converted mill by the old bridge with great views in summer. *11am-11pm* €€

Bürgerspital Weinstube: This medieval dining experience offers up superb regional dishes, including *Mostsuppe* (tasty wine soup). *11am-midnight* €€

EXPLORING WÜRZBURG ON FOOT

Trace Würzburg's remarkable post-WWII rebirth from the narrow streets of the old town to the fortress on high.

START	END	LENGTH
Hauptbahnhof	Festung Marienberg	2.5km; 2 hrs

Begin at ❶ **Hauptbahnhof**, north of the city centre, then head west and follow the Röntgenring to 8a where you'll find the ❷ **Röntgen-Gedächtnisstätte (Röntgen Memorial)**, the preserved laboratory of Nobel Prize in Physics winner Wilhelm Conrad Röntgen, with an exhibition and film about his life and work. From Röntgenring, head south along Koellikerstrasse, then follow the tramlines across Dominikanerplatz to the Oberer Markt and Unterer Markt. Behind the rococo facade of the ornately stuccoed ❸ **Falkenhaus**, you'll find the main tourist office. Head back to the tramlines, then south for 100m to the satisfyingly symmetrical ❹ **Neumünster**, whose Romanesque original was given a typical baroque restyle by the Zimmermann brothers. Next door to the Neumünster rises ❺ **Dom St Kilian (Würzburg Cathedral)**, possibly Germany's oddest cathedral with its incongruous mishmash of architectural styles. Balthasar Neumann's Schönbornkapelle (a chapel within the cathedral) returns a little baroque order to things. From the cathedral, walk west along Domstrasse to the ❻ **Grafeneckart**. Dating to 1659, it houses a scale model and an exhibition on the WWII bombing. Climb the tower to appreciate the city's remarkable recovery from above. At the foot of the Grafeneckart begins the Alte Mainbrücke, the 16th-century bridge spanning the River Main. A 1km uphill walk brings you to the ❼ **Festung Marienberg** (p121), a huge fortress housing two museums.

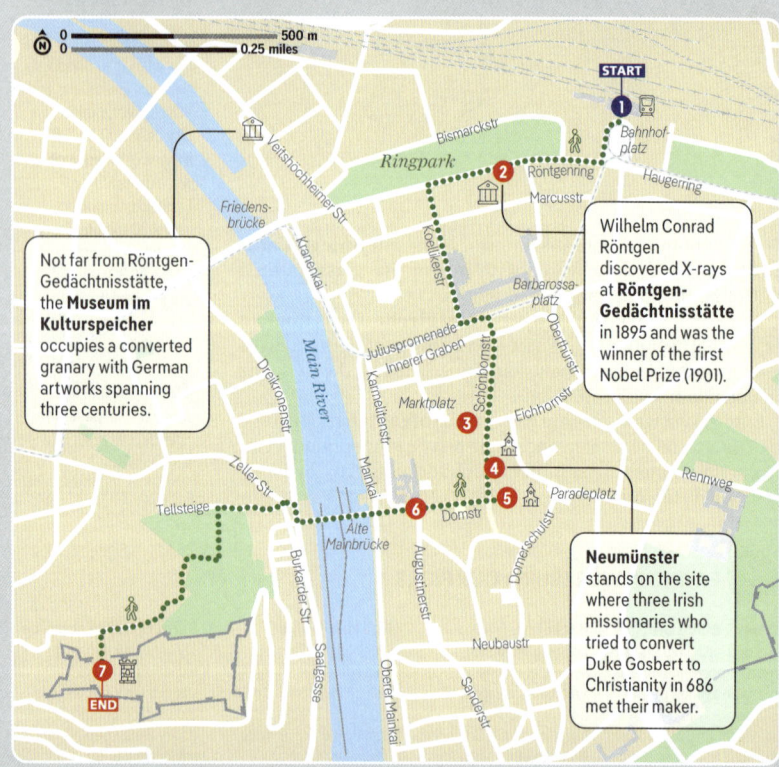

Not far from Röntgen-Gedächtnisstätte, the **Museum im Kulturspeicher** occupies a converted granary with German artworks spanning three centuries.

Wilhelm Conrad Röntgen discovered X-rays at **Röntgen-Gedächtnisstätte** in 1895 and was the winner of the first Nobel Prize (1901).

Neumünster stands on the site where three Irish missionaries who tried to convert Duke Gosbert to Christianity in 686 met their maker.

Discover the World of Würzburg Wines
Sample local wines in summer

Few regions of Europe have such a full calendar of wine festivals and celebrations of the humble grape. The actual grape harvest happens in the autumn, with a whole host of parties and minor village festivals taking place around this time. Otherwise, summer is undoubtedly the best time for wine lovers to visit, with the spectacularly sited **Hofgarten Wine Festival** in early July barely over before the **Wein am Stein** festival gets underway (around the middle of July), adding live music to the mix.

Climb to Würzburg's Fortress
Enjoy river and city views

When you first glimpse the **Festung Marienberg** (schloesser. bayern.de; adult/child €4/free), across the river from the old town, this imposing fortress makes perfect sense. Commanding the highest ground for kilometres around and able to keep an eye on all traffic along the river, the dual purpose of the castle, as both military stronghold and seat of royalty, is evident from the structure – an exterior ring of forbidding defensive fortifications, with a multistorey palace presiding over the heights.

Archaeological finds suggest that there was a much smaller fortress here from the 8th century. The construction of what you see today took place over more than five centuries, first initiated around 1200 by the local prince-bishops who governed here, right through until 1719. And the fortress is as impregnable as it looks – its defences were only breached once, by Swedish troops during the Thirty Years' War, in 1631.

Access to the ramparts and some of the rooms means that you get some of the best views in this part of Germany: out over the town, river and vineyard-clad hills. The other is to enjoy the palatial interior. The main focal point of any visit is the **Fürstenbaumuseum** (closed November to mid-March), which documents and showcases the lavish lifestyle of those who lived here. Also worth lingering over is the **Mainfränkisches Museum**, with its exhibitions around Würzburg's history as well as works by local late-Gothic master carver Tilman Riemenschneider.

The castle is at its most spectacular at night, when the whole complex is dramatically illuminated. To get here, it's a pretty 25-minute walk up through the vineyards that surround the town; the path begins from the Alte Mainbrücke via the Tellsteige trail.

WÜRZBURG FESTIVALS

Africa Festival: Held on the meadows northwest of the river at Mainwiesen, this is Europe's largest festival of Afro music and culture. Late May (africafestival.org)

Mozart Fest: Germany's oldest Mozart festival, takes place at the Residenz and several other venues. June (mozartfest.de)

Hofgarten Wine Festival: Top local wine festival held on the grounds of the Residenz and organised by the Staatlicher Hofkeller. Early July (hofkeller.de)

Wein am Stein: A superb wine and music festival held at the Weingut am Stein. July (wein-am-stein.de)

Stramu: Early September sees Würzburg host Stramu, Europe's largest street-music event. Early September (stramu-wuerzburg.de)

 DRINKING IN WÜRZBURG: SAMPLING LOCAL WINES

Juliusspital: This appealing wine tavern has a fabulous wine list of Franconian wines paired with excellent local dishes. *10am-7pm Mon-Sat*

Bürgerspital Weinstube (p119): One of the most extensive lists of local wines in Bavaria, with Franconian wines (and food). *11am-midnight*

Wohlsein Weine Würzburg: This modern wine bar is an antidote to stately old wine cellars. *4-9pm Wed & Thu, 10am-9pm Fri & Sat*

Heinrich: Another cool modern wine bar serving Franconian and other German wines in the city centre. *5pm-2am Tue-Sat*

The Romantic Road

Welcome to Germany at its most enchanting, with storybook, medieval gems cutting a swathe through the heart of Bavaria.

Places
Würzburg p122
Tauberbischofsheim p122
Weikersheim p123
Rothenburg ob der Tauber p124
Dinkelsbühl p128
Nördlingen p130
Harburg p131
Donauwörth p131
Augsburg p132
Landsberg am Lech p132
Füssen p133

From the vineyards of Würzburg to the foot of the Alps, the almost 400km-long Romantic Road (Romantische Strasse) is by far Germany's most popular tourist route. It passes through more than two dozen cities, towns and villages in a ribbon of half-timbered quaintness that just keeps on coming. This is the Germany many expect to see, with the Romantic Road's perfectly conserved towns delivering on all the clichéd promises seen pre-trip on Instagram. Yes, the towns were long ago discovered and can be crowded, never more so than on a summer weekend. But walking the cobbled streets of places like Rothenburg and Nördlingen in the evening captures the magic of this remarkable route.

Würzburg

The Romantic Road's northernmost starting point or stop, Würzburg (p118) is a dynamic city reborn from a catastrophic bombing raid in the final year of WWII. It's a wonderful place to spend a few days before setting out along the Romantische Strasse, walking its pretty old town, visiting its museums and surveying the view from high above the river on the ramparts of the imposing fortress. Würzburg is also something of a culinary star and an excellent place to sample some of Germany's best wines paired with regional Franconian dishes.

Tauberbischofsheim   TIME FROM WÜRZBURG: **30 MINS** 🚗
Walk quiet medieval streets

Set in a low valley, **Tauberbischofsheim** is a charming introduction to what may be the most memorable feature of the Romantic Road: small villages radiating out from a medieval core. Because it's less well-known than most other towns

---

GETTING AROUND

Your own hire car is the most obvious way of tackling the Romantic Road – this usually means parking in parking areas just outside town centres. Cycling is also an enjoyable way to explore. If you don't have your own wheels, semi-regular trains and buses link most stops on the route. Otherwise the **Romantic Road Coach** (romanticroadcoach.de) plies the route every day in both directions and has different packages as far as Rothenburg, whereafter the train takes over; check the website for times and prices.

THE ROMANTIC ROAD

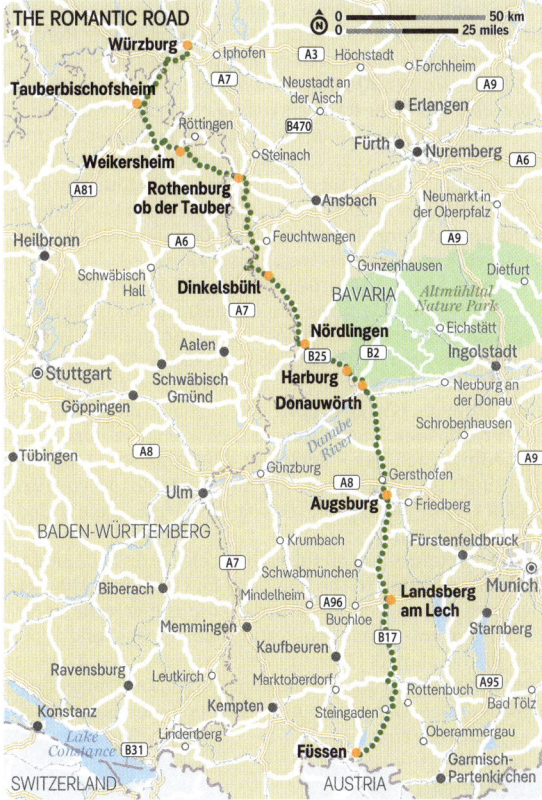

THE ROMANTIC ROAD: VITAL STATS

There are around 200 'holiday routes' in Germany, but the Romantic Road is by far the best known. Here are some of its key statistics:

Length 460km

Visitors Approximately 30 million people annually

Year created 1950

Number of official stops 29

Official website *romantischestrasse.de*

Number of castles and palaces 22

Number of UNESCO sites 4

Largest city Augsburg (population 301,000 people)

Smallest stop Röttingen (1681 people)

Number of autobahns 0

Most visited town Rothenburg ob der Tauber

along the route, Tauberbischofsheim feels more timeless than most: we've been here on days when the only other people here are locals.

The handsome, perfectly symmetrical brick **Rathaus** is an understated gem, benefiting from the absence of the ornate flourishes that adorn so many such buildings across Bavaria. The Rathaus overlooks the town's centrepiece, **Marktplatz**, a real village square with its tall, half-timbered facades, turreted windows and trees. From Marktplatz, it's a short amble through the pretty medieval lanes to **Schlossplatz**. The 13th-century Kurmainzisches Schloss looms over Schlossplatz, which is another quiet, pretty square, and houses the **Tauberfränkisches Landschaftsmuseum** *(tauberfraenkisches-landschaftsmuseum.de; adult/child €5/free),* where Tauberbischofsheim's historical story is told well in exhaustive detail.

Weikersheim TIME FROM TAUBERBISCHOFSHEIM: 40 MINS

Visit a beautiful palace

A pretty town of 7500 straddling the River Tauber amid low hills (it actually just sneaks into Baden-Württemberg but we won't tell if you don't), **Weikersheim** is a stunning little place.

The small tangle of streets coming off the old Marktplatz is pretty enough, but the main reason to stop here is **Schloss Weikersheim** *(schloss-weikersheim.de; adult 60/80min tour €9/11, family €22.50/27.50, gardens only adult/child/family €5/2.50/12.50)*. Some travellers consider this extravagant palace the finest of its kind along the Romantic Road (not counting Neuschwanstein of course). As with so many central European palaces built around the late 15th and early 16th centuries, Schloss Weikersheim is surrounded by formal ornamental gardens that were inspired by Versailles and is Renaissance to the core, with various local twists, of course.

Looking a little like an oversized Bavarian country manor, the exterior of this three-gabled masterpiece is less elaborate than grand and harmonious. The interior is more richly decorated, with notable nods to the baroque styles that lay just around the historical corner. Of rare beauty, the enormous **Knights Hall** dates from around 1600 and is over 40m long. The rich decor here includes a huge painted ceiling, each panel depicting a hunting scene, and the amazingly ornate fireplace. The unforgettable rococo mirror cabinet, with its gilt-and-red colour scheme, is a highlight of the guided tour.

And don't miss a stroll through the elegantly laid-out **gardens**. In addition to the fountains and pathways that lead between manicured flowerbeds, note the eclectic collection of statues – from Apollo and Diana to symbolic allegories of the planets (Mercury, Saturn, Venus and Mars), to the rather enigmatic Weikersheimer Zwerge (Weikersheim dwarfs) ,each one of whom represents a member of Count Carl Ludwig's court.

Rothenburg ob der Tauber

TIME FROM WEIKERSHEIM: **30 MINS**

Walk Rothenburg's medieval streets

Rothenburg ob der Tauber is archetypal fairy tale Germany. Few large villages or small towns in Germany are so uniformly and impressively medieval as Rothenburg. Partly this is because of the architecture, which has been painstakingly preserved thanks to some of the strictest urban-conservation orders in Germany. As a result, Rothenburg is a period piece of gables, turrets and half-timbered-facades, a tangle of lanes watched over by higgledy-piggledy houses – all encircled by tower-dotted protective stone walls. But it's also because the

BEST VIEWS ALONG THE ROMANTIC ROAD

Plönlein: One of the most recognisable images of Bavaria, this small square is a magical evocation of Rothenburg's charm in one view.

Rathausturm: Take in all of Rothenburg, including its medieval walls and rural surrounds, in one panorama from the summit of the town hall.

Stone Bridge: A fabulous panorama of Harburg village and castle can be admired from the 1702 Stone Bridge spanning the Wörnitz.

Marienbrücke: There's no such thing as a bad view of Schloss Neuschwanstein, but this one's both spectacular and iconic.

Augsburger Strasse Bridge: Get an all-in-one view of the Danube, the town of Donauwörth and the Wörnitz River from this bridge at the southeastern end of town.

EATING IN ROTHENBURG OB DER TAUBER: OUR PICKS

Zur Höll: Medieval wine tavern in Rothenburg's oldest original building, offering regional specialities and Franconian wines. *5-11pm Mon-Sat* €€

Gasthof Butz: Family-run inn in a former brewery serving no-nonsense southern German dishes. *11.30am-2pm & 6-9pm Fri-Sun, Tue & Wed* €€

Mittermeier: Savour a finely crafted menu at one of Rothenburg's longest-standing fine-dining establishments. *6-9pm Tue-Sat* €€€

Weinstube zum Pulverer: Ancient, wood-panelled treat serving classic German cooking in a tranquil, untouristy atmosphere. *5-11pm Wed-Fri, noon-11pm Sat & Sun* €€€

ROTHENBURG OB DER TAUBER

★ HIGHLIGHTS	5 Jakobskirche	11 Burg-Hotel	18 Zur Höll
1 Plönlein	6 Marktplatz	12 Historik Hotel Gotisches Haus Garni	● SHOPPING
2 Rathausturm	7 Mittelalterliches Kriminalmuseum	13 Hotel Herrnschlösschen	19 Käthe Wohlfahrt Weihnachtsdorf
3 Stadtmauer	8 Röderturm	● EATING	● INFORMATION
● SIGHTS	9 Sieberturm	14 Diller's Schneeballen	20 Tourist Office
see 19 Deutsches Weihnachtsmuseum	● SLEEPING	15 Gasthof Butz	
4 Doppelbrücke	10 Altfränkische Weinstube	16 Mittermeier	
		17 Weinstube zum Pulverer	

town centre just *feels* medieval, thanks to the cobblestones, the near-absence of vehicular traffic in Rothenburg's old core, and the special something that has long held visitors in its thrall.

If you were to only visit one town along the Romantic Road – what were you thinking? – Rothenburg ob der Tauber would be our first choice. Yes, this is the main tourist stop along Germany's most popular tourist route, and can be crowded year-round. But even with the crowds, Rothenburg is undeniably worth it. If at all possible, plan to stay overnight and experience the town as lamplight casts its spell long after the last tour buses have left. Do so in winter when mists swirl mysteriously through the empty streets, and you'll wonder if you've wandered into some magical, medieval fable.

ROTHENBURG FESTIVALS

Rothenburg puts on a full calendar of events for locals and visitors alike. On the cusp of summer's arrival the **Historisches Festspiel 'Der Meistertrunk'** *(meistertrunk.de)* is Rothenburg's biggest event of the year. It takes place over Whitsuntide (late May), with parades, dances and a medieval market; it commemorates the mayor's epic drinking feat that saved the town in 1631. The traditional local 'Shepherds' Dance' known as **Historischer Schäfertanz** *(schaefertanz rothenburg.de)* is performed in the main square several times from April to October. And, of course, this being Rothenburg, the weeks leading up to Christmas are a special time to visit. The town's Advent **Christmas Market** *(rothenburg.de)* is one of the prettiest in Germany and takes place on the Marktplatz.

Doppelbrücke

The best way to explore Rothenburg, especially if this is your first time, is to simply wander with no purpose other than to walk with wonder. There is so much fun to be had just from following your curiosity down any ancient laneway that captures your attention, admiring the quaint architecture, ducking (literally) in and out of half-timbered novelty shops and eating snowballs(!) as you go.

Having thus wrapped yourself somewhat randomly in its warm and charming embrace, you can add a little more focus to your explorations: Rothenburg has the most worthwhile collection of visitable sights outside the main Romantic Road cities and it's well worth digging a bit deeper here.

A good place to start is the **Marktplatz**, the central, irregularly shaped piazza whose expanse of cobbles buzzes all day long with tourist chatter and selfie scenarios. At the crossroads of the four main streets through town, this epicentre is where you'll find the town hall and its climbable tower – a useful experience for the view and for getting your bearings. In the same building, you'll also find the town's busy tourist office.

Bavaria's most photographed and Instagrammed structure must be the **Plönlein**, a small square where a slightly crooked, half-timbered building sits at a divide in the road and is backed by the tall **Siebersturm** (one of the town's many defensive towers). It's a prime selfie spot, though you may have to join a queue.

Follow the ramparts

We're all for getting as many different perspectives on Rothenburg's medieval core as you can, and walking the town's defensive walls, or **Stadtmauer** *(free),* is one of the best ways to get an overview of the town.

Rothenburg never demolished its system of town walls and 42 gates and towers that enclose the entire old centre. The walls are almost as old as the town itself, having been built of sturdy stone in 1142. These days, it's possible to walk the full 2.5km around the unbroken ring of defensive battlements. Apart from offering the opportunity to look down into some of the lesser visited laneways of the old town, such a walk reinforces the sense of the importance medieval people placed on defending their settlements. It's also easy to imagine the gates being closed every night and the townsfolk huddling behind the walls, feeling themselves to be safe from the uncertainties of the outside world.

It's all worth lingering over, but a couple of vantage points in particular are worth seeking out. One of these is the eastern tower, the **Röderturm**. But for the most impressive views head to the western side of town, where a sweeping vista of the Tauber Valley includes the **Doppelbrücke**, a superb double-decker bridge.

Look down on Rothenburg

Arguably the best view in Rothenburg is from the **Rathausturm** *(adult/child/family €4/2/10)*, the tower of the town hall. The building it rises above dates back to the 14th century, and you can climb the 220 steps for cinematic views down upon Marktplatz, the terracotta roofs of the Altstadt, and beyond the walls to the surrounding countryside. While views are sweeping and superb, the viewing platform is narrow, often crowded and not for those with a fear of heights!

Attend a church concert

There are several churches in town but the main place of worship is the **Jakobskirche** *(adult/child/student/family €3.50/free/2/7)*, in Klingengasse. This 15th-century Lutheran church has some wonderfully aged stained-glass windows, including one that depicts Moses leading the Jews out of Egypt; in one endearing local touch, pretzels fall from the sky rather than manna as in the Old Testament story. The windows are at their best on the morning of a sunny day when light floods the inner sanctuary and brings out the detail of the scenes created in glass.

But the top attraction is Tilman Riemenschneider's gilded and extravagant *Heilig Blut Altar* (Altar of the Holy Blood). The gilded cross above the main scene depicting the Last Supper incorporates Rothenburg's most treasured reliquary – a rock crystal capsule said to contain three drops of Christ's blood. Not surprisingly, the church is popular with pilgrims.

The church also has one of Bavaria's largest and most impressive organs (which, unusually, can be played from both sides), and to hear it played is a Rothenburg highlight. Ask at the church or **tourist office** about the free concerts that run throughout the year, including nightly performances during the pre-Christmas Advent season.

Catch the spirit of Christmas

Christmas and Rothenburg seem like a match made in heaven, and this is one place where we don't mind contemplating the joys of Christmas all through the year. The centrepiece, and one of the town's top attractions, is **Käthe Wohlfahrt Weihnachtsdorf** *(Christmas Village; wohlfahrt.com; free)*, a year-round Yuletide superstore offering a mind-boggling assortment of (pricey) decorations and ornaments. Begun near Stuttgart as a family-run store in 1966, and having called Rothenburg

CHRISTMAS & SNOWBALLS YEAR-ROUND

If the mere mention of 'Christmas' in summer might annoy you, you've probably already reached the conclusion that Rothenburg is not for you. But perhaps the best way to change your mind (or at least forget your principles for a while) is to highlight the town's only contribution to world gastronomy: the *Schneeball,* the famous snowball – ribbons of dough loosely shaped into balls, deep-fried then coated in icing sugar or cinnamon. You'll see them on sale all over town no matter the month. **Diller's Schneeballen** *(schneeballen.eu)*, a few steps down the hill from Marktplatz on Obere Schmiedgasse, takes it to the next level, with 27 different varieties and flavours baked fresh every morning.

KINDERZECHE

Dinkelsbühl's biggest annual party happens in the third week of July, when the town comes together for the 10-day **Kinderzeche** *(kinderzeche.de)*. This event celebrates how, during the Thirty Years' War, the town's children persuaded the invading Swedish troops to spare Dinkelsbühl from a ransacking. The festivities include a pageant, re-enactments in the festival hall, lots of music and other merriment, and involve all of the town's schoolchildren as well as around 10% of the rest of the population. It's by far the best time to be in town, but if you can't make it, throughout the year you can at least learn about the event and see the costumes used by visiting the **Zeughaus der Kinderzeche** *(kinderzeche.de; adult/student/child €4/2/free)* in Bauhofstrasse in the Old Town.

home since 1977, this Aladdin's Cave is at its best in the handmade wooden decorations that dominate the displays. There's a smaller sister store right across the road, with other small stores in Nuremberg, Bamberg, Oberammergau and elsewhere.

Right next door to the main store is the **Deutsches Weihnachtsmuseum** *(German Christmas Museum; weihnachtsmuseum.de; adult/concession/child/family €5/4/2/11)*. This place traces the development of various Christmas customs and decorations, and includes a fascinating exhibition of 150 Santa figures, plus lots of yesteryear baubles, tinsel and hand-crafted Christmas items.

Visit a museum of medieval crime

Rothenburg has a smattering of museums, the most rewarding of which (unless you are a diehard Christmas fan) is the **Mittelalterliches Kriminalmuseum** *(kriminalmuseum.eu; adult/concession/child €9.50/6.50/5)*, Europe's largest museum dedicated to medieval crime and punishment. Perhaps not for the squeamish, this display of torture instruments, masks of shame, executioners' swords and other gory paraphernalia sheds light on how ne'er-do-wells were disciplined for their misdemeanours. There are also exhibitions on the development of law since the Middle Ages and a replica of the imperial crown jewels of the Holy Roman Empire.

To really scare yourself witless, ask at the tourist office about after-dark **walking tours** through the dimly lit streets, led by a guide in the uniform of an old-school executioner...

Dinkelsbühl

TIME FROM ROTHENBURG: **45 MINS**

Discover a medieval masterpiece

A tranquil town of just under 12,000 souls, **Dinkelsbühl** has managed to duck the cannon balls and mortar rounds of European history to emerge as a rival to Rothenburg for the title of the Romantic Road's most authentically medieval stop.

The town's incredibly well-preserved, liver-shaped core is best appreciated during a circuit of the fortified **walls**, which kept out intruders over the centuries. These boast 18 towers and four hefty gates, and at around 2.5km in length it'll take you an hour to circumnavigate the lot. Parks and various watercourses provide ample opportunity for a break and/or picnic. Paths also surround the old town outside the walls – great for getting a view of the walls themselves.

The Altstadt here is smaller than Rothenburg's, and exploring within the walls focuses on three main thoroughfares:

EATING IN DINKELSBÜHL: OUR PICKS

Café Central: Want to sample Bavaria's best apple strudel or Black Forest cake? Climb the steps or take a streetside table. *9am-10pm Mon-Sat, 11am-10pm Sun* €

Weib's Brauhaus: A female brewmaster presides over the copper vats at this Dinkelsbühl half-timbered pub-restaurant. *5.30-11pm Wed, 11am-11pm Thu-Mon* €€

Haus Appelberg: Local fish, Franconian sausages and *Maultaschen* (pork-and-spinach ravioli) paired with Franconian wines. *6-9.30pm Tue-Sat* €€

Altdeutsches Restaurant: Recommended by Michelin, enjoy minimalist, flavour-packed traditional food at this restaurant. *11.30am-2pm & 5.30-11pm* €€€

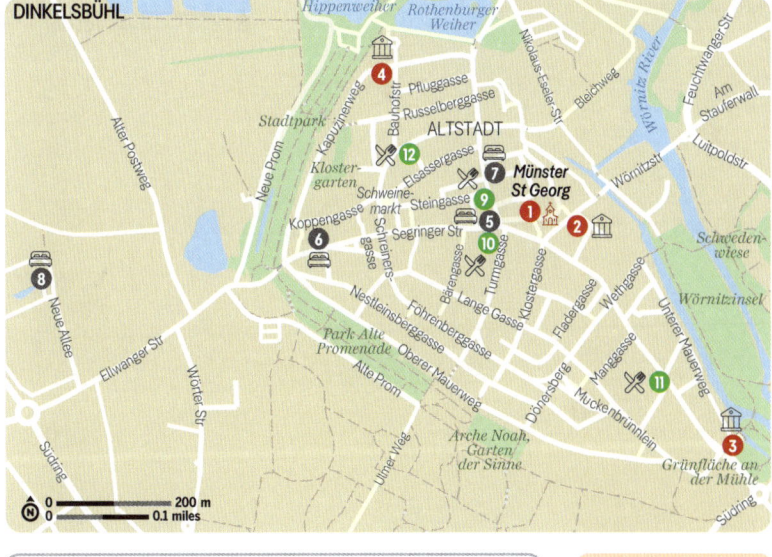

- ⭐ **HIGHLIGHTS**
- 1 Münster St Georg
- 🔴 **SIGHTS**
- 2 Haus der Geschichte
- 3 Museum of the 3rd Dimension
- 4 Zeughaus der Kinderzeche
- ⚫ **SLEEPING**
- 5 Deutsches Haus
- 6 Dinkelsbühler Kunst-Stuben
- 7 Meiser Altstadt Hotel
- 8 Meiser Design Hotel
- 🟢 **EATING**
- 9 Altdeutsches Restaurant
- 10 Café Central
- 11 Haus Appelberg
- 12 Weib's Brauhaus

Seringer Strasse, Nördlinger Strasse and Dr Martin Luther Strasse. Each is lined with uniformly stunning half-timbered facades, with enticing laneways leading off at all angles.

Where those three roads converge, on the central Marktplatz, **Münster St Georg** (st-georg-dinkelsbuehl.de; free) is both a historical timepiece and the town's main place of worship. One of southern Germany's purest late-Gothic hall churches, it has an exterior that's rather austere but an interior that astounds with its incredible fan-vaulted ceiling. A curiosity is the Pretzl Window donated by the bakers' guild; it's located in the upper section of the last window in the right aisle.

Learn about Dinkelsbühl's past

It's easy to wander the streets of many Romantic Road towns and get caught up in the spirit of medieval time travel. But if you're eager to learn more detail about Dinkelsbühl's historical story, spare an hour or two for the excellent **Haus der Geschichte** (House of History; hausdergeschichte-dinkelsbuehl.de; adult/child/family €5/2/10). You'll find it in the Old Town Hall, a complex dating from the 14th to 16th centuries. The well-curated and easily digestible exhibition traces the town's 800 years of trials and tribulations at the hands of various troublemakers (Swedes, Napoleon), and examines trades and traditions practised by the locals.

NÖRDLINGEN FROM THE WONKAVATOR

If you've seen the wonderful 1970s film *Willy Wonka & the Chocolate Factory*, you've already had a bird's-eye view of Nördlingen. At the end of the movie, Wonka, Charlie and his grandpa smash through the chocolate factory's glass roof in the Wonkavator and the scenes that follow feature an aerial view of the town. Interestingly, most of the movie was shot in and around Munich, with huge Technicolour sets built specially at the Bavaria Filmstadt. However, only one local featured in the film: Munich boy Michael Bollner, who played Augustus Gloop. You can check the Nördlingen scenes out on YouTube.

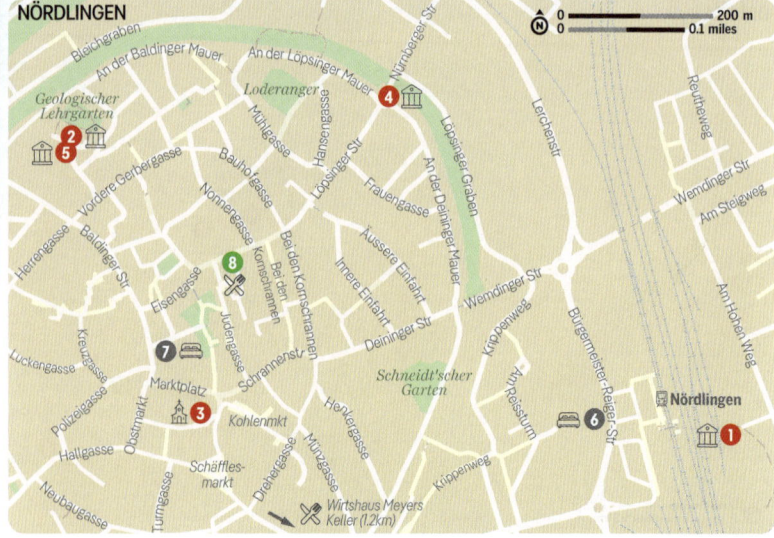

NÖRDLINGEN

SIGHTS
1. Bayerisches Eisenbahnmuseum
2. RiesKrater Museum
3. St Georgskirche
4. Stadtmauermuseum
5. Stadtmuseum

SLEEPING
6. Art Hotel Ana Flair
7. Kaiserhof Hotel Sonne

EATING
8. Café Radlos

For a refreshingly modern take on Dinkelsbühl and the Romantic Road, the **Museum of the 3rd Dimension** (*3d-museum.de; adult/youth/child/family €10/8/6/28*), just outside the easternmost town gate, offers three floors of holographic images, stereoscopes and attention-grabbing 3D imagery.

Nördlingen

TIME FROM DINKELSBÜHL: **40 MINS**

Medieval walls and ancient craters

Dreamily medieval, **Nördlingen** receives slightly fewer tourists than its better-known neighbours. And more so than most other Romantic Road towns, it manages to retain an air of gritty authenticity.

The town lies within the Ries Basin, a massive impact crater carved out by a meteorite over 15 million years ago. The crater – some 25km in diameter – is one of the best preserved on Earth, and has been declared a special 'geopark'. The story of the meteorite's impact and what it left behind can be discovered at the **RiesKrater Museum** (*rieskrater-museum.de; adult/child/family €5/2/11*) on Eugene-Shoemaker-Platz.

For reasons unknown, and all the more intriguing because of that fact, Nördlingen's original 14th-century defensive walls mimic the crater's rim and are almost perfectly circular. A popular activity for visitors is 'going full circle' – access points are near the

EATING IN NÖRDLINGEN & DONAUWÖRTH: OUR PICKS

| **Café Bistro Simple**: Donauwörth spot that blends salads with light-touch Mediterranean and Bulgarian flavours. *11am-8pm Mon-Fri, 10am-5.30pm Sat* € | **Posthotel Traube**: A hotel restaurant that rolls cafe, restaurant and beer garden all into one in Donauwörth. *11.30am-2pm & 5-10pm* €€ | **Cafe Radlos**: This been-here-forever, multitasking Nördlingen hangout has pizza, coffee, events and a kids corner. *11.30am-9pm Thu-Mon, 5-9pm Wed* €€ | **Wirtshaus Meyers Keller**: A Michelin-starred Nördlingen institution, where local market-fresh ingredients and imagination are the watchwords. €€€ |

five Old Town gates. One of these, the Löpsinger Torturm, is home to the **Stadtmauermuseum** *(adult/child/family €3/2/7)*. Head up the spiral staircase for an interesting exhibition on the walls.

To get a perspective on the town's circular shape, climb the 90m-high Daniel Tower attached to the huge **St Georgskirche** *(kirchengemeinde-noerdlingen.de; tower adult/child €4/3)*, which is Nördlingen's tallest structure. On a clear day, you may also be able to see the perimeter of the crater itself.

Rainy-day museums

If you find yourself in Nördlingen on a rainy afternoon or morning – not entirely out of the question in these parts – two museums exist to keep you occupied.

In the Old Town, you'll find the worthwhile **Stadtmuseum** *(stadtmuseum-noerdlingen.de; adult/child/family €5/2/11)*, Nördlingen's municipal museum. Set up to tell the story of Nördlingen's past, it goes much further with an exhaustive exhibition that covers an ambitious sweep of human existence on the planet, from the early Stone Age to 20th-century art.

Kids and train buffs also won't want to miss the **Bayerisches Eisenbahnmuseum** *(Bavarian Railway Museum; bayerisches-eisenbahnmuseum.de; adult/child €8/4)*, which is right by the train station. It's half museum, half graveyard for locos that have puffed their last. The museum runs **steam trains** *(adult/child/family €12/6/30)* up to Dinkelsbühl, Feuchtwangen and Gunzenhausen several times a year; see the website for details.

Harburg
TIME FROM NÖRDLINGEN: **25 MINS**

Explore a storybook castle

Harburg looms above the road between Nördlingen and Donauwörth. Literally so: the road runs through a tunnel directly beneath the fortress.

Schloss Harburg *(burg-harburg.de; adult/child €3.50/2.50, guided tour €5/2.50)* is the Romantic Road's most dramatic medieval castle. Looming over the Wörnitz River, the medieval covered parapets, towers, turrets, keep and red-tiled roofs of the 12th-century castle are so perfectly preserved they almost appear to be from a film set. Take a tour or stay the night at the **Schlosshotel Harburg** in a converted part of the castle, surely the Romantic Road's most impressive place to stay.

Donauwörth
TIME FROM HARBURG: **15 MINS**

The meeting of the waters

Between Augsburg and Nördlingen, **Donauwörth** is the spot where the Danube and the Romantic Road come to their inevitable collision. In fact, this town of around 20,000 people sits at the confluence of the Danube and Wörnitz Rivers, with some of the Old Town located on an island. The best views of the river and Old Town together are from Augsburger Strasse and the bridge over the Danube at the southeastern edge of the Old Town.

Unlike other places on the route, Donauwörth is a post-WWII rebuild, the war having obliterated 75% of the medieval

ROMANTIC ROAD COACH

Designed as a way to help visitors travel along the Romantic Road, many of whose towns aren't connected by regular rail services, the **Romantic Road Coach** *(*p122; romanticroadcoach.de)* is an excellent choice. These days, rail covers half the route. The most popular bus or minibus routes operate as day trips from Würzburg or Frankfurt am Main to Rothenburg ob der Tauber; some of these day tours include wine tasting along the way. Also possible is simply a bus ticket (without the tour, although most buses have audioguides). The bus runs as far as Rothenburg, whereafter trains (bookable through Deutsche Bahn at *bahn.de*) continue through 15 stations, including Dinkelsbühl, Harburg, Nördlingen, Donauwörth, Augsburg, Landsberg am Lech, Füssen and Munich.

ROMANTIC ROAD CASTLES

Schloss Neuschwanstein: Surely the world's most famous castle, and certainly one of its most beautiful, Neuschwanstein is simply unmissable.

Schloss Hohenschwangau: A less extravagant complement to Neuschwanstein, this former home of King Ludwig II feels like the monarch just stepped out for a walk.

Schloss Harburg: Looking like it was custom built for a film set, Harburg's castle has every flourish you'd expect from a medieval fortress.

Schloss Weikersheim: More palace than castle, Schloss Weikersheim has a bejewelled interior that dazzles in its extravagance.

Festung Marienberg: Fabulous town, river and vineyard views to go with 800-year-old bastions make for a fine Würzburg afternoon.

original. After wandering the main **Reichstrasse** with its tall, colourful townhouses, cafes and shops, you'll find the town has a handful of other attractions.

The **Rathaus** is a mix of styles from the last 800 years and is of interest to visitors for two reasons. Firstly, it's home to the **tourist office** *(donauwoerth.de)*. Secondly, at 11am and 4pm daily, the carillon on the ornamented step gable plays a composition by local legend Werner Egk (1901–83) from his opera *Die Zaubergeige* (The Magic Violin).

Germany's favourite dolls

Across Germany, Donauwörth is known as the home of the doll factory **Kaethe Kruse**, and the **Käthe-Kruse-Puppenmuseum** *(kaethe-kruse.de; adult/child/family €2.50/1.50/4.50)* on Pflegstrasse is a nostalgia-inducing experience that fills a former monastery with dolls and dollhouses. The museum has more than 150 hand-made dolls in residence, alongside life-sized mannequins and even toy soldiers; the oldest items in the collection date back to 1912. Dolls are still made here, as they have been since Kaethe Kruse moved to the town after WWII.

Augsburg
TIME FROM DONAUWÖRTH: **45 MINS**

Ranking among Germany's oldest towns – its story dates back around 2000 years – **Augsburg** (p134) is worth as much time as you can give it. Its offerings are varied, from the fascinating Fuggerei and its social and architectural history, to memorable churches and great food. Its puppet or marionette theatre is one of southern Germany's most underrated museums. And as the largest town along the Romantic Road, it's also an important regional centre.

Landsberg am Lech
TIME FROM AUGSBURG: **40 MINS**

Explore a little-known old town

Lovely little **Landsberg am Lech** is often overlooked by travellers of the Romantic Road as they town-hop between Füssen in the south and Augsburg in the north. But it's because of this very absence of tourists and a less commercial ambience that this walled town, prettily set on the River Lech, is worth closer inspection.

The Old Town sits on the east bank of the river. Centred on the triangular Hauptplatz, the Altstadt has a smattering of sights, beyond which lie interrupted sections of the town's original defences, interspersed with towers that somehow avoided the

EATING & DRINKING IN LANDSBERG: OUR PICKS

Lechgarten: Beer garden by the River Lech with 250 seats, pub food and beer from Andechs Monastery. *3-11pm Mon-Fri, noon-11pm Sat & Sun* €

LuSy's Lechcafe: Small powder-blue cafe by the river with outdoor seating, good coffee and even better cakes. *1-7pm Fri-Sun* €

Restaurant am Hexenturm: Fresh ingredients and dishes like roast pork with bread-roll dumplings, gravy and coleslaw. *11.30am-2.30pm & 5-11pm* €€

Lech-Line: Arguably Landsberg's best kitchen, this fine-dining bistro has assured seasonal cooking from Bavaria and beyond. *6pm-midnight Wed-Sat* €€€

LANDSBERG AM LECH

● **SIGHTS**
1 Heilig-Kreuz-Kirche
2 Johanniskirche
3 Schmalzturm
4 Stadtpfarrkirche Mariä Himmelfahrt

● **SLEEPING**
5 Stadthotel Augsburger Hof

● **EATING**
6 Lechgarten
7 Lech-Line
8 LuSy's Lechcafé
9 Restaurant am Hexenturm

BAVARIA'S MEDIEVAL CITY WALLS

Rothenburg ob der Tauber: Extending over 2.5km, Rothenburg's ancient walls (p124) encircle the town.

Dinkelsbühl: Also 2.5km long, the walls at Dinkelsbühl (p128) are much quieter than Rothenburg's but just as beautiful.

Nördlingen: Dating back to the 14th century, Nördlingen's walls (p130) are almost perfectly circular.

Landsberg am Lech: One of Bavaria's least-known walled cities, Landsberg has fine, 15th-century fortified gates and imposing stone ramparts.

Nuremberg: Beginning opposite the Hauptbahnhof and extending around the Altstadt, the walls in Nuremberg (p100) are a constant presence in the city.

ravages of Bavarian history. One of the towers stands just off the northeastern side of Hauptplatz – the heftily Gothic **Schmalzturm**, built in the 13th or 14th century and squeezed on both sides by tall baroque townhouses; above the passageway between the arches is a cannon ball that marks the 1796 occupation of the town by Napoleon and his troops.

Also on the square is the town's main church, the **Stadtpfarrkirche Mariä Himmelfahrt** *(free)*, a huge 15th-century building with a slender bell tower built by Matthäus von Ensingen, architect of the Bern Cathedral in Switzerland. The barrel nave is stuccoed to baroque perfection. Landsberg's 'other' church is a tiny but much more architecturally valuable affair. If you've already seen the Wieskirche (p141) near Füssen, you'll instantly recognise the baroque **Johanniskirche** *(free)* as a creation by the same architect, Dominikus Zimmermann.

Rounding out the trio of old-town churches, **Heilig-Kreuz-Kirche** *(free)*, a short walk uphill from the Schmalzturm, is a beautiful baroque Jesuit church, the interior of which is a hallucination in broodily dark gilding and glorious ceiling decoration.

Füssen

TIME FROM LANDSBERG AM LECH: **1 HR**

One of Germany's most storied pre-Alpine towns, **Füssen** (p138) combines a glorious setting with world-class attractions. The town's location is special, occupying the spot where the plains of southern Germany meet the Alps in all their glory – there are exceptional views at every turn. The town itself has a medieval core that's intimate and rewards quiet and inquisitive strolling. But it's the presence of two astonishing castles – Schloss Neuschwanstein and Schloss Hohenschwangau – that elevates it into the realm of Bavaria's must-sees.

Augsburg

MEDIEVAL ARCHITECTURE | FASCINATING HISTORY | CULINARY EXCELLENCE

☑ TOP TIP

As a centre of business, Augsburg has a lot of accommodation for a city of its size. This makes it a good alternative to booked-out Munich during Oktoberfest. This secret got out long ago, but it's still easier to find a bed here than in the state capital.

Steeped in history and by far the biggest settlement on the Romantic Road, Augsburg is Bavaria's third-largest city and one of its most agreeable. Moulded by Romans, then medieval artisans, bankers and traders, it's also one of Germany's oldest cities, dating back more than 2000 years, and it shows. The city's medieval core is watched over by a dense collection of spires, while at ground level colourful facades and cobbled laneways lend much atmosphere to a city that feels much more intimate than its size would suggest. And Augsburg is no museum piece: as a regional centre for industry and technology, it has a real dynamism, with lively culinary and arts scenes. Augsburg is an easy day trip from Munich. Or if you're looking for an alternative Bavarian base to Munich or Nuremberg, staying here puts you within easy reach of the Bavarian capital, the Romantic Road, Ulm and the Alps.

Wander Augsburg's Fuggerei
Architecture with a history

The legacy of Jakob Fugger 'The Rich' lives on at Augsburg's Catholic welfare settlement, the **Fuggerei** *(fugger.de; adult/concession/child/family €8/7/4/18)*, which is the oldest of its kind in existence. Around 150 people call this place home today, and their rent remains frozen at the equivalent of just 1 Rhenish guilder (less than €1) per year, plus utilities and three daily prayers.

 GETTING AROUND

Getting here is easy: by car, it's just off the A8 equidistant from Ulm and Munich, and Augsburg is also well-connected to the rest of Bavaria by rail. Regular train connections include Donauwörth (20 to 40 minutes), Munich (30 to 50 minutes), Nuremberg (one to two hours), Ulm (45 minutes to one hour) and Füssen (two hours). Once you're here, take tram 3 or 6 from the Hauptbahnhof to the central interchange at Königsplatz, where all of Augsburg's tram routes converge. Tram 2 runs from here to Rathausplatz. From here the entire city centre can be comfortably explored on foot.

HIGHLIGHTS
1 Dom Mariä Heimsuchung
2 Fuggerei

SIGHTS
3 Fuggereimuseum
4 St Anna Kirche

SLEEPING
5 Dom Hotel
6 Hotel am Rathaus
7 Steigenberger Drei Mohren Hotel

EATING
8 Antico Duomo
9 Bauerntanz
10 Perlacht Acht

RICH FUGGER

In medieval times, the Fuggers were a prominent, wealthy Augsburg family, and it was one Jakob Fugger (1459–1525; aptly nicknamed 'the Rich') who bequeathed Augsburg its most famous sight, the Fuggerei, the world's oldest social-housing project. Jakob would have topped the 2023 Forbes list with an estimated fortune of US$400 billion in today's money, earned from a global trading empire. He counted the Habsburgs in both Austria and Spain as family friends. Deeply religious, Jakob took to heart the story of Jesus telling a rich man that it was more difficult for a camel to pass through the eye of a needle than it was for a rich man to enter heaven, hence his gift to the poor and needy of Augsburg.

Apart from the Fuggerei's story, it's an appealing complex to explore, with its vine-clad homes featuring Bavarian-style steepled facades. Residents might wave to you as you stroll through the car-free lanes of this gated community, flanked by its 67 pin-neat houses (containing 140 apartments) and little gardens. If you are curious about what the dwellings once looked like on the inside, visit the **Fuggereimuseum** *(fugger.de; adult/concession/child/family €8/7/4/18)* at Mittlere Gasse 13 and 14, a typical Fuggerei apartment as it would have looked a couple of centuries ago.

The sober, modest place sports painted timber furniture so typical for the Alps, and whitewashed walls. A film next door tells the Fuggerei's story. There's another branch at Ochsengasse 46 and 47, which looks at everyday life at the Fuggerei, including the hardships of WWII, and there's more war heritage on show at the War Bunker, where an interesting exhibition documents the destruction of much of the complex in a 1944 air raid.

Another location associated with the Fuggers is **St Anna Kirche** *(st-anna-augsburg.de; free)*. Well hidden and rather plain from the outside, the sumptuous Fuggerkapelle, where Jakob Fugger and some of his relatives lie buried, and the lavishly frescoed Goldschmiedekapelle (Goldsmiths Chapel; 1420), come as a somewhat overwhelming surprise.

Admire the Art in Augsburg's Cathedral
Paintings and stained-glass windows

With all of the attention on the Fuggerei as Augsburg's standout attraction, the handsome **Dom Mariä Heimsuchung** *(free)* is something of an unknown treasure. Anchoring the heart of the medieval Altstadt, the cathedral lacks the solemn

AUGSBURG ON FOOT

Take a stroll through the heart of medieval Augsburg, tracing the city's story through squares, churches and museums.

START	END	LENGTH
Hauptbahnhof	Brechthaus	2km; 1½ hrs

The ❶ **Hauptbahnhof** is Augsburg's gateway, the point at which most visitors arrive in the city. From the tangle of streets in front of the station, it's a short walk to the ❷ **Jüdisches Museum Augsburg Schwaben (Jewish Museum Augsburg Swabia)** on Halderstrasse, housed in an Art Nouveau synagogue.

From the synagogue, cross Königsplatz towards ❸ **St Anna Kirche** (p135), often regarded as Germany's first Renaissance church. Nearby, the ❹ **Maximilianmuseum** has a permanent exhibition of treasure but also holds some excellent temporary shows on a Bavarian theme.

From the museum it's a short stroll north to irregularly shaped ❺ **Rathausplatz**, with its trams and cobbles. The Rathaus (town hall) stands on the western side and is home to the impressive Goldener Saal, a grand banqueting hall that is a dazzling, frescoed space canopied by a gilded and coffered ceiling.

Next door to the town hall rises the ❻ **Perlachturm**, the tower belonging to St Peter's Church. The newly renovated 70m-tall tower is the best place in Augsburg from which to get a bird's-eye view of the town's comings and goings.

Leaving the Rathausplatz via a street called Am Perlachberg, cross Metzgplatz and take the next street on the left, Auf dem Rain. At number 7 you will discover the ❼ **Brechthaus**, opened in 1998 to celebrate the 100th birthday of Bertolt Brecht, the local-born playwright and poet.

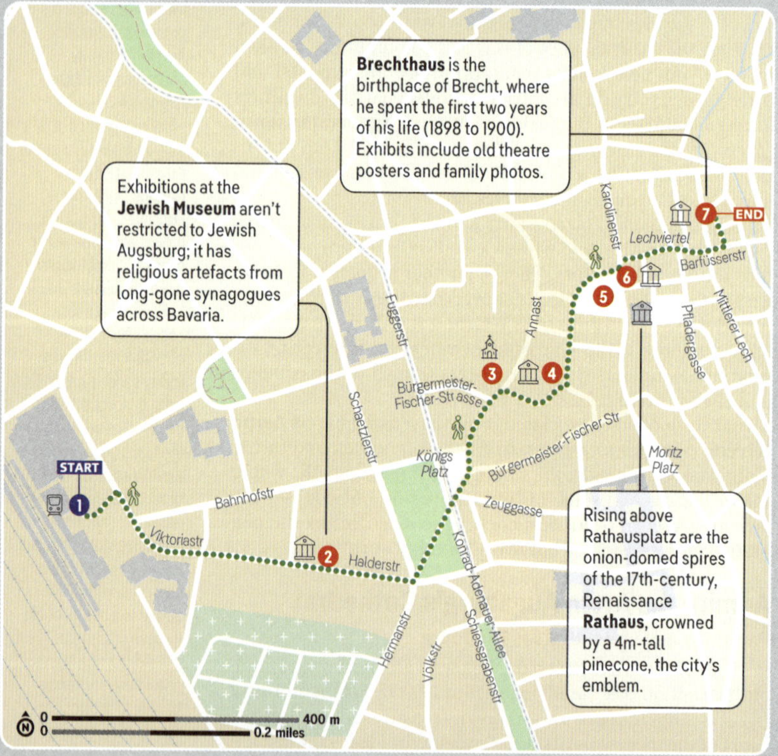

Brechthaus is the birthplace of Brecht, where he spent the first two years of his life (1898 to 1900). Exhibits include old theatre posters and family photos.

Exhibitions at the **Jewish Museum** aren't restricted to Jewish Augsburg; it has religious artefacts from long-gone synagogues across Bavaria.

Rising above Rathausplatz are the onion-domed spires of the 17th-century, Renaissance **Rathaus**, crowned by a 4m-tall pinecone, the city's emblem.

grandeur of so many European cathedrals, surrounded as it is by trees and with a mix of whitewash and brick covering its exterior. But it's the interior that really elevates this ancient house of worship into something special.

The first church on this site was built nearly 1300 years ago, in the 7th century, but nothing remains of that original. Most of what you see today began to take shape in the 14th and 15th centuries as the Gothic style took hold across Europe and left its mark here. The austerity of the Gothic form superbly frames and offsets Bavaria's most magnificent stained-glass windows. Depicting some of the towering figures of the Old Testament (David, Daniel, Jonah, Hosea and Moses) and known as the 'Prophets' Windows', the windows depict the prophets in rich colours and intricate detail. The windows are among the oldest figurative stained-glass windows in Germany, having been created in the 12th century.

Other highlights include the 11th-century, 35-panel bronze door, the unusual use of two choir stalls, and the four paintings by Hans Holbein the Elder, one of Europe's most revered medieval painters, including one of Jesus' circumcision.

Visit Augsburg's Puppet Theatre
Take in a performance, enjoy the museum

You don't have to be a child to enjoy **Augsburger Puppenkiste** *(puppenkiste.de; tickets from €10, museum adult/child/family €5/3.30/12.90)*. On the southeastern fringe of the old town, this much-loved theatre, museum and shop is one of Europe's most beloved centres for the genre. Performances range from adult storylines (recent shows have included *Doktor Faust, The Little Prince* and adaptations of Mozart scores such as *The Magic Flute*) to child-focused fairy tales that have included *Aladdin, Rapunzel* and *Hansel & Gretel*. Advance bookings for the shows are essential.

The museum, which is well worth visiting before your performance, takes your through the history of puppetry, exhibits of the extraordinary puppets used in performances down through the years, and archive footage of past performances of modern and classic fairy tales that even non-German speakers will enjoy. Stop by the shop afterwards; there's also a restaurant.

The box office and museum are open noon to 6pm Wednesday to Sunday. Most performances are at child-friendly times, but check the website under 'Spielplan' for timings.

AUGSBURG HISTORY

For much of its history, Augsburg's story has followed a parallel path to that of Bavaria, to which it now belongs. According to local legend (and most historians), the city was founded (and given its name) by the stepchildren of Roman Emperor Augustus over 2000 years ago. As an independent city state from the 13th century, it was also one of the region's wealthiest, free to raise its own taxes, with public coffers bulging from the proceeds of the textile trade. Banking families such as the Fuggers and the Welsers even bankrolled entire countries and helped out the odd skint monarch. However, from the 16th century, religious strife and economic decline plagued the city. Augsburg finally joined the Kingdom of Bavaria in 1806.

 EATING IN AUGSBURG: OUR PICKS

Antico Duomo: Italian food opposite the cathedral and with a pink Vespa scooter in the window. *noon-2.30pm & 5.30-10.30pm Wed-Mon* €€

Bauerntanz: Large servings of Swabian and Bavarian food (*Spätzle* every which way) amid lace curtains and dark timber. *noon-11pm Tue-Sat, noon-9pm Sat, 5-11pm Mon* €€

Perlacht Acht: Light, tasty dishes with a sunny Mediterranean focus (handmade pastas, risottos and the like). *5-11.30pm Tue-Fri, noon-2.30pm & 5-11.30pm Sat & Sun* €€

August: Two-Michelin-starred chef Christian Grünwald produces some of Bavaria's most innovative cooking; reservations a must. *6.30pm-midnight Thu-Sat* €€€

Füssen

FAIRY TALE CASTLES | HISTORIC ARCHITECTURE | MOUNTAIN VIEWS

GETTING AROUND

It's just under 4km from the centre of Füssen to the car parks, bus stop and ticket office for Schloss Neuschwanstein and Schloss Hohenschwangau. You can walk, cycle, drive, or take a bus or taxi (€12 to €20 one way). If you're taking the bus, buses 73 and 78 *(bahn. de)* serve the castles from Füssen Bahnhof (€6 return, five minutes, at least hourly). Buy tickets from the driver and make sure it's a direct service. Munich tour companies run day excursions out to the castles.

☑ TOP TIP

If you want to do Neuschwanstein and Hohenschwangau in a single day from Munich, you'll need to start very early. The first train leaves Munich at 4.39am (change in Buchloe), reaching Füssen at 7.21am.

The gateway town to Germany's most famous castle, Ludwig II's Neuschwanstein, Füssen bustles with tourists year-round, some emerging from the train station on DIY day trips from Munich, searching for the bus to the castles, others checking into luxury hotels before enjoying a spot of apres-ski, with or without the skiing beforehand. Even without Neuschwanstein's presence just over 5km to the southeast, Füssen would attract a fair number of visitors to its lakes and ski slopes, acting as a base from which to enjoy this strip of the German Alps. The town itself is worth a couple of hours' exploration, but it's really the surroundings that draw travellers – and it's easy to escape the crowds amid a landscape of gentle hiking trails and Alpine vistas.

Füssen is also the climax of the Romantic Road, with the Neuschwanstein and Hohenschwangau castles the definite crescendo to the ribbon of quaintness and *echt* (genuine) German character that starts way off to the north in distant Würzburg.

Discover Old Füssen

Füssen's in-town castle

For the vast majority of visitors, Füssen really is just a jumping-off point for the stellar attractions a short distance to the southeast. But the town does have a few worthwhile draws that reward those who decide to linger longer, or if you're looking to explore a little and see the town itself either side of a visit to the castles.

The old town is compact and a pleasure to walk around: the lack of tourists and crowds of any kind is an appealing counterpoint to the busyness of the castles and surrounding trails. Towering over the old town's compact historical centre is the **Hohes Schloss** *(High Castle; adult/child €8/free),* Füssen's very own castle. This late-Gothic confection was a one-time retreat for the bishops of Augsburg. The north wing of the palace contains two galleries, the **Staatsgalerie** (State Gallery) and the **Städtische Gemäldegalerie** (City Paintings Gallery) with paintings and sculpture from the 15th to the 19th centuries. The inner courtyard

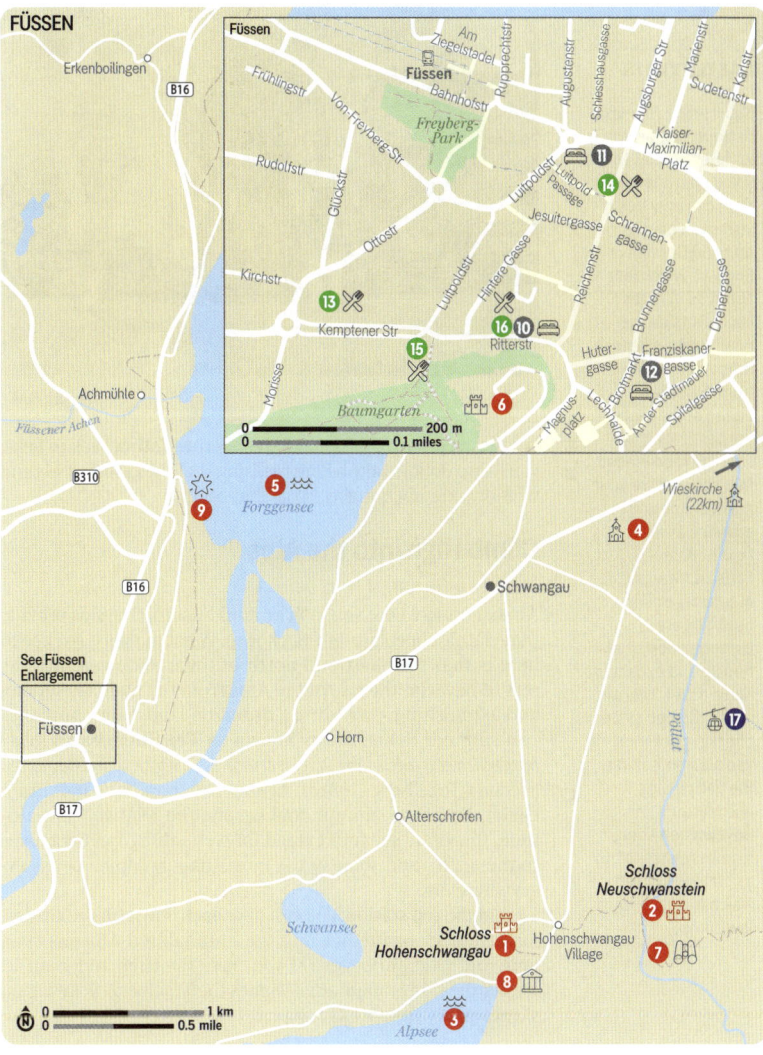

🟆 HIGHLIGHTS
1. Schloss Hohenschwangau
2. Schloss Neuschwanstein

🔴 SIGHTS
3. Alpsee
4. Church of St Coloman
5. Forggensee
6. Hohes Schloss
7. Marienbrücke
8. Museum der Bayerischen Könige

🔴 ACTIVITIES
9. Forggensee-Schifffahrt

⚫ SLEEPING
10. Altstadthotel Zum Hechten
11. Hotel Sonne
12. Old Kings Hostel

🟢 EATING
13. Beim Olivenbauer
14. Vinzenzmurr Metzgerei
15. Zum Franziskaner
16. Zum Lechten

🔵 TRANSPORT
17. Tegelbergbahn

Wieskirche

CASTLE VISITS

You'll enjoy your visit to Neuschwanstein and Hohenschwangau if you plan ahead. Both can only be visited on guided tours (in German or English), which last about 35 minutes each. Outside the peak summer season, tickets are available from the ticket centre at the foot of the castles, but we *strongly* recommend that you reserve your ticket online and in advance at *shop.ticket-center-hohenschwangau.de*; in summer online bookings are essential: don't just turn up and expect to find a ticket. There is a complicated system of ticket packages – if you plan on visiting the two castles and Museum der Bayerischen Könige, it makes sense to buy a combined ticket, which will save you a few euros.

is a masterpiece of illusionary architecture dating back to 1499; you'll do a double-take before realising that the gables, oriels and windows are not quite as 3D as they seem.

Climb High into the Alps

Take a cable car

Almost everywhere you look around Füssen, the Alps provide that classic chocolate-box backdrop. What makes it so special here is that plains extend north of town and deep into the rest of Bavaria; the rise of the Alps from the plains is sudden and astonishing, providing a dramatic landscape contrast.

In summer the cable car known as **Tegelbergbahn** *(tegelbergbahn.de; adult one-way/return €20.50/31, child €8.50/13)* ascends Tegelberg (1881m) to the Tegelberghaus mountain chalet. From the summit, and despite the relatively low altitude, the views seem to extend forever, taking in Forggensee to the north, and some of the most shapely Alpine peaks everywhere else.

From the top station, you can hike back down (to the castles, for instance), or further into the uninhabited Alps between here and Oberammergau if you have the time and gear. In winter the same mountain becomes the Tegelberg–Schwangau ski resort, with five easy slopes.

Go Boating with Alpine Views

Chill around Forggensee

Füssen is encircled with pretty Alpine lakes, adding to the postcard-perfect scenery of the area. It's not difficult to see why Ludwig was so obsessed with building his castle in these parts.

The largest lake in the area is 15-sq-km **Forggensee** to the north. The lake, actually a reservoir (Germany's largest), is named after Forggen, a village that disappeared when the area was flooded.

Pleasure boats belonging to the **Forggensee-Schifffahrt** *(forggensee-schifffahrt.de; adult/child/family/dog return trips from €13/6.50/33/3)* ply the waters here regularly from June to mid-October. The Alpine views are unforgettable, especially on a clear sunny day when the waters take on an almost hallucinatory shade of blue.

If lakes get you excited (and they *do* offer some of the region's loveliest views), another magical place is **Alpsee** near the castles. A path goes all the way round the lake (Alpsee Rundweg – around 5km), with photogenic views back to the castles in numerous places along the way.

Visit a UNESCO World Heritage-Listed Church

Take a trip to Wieskirche

When it comes to architectural treasures, one close to Füssen flies a little under the radar for tourists. One of four Romantic Road UNESCO-listed sites, the pilgrimage church **Wieskirche** *(wieskirche.de; free)* lies around 25km northeast of Füssen. It is one of Bavaria's best-known baroque churches, the monumental work of Dominikus and Johann Baptist Zimmermann.

The story goes that in 1730, a farmer in Steingaden, about 30km northeast of Füssen, witnessed the miracle of his Christ statue shedding tears. Pilgrims poured into the town in such numbers over the next decade that the local abbot commissioned a new church to house the weeping work. Inside the almost circular structure, eight snow-white pillars are topped by gold capital stones and swirling decorations. The unsupported dome's surface is adorned with a pastel ceiling fresco that vividly recreates the resurrection of Christ.

The large number of pilgrims that visit here more than makes up for the lack of tourists, and it gives the church a powerful sense of spiritual clamour utterly unlike any other church in Bavaria. Buses head here from Füssen, or it's a 20-minute drive.

Füssen's Best View

Camera at the ready

There are many wonderful views in the vicinity of Füssen, from the castles to the Alps and Alpine lakes. But there is one view that we recommend above all others. Some 5km northeast of town, off Rte 17 (which connects Füssen with Steingaden), lies the small baroque **Church of St Coloman**. The church itself dates back to the 17th century and has an extravagant baroque interior, although the door is rarely open. But the view from the road between Rte 17 and the church is extraordinary – of the church, the Alps, even a distant Neuschwanstein. If you're lucky enough to be here on a day when the sun is shining, the results are magnificent.

CLIMBING THE NEUSCHWANSTEIN HILL

There are a number of ways to get up to Neuschwanstein. The cheapest is to walk – it costs nothing, but it's a long and relentless climb. If you want to visit Marienbrücke first, as we suggest you do, follow the signs as you near the top – there's a steep cut-through to the bridge. The other options are to take a horse-drawn carriage, but it takes you directly to the castle, which means you need to climb past Neuschwanstein and then back again. Unless you like the walk up, we recommend taking the shuttle bus up (it drops you at the start of the short trail to Marienbrücke), then walk down to the castle before following the road down on foot.

EATING IN FÜSSEN: OUR PICKS

Vinzenzmurr Metzgerai: *Leberkäse* in a bun, goulash soup, *Saures Lüngerl* (goat or beef lung with dumplings), bratwurst and schnitzel. *9am-6pm Mon-Fri, 8am-1pm Sat* €

Beim Olivenbauer: Tyrol meets the local Allgäu region at this fun eatery. Try the *Maultaschen* with a mug of local beer. *noon-11pm* €€

Zum Franziskaner: Specialises in *Schweinshaxe* (pork knuckle) and schnitzel as well as other meaty Bavarian and Allgäu staples. *11.30am-10pm Thu-Tue* €€

Zum Hechten: Füssen's best hotel restaurant keeps things regional with Allgäu favourites like schnitzel, noodles and venison goulash. *11am-10pm* €€

Schloss Neuschwanstein

TOP EXPERIENCE

Schloss Neuschwanstein

Rising amid the forested peaks like a fantasy vision, Schloss Neuschwanstein was the model for Disney's *Sleeping Beauty* castle. King Ludwig II planned this fairy tale pile himself, with the help of a stage designer rather than architect: the result is pure theatre, a giant platform on which he hoped to recreate the world of Germanic mythology, inspired by the operatic works of his friend Richard Wagner.

DON'T MISS

Schloss Hohenschwangau

Museum der Bayerischen Könige

Marienbrücke

Alpsee

Sängersaal

Thronsaal

Schloss Neuschwanstein

Ludwig II's fairy tale **Schloss Neuschwanstein** is Bavaria's most visited attraction, and as it comes into view for the first time, it is instantly obvious why. This is the castle of Disney inspiration, the one that kids might draw with princesses letting down their hair from a tower or with a dragon climbing the ramparts. Some have described it as the world's best castle.

History

Neuschwanstein was built as a romantic medieval fortress: work started in 1869 and, like so many of Ludwig's grand schemes, was never finished.

So where did the grandiose vision that gave birth to Neuschwanstein come from? Prinz Otto Ludwig Friedrich Wilhelm

PRACTICALITIES

● neuschwanstein.de ● adult/child €23.50/2.50 ● combined ticket with Hohenschwangau €48.50/17 ● with Hohenschwangau & museum €63.50/19.50

was a sensitive soul, fascinated by romantic epics, architecture and music, but his parents, Maximilian II and Marie, took little interest in his musings and he suffered a lonely and joyless childhood. In 1864, at the age of 18, the prince became king.

At first, Ludwig was an enthusiastic leader. But Bavaria's days as a sovereign state were numbered, and he became a puppet king after the creation of the German Reich in 1871 (which had its advantages, as Bismarck gave Ludwig a hefty allowance). Ludwig withdrew completely to drink, draw up castle plans and view concerts and operas in private. His obsession with French culture and the Sun King, Louis XIV, inspired the fantastical palaces of Neuschwanstein, Linderhof (p150) and Herrenchiemsee (p157) – lavish projects that left a legacy that rippled down through the centuries, even as they doomed the monarch during his lifetime.

Contrary to popular belief, it was only Ludwig's purse – and not the state treasury – that was being bankrupted through all this castle construction. However, by 1886 his ever-growing mountain of debt and unpredictable behaviour put him at odds with his cabinet. The king, it seemed, needed to be 'managed'. In January 1886, several ministers and relatives arranged a hasty psychiatric test that diagnosed Ludwig as mentally unfit to rule (this was made easier by the fact that his brother had been declared insane years earlier). That June, he was removed to Schloss Berg on Lake Starnberg.

And did he ever get to enjoy the architectural confections that would ultimately lead to his downfall? For all the coffer-depleting sums spent on it, the king spent just over 170 days in residence at his beloved Schloss Neuschwanstein.

Highlights

The most impressive room is the **Sängersaal** (Minstrels' Hall), whose frescos depict scenes from the opera *Tannhäuser*. Don't miss Ludwig's *Tristan and Isolde*-themed bedroom, dominated by a huge Gothic-style bed crowned with an intricately carved cathedral-like spire, and the grotto, with more references to *Tannhäuser*. The Byzantine-style **Thronsaal** (Throne Room) boasts an incredible mosaic floor containing over two million stones. The tour ends with an interesting 20-minute **film** before you're unleashed into the gift shop.

Marienbrücke

For the postcard view of Neuschwanstein, take a steep, 15-minute walk up to **Marienbrücke** (Mary's Bridge), which spans the spectacular Pöllat Gorge over a waterfall just above the castle. Ludwig apparently enjoyed coming up here after dark to watch the candlelight radiating from the Sängersaal. The bridge rises high above the gorge – not one for those with a fear of heights, especially when thronging with visitors.

Schloss Hohenschwangau

You get two for your money here and Hohenschwangau's 'other' castle is just as interesting, if not as dreamily storybook-ish as Neuschwanstein. King Ludwig II grew up at **Schloss Hohenschwangau** (*hohenschwangau.de; adult/child €26/14.50*) and later enjoyed

---

THE DEATH OF LUDWIG II – PART 1

Every year on 13 June, a stirring ceremony takes place on the eastern shore of Lake Starnberg. A small boat glides towards a cross just offshore and a plain wreath is fastened to its front. A single trumpet cuts the silence as the boat returns from this solemn ritual in honour of the most beloved king ever to rule Bavaria: Ludwig II.

TOP TIPS

● Book your tickets online and in advance.

● The castles are located in a place called Hohenschwangau.

● It is feasible to make a day trip to the castles from Munich using public transport.

● All Munich's tour companies run day excursions out to the castles.

● There's no need to buy tickets for the Museum der Bayerischen Könige online beforehand.

● Enough time is left between tours for the steep 30- to 40-minute walk between the castles.

● Bring a picnic to have by the Alpsee and enjoy its pretty views.

● Visit on weekdays in spring and autumn for a more tranquil experience.

THE DEATH OF LUDWIG II – PART 2

The cross marks the spot where Ludwig died under mysterious circumstances in 1886. No-one knows what happened that night, except that Ludwig and his doctor took a Sunday evening lakeside walk and were found several hours later, drowned in just 1m of water. Ludwig had been exiled because of his erratic behaviour and extravagant spending. That summer the authorities opened Neuschwanstein to the public to help pay off Ludwig's huge debts.

long summers here until his death in 1886. It was converted into a summer residence by Ludwig's father Maximilian II on the site of a 12th-century fortress. Far less ostentatious, this castle was actually inhabited for long periods of time. It was at Hohenschwangau that Ludwig first met Richard Wagner. The **Hohenstaufensaal** features a piano where the composer would entertain Ludwig with excerpts from his latest works. Some rooms have frescos from German mythology, including the story of the Swan Knight, Lohengrin. The swan theme runs throughout.

Museum der Bayerischen Könige

After the castles, many visitors head straight for the tour bus, but there's one other attraction here that's well worth seeing before you go – the **Museum der Bayerischen Könige** *(Museum of the Bavarian Kings; hohenschwangau.de/museum-der-bayerischen-koenige; adult/child €17/2.50)*. Be sure to pick up the detailed audioguide with your ticket.

The Exhibition

Opened in 2011, this architecturally impressive building tells the story of the Wittelsbach dynasty, from its very beginnings to its last members. Naturally the focus is skewed towards those who had the greatest influence on the location in which the museum is situated – Maximilian II and his son, King Ludwig II. One of the dramatically illuminated highlights of the blingy exhibition includes Ludwig II's famous blue-and-gold robe.

Alpsee Views

The museum's huge windows provide impressive views of the Alpsee (p140), one of the many lakes to be found around Füssen. The path that circumnavigates the lake offers up dramatic views back towards Hohenschwangau, especially from the furthest points.

Schloss Hohenschwangau (p143)

Garmisch-Partenkirchen

ALPINE SCENERY | CANYON HIKING | PICTURESQUE VILLAGE

With its double-barrelled name and privileged position amid the highest of the German Alps, there's something aristocratic about Ga-Pa (as some locals call it). Wintering in Garmisch still has an old-money ring to it and Bavaria's top ski centre doesn't disappoint, even in the 21st century. From December through to April this is the top hangout for avid skiing fans, who come to carve slopes on Germany's highest peak, the Zugspitze. In the warmer months hikers take over to hit the Alpine meadows that extend south in a seemingly endless parade of limestone peaks. Whether you arrive as a day-tripper from Munich or on a fortnight's skiing holiday, Ga-Pa is one of the definite highlights of the Free State.

Walk along the Partnachklamm
Dramatic gorge hike

One of the best days out you can enjoy without climbing a mountain in these parts is a hike along a beautiful gorge called the **Partnachklamm** *(partnachklamm.eu; adult/child €10/5)*. This is where the River Partnach squeezes through a very narrow rock crevice, its green snowmelt waters surging through a 700m-long slit that at some points is 80m deep.

To reach the gorge, head along the river south from the train station, following the signs. On the way you'll pass the old Olympic Stadium from the 1936 Winter Games and Ga-Pa's giant ski jumps. At the entrance to the gorge you'll have to buy a ticket to enter and it's best to have cash. A narrow walkway above the gushing river guides you along. It's an enjoyable hike year-round.

Before you know it, the Partnachklamm spits you out into the narrow valley of the River Partnach. You can just turn back and enjoy it all again in the opposite direction.

Hike to Ludwig II's Former Hunting Lodge
Jagdschloss Schachen

If you've hiked the Partnachklamm, and even if you haven't, it's worth paying a visit to **Königshaus am Schachen** *(adult/*

GETTING AROUND

Garmisch-Partenkirchen has hourly rail connections from Munich; special packages, available from Munich Hauptbahnhof, combine the return trip with a Zugspitze day ski pass. The train station and Zugspitzbahn station lie in the centre of town, essentially dividing the erstwhile towns of Garmisch and Partenkirchen. Once in town, you can easily get around on foot. To reach Zugspitze, you can either catch the train in town, or drive to Elbsee and catch the train or cable car from there. For bike hire, try **Bikecenter**.

☑ TOP TIP

A **Top Snow Card** covers all the slopes around Garmisch as well as over the border in the Austrian Tyrol (altogether 214km of pistes and 89 cable cars and ski lifts). It can be purchased at any cable-car station. See *zugspitzarena.com* for details.

HIGHLIGHTS
1. Partnachklamm
2. Zugspitze

SIGHTS
3. Königshaus am Schachen

ACTIVITIES
4. Zugspitzbahn

SLEEPING
5. Gasthof zum Rassen
6. Hotel Rheinischer Hof
7. Reindl's Partenkirchner Hof

EATING
8. Gasthof Fraundorfer
9. Hobi's Backstube
10. Hofbräustüberl
11. Zum Wildschütz

TRANSPORT
12. Bikecenter
13. Eckbauerbahn

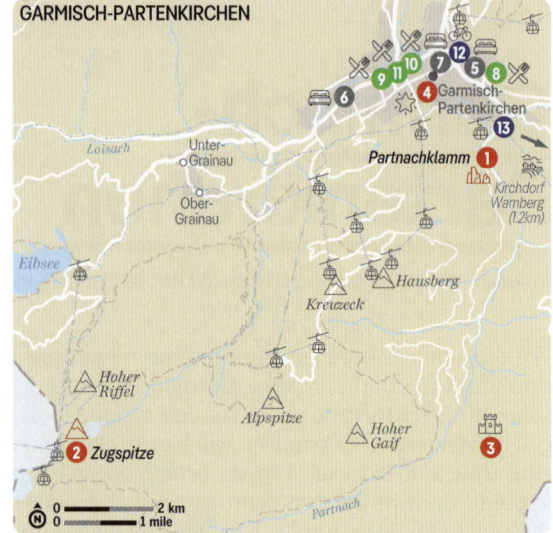

BEST EVENTS IN GA-PA

Four Hills Ski Jumping: New Year's Day ski-jumping event at the Olympic Ski Stadium.

Hornschlittenrennen: Traditional 6 January sledge race. *(hornschlitten.de)*

Zugspitz Ultratrail: In mid-June, Germany's biggest trail-running event. *(zugspitz-ultratrail.com)*

Heimatwochen: Garmisch holds its folksy festival in early August, and Partenkirchen in late August.

AlpenTestival: August outdoors festival. *(alpentestival.de)*

concession/child €5/4/free), which is sometimes called Jagdschloss Schachen. Wonderfully remote (it's 10km further along the river valley from where Partnachklamm ends), it's the least-visited of all Ludwig II's projects. A quite plain wooden structure from the outside, the interior is surprisingly magnificent; the Moorish Room in particular seems to spring from the pages of *Arabian Nights* and is a fitting monument to the fantastical vision of Ludwig II. Note that entry tickets can be purchased in cash only.

The nearby **Schachenhaus** hut has welcome refreshments and basic beds for the night (cash only).

Visit a Mountain Church-Village

Detour to Kirchdorf Wamberg

Southeast of Garmisch but so close it's effectively an extension of town, **Kirchdorf Wamberg** is quaint and Germany's highest *Kirchdorf* (church-village). You can walk from near the hospital (around 45 minutes) or take the cable car **Eckbauerbahn** (eckbauerbahn.de; adult one-way/return €16.50/26, child €9.50/13) then walk along the path heading northeast through some exquisite Alpine scenery. The views from the village are definitely worth the effort.

EATING IN GARMISCH-PARTENKIRCHEN: OUR PICKS

Hobi's Backstube: Easily Ga-Pa's best bakery with *Kaffee* (coffee), *Kuchen* (cake), sandwiches and all-day soups. *6.30am-1pm Mon, Tue & Fri, 7am-noon Sat, 7-11am Sun* €

Gasthof Fraundorfer: Come here for *Steins* of frothing ale and monster portions of plattered pig meat. *noon-midnight Thu-Mon, 5-11pm Wed* €€

Zum Wildschütz: The best place in town for fresh venison, rabbit, wild boar and other seasonal game dishes. *noon-11pm Thu-Sun, 5-11pm Wed* €€

Hofbräustüberl: Central restaurant offering big portions of Bavarian food in a traditional dining room. *5.30-10.30pm Tue-Thu, 11.30am-10.30pm Fri-Sun* €€

TOP EXPERIENCE

Zugspitze

At 2962m, the Zugspitze is Germany's tallest mountain and boasts Germany's only (and shrinking) glacier. But talking about its height only tells half the story. The views from the summit are simply superb and some of the most magical anywhere in the German Alps. Dedicate at least half a day to the experience, which includes a glorious cable-car ride.

Head for the Summit of Zugspitze

A cogwheel train (Zahnradbahn) called the **Zugspitzbahn** chugs all the way from a special station next to Ga-Pa's main train terminus once an hour (until 2.15pm). The journey takes 75 minutes along the plain and up into the tunnel at Riffelriss. The views as you travel along the valley are superb, but the climb itself is largely through enclosing forest and tunnel.

When you alight at the end of the line, you'll find yourself on the **Zugspitzplatt**, a plateau below the summit. From here the views are superb, and you can rent skis and snowboards *(skiverleih-garmisch.com)*. When you're ready, a 10-minute cable car takes you up the final vertical metres to the top.

The second way up is to take the train (or drive) to **Eibsee**, an idyllic Alpine lake around 10km southwest of Ga-Pa. From here, the **Eibsee-Seilbahn**, a super-steep cable car, swings to the top. You can then either take the cable car or the train back.

The summit is no lonely, windswept spot: here you'll find a chalet, snack bars and even a museum. Part of it is on Austrian territory. And the views are simply stupendous.

TOP TIPS

- In summer, make an early start or go on a weekday to beat at least some of the crowds.

- You can save money by driving to Eibsee, parking your vehicle (per day €5) and catching the train or cable car from there.

PRACTICALITIES

- zugspitze.de
- adult/child €75/37.50
- 10am-5pm Mon-Sat, noon-5pm Sun, after dark 6-10pm Thu

Beyond Garmisch-Partenkirchen

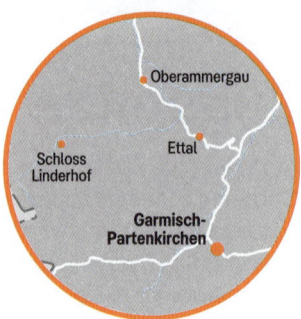

Head into high-altitude valleys for the world-famous Passion Play in beautiful Oberammergau, with a monastery and King Ludwig castle nearby.

Places
Oberammergau p148
Ettal p150
Schloss Linderhof p150

High in a lovely north-facing valley of the Ammergauer Alps close to Garmisch-Partenkirchen, Oberammergau has great beauty to go with its world-famous calling card: the once-a-decade Passion Play (it's next held in 2030 with related events echoing down through intervening years). The setting of this quietly quaint town, where traditional painted houses and woodcarving shops crowd the town centre, is superb. Dark forests and mountains that remain snow-dusted until well into summer surround Oberammergau, which is a starting point for hikes and cross-country-skiing trips into easily accessible Alpine backcountry. And, of course, there are some superb attractions just a short drive away, among them Linderhof and Kloster Ettal. But it's the Passion Play that draws most visitors.

Oberammergau

TIME FROM GARMISCH-PARTENKIRCHEN: 30 MINS

Admire Oberammergau's painted buildings

Any visit to **Oberammergau**, a small town of around 5000 people should begin with a wander around the centre to admire the numerous examples of *Lüftlmalerei*. This practice of painting huge, decorative murals on house facades can be found throughout the Alps, but the style was actually invented here. A *trompe l'oeil* fresco technique is used, with the paint fusing with the plaster below to create an image that lasts many years.

Common motifs include biblical stories, hunting scenes, agricultural cameos and other representations of traditional folk life. One of the best examples in town is the **Pilatushaus**, where painted columns snap into 3D as you approach. It contains a gallery of traditional glass painting on the 1st floor and several workshops at ground level where you can watch demonstrations of local crafts.

Fairy tales are also popular. Near the southeastern end of the town centre, the **Little Red Riding Hood House** has

GETTING AROUND

Oberammergau lies a mere 11km as the crow flies from Garmisch-Partenkirchen (or 20km by road). Hourly bus 9606 goes direct to Garmisch-Partenkirchen via Ettal. Bus 9622 connects Oberammergau with Linderhof. Hiking the 12.5km back to Oberammergau from Linderhof is a pleasant way to end a day out. It's an easy drive between all three, with a good road (B2 and B23) also up and over the mountains to Garmisch.

Pilatushaus

scenes from one of the Brothers Grimm's best-known tales. Also across the road is **Hansel & Gretel House**, with more fine scenes from that story.

Discover Oberammergau's woodcarving traditions

Oberammergau is known throughout Germany for its wood carving – many of the more elaborate nativity scenes you see around the country were carved here. Shops around town sell examples for tens to thousands of euros, but some of the best works can be viewed at the **Oberammergau Museum** *(oberammergaumuseum.de; adult/child €5/2, combined ticket with Passionstheater €9/3).* The intricacy of many of the pieces is astonishing, from children's toys and Christmas decorations to larger scenes of local life. Nativity scenes, some examples of Blue Rider works, and exhibitions on the Passion Play complete this very worthwhile museum's offerings.

Learn about the Passion Play

Another artistic discipline the town gets 'passionate' about is acting. Many people have heard of the world's most famous Passion Play, which takes place every 10 years at the 4500-seat **Passionstheater** *(passionstheater.de; adult/child €5/2, combined ticket with Oberammergau Museum €9/3).*

The Passion Play Theatre doesn't lie dormant in the decade between the main performances. Ask the tourist office about music, plays and opera performances that take place here over the summer. You can also consult the theatre's website for more information. Additionally, this venue can be visited as part of a **guided tour** *(adult/child €9/3),* which provides a lot of fascinating background info on the play's history and also lets you take a peek at the costumes and sets.

There are various versions of the tour. If you plan on visiting the Oberammergau Museum as well, you can get a **combined ticket** *(adult/child €9/3)* that includes entry to the theatre and the tour. And if for some reason you don't want to tour

OBERAMMERGAU'S PASSION PLAY

A blend of opera, ritual and Hollywood epic, the **Passion Play** has been performed every year ending in a zero (plus some extra years for a variety of reasons) since the late 17th century as a collective 'thank you' from the villagers for being spared the bubonic plague. One exception was 2020, when the town wasn't spared from COVID-19, though it was held in 2022.

Over half of Oberammergau (a cast of around 2000) takes part, sewing amazing costumes and growing hair and beards for their roles. The whole performance lasts over five hours and usually takes place in the evening. The next performances are scheduled for between May and October 2030, but tours of the Passionstheater enable you to experience a taste of the play any time.

AN ETTAL BREW

Some might argue that the real high point of a visit to Kloster Ettal is sampling the **Ettaler Klosterlikör**, a sugary herbal digestif that has been made by the monks here for centuries. It's available in two colours – Ettaler Klosterliqueur Gelb (yellow) and Ettaler Klosterliqueur Grün (green); only natural colourings and herbs are used. Its taste is enhanced by the on-site maturing process for six months in oak barrels, and the monastery even has its own bottling plant. You can learn more about the whole production on the twice-weekly, 45-minute guided tour of the liqueur factory. The end product is available from the in-house shop, and you can even buy it online and have it shipped around the world.

---

the theatre, you can take a **village tour** for the same price. Bookings for the tours can be made at the theatre or ask at the **tourist office** *(ammergauer-alpen.de)*.

Ride the Laber-Bergbahn cable car

From Oberammergau's eastern suburbs take the **Laber-Bergbahn** *(laber-bergbahn.de; adult one-way/return €13/21.50, child €7/12)* cable car to Mt Laber (1682m). For most visitors, it's worth it just for the special views of Oberammergau and down into the next valley to Kloster Ettal. But the top station is also the starting point for some fine walking trails, including a picturesque route back down into Oberammergau.

Ettal
TIME FROM GARMISCH-PARTENKIRCHEN: **20 MINS**

Explore a Benedictine monastery

Just 7km southeast of Oberammergau, the pretty hamlet of **Ettal** would be just another bend in the road heading south to Garmisch were it not for the famous Benedictine monastery, **Kloster Ettal** *(kloster-ettal.de; entry free, monastery tour adult/child €5/free)*. The definite highlight of this astonishing confection high in the Alps is the sugary rococo basilica housing the monks' prized possession, a marble Madonna brought from Rome by Ludwig der Bayer in 1330.

Kloster Ettal continues to function as a monastery, and attending a service or 'vespers' is a moving reminder of the simplicity of the monastic life, in stark contrast to the lavish surrounds. Service times are listed on the website. A 45-minute **guided tour** *(3pm Mon & Thu)* is another fine way to see the inner workings and architecture of the monastery. All tours are in German only. Guided tours for the monastery's **beer brewery** *(adult/child €12/free; 3pm Fri & Tue)* and **liqueur factory** *(adult/child €12/free; 4pm Mon & Thu)* are also possible.

Schloss Linderhof
TIME FROM GARMISCH-PARTENKIRCHEN: **45 MINS**

Marvel at Ludwig II's Alpine escape

To the south of Oberammergau, in a wide valley hemmed by peaks rising over 1700m in places, UNESCO-listed **Schloss Linderhof** *(schlosslinderhof.de; adult/concession €10/9)* is the most remote of all Ludwig II's bizarre yet unforgettable castles; this one is set far from human habitation (just as

---

EATING IN OBERAMMERGAU: OUR PICKS

Altes Sägewerk: This slick place does Bavarian classics with the occasional twist. *5.30–11pm Thu-Sat & Mon, 10am-3pm Sun* €€

Trattoria Sardegna: Craving a break from Bavarian meals? This Italian spot is outstanding. *5.30-9pm Mon & Tue, noon-2pm & 5.30-9pm Thu-Sun* €€

Kofel Aussicht: This Russian-Ukrainian spot is terrific; try the Siberian fish soup or the *Pelmeni* (dumplings). *5-9pm Mon, Tue & Thu, noon-9pm Fri-Sun* €€

S'Wirtshaus: Long-standing Oberammergau favourite for traditional Bavarian plates and fine desserts. *11am-8pm Wed-Sun* €€

Kloster Ettal

Bavaria's crazy king liked things), seemingly in the middle of Alpine nowhere.

A compact jewel-encrusted safe box of weird and wonderful trinkets, Schloss Linderhof is Ludwig II's smallest but most extravagant palace, and the only one he lived to see fully built. Completed in 1878, the palace climbs a steep hillside in a fantasy landscape of French gardens, fountains and follies. The reclusive king used the palace as a retreat and hardly ever received visitors here. Linderhof was clearly inspired by Versailles and was dedicated to France's Louis XIV, the Sun King.

Linderhof's myth-laden, highly decorative chambers are a monument to the king's excesses, which so unsettled the penny counters in Munich. The private bedroom is the largest room, heavily ornamented and anchored by an enormous 108-candle crystal chandelier weighing 500kg. An artificial waterfall, built to cool the room in summer, cascades just outside the window. The dining room reflects the king's fetish for privacy and inventions. The king would eat from a mechanised dining board, whimsically labelled 'Table, Lay Yourself', that sank through the floor so that his servants could replenish it without being visible. The gilded **Audience Room** and the **Hall of Mirrors** are two of the most extravagant of all the salons, positively awash in elaborate gold.

Laid out by the famous court gardener Carl von Effner, the gardens and outbuildings, open April to October, are as fascinating as the castle itself. The highlight is the **Moorish Kiosk** where Ludwig, dressed in Asian-style garb, would preside over nightly entertainment from a peacock throne. Underwater light dances on the stalactites at the **Venus Grotto**, an artificial cave inspired by a stage set for Wagner's *Tannhäuser*. Ludwig's fantastic conch-shaped boat is moored by the shore.

ALPINE INFORMATION

For information about Alpine regions (and the rest of Bavaria), the following tourist offices are filled with handy brochures and advice.

Oberammergau Tourist Office: Close to the Passionstheater, this is one of the better such places in southern Bavaria; don't forget to pay for parking before you go in.

Garmisch-Partenkirchen Tourist Office: One of the largest in the Alps; staff are happy to talk you through Zugspitze options.

Berchtesgaden Tourist Office: In Berchetsgaden town, with a second option, **Schönau am Königssee Tourist Office**, near the car park for Königssee.

Füssen Tourist Office: Good at distilling all of the possible ways to see the castles and finding the right one for you.

Berchtesgaden

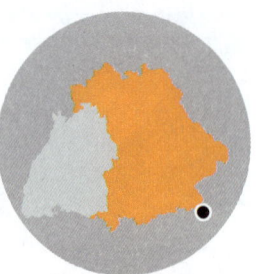

ALPINE SCENERY | FASCINATING HISTORY | BEAUTIFUL KÖNIGSEE

GETTING AROUND

It's around 7km from downtown Berchtesgaden to the boat jetties at the village of Schönau am Königssee.

Without a car, you'll need to use the local **RVO** *(dbregiobus-bayern.de)* bus network to reach its shores. Bus 841/842 makes the trip out here from the Berchtesgaden train station below the centre of town roughly twice an hour. If arriving by car, the good news is there's ample paid parking in a huge car park just back from the lake.

☑ TOP TIP

If travelling from elsewhere in Bavaria, make sure you set your GPS to avoid Austria. A tiny stretch of the motorway between Salzburg and the border includes a short segment of Austrian motorway (one/10 days €9.30/12.40), and the €120 fine (€65 for motorcycles) makes this an expensive shortcut. Many get snared'.

A little arrowhead of Germany piercing northern Austria, the Berchtesgadener Land plunges deep into Bavaria's southern neighbour. Encircled by six soaring mountain ranges, this is a dreamy corner of Central Europe and the ideal spot to experience the Alps just a couple of hours from Munich's Hauptbahnhof and right on Salzburg's doorstep. There's some top-level hiking here as well as skiing, but the main draw for most is the Königssee, Germany's highest lake (603m), its pristine waters plied by silent electric pleasure boats. The town of Berchtesgaden itself is the obvious base, with trains arriving direct from Munich and countless hotels, guesthouses, restaurants, supermarkets, gear shops and an avalanche of souvenir outlets.

Away from the trails, the area has a more sinister aspect – the mountaintop Eagle's Nest was a lodge built for Hitler and is now a disturbing dark-tourism destination; the Dokumentation Obersalzberg ably chronicles the region's Nazi past.

Sailing the Königssee
Gliding across an Alpine lake

The thing do to in Berchtesgaden is to take a pleasure boat along the shimmering, fjordlike depths of the **Königssee**. Purring electric vessels operated by **Bayerische Seen-Schifffahrt** *(seenschifffahrt.de)* make the trip to the **St Bartholomä** hamlet in around 30 minutes. The highlight, apart from the elemental colours and superb scenery, is when the boat stops for the captain to play a trumpet towards the Echo Wall – the sound bounces off the rock in a perfect reproduction.

Once at St Bartholomä, visit the unusual pilgrimage church with its triple-barrelled form that took on its current shape in 1697. Many retreat to the beer garden and **Gaststätte St Bartholomä** for some filling Alpine dishes – try the venison, dumplings or red sauerkraut. More active visitors can take a 3.5km-long trail up to the **Eiskapelle**, a cave where the ice

BERCHTESGADEN

🟠 HIGHLIGHTS
1 Dokumentation Obersalzberg
2 Eagle's Nest
3 Jennerbahn am Königssee
4 Königssee
5 Rossfeld Scenic Road

🟠 SIGHTS
6 Königsblick

7 Malerwinkel
8 Salzbergwerk
9 St Bartholomä

🟠 ACTIVITIES
10 Bayerische Seen-Schifffahrt
11 Eiskapelle
12 MTR Tour
13 Salet
see 10 Sport Renoth

⚫ SLEEPING
14 Alpinhotel Berchtesgaden
15 DJH Hostel
16 Hotel Edelweiss

🟢 EATING
17 Berchtesgadener Esszimmer
18 Bräustübl

19 Café Graflhöhe 'Windbeutelbaron'
see 9 Gaststätte St Bartholomä

🔵 INFORMATION
20 Berchtesgaden National Park Office
21 Berchtesgaden Tourist Office
22 Schönau am Königssee Tourist Office

KÖNIGSSEE PRACTICALITIES

At busy times (weekends between May and September, all July and August) buy tickets ahead online. Boats run at regular intervals from around 8am to 5pm from mid-June to mid-September, with fewer departures throughout the rest of the year.
Berchtesgaden Tourist Office (p151) (*berchtesgaden.com*), close to the train station, has detailed information on the entire Berchtesgaden region.
Schönau am Königssee Tourist Office (p151) (*koenigssee.de*) has two similarly helpful branches, including one at the lake car park and the other at Rathausplatz 1, which is the nearest tourist office to the Königssee. In town, at the modern 'Haus der Berge',
Berchtesgaden National Park Office (*nationalpark-berchtesgaden.bayern.de*) is good for info about hiking and wildlife, and has an exhibition about the national park.

survives year-round. After big snow years, the entrance can be blocked by avalanche debris until high summer. More relaxing strolls can be enjoyed north and south of St Bartholomä, but the going gets tough as the paths wander up and away from the shore.

Don't miss the last boat back from St Bartholomä, as there's no other way back.

Take the Jennerbahn Cable Car
Look down on Königssee

Riding the **Jennerbahn am Königssee** (*jennerbahn.de; adult/child €45/27*) is a stunning complement to a boat ride on the lake – the views of the lake from above are magnificent. The cable car is beloved by skiers in winter and hikers in summer, taking you as it does up to all manner of enticing trailheads. Ask at the tourist office near the car park for maps and advice. The *Nationalpark Berchtesgaden* brochure has some suggested hikes both from here and in the wider area.

For the casual, less active visitor, it's all about the views. The cable car passes through Middle Station at an altitude of 1200m, and you then ride a different cable car to Mountain Station (1800m); both have restaurants and fine views. But for the best views of Königssee, walk 550m (20 minutes) to the lookout at **Königsblick** (1874m).

Tickets are cheaper after 3pm in summer.

Hike & Ski Berchtesgadener Land
Get active outdoors around Königssee

From St Bartholomä, boats continue 10 minutes further to **Salet**, where there's a jetty and a shelter. From here hikers can make their way back to **Schönau**, a relatively challenging hike of 17km. From Schönau it's a 25km, two-day adventure to St Bartholomä via Mt Watzmann (2713m), staying at the high-perched hut Watzmannhaus en route. This is a serious mountaineering hike and not for first-timers. For a short hike, take the **Malerwinkelrundweg** from behind the boathouses in Schönau am Königssee to the **Malerwinkel**, a viewpoint enjoying Königssee panoramas. The full circuit is 3km.

The **Jenner-Königssee** (*jennerbahn.de*) ski area is the biggest and most varied of the five local ski fields. Take the Jennerbahn to access the runs. For ski equipment and advice, try **Sport Renoth** (*sport-renoth.de*); you can book your equipment online.

Descend into the Region's Salt Mines
Berchtesgaden's white gold

A change of pace from the bigger-ticket Berchtesgaden attractions, **Salzbergwerk** (*salzbergwerk.de; adult/student/child €25.50/22.50/13*) has thrown open its salt mine for fun-filled 1½-hour tours. Kids will especially love donning miners' garb and whooshing down a wooden slide into the depths of the mine. Down below, highlights include the mysteriously glowing salt grottoes and crossing a 100m-long subterranean salt lake on a wooden raft.

The Salzbergwerk is 2.8km northeast of the Berchtesgaden Hauptbahnhof; take bus 840 from the station.

Berchtesgaden's Dark Nazi Heritage
Signposts to the Nazi past

In 1933 the tranquil Alpine settlement of **Obersalzberg** (3km southeast from Berchtesgaden) in essence became the second seat of Nazi power after Berlin. This dark period is given the full historical treatment at the superb exhibition at the **Dokumentation Obersalzberg** *(obersalzberg.de; adult/child €3/free)*. Various rooms document the forced takeover of the area, the construction of the Berghof compound that Hitler commandeered and the daily life of the Nazi elite. All facets of Nazi terror are dealt with, including Hitler's near-mythical appeal, his racial politics, the resistance movement, Nazi Germany's foreign policy and the death camps. A section of the underground bunker network is also open for exploration. Hourly RVO bus 838 from Berchtesgaden train station will get you here. Alternatively, you can drive up and pay for parking.

Much better known than the Dokumentation Obersalzberg is Hitler's mountain hideout, the hard-to-reach **Eagle's Nest** *(kehlsteinhaus.de; adult/child €31.90/16.50)*, aka Kehlsteinhaus. At 1834m above sea level, this high-perched chalet was built as a mountaintop retreat for Hitler and gifted to him on his 50th birthday. It took around 3000 workers a mere two years to carve the precipitous 6km-long mountain road, cut a 124m-long tunnel and a brass-panelled lift through the rock, and build the lodge itself (now a seasonal restaurant). Note that Eagle's Nest is open only from early May to late October, depending on weather conditions.

The lift can only be reached by special bus RVO 849 from the Dokumentation Obersalzberg. As you need to book a ticket time online for Eagle's Nest, get to the bus stop at least half an hour before the scheduled departure time. On foot it's a very steep climb.

On clear days, the views from Eagle's Nest are simply breathtaking, with the mountains ringing Berchtesgaden rising all around. Allow at least two hours to get through queues, explore the lodge and the mountaintop, and perhaps have a bite to eat. Some choose to hike back down to Dokumentation Obersalzberg (around two hours).

BERCHTESGADEN'S TRADITIONAL ALPINE EVENTS

Palm Sunday: On the Sunday before Easter the incredibly colourful *Palmbosch'n'* (palm bushes) are blessed – they then adorn homes for several weeks afterwards.

St John's Day: On this day (24 June) dramatic bonfires are lit on the mountaintops.

Schellenberger Dult: This traditional fair is held in Markt Schellenberg to the north in early July.

Almabtrieb: Cows return from summer pastures – a real Alpine spectacle in early autumn, depending on the weather.

Buttnmandl: Just before Christmas, a 'straw man' wearing a huge cowbell visits children to see if they've been good.

 EATING IN BERCHTESGADEN: OUR PICKS

Bräustübl: This brewery-run beer hall does a mean pork roast. the house speciality, breaded calf's head, and there's an oompah band weekends. *11am-11pm* €€

Gaststätte St Bartholomä (p152): Serves hearty meat and fish dishes and HB lager on the inner reaches of Königsee, reachable only by boat. *hours vary* €€

Café Graflhöhe 'Windbeutelbaron': For wow factor, look no further than this high-seated, panorama-rich, traditional restaurant-cafe. *10am-6pm Thu-Tue* €€

Berchtesgadener Esszimmer: Berchtesgaden's Michelin-starred restaurant offers regional dishes served in a traditional dining room. *6-10pm Tue-Sat* €€€

BERCHTESGADEN – A NAZI STRONGHOLD

Of all the German towns tainted by the Third Reich, Berchtesgaden has a burden heavier than most. Hitler fell in love with nearby Obersalzberg in the 1920s and bought a small country home, later enlarged into the imposing Berghof.

After seizing power in 1933, Hitler established a part-time headquarters here and brought much of the party brass with him. They bought, or confiscated, large tracts of land and tore down farmhouses to erect a 2m-high barbed-wire fence, and Obersalzberg became the fortified southern headquarters of the NSDAP (National Socialist German Workers' Party). In 1938 British Prime Minister Neville Chamberlain visited for negotiations, which led to the infamous promise of 'peace for our time' at the expense of Czechoslovakia's Sudetenland.

Rossfeld Scenic Road

Drive Germany's Highest Scenic Road

Drive into the clouds

One of Berchtesgaden's best-kept secrets, the **Rossfeld Scenic Road** *(rossfeldpanoramastrasse.de; toll for car/motorcycle €9/5.50)* is a glorious 15.4km drive. It's one of the prettiest drives anywhere in the Alps, with views to Salzburg, Eagle's Nest and some of Germany's highest peaks. It's also the highest place you can reach in a private vehicle in Germany, and is open year-round. You can drive it in either direction, from either Oberau or Obersalzburg. Not surprisingly, the road is often used for film shoots and for test driving vehicles; ask **MTR Tour** *(mtr-tour.de),* which is based in Winkl, about renting or taking a tour on a latest-model BMW motorbike. There are plenty of parking pullovers, and there's a restaurant at the summit.

Chiemsee

BOAT & CYCLE TRIPS | LUDWIG CASTLE | HISTORIC ISLAND

As you approach the Alps from the north, the mountains rise sheer from the plains: they're visible from at least 40km away. It can be tempting to rush towards them, but they're not going anywhere. Pause instead for a day or two to explore the lakes and forests that extend over the adjacent area and all of which offer spectacular mountain views on a clear day. If you only stop at one lake, make it Chiemsee – at 80 sq km it's the largest lake in the Free State (and nicknamed the Bavarian Sea). A mere hour from Munich's Hauptbahnhof, this is an easily accessible, day-tripper magnet. Crowds can overwhelm on weekends, but weekdays are often surprisingly quiet, and the shoreline is long enough that there's usually a quiet corner to sit and take it all in. Locals come for a swim, while tourists arrive to see one of Bavaria's top attractions: Ludwig II's Schloss Herrenchiemsee.

Discover Ludwig II's Island Palace
Complete your set of Ludwig's fantasy castles

Often the last of Ludwig II's mad mansions that tourists see, **Schloss Herrenchiemsee** (*herrenchiemsee.de; adult/child €11/ free*) is the most Versaille-like of all his pads. Begun in 1878, this ostentatious pile on the lake island of **Herreninsel** was never intended as a residence, but as homage to absolutist monarchy, as epitomised by Ludwig's exemplar, Louis XIV, the Sun King.

Incredibly, Ludwig blew more cash on this castle than on Neuschwanstein (p142) and Linderhof (p150) put together, but when the coffers ran dry in 1885, one year before his death, 50 rooms remained incomplete. Those that were finished outdo each other in opulence. The vast **Gesandtentreppe** (Ambassador Staircase), a double staircase leading to a frescoed gallery and topped by a glass roof, is the first visual knockout on the guided tour, but that fades in comparison with the spectacular **Grosse Spiegelgalerie** (Great Hall of Mirrors). This tunnel of light extends the length of the garden (98m; 10m longer than Versailles'). It sports 52 candelabras and 33 great glass chandeliers with 7000 candles, which used to take 70 servants half an hour to light.

GETTING AROUND

Chiemsee-Schifffahrt (*chiemsee-schifffahrt. de*) operates half-hourly to hourly ferries from Prien with stops at Herreninsel, Fraueninsel, Seebruck and Chieming on a schedule that changes seasonally. You can circumnavigate the entire lake and make all these stops, getting off and then catching the next ferry that comes your way. For exploring the other lakes in the area, you'll need your own wheels.

☑ TOP TIP

Pretty Waginger See, around 28km northeast of Chiemsee, is a tranquil, seldom-visited lake surrounded by campgrounds. In summer, if the crowds begin to spoil the effect of Chiemsee's natural beauty, escape via a 30-minute drive to Waginger See.

HIGHLIGHTS
1 Frauenwörth Abbey
2 Schloss Herrenchiemsee

SIGHTS
3 Fraueninsel
see 3 Torhalle

ACTIVITIES
see 3 Inselführungen Fraueninsel

INFORMATION
4 Chiemsee Tourist Office

TRANSPORT
see 4 Bike Rental Fritz Müller
5 Chiemsee-Schifffahrt

FÜNF-SEEN-LAND

On the way to Ga-Pa you are likely to pass through the Bavarian lake district, the Fünf-Seen-Land (Five Lakes District), south of Munich. It's hugely popular (especially for people from Munich on weekends).

Starnberger See: On the S6 S-Bahn line, this lake was once the haunt of Bavaria's royal family and it still has a patrician air.

Kloster Andechs: This gorgeous hilltop monastery is famous for its monk-brewed lagers, which can be slurped in its *Bräustüberl*.

Schloss Berg: On Starnberg See, it was near this castle that Ludwig II and his doctor mysteriously drowned. Hike here from Starnberg town.

The **Paradeschlafzimmer** (State Bedroom) contains a canopied bed perching altar-like on a pedestal behind a golden balustrade. This was the heart of the palace, where morning and evening audiences were to be held. But it's the king's bedroom, the **Kleines Blaues Schlafzimmer** (Little Blue Bedroom), that really steals the show. The decoration is sickly, encrusted with gilded stucco and wildly extravagant carvings. Incredibly, Ludwig only spent 10 nights here.

Visit an 8th-Century Abbey on Fraueninsel
Explore a 1300-year-old island monastery

Northeast of Herreninsel and much smaller, **Fraueninsel** is a fine way to escape the worst of the summer crowds on Chiemsee. One-third of the island is given over to **Frauenwörth Abbey** *(frauenwoerth.de; tours per person €6)*. Most of the buildings here date from later centuries. The 10th-century church, for example, has a free-standing, 11th-century bell tower with a distinctive onion-dome top. Across from the church is the 860 CE Carolingian **Torhalle**, a museum with medieval *objets d'art*, sculpture and changing exhibitions of regional paintings from the 18th to the 20th centuries. Arrange a tour through **Inselführungen Fraueninsel** *(fraueninsel-fuehrungen.de; tours from €70)*; prices vary according to the number of people.

Cycle the Lakeshore
Ride around Chiemsee on two wheels

One of the best ways to explore Chiemsee and leave the boating crowds behind is to rent a bike and cycle; a full circumnavigation of the lake would be 64km. Head for the lakeside town of Bernau to **Bike Rental Fritz Müller** *(fahrradverleih-chiemsee.de; half/full day from €9/15)*, opposite the **Chiemsee Tourist Office**.

Regensburg

UNESCO SITE | RIVERSIDE CITY | HISTORIC ARCHITECTURE

Sitting pretty astride the Danube, Regensburg is the capital of the Oberpfalz region (Upper Palatinate), which runs along the border with Czechia to the east. A laid-back, youthful kind of place, this architecturally alluring city lies slightly in the shadow of bigger names such as Munich and Nuremberg, meaning visitors are generally taken aback at what they find here. The tangle of old streets makes it feel like some some kind of hidden treasure, and the old bridge across the Danube sets up a magnificent panorama. Regensburg actually dates back to Roman times and the city's 2000 years of architectural heritage was recognised by UNESCO in 2006 with a place on its World Heritage list.

Regensburg is best approached as a day trip or by hopping off the train when en route elsewhere. However, a considerable share of tourist footfall arrives on the absurdly long cruise boats that tie up along the Danube ready to take you up and downriver.

Explore a Private Palace
Regensburg's Schloss Thurn und Taxis

In parkland near the train station you will find one of Regensburg's highlights, the **Schloss Thurn und Taxis** *(thurnundtaxis.de; adult/child €17/14, treasury & carriage museum adult/child €6/4)*. In the 15th century, Franz von Taxis (1459–1517) assured his place in history by setting up the first European postal system, a monopoly until the 19th century. In recognition of his services, the family was gifted a spare Benedictine monastery (then known as St Emmeram), which was from then on the family home. It was soon one of the most modern palaces in Europe with such luxuries as flushing toilets.

After touring the grand State Rooms and cloisters on the compulsory 80-minute guided tour, you can also access the **Schatzkammer** (Treasury) and carriage museum. The treasures on display belonged for many years to Germany's wealthiest dynasty.

GETTING AROUND

Regensburg is around one hour southeast of Nuremberg and northwest of Passau via the A3 autobahn. The A93 runs south to Munich. The town is well served by rail connections, including with Frankfurt am Main (three hours), Landshut (40 minutes), Munich (1½ hours), Nuremberg (one to two hours), Passau (one hour) and elsewhere. Once in Regensburg, the weekday-only Altstadtbus connects the Hauptbahnhof and the Altstadt every 10 minutes. The town centre is ideal for walking.

☑ TOP TIP

Regensburg is a cycling city, with locals whizzing around by pedal power. Join them by renting two-wheelers from **Bikehaus** *(fahrradverleih-regensburg.de)* at the train station. There are also various e-scooters (part of the city's scootershare scheme) scattered across the city.

REGENSBURG

HIGHLIGHTS
1. Dom St Peter
2. House of Bavarian History

SIGHTS
3. Alte Kapelle
4. Document Neupfarrplatz
5. Schloss Thurn und Taxis
6. Schottenkirche St Jakob

ACTIVITIES
7. Schifffahrt Klinger

EATING
8. Dicker Mann
9. Historische Wurstkuchl
10. Leerer Beutel
11. Storstad

DRINKING & NIGHTLIFE
12. Cafebar
13. Kneitinger
14. Paletti
15. Spitalgarten

INFORMATION
16. Regensburg Tourist Office

TRANSPORT
17. Bikehaus

Follow Bavaria's Story

Visit the House of Bavarian History

Opened in 2019 around 250m east of the Steinerne Brücke, the **House of Bavarian History** *(hdbg.de; adult/concession/child €7/5/free)* is one of the better museums to open in Germany in recent years. This journey into Bavaria's past begins with the Romans and takes you through nearly two millennia of history, right up to the founding of the Kingdom of Bavaria in 1806. The commentary, by cabaret artist Christoph Süss, is endlessly entertaining, making for an anything-but-staid museum experience. Upstairs, the permanent collection is similarly as much performance art as museum, with a historical theatre and all manner of multimedia displays and interactive exhibits. There's an excellent store at the exit, and this being Bavaria, there's even a Bavarian pub…

Explore Religious Regensburg

City of churches

Regensburg's austere Catholic **Dom St Peter** *(bistum-regensburg.de; free)* dominates the city skyline and is a masterpiece of the Gothic style with few rivals for grandeur in Bavaria. A church has existed here since CE 700, but what you see today took 240 years to build; begun in 1280 after its predecessor burned down, it was finally finished in 1520. After admiring the soaring facade, step inside and enjoy the exquisite, luminous stained-glass windows and extravagant main altar all sheathed in silver. The **Domspatzen** is a boys' choir that has been around for over 1000 years; they accompany the 10am Sunday service during the school year. Attached to the church is the **Domschatzmuseum** (Cathedral Treasury), which overflows (and overwhelms) with lavish monstrances, tapestries and other church treasures.

Southeast of the cathedral, the old-style religious opulence continues with the **Alte Kapelle** *(free)*: don't be fooled by the rather humble facade. With over-the-top rococo adornments, a 1000-year-old core and vaulted Gothic ceilings, it's one of Regensburg's biggest surprises. You may enter only during church services, but you can always see inside through the wrought-iron grill.

Rounding out Regensburg's portfolio of houses of Christian worship, the **Schottenkirche St Jakob** *(free)* has a superb 12th-century portal that is widely considered to be the pinnacle of Romanesque architecture in Germany. Head inside for more graceful Romanesque simplicity.

REGENSBURG FESTIVALS

Regensburg loves its beer so much that it celebrates local, wider Bavarian and German brews, and even the odd international tipple twice each year. **Dult** *(r-dult.de)* is a major event and an Oktoberfest-style beer party with brewery tents, carousel rides, entertainment, bratwurst aplenty and all kinds of vendors on the Dultplatz. It's held in May, and again in August–September; book months ahead if you plan on visiting at this time. And this being Germany in general and Bavaria in particular, the December **Weihnachtsmarkt** is one of the region's best, with stalls selling roasted chestnuts, *Glühwein* (mulled wine), gingerbread and traditional wooden toys during Advent at Neupfarrplatz and Schloss Thurn und Taxis.

 EATING IN REGENSBURG: OUR PICKS

Historische Wurstkuchl: Traditional finger-size sausages, grilled over beech wood, with its own sauerkraut and sweet grainy mustard. *10am-7pm* €

Dicker Mann: Here since the 14th century, this traditional inn is a relative newcomer, serving Bavarian staples. *9am-1am* €€

Leerer Deutel: A mixed menu of Bavarian, Tyrolean and Italian dishes; ask about the weekday lunch specials. *11am-10pm Tue-Fri, 5-10pm Sat* €€

Storstad. Storstad does lamb, cod and mackerel, paired with wines in an ultramodern setting. *6.30pm-midnight Tue & Wed, noon-4pm & 6.30pm-midnight Thu-Sat* €€

BAVARIA'S UNESCO SITES

Regensburg is one of 10 UNESCO World Heritage–listed sites in Bavaria, out of German's total of 54. In addition to Regensburg, Bavarian sites inscribed on the list include the old town of Bamberg (p112), the Würzburg Residenz (p118), Bayreuth's opera house (p117), the Romantic Road's Wieskirche (p141) and the Beahim Globe in the Germanisches Nationalmuseum (p108) in Nuremberg. Germany has also nominated for recognition what it calls 'Dreams in Stone', a collection of castles built by Ludwig II and including Schloss Neuschwanstein (p142), Schloss Hohenschwangau (p143), both near Füssen, and Schloss Linderhof (p150), near Ettal and Oberammergau.

Neupfarrplatz

Return to Regensburg's Jewish Past
Visit the Document Neupfarrplatz

In the 16th century, Regensburg had a thriving Jewish Quarter that was one of the largest and most significant in Bavaria. This period was one of the least known parts of the city's past, and largely lay buried until excavations in the 1990s unearthed traces from the period, as well as Roman buildings, gold coins and even a Nazi bunker. The underground **Document Neupfarrplatz** *(tour adult/concession/family €8/5/16)* only provides access to a small portion of the excavated area, but tours feature a worthwhile multimedia presentation (in German) about the square's history. Back up above, on the square itself, a work by renowned Israeli artist Dani Karavan graces the site of the former synagogue.

Contact the **Regensburg Tourist Office** for tickets and tour details.

DRINKING IN REGENSBURG: OUR PICKS

Cafebar: Swathed in Jugendstil tile, cast iron and stained glass, Cafebar has been serving locals for over 30 years. *8am-2am Mon-Fri, 9am-2am Sat, 1pm-2am Sun*

Kneitinger: Kneitinger is Regensburg's local beer and there's no better place to sample it than the brewery's own tavern, in business since 1530. *11am-midnight*

Paletti: In a passageway off Gesandtenstrasse, this Italian place dates back to the 1960s. *8am-midnight Mon, to 1am Tue-Thu, to 2am Fri & Sat, 1pm-midnight Sun*

Spitalgarten: Take up an outdoor table and ponder how they've brewed beer (called Spital) here since 1350. *11am-11pm*

A WALK IN REGENSBURG

Regensburg's old town is like an invitation to get out and walk – steeped in history, and recognised by UNESCO, the Altstadt is a gem.

START	END	LENGTH
Steinerne Brücke	Golf Museum	2km; 2 hrs

Begin your tour of Regensburg at the 900-year-old **1 Steinerne Brücke** (Old Stone Bridge), once the only fortified crossing of the Danube.

From the town end of the bridge, head west into Fischmarkt to see the **2 Kepler-Gedächtnishaus** (Kepler Memorial House). Double back along Fischmarkt then veer south into Schmerbühl alley to see the **3 Altes Rathaus** (Old Town Hall).

From the Old Town Hall, it's a short walk along Watmarkt, where you will find the **4 Oskar Schindler Plaque**. From 20th-century history, go back 2000 years to Regensburg's days as the Roman garrison Castra Regina at the hefty **5 Porta Praetoria** (179 CE), commissioned by Emperor Marcus Aurelius. Roman walls continue the length of **6 Unter den Schwibbögen**. At the end of this street is the latest addition to Bavaria's tourist offerings, the exceptional **7 House of Bavarian History** (p161), housed in a purpose-built, sustainable wedge of contemporary architecture.

Go back along Unter den Schwibbögen and pass again through the Porta Praetoria to reach the **8 Dom St Peter** (p161), a soaring landmark and one of Bavaria's grandest Gothic cathedrals.

Off the cathedral square (Domplatz), Tändlergasse boasts Europe's best **9 Golf Museum**, a fine repository of wooden clubs, ivory tees and yellowing score cards.

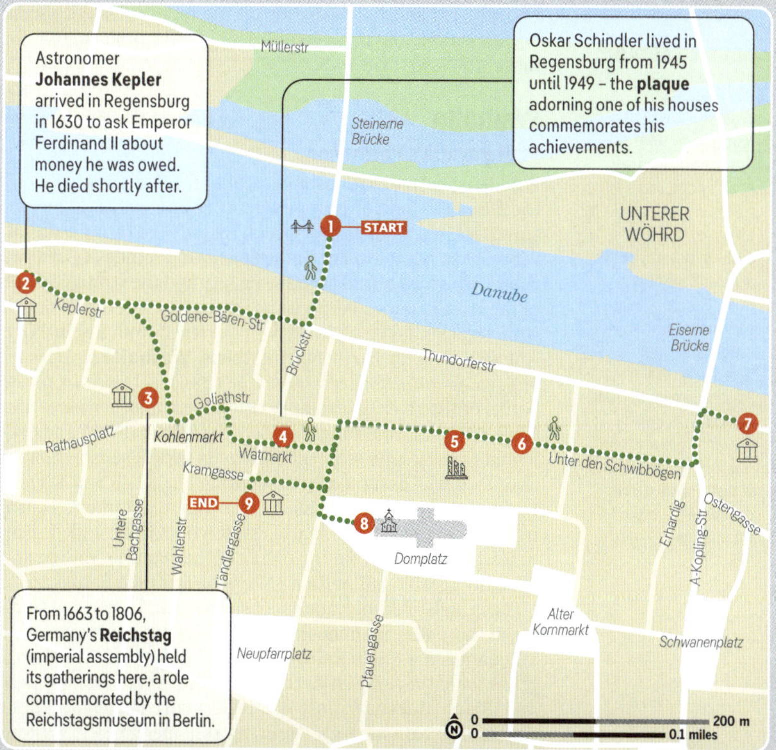

Astronomer **Johannes Kepler** arrived in Regensburg in 1630 to ask Emperor Ferdinand II about money he was owed. He died shortly after.

Oskar Schindler lived in Regensburg from 1945 until 1949 – the **plaque** adorning one of his houses commemorates his achievements.

From 1663 to 1806, Germany's **Reichstag** (imperial assembly) held its gatherings here, a role commemorated by the Reichstagsmuseum in Berlin.

Beyond Regensburg

Trips along the Danube are the highlight beyond Regensburg. Landshut, Ingolstadt and Straubing also make engaging day trips.

Places
Walhalla p164
Danube Gorge p165
Landshut p166
Ingolstadt p167

With Regensburg's UNESCO-listed cityscape fresh in your memory, use the city as a base for some excellent forays into the hinterland. Trips in pleasure boats along the Danube are a huge attraction and glorious Walhalla and the dramatic riverscape and cliffs at the Weltenburg Narrows are a brilliant way to see a different side to this, one of Europe's grandest old rivers. Even if you've already seen Walhalla, Weltenburg is still very much worth the excursion. Also on the Danube, Straubing has a beer festival that almost rivals Munich's Oktoberfest. To the south, straddling the Isar (the river that runs through Munich), is Landshut, a slightly off-the-radar town with some big attractions and many a traditional tavern. Ingolstadt is for those who love their Audi.

GETTING AROUND

Weltenburg and Walhalla are best reached by boat, though you can get near by car, too – to experience the full effect of the river's sudden drama, boats are undoubtedly best. The best way to access Landshut, Ingolstadt and Straubing is by train – all have regular rail connections with Regensburg and with each other. But if time is tight, having your own wheels makes a lot of sense.

Walhalla

TIME FROM REGENSBURG: **1 HR**

Visit Bavaria's Parthenon

Exploring beyond Regensburg means travelling by boat along the Danube – one of Europe's great rivers, whose name, for travellers, seems to have a special magic. The Danube has always held a notable place in the hearts and minds of Bavaria's rulers, who recognised both the beauty and the strategic value of the river's course. Perhaps the strangest of all the Danube's royal legacies lies just 12km downriver (east) from Regensburg.

Modelled on the Parthenon in Athens, **Walhalla** (*schloesser. bayern.de; adult/concession/child €5/4/free*) rises from the banks of the river like an apparition from another place and time. This breathtaking monument built by Ludwig I and dedicated to the giants of Germanic (in its widest sense) thought and deed was designed by none other than Leo von Klenze, Ludwig I's architect of choice, who rebuilt Munich's centre in neo-Greek style. The marble steps von Klenze added seem to lead up forever from the banks of the Danube, ending at a dazzling marble hall with a gallery of Teutonic heroes.

The grandeur of the monument seems fitting when you think about those who are honoured here. Faces you might recognise and names you might know include Wilhelm Conrad Röntgen (inventor of the X-ray), Albert Einstein (no explanation needed) and Konrad Adenauer, post-WWII German chancellor. Printer Gutenberg, Nuremberg's Dürer, astronomer Kepler, warlord

Walhalla

Wallenstein, Mozart and Catherine the Great are all honoured too. And just because Ludwig I is no longer on the scene doesn't mean the list is complete: the most recent addition (2022) was Max Planck, winner of the Nobel Prize in Physics in 1918.

The collection also includes a few luminaries whose presence among the heroes of ancient Germany seems like a dubious territorial grab from neighbouring countries and to reflect a wish that such people *were* German. Among these are astronomer Copernicus, who was born in Toruń in present-day Poland, and a handful of Flemish painters.

There are lots of ways to reach Walhalla, a dozen kilometres along the river from Regensburg's Old Town. If you're going by car, take the Danube Valley country road via Tegernheim to the village of Donaustauf, then follow the signs. Bus 5 from Regensburg Hauptbahnhof also runs here. But if you've even a vague notion of the romance of river travel, easily the best way to reach the memorial is on a boat cruise with **Schifffahrt Klinger** *(schifffahrtklinger.de; adult one-way/return €15/20, child €7/10, family €40/55)*, which includes a one-hour stop at Walhalla.

Danube Gorge
TIME FROM REGENSBURG: **3-4 HRS**

Up the Danube to Weltenburg

If your idea of the Danube is a wide, sluggish river flowing across the plains of Central and Eastern Europe, then prepare yourself for a shock. Possibly the best trip you can make from Regensburg is along the Danube to the **Danube Gorge** (also called Weltenburg Narrows, or Weltenburger Enge) and Weltenburg Monastery, around 40km to the southwest.

The tour by Schifffahrt Klinger *(adult one-way/return €36/55, family €109/149)* runs on Saturdays only from late May until mid-September, although you can still visit the monastery at other times. It's a full-day trip, setting out from Regensburg at 9am, and returning around 6pm. You'll get to

THE BIRTH OF FRANKENSTEIN

Mary Shelley's novel *Frankenstein* (1818) set a creepy precedent in the world of monster fantasies. The story is well known: young scientist Victor Frankenstein travels to Ingolstadt to study medicine. He becomes obsessed with the idea of creating a human being and goes shopping for parts at the local cemetery. Unfortunately his creature is a problem child and sets out to destroy its maker.

Shelley picked Ingolstadt because it was home to a prominent university and medical faculty. In the 19th century, a laboratory for scientists and medical doctors was housed in the Alte Anatomie (now the **Deutsches Medizinhistorisches Museum**). In the operating theatre, professors and their students carried out experiments on corpses and dead tissue.

spend just over three hours enjoying the gorge and monastery, before beginning the return journey.

The tour takes you from Regensburg to **Kelheim**, a journey that hints little at what lies ahead where, just after Kelheim, one of Europe's major waterways squeezes through a narrow gorge with limestone cliffs rising up to 80m on both sides; scan the cliffs for statues carved from the rock. Where the terrain allows, there are small pebble beaches, while dense woodlands rise from the water's edge elsewhere. The alternative name, the 'Weltenburg Narrows', is a fitting label – it's quite a sight to see large vessels negotiating this stretch of the river.

The final destination of the trip is **Weltenburg Monastery**, which sits on a promontory at a tight bend in the river. This is believed to be Bavaria's oldest monastery, with some sources claiming it was established as early as 617. The visitable highlight here is the monastery church, a baroque confection built by the Asam brothers between 1716 and 1739.

In good old monastic style, Weltenburg is famous for its brewery, said to be the world's oldest monastic beer-producing facility. The monks famously brew up the Weltenburger Kloster Barock Dunkel, a supreme dark beer, said by some to be unsurpassed in Central Europe. See what all the fuss is about yourself at the **Klosterschenke Weltenburg** *(klosterschenke-weltenburg.de),* a large restaurant and beer hall that's open mid-March to mid-December and occupies one wing of the monastery complex. It's where most passengers end up.

Landshut

TIME FROM REGENSBURG: **45 MINS**

Visit Landshut's castle

Around 65km south of Regensburg by road, **Landshut** is a workaday town with a pretty Altstadt, making it a stimulating stop-off on your way to the Bavarian capital. With direct bus connections to Munich Airport, this is also a good place to spend half a day or a night before a flight.

Landshut has a duo of sights worth your attention. Top billing in town goes to **Burg Trausnitz** *(burg-trausnitz.de; adult/child €6/free),* roosting high above the Altstadt. The compulsory hour-long guided tour takes you through the Gothic and Renaissance halls and chambers, ending at a terrace with bird's-eye views of the town below. It also includes the **Kunst- und Wunderkammer** (Room of Art and Curiosities), a typical Renaissance-era display of exotic curios that was assembled by the local dukes.

GÄUBODENFEST

Around 30 minutes by road southeast of Regensburg, small-town Straubing is another perfectly renovated, affluent Bavarian town that goes about its busy Central European life largely unnoticed by the outside world. Unnoticed, that is, until it hosts Bavaria's second-largest beer festival, the **Gäubodenfest** *(ausstellungs-gmbh.de/gaeubodenvolksfest).* This 10-day blow-out in mid-August started, like the Oktoberfest, as an agricultural show and elements of the original event do survive. But the main reason over one million drinkers descend on this small town is to swill the often obscure beers on tap in Oktoberfest-style marquees, all supplied by six local breweries. If you can't make it to Oktoberfest, this lesser-known sibling takes place conveniently during the summer holidays and is a good alternative.

EATING IN LANDSHUT: OUR PICKS

Firmer Bräu: It's all about good old-fashioned bratwurst with sauerkraut or golden schnitzels here. *10am-10pm Mon-Sat, to 3pm Sun* €€

Augustiner an der St Martins Kirche: This tavern at the foot of St Martin's spire serves Bavarian platters and Munich lager. *10am-11pm Tue-Sat, to 9pm Sun* €€

Heilig-Geist-Stuberl: The conservative menu at this Landshut tavern includes the best schnitzel far and wide. *10am-10.30pm* €€

Rauchensteiner: Artfully presented Bavarian staples with subtle twists and fresh salads by the Isar. *11.30am-2.30pm & 5.30-11pm Tue-Sat* €€

Experience a Gothic masterpiece

Landshut's other unmissable sight is **St Martin Church** *(st.martin-landshut.de)*, which rises in Gothic splendour at the southern end of the Altstadt. The church's spire is the tallest brick structure in the world at 130.6m high, and took 55 years to build. It's by far Bavaria's tallest church, with Regensburg's Dom 25m shorter. There is a pleasing simplicity about the soaring main sanctuary, and whatever your beliefs, attending one of the daily worship services (10am Monday to Saturday, 11am and 6.30pm Sunday) is a wonderful way to start the day.

Ingolstadt

TIME FROM REGENSBURG: 1¼ HRS

Discover the home of Audi

The overwhelming number of visitors to the affluent town of **Ingolstadt** are here for one thing: cars. Ingolstadt is the headquarters of Audi, the third member of the southern luxury motoring trio (after BMW in Munich and Mercedes in Stuttgart). Arriving by rail, you'll likely see long trains waiting to transport the latest e-models to all corners of the globe.

If you're a devotee of the four rings, head straight for the **Audi Factory** *(audi.de/audi-forum-ingolstadt/en/discovery-tours; tours per person €9-21)*. This is where you find the **Audi Museum Mobile** *(audi.de/audi-forum-ingolstadt/de/#Audi-museum-mobile; per person €5-10)*, which charts the company's history from its humble beginnings in 1899 to its latest dream machines, such as the R8. Some 50 cars and 20 motorbikes are on display, including prototypes that glide past visitors on an open lift. You can then take one of the tours of the production facility. Buy tickets online and in advance to avoid disappointment. If you don't have your own wheels, take bus 11 from the Hauptbahnhof or Paradeplatz.

Wander Ingolstadt's Altstadt

At its heart is easily Ingolstadt's most valuable piece of architecture, the **Asamkirche Maria de Victoria** *(adult/child €5/3.50)*, an overwhelming baroque masterpiece designed by the Asam brothers between 1732 and 1736. The church's *trompe l'oeil* ceiling, painted in just six weeks in 1735, is the world's largest fresco on a flat surface.

Other highlights of the old town include two superb Gothic structures: the Gothic **Kreuztor** (1385), which was one of the four main gates into the city until the 19th century, and the **Liebfrauenmünster** (1425), with its pair of strangely oblique square towers outside and an ethereal interior.

THE LANDSHUT WEDDING

Within Bavaria locals know Landshut best for its top event, the famous **Landshuter Hochzeit** *(Landshut Wedding; landshuter-hochzeit.de)*. One of Europe's biggest medieval celebrations, it takes place every four years in July and attracts a staggering 120,000 visitors. The celebrations were first held in 1902, inspired by a painting of the lavish 1475 marriage of Duke Georg der Reiche of Bavaria-Landshut to Princess Jadwiga (sometimes called Hedwig) of Poland in Landshut's Rathaus. Locals take great pride in the authenticity of costumes, performances and even food when it comes to take the town and its guest revellers back to 1475. The next Landshut Wedding is scheduled to run in 2027.

EATING & DRINKING IN INGOLSTADT

Little Kitchen – Ingolstadt: No-nonsense but excellent hot dogs, burgers and fries with a devoted local following. *10am-6pm* €

Weissbräuhaus. A beer hall with a modern feel serving the delicious signature *Weissbräupfändl* (pork fillet with homemade noodles). *9am-11pm* €€

Gasthaus Daniel: In a wonderfully Bavarian step-gabled townhouse, Ingolstadt's oldest inn is a lovingly run, Michelin-reviewed local institution. *11am-11pm Wed-Sun* €€

Neue Galerie Das MO: This trendy haunt has occasional art exhibitions and a shaded, walled beer garden. *11am-11pm Sun-Thu, to midnight Fri & Sat*

Passau

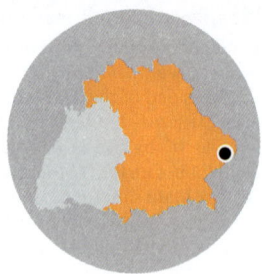

RIVERSIDE CITY | ITALIANATE ARCHITECTURE | PRETTY OLD TOWN

☑ TOP TIP

The **PassauRegioCard** *(passauregiocard.de; 3-/5-/7-day pass €38.50/48.50/55.50)* is the region's tourist pass. It's valid for all the town's museums and gives a modest discount on Danube cruises. It also provides savings at various spas and on dozens of other experiences across the Bavarian Forest and even over the border in South Bohemia.

Stacked along a narrow peninsula at the confluence of three rivers, Italianate Passau, near the border with Austria, is one of Bavaria's secret spots. A joy to explore, its Altstadt is a knot of cobbled lanes, pretty piazzas, medieval passageways, baroque churches and street cafes. The rivers here have shaped Passau's fate, bringing both wealth as a trading post for Bohemian salt, a precious medieval commodity, and ruin via inevitable floods (look out around town for high-water markers on facades). And wherever you head in Passau, you will eventually come to water. Christianity also conferred much prestige on Passau, which was once the largest bishopric in the Holy Roman Empire. Today, Passau is a Danube river-cruise stop and the convergence point of several long-distance cycling routes. But stay overnight to immerse yourself in Passau after the day-trippers have moved on and you'll soon find yourself falling in love with this gorgeous city.

Explore Where Three Rivers Meet Dreiflusseck

A watery spectacle

If you head along the Danube until you can't go any further, you'll end up at the **Dreiflusseck**, one of Central Europe's more accessible geographic features. This is the spot on the

GETTING AROUND

Regular rail connections from Passau include Munich (2¼ hours), Nuremberg (two hours), Regensburg (one hour) and Vienna (2¾ hours). Once you're here, Passau's central Altstadt is compact enough to get around on foot. The train station is 1.8km as the crow flies from the Dreiflusseck; the CityBus links the Bahnhof with the Altstadt twice an hour. The walk up the hill to the Veste Oberhaus, via the Luitpoldbrücke and Ludwigsteig path, takes about 30 minutes. From April to October a shuttle bus operates every 30 minutes from Rathausplatz.

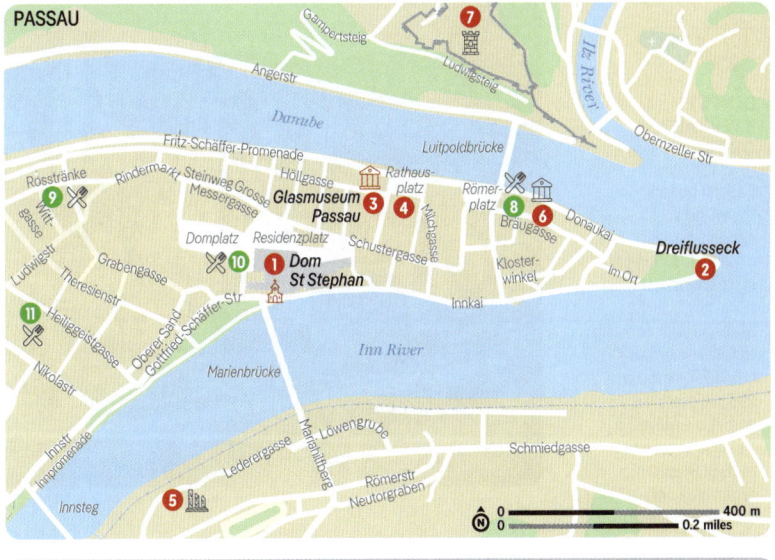

HIGHLIGHTS
1 Dom St Stephan
2 Dreiflusseck
3 Glasmuseum Passau

SIGHTS
4 Altes Rathaus
see 4 Grosser Rathaussaal
5 Kastell Boiotro
6 Museum Moderner Kunst
see 5 Römermuseum
7 Veste Oberhaus

EATING
8 Altes Bräuhaus
9 Café Greindl
10 Cafe Stephan's Dom
11 Heilig-Geist-Stifts-Schenke

map where three rivers converge: the Ilz, the Danube and the Inn. From the north the Ilz sluices brackish water down from the peat-rich Bavarian Forest, meeting the cloudy brown of the Danube as it flows from the west, and the pale snowmelt jade of the Inn from the south. The result is a unique tricolour. Although just about visible from the Dreiflusseck, the effect is best observed from high up on the ramparts of the Veste Oberhaus (p171).

Romans by the Danube
Explore the town's Roman heritage

Across the river from the Altstadt is where you will find the remnants of Passau's short stint in the Roman Empire. To get here, cross the Innsteg footbridge, which was once the only crossing between the north bank of the River Inn and the Altstadt.

Allow yourself to be distracted by the views back towards the Altstadt for a moment, then head to the top attraction here on the south bank, **Kastell Boiotro**, the ruins of a Roman fort that stood here from 250 to 400 CE. Incredibly, some of the Roman towers are still inhabited. There's a castle-themed kids' playground nearby. The site's **Römermuseum** *(stadtarchaeologie. de; adult/child €5/2.50)* displays artefacts unearthed here and elsewhere across Eastern Bavaria.

DOM ST STEPHAN'S ORGAN

Passau boasts the world's second-largest organ – the musical instrument that fills the city's Dom St Stephan with echoing tones. The organ has 17,774 pipes and 233 registers, all somehow played by a single organist. In fact, St Stephan's organ was only denied *Guinness Book of World Records* status in 1994 when a similar instrument in Los Angeles was expanded. If you are visiting between May and October or in the week leading up to Christmas you might be able catch the organ in action. Recitals take place several times a month – scan the DR code for for more details and a recital schedule.

SINA ETTMER PHOTOGRAPHY/SHUTTERSTOCK

Passau's Top Temple
Visit the city's cathedral

Completely dominating Domplatz, the Altstadt's biggest square, is the city's cathedral, the **Dom St Stephan** *(bistum-passau. de; free)*. There's been a church on this spot since the late 5th century, but what you see today is much younger thanks to the fire of 1662, which ravaged much of the medieval town, including the cathedral. This baroque marvel is the work of Italians Carlo Lurago and the stucco master Giovanni Battista Carlone. The interior is a cornucopia of saints and cherubs that gaze down at the congregation from countless cornices and capitals. However, the cathedral is best known for its monster organ, which is best appreciated and enjoyed during one of the concerts that take place here during the summer months.

See a Top Glass Collection
The continent's biggest glass exhibition

Within the Hotel Wilder Mann, the **Glasmuseum Passau** *(glasmuseum.de; adult/concession €8/6)* claims to be Europe's largest museum dedicated to European glass. This warren-like exhibition is packed with some 30,000 priceless pieces of glass and crystal from over the centuries. There are delicate

EATING IN PASSAU: OUR PICKS

Café Greindl: The Kaffee-und-Torte society meet daily at this bright, flowery cafe, which oozes Bavarian *Gemütlichkeit* (cosiness). *8am-6pm Mon-Sat, 11am-6pm Sun* €

Cafe Stephan's Dom: A Central European classic with plush padded seats, tiny tables and chandeliers under which to enjoy your coffee and cake. *10am-6pm* €

Heilig-Geist-Stifts-Schenke: Walnut-panelled dining rooms, local wines and fish, and a vine-shaded garden make this a Passau special. *11am-10pm Fri-Tue* €€

Altes Bräuhaus: A cheap set lunch menu attracts the midday crowds to this traditional tavern. *11am-midnight* €€

Passau

pieces from Murano alongside Czech crystal, and 17th-century Bavarian bottles next to Art Deco vases from Saxony. If you weren't an admirer of the material before your visit, you might just be upon leaving.

Ascending to History

Look down on Passau

From the **Rathausplatz**, the main town square and location of the town hall, on the opposite side of the Danube you'll see the towering **Veste Oberhaus** *(oberhausmuseum.de; adult/child €7/5)*, a 13th-century fortress built by the region's prince-bishops. The views from the hill are superb and the fortress itself houses a regional history museum. It's a strenuous uphill slog here from the Rathausplatz, but a shuttle bus runs here and back in summer when it can get surprisingly hot.

Take in Bavaria's Artistic Heritage

Art museums and more

Presiding over the main Rathausplatz, the **Altes Rathaus** *(free)* is notable as a grand Gothic structure, crowned by a 19th-century painted tower from which a carillon chimes several times daily. Inside, the **Grosser Rathaussaal**, or Great Assembly Room, is adorned by paintings by 19th-century local artist Ferdinand Wagner, who took Passau's history as his muse. If the door is open to the Small Assembly Room, check out the ceiling fresco – an allegory of the three rivers that converge at Passau.

Elsewhere, Gothic architecture contrasts with 20th- and 21st-century artworks at **Museum Moderner Kunst** *(mmk-passau.de; adult/family/child €10/15/free),* Passau's Modern Art Museum; highlights include cubist and expressionist works by Georg Philipp Wörlen, who died in Passau in 1954.

PASSAU'S HISTORY

There has been a settlement here since Roman times, and from around the 2nd century BCE, Passau was Roman Batavis, an important regional centre and home to many Germanic locals (known as the Batavi) who served in the Roman army. As Rome's power waned, Passau was vulnerable to attack and often changed hands in the centuries that followed. In the 5th century CE, a monastery was built – although nothing remains of this original structure, it was located at the site now occupied by Dom St Stephan. From the founding of the monastery until recent times, the bishops of Passau wielded great power in Bavaria, and it was an important centre of learning and ecclesiastical might. A young Adolf Hitler lived in Passau with his family from 1892 to 1894.

Bavarian Forest

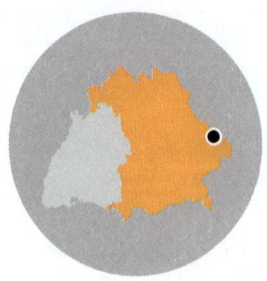

WILD NATURE | BEAUTIFUL FOREST | ARTS & CRAFTS

Unfurling along the border with neighbouring neighbouring Czechia, the Bavarian Forest is one of the wildest remaining parts of Germany. With the Nationalpark Bayerischer Wald (Bavarian Forest National Park) at its heart, this is a densely forested paradise for fresh-air lovers, hill hikers, mushroom pickers, mountain bikers, wildlife watchers and cross-country skiers. It coexists with the larger Šumava National Park on the Czech side, which, along with the Bohemian Forest and the Slavkovský Forest, represents one of Europe's largest forested areas, extending almost from Saxony into Austria. It goes without saying that the whole area is riddled with trails of all kinds, many now linking to those across the old Iron Curtain.

But the Bavarian Forest isn't known solely for its mysterious wooded peaks and uninhabited valleys. This is glass-producing country, and there are several glass-related attractions spread across the wider area.

Get Outdoors in Summer

Hiking and biking in the Bavarian Forest

Apart from the obvious attractions of the Bavarian Alps, there's no better place in the Free State to pull on hiking boots or snap on cross-country skis than the **Bavarian Forest National Park** *(nationalpark-bayerischer-wald.de)* and surrounding areas. The park extends around 24,250 hectares along the Czech border, from Bayerisch Eisenstein in the north to Finsterau in the south. No matter whether you come to enjoy the warmer months or the snow, unlike the Alps you'll encounter far fewer people on the trails here and there's also more wildlife to spot.

The European long-distance E6 hiking route cuts through the Bavarian Forest, but with over 350km of trails amid thick mountain spruce in the park, there are countless other routes to follow. Popular hikes include those to the summit of **Mt Lusen** (1373m), to the top of **Mt Grosser Arber** (1456m), the park's highest, and along the ridge that divides Bavaria from

GETTING AROUND

In summer, the **Igel-Bus** *(bayerwald-ticket.com)* navigates around the national park on three routes. The **Bayerwald-Ticket** *(per person €15.50)*, a day pass good for unlimited travel on buses and trains across the forest area, is available from the park visitor centres, stations and tourist offices. However, public transport is rather sketchy in these parts and you'll see much more with your own car.

☑ TOP TIP

The national park has various information and exhibition centres. The first is the **Hans-Eisenmann-Haus** in Lusen, the second the **Haus zur Wildnis** in Falkenstein. See *nationalpark-bayerischer-wald.bayern.de* for more details on what these places offer, along with heaps of information on the park itself.

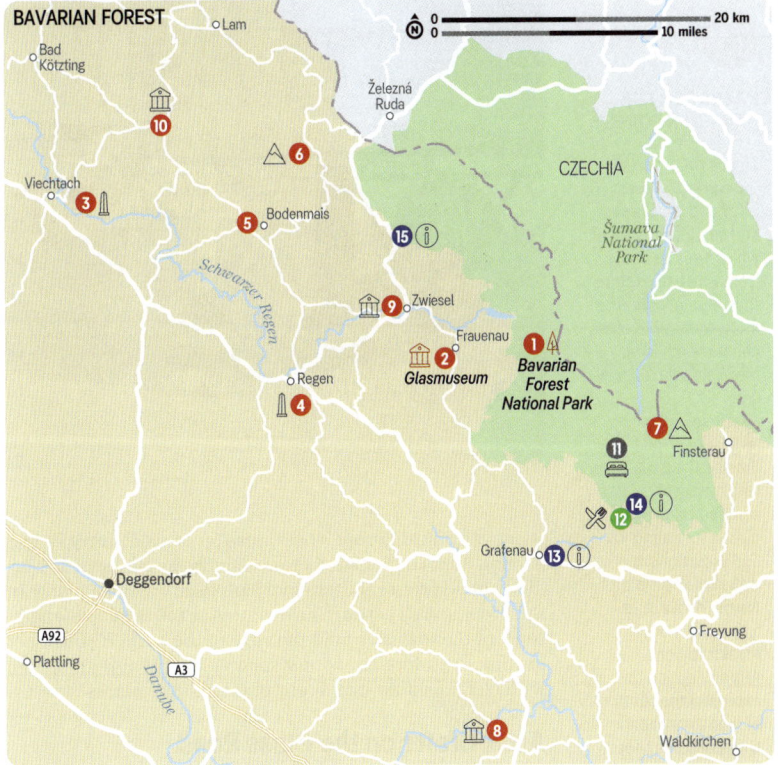

HIGHLIGHTS
1 Bavarian Forest National Park
2 Glasmuseum

SIGHTS
3 Gläserne Scheune
4 Gläserne Wald
see 2 Gläsernen Gärten
5 JOSKA
6 Mt Grosser Arber
7 Mt Lusen
8 Museumsdorf Bayerischer Wald
9 Waldmuseum
10 Weinfurtner Glasdorf

SLEEPING
11 DJH Waldhäuser Hostel
see 9 Hotel Zur Waldbahn

EATING
see 9 Dampfbräu
12 Euler Landgasthof Neuschönau

see 8 Gasthaus Mühlhiasl
see 9 Hotel Zur Waldbahn

INFORMATION
13 Grafenau Tourist Office
14 Hans-Eisenmann-Haus
15 Haus zur Wildnis
see 9 Zwiesel Tourist Office

West Bohemia. Note that some paths in the national park are out of bounds from November to July.

Other activities include mountain biking, trail running and geocaching. Whatever route you're planning or activity you are doing, maps produced by Kompass – sheets 195, 196, 197 and 198 – are invaluable companions. They are available from tourist offices, some bookshops, the park visitor centre and online.

Ski the Bavarian Forest

Explore the winter forest

The Bavarian Forest has seven ski areas. Although there is some downhill skiing – especially around the Grosser Arber, which sometimes hosts European and World Cup ski races – the forest

NADEZDA MURMAKOVA/SHUTTERSTOCK

BASES FOR THE BAVARIAN FOREST

The German part of the Bavarian Forest is fringed by villages and small towns, all of which work as bases from which to explore the national park. The more accessible ones can be reached via the Waldbahn railway line.

Zwiesel is the largest town just outside the park, with plenty of accommodation, places for eating and provisioning, a well-stocked, helpful **tourist office**, and a museum about local traditions. Another option for exploring the south of the national park, **Grafenau** has shops, accommodation, a spa and a **tourist office**. And if you're looking to combine the region's glass-making traditions with time spent exploring the park, **Frauenau**, very near the park's boundary, boasts the Glasmuseum.

is one of Central Europe's best areas for cross-country skiing. Around 80km of prepared cross-country (also known as Nordic) routes traverse the national park itself, with and more in the wider area. There are hire centres at the ski slopes and in some of the towns around the edge of the park. If you're not looking to go very far, winter snowshoeing is also an option, with equipment for hire at any of the ski-hire places.

Art & Crafts on the Glass Road
A crystal trail across Bavaria's east

Away from the outdoor activities in the forested hills of Eastern Bavaria, the region has a centuries-old glass-blowing tradition (as do West and North Bohemia across the border). These traditions still thrive in many of the towns along the **Glasstrasse** *(Glass Road; dieglasstrasse.de)*, a 250km holiday route connecting Waldsassen in the Oberpfalz region with Passau on the border with Austria. You can visit the studios, workshops, museums and shops, try your hand at glass-blowing and buy some attractive pieces as souvenirs.

There are almost 50 stops on the Glass Road, so plan your route carefully. The definite centre point of the whole route is Frauenau's must-see **Glasmuseum** *(glasmuseum-frauenau.de; adult/concession/child €5/4/free, Sun €1)*. This dazzlingly modern museum covers four millennia of glass-making history, starting with the ancient Egyptians and ending with modern glass art from around the world. Demonstrations and workshops for kids are regular features. **Frauenau** also has several glass factories where you can watch blowers at work.

For some of the best hands-on glass experiences head to **JOSKA** *(joska.com; free)* in Bodenmais and the **Weinfurtner Glasdorf** *(weinfurtner.de; free)* in Arnbruck. At these places and many more, even children can blow their own souvenirs along with watching the professionals work their magic.

Grosser Arber (p173)

The Glass Road is also lined with pieces of glass art – a unique collection not found anywhere else on Earth. Check out the incredible **Gläserne Wald** *(Glass Forest; regen.de; free)* in Regen, the amazing **Gläserne Scheune** *(Glass Barn; glaeserne-scheune.de; adult/youth/child €7.50/3.50/free)* in Rauhbühl, and the **Gläsernen Gärten** *(Glass Gardens; free)* next to the Glasmuseum in Frauenau.

Learn the Story of Bayerischer Wald

Visit Bavarian Forest museums

As you explore the Bavarian Forest, it's not just the dense carpet of trees that has the power to fascinate. The human story here dates back millennia, and some of the smaller villages and isolated structures beg further explanation. Part of that story is told in the **Museumsdorf Bayerischer Wald** *(museumsdorf.com; adult/child €7/5)*, a 20-hectare open-air museum in Tittling, on the southern rim of the Bavarian Forest, with 150 traditional timber cottages and farmsteads that date from the 17th to the 19th centuries. And in Zwiesel, the **Waldmuseum** *(waldmuseum.zwiesel.de; adult/concession/child/family €8/6/2/16)* occupies a former brewery and has exhibitions on local traditions, wildlife and life in the forest.

OPERATION KÁMEN

Czech researcher and historian Václava Jandečková is the author of *Kámen* (2013), a book that tells the story of a Cold War scheme implemented by the Czechoslovak communists that played out in the forests dividing Bohemia from Bavaria. Jandečková explains that operatives were employed by the Czechoslovak secret police to set up false borders, then lured unsuspecting individuals to these fake crossing points into Bavaria in order to glean information about possible resistance to the communist regime before arresting them. The scheme ran from 1948 to the early 1950s and became known as the 'Kámen operations'. None of the perpetrators were brought to justice. A 2023 English-language graphic novel also tells the story of this Cold War cross-border scam.

EATING IN THE BAVARIAN FOREST: OUR PICKS

Euler Landgasthof Neuschönau: A fresh take on regional dishes make this Neuschönau place stand out, with lots of veg options. *11.30am-10pm Wed-Mon, 5-10pm Tue* €€

Dampfbräu: Large servings of East Bavarian fare (meat and dumplings) and excellent 'steam' beer. In Zwiesel. *noon-2.30pm & 5.30-10.30pm Tue-Sat* €€

Gasthaus Mühlhiasl: The in-house restaurant at Tittling's Museumsdorf Bayerischer Wald, with forest inhabitants, mushrooms and dumplings. *11.30am-5pm Wed-Sun* €€

Hotel Zur Waldbahn: Locally foraged asparagus and local meats dominate this fine hotel-restaurant in Zwiesel. *11.30am-2.30pm & 5.30-10.30pm Tue-Sun* €€€

Places We Love to Stay

€ Budget €€ Midrange €€€ Top End

Nuremberg
MAP p101

Probst-Garni Hotel € The last sensibly priced hotel in the Altstadt, with basic rooms and breakfast (extra).

Five Reasons € This neat, well-located hostel-hotel has small dorms, some doubles, 24-hour reception and breakfast till lunchtime.

DJH Hostel € Nuremberg's youth hostel in the ancient Kornhaus is a renovated affair with many facilities and services.

Hotel Deutscher Kaiser €€ Castle-like granite stairs lead to rooms with Italian porcelain, silk lampshades and period furniture in this central historic hotel.

Hotel Elch €€ Inhabiting a 14th-century, half-timbered house near the Kaiserburg, the Elch offers a choice between fairy tale 'historic' and slick 'boutique'.

Agneshof €€ In a quiet spot near the St Sebalduskirche, sophisticated, artsy Agneshof comes with a wellness centre and a deckchair-strewn courtyard.

Leonardo Royal Hotel €€ A stone's throw from the Hauptbahnhof and walking distance from the Altstadt, the Royal has slick rooms and great service.

Art & Business Hotel €€ This contemporary place close to the Hauptbahnhof has a trendy bar, slate bathrooms and cool rooms.

Hotel Drei Raben €€€ This classy charmer plays with stories from Nuremberg lore, everything from Albrecht Dürer to the first railway. Loads of character.

Bamberg
MAP p113

Hotel Residenzschloss €€ High ceilings and palatial surrounds define this contemporary place in a quiet setting by the river.

Hotel Sankt Nepomuk €€ Occupying a half-timbered one-time mill by the Regnitz, this place has a good restaurant and super-modern rooms.

Würzburg
MAP p119

Babelfish € This uncluttered, deep-clean hostel has a sunny rooftop terrace and is a great traveller hangout.

Hotel Zum Winzermännle €€ Family-run converted winery in the heart of the city with old-fashioned rooms, some with balconies.

Hotel Rebstock €€€ Würzburg's best hotel inhabits a renovated rococo townhouse, with great facilities, service and Altstadt location.

Rothenburg ob der Tauber
MAP p125

Burg-Hotel €€€ The eight rooms at this Rothenburg hotel have boutique finishes and wonderful views from the four-poster beds.

Hotel Herrnschlösschen €€€ Occupying a 900-year-old Rothenburg mansion, this top-class hotel is a blend of ancient and new, Gothic and faux-retro.

Altfränkische Weinstube €€€ This 650-year-old Rothenburg inn has heaps of medieval character and an excellent restaurant.

Historik Hotel Gotisches Haus Garni €€€ Renovated rooms with wooden period furnishings, exposed brickwork and a medieval sensibility.

Dinkelsbühl
MAP p129

Dinkelsbühler Kunst-Stuben €€ Owner-run art-themed Dinkelsbühl guesthouse with loads of extras, hand-picked furniture and character by the lorry load.

Deutsches Haus €€ Hidden behind an ornate, leaning facade, the elegant rooms here have antique touches and slick bathrooms.

Meiser Design Hotel €€€ This uber-modern design hotel has bold colour schemes and top facilities within walking distance of the town walls. It has more traditional digs inside the old town.

Meiser Altstadt Hotel €€€ The old-school alter ego of the Meiser Design Hotel, this luxury place has period furnishings in the Altstadt's heart.

Nördlingen & Harburg
MAP p130

Kaiserhof Hotel Sonne €€ A mix of old and new rooms awaits at this historical old hotel right on Nördlingen's main square.

Art Hotel Ana Flair €€ Outside the Nördlingen town walls and opposite the train station, this stylish place has modern flair.

Schlosshotel Harburg (p131) **€€** Part of Schloss Harburg has been transformed into a very comfortable and romantic hotel.

Landsberg am Lech MAP p133

Stadthotel Augsburger Hof €€ The best option in Landsberg is this traditional inn with modern bathrooms and pine-rich rooms.

Landhotel Endhart €€ You're not exactly spoiled for choice in Landsberg, but this place does spacious, modern rooms in a decent location.

Augsburg MAP p135

Dom Hotel €€ Martin Luther and Kaiser Maximilian I both stayed in this renovated, 500-year-old former bishop's guesthouse with pristine upkeep; some rooms have cathedral views.

Hotel am Rathaus €€ In the heart of Augsburg, this boutique offering has clean-lined neutral decor and a sunny little breakfast room.

Steigenberger Drei Mohren Hotel €€€ Proud dad Leopold Mozart stayed here with his prodigious offspring in 1766. It remains Augsburg's oldest and grandest hotel.

Füssen MAP p139

Old Kings Hostel € Just because you're paying budget prices doesn't mean you have to forgo style – it's in the old town with quirky, themed rooms and great communal facilities.

Altstadthotel Zum Hechten €€ Friendly and one of the town's oldest hotels, this place has bright, modern rooms and a small but lovely spa.

Hotel Sonne €€ Design features surprise at every turn here at this stunning Altstadt design hotel where every room is different and gorgeous.

Garmisch-Partenkirchen MAP p146

Reindl's Partenkirchner Hof €€ Five-star everything here includes wine bar, gourmet restaurant and folk-themed rooms.

Gasthof zum Rassen €€ Behind a 14th-century frescoed facade, this guesthouse has modern rooms, antique public areas and Bavaria's oldest folk theatre.

Hotel Rheinischer Hof €€ This four-star place southwest of the centre is excellent, with Zugspitze views from the more expensive rooms.

Berchtesgaden MAP p153

DJH Hostel € Modern youth hostel, in the nearby village of Strub, with great facilities and views.

Hotel Edelweiss €€ The central, sleek Edelweiss is a combination of traditional timber flair and 21st-century luxury.

Alpinhotel Berchtesgaden €€ A typical Alpine guesthouse with lots of pine, hearty breakfasts and amiable owner-managers. It's in Oberau, northeast of Berchtesgaden.

Oberammergau

Gästehaus Richter € Central, family-run guesthouse with an Alpine welcome and a day-launching breakfast.

Hotel Alte Post €€ A superb choice with its *Lüftlmalerei* facade, faultlessly traditional restaurant and comfortable (if slightly bland) rooms.

Hotel Turmwirt €€ Pristine rooms, Alpine views, traditional furniture and delicious southern German food.

Bavarian Forest MAP p173

DJH Waldhäuser Hostel € The only DJH accommodation in the national park, this stone-built hostel near Neuschönau is surprisingly modern inside.

Hotel Zur Waldbahn €€ This traditional inn opposite Zwiesel train station has plenty of *Gemütlichkeit*.

Hotel Residenzschloss

Researched by
Kerry Walker

Salzburg & Around

BAROQUE BRILLIANCE AND ALPINE HIGHS

With uplifting Alps and rousing Mozart symphonies, hilltop castles and cultural cachet, this bite-sized region is Austria's scene-stealer.

One of Austria's smallest provinces, Salzburgerland is proof that size really doesn't matter. Well, not when you have Mozart, Maria von Trapp and the 600-year legacy of the prince-archbishops behind you. This is the land that grabbed the world spotlight and shouted 'Austria!' with Julie Andrews skipping joyously down the mountainsides. This is indeed the land of crisp apple strudel, dancing marionettes and high-on-a-hilltop castles. This is the Austria of your wildest childhood dreams.

Spread at the foot of wooded cliffs and along the banks of a turquoise river, Salzburg's baroque-in-overdrive Altstadt rolls back a millennium of history, with its parade of palaces, churches, abbeys and domes, where the prince-archbishops once dreamed big and horse-drawn carriages clip-clop past evoking the glory days of the Habsburg Empire. Here you're constantly looking up in wonder: at the whopping hilltop fortress, at lavish concert halls where Mozart once performed, and at the mountains ripping across the horizon.

But Salzburg is just the prelude to the region's sensational beauty. Just outside the city, the landscape is etched with deep ravines, glinting ice caves, karst plateaux, waterfall-splashed gorges and mountains of myth – in short, the kind of alpine gorgeousness that no well-orchestrated symphony or yodelling nun could ever quite capture. Culturally the region beyond Salzburg hits high notes, too, with grand baroque palaces, Celtic salt mines and medieval castles ripe for a fairy tale.

FROM LEFT: CANADASTOCK/SHUTTERSTOCK, GIMAS/SHUTTERSTOCK

THE MAIN AREAS

SALZBURG
Baroque majesty and Mozart.
p182

HELLBRUNN
Summer palace, landscaped park and trick fountains. **p201**

HALLEIN
Celtic heritage and salt mines.
p202

For places to stay in Salzburg & Around, see p207

SALZBURG & AROUND

THE GUIDE

Schloss Hellbrunn (p201)

WERFEN
Ice caves, medieval castles and cinematic backdrops. **p203**

FILZMOOS
Mountain drama and high-level hiking. **p205**

LIECHTENSTEINKLAMM
Photogenic gorge carved deep into the alps. **p206**

Find Your Way

In Salzburg, it's a cinch to visit most places on foot or by bike; indeed, the Altstadt is pedestrian-only. Trains journeying deeper into Salzburgerland are frequent, reliable and scenic, but your own wheels are recommended for reaching the region's most remote corners.

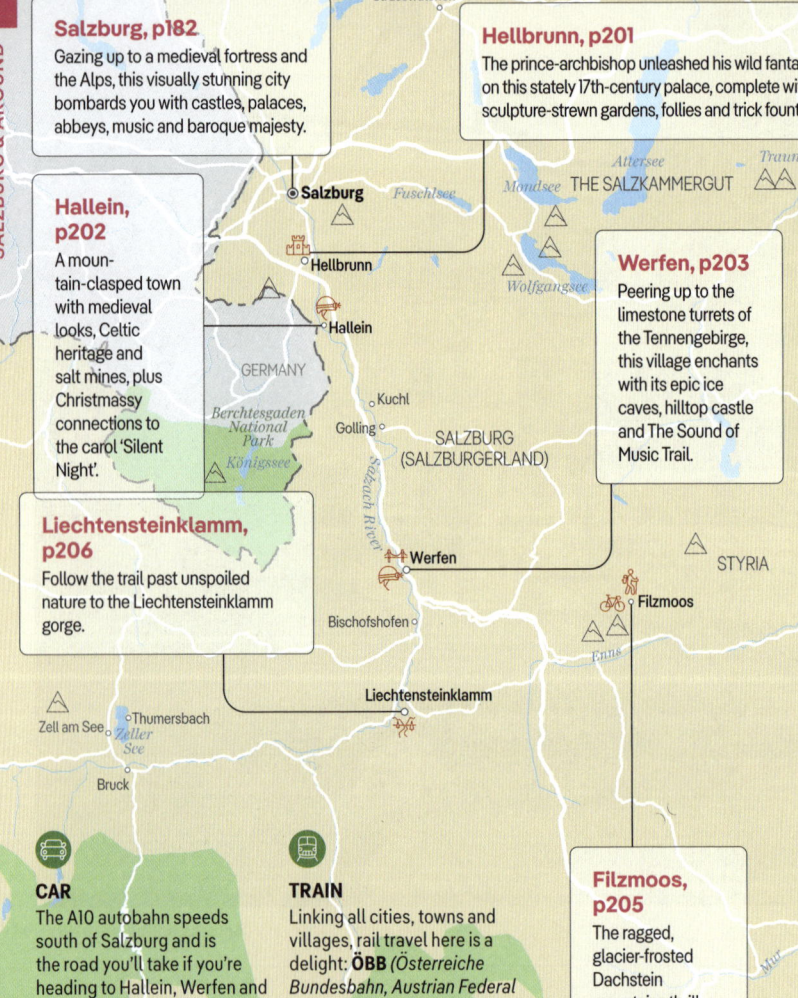

Salzburg, p182
Gazing up to a medieval fortress and the Alps, this visually stunning city bombards you with castles, palaces, abbeys, music and baroque majesty.

Hellbrunn, p201
The prince-archbishop unleashed his wild fantasy on this stately 17th-century palace, complete with sculpture-strewn gardens, follies and trick fountains.

Hallein, p202
A mountain-clasped town with medieval looks, Celtic heritage and salt mines, plus Christmassy connections to the carol 'Silent Night'.

Werfen, p203
Peering up to the limestone turrets of the Tennengebirge, this village enchants with its epic ice caves, hilltop castle and The Sound of Music Trail.

Liechtensteinklamm, p206
Follow the trail past unspoiled nature to the Liechtensteinklamm gorge.

Filzmoos, p205
The ragged, glacier-frosted Dachstein mountains thrill with high-level hiking and biking.

CAR
The A10 autobahn speeds south of Salzburg and is the road you'll take if you're heading to Hallein, Werfen and Filzmoos. E-vehicle charging points are ubiquitous (there's even one in the national park).

TRAIN
Linking all cities, towns and villages, rail travel here is a delight: **ÖBB** *(Österreiche Bundesbahn, Austrian Federal Railway; oebb.at)* trains are smooth, efficient and inexpensive, and the views are magic. Where trains stop, Postbus services take over.

Mountain landscape, Filzmoos (p205)

Plan Your Time

Salzburgerland looks tiny on the map, but there's a lot of vertical to consider. You can't do it all, so choose wisely, combining a short city break in Salzburg, say, with forays into the great outdoors.

On a Long Weekend

● Stay in **Salzburg** (p182) for a feast of castles, palaces and gallery visits in the UNESCO-stamped baroque **Altstadt** (p191) and a soul-soaring walk in the woods above the city rooftops at **Mönchsberg** (p184). Pack in Mozart and Maria fun, with everything from *The Sound of Music* **bike rides** (p187) to chamber concerts. Hitch a cable car up to **Untersberg** (p185) for riveting views and a flavour of the Alps.

With a Week or More

● Begin by exploring Salzburg's decorous **Altstadt** (p191), where uplifting views of the Alps will have you itching to venture beyond. Waft around regal gardens and a palace at **Schloss Hellbrunn** (p201). **Werfen** (p203), with the world's biggest **ice caves** (p203) and a knockout **castle** (p204), and **Hallein** (p202), with Celtic heritage and **salt mines,** (p202) are easy day trips. For a shot of the Alps and hiking trails, **Filzmoos** (p205) beckons.

SEASONAL HIGHLIGHTS

SPRING
Snow on summits but valleys bloom at lower elevations. Salzburg reverberates with music at **Osterfestspiele** (Easter Festival).

SUMMER
Salzburger Festspiele (p197) is in full swing. Music and theatre in Zell am See. Hikers take to trails in the Tennen and Dachstein mountains.

AUTUMN
Quieter days, colourful foliage and excellent wildlife-spotting in the Alps. It's a terrific time for outdoor activities.

WINTER
Christmas waves a winter wonderland wand, snow draws skiers and **Mozart Week** (p188) pulls in world-renowned orchestras.

Salzburg

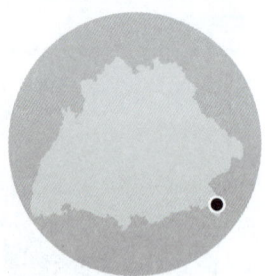

BAROQUE BRILLIANCE | MOZART'S BIRTHPLACE | ALPINE BACKDROP

☑ TOP TIP

Salzburg has two peak seasons. During the summer holidays (July and August), the city gets swamped. In December, when the city brims with Christmas markets and festival sparkle, it can get busy and expensive, too. To save, come in spring or autumn for cheaper flights, lower room rates and fewer crowds.

The joke, 'If it's baroque, don't fix it,' could be a perfect maxim for Salzburg: the storybook Altstadt burrowed below steep hills looks much as it did when Mozart lived here 250 years ago. Beside the fast-flowing Salzach River which divides the city in two, your lifted gaze is raised inch by inch to graceful domes and spires, the formidable clifftop fortress and the mountains beyond. It's a backdrop that did the lordly prince-archbishops and Maria proud.

Beyond Salzburg's two biggest money-spinners – Mozart and *The Sound of Music* – hides a city with a burgeoning arts scene, wonderful food, manicured parks, quiet side streets where classical music wafts from open windows, and concert halls that uphold musical tradition 365 days a year. Everywhere you go, the scenery, the skyline, the music and the history send your spirits soaring higher than Julie Andrews' octave-leaping vocals.

GETTING AROUND

Salzburg's sight-packed Altstadt is a joy to explore on foot, and walking is the only way to get a true feel for its pedestrianised backstreets. Unless you're going further afield, you need never set foot in a bus or train. This is one of Austria's most cycle-friendly cities, with a superb network of bike paths along the river, making the transition from city to mountains seamless. Touring and e-bikes can be rented at **aVelo** *(avelosalzburg.com)* at Staatsbrücke.

Getting around by public transport (SVV) is quick, easy and inexpensive. It's cheaper to buy tickets online or at the ticket machine than on board. If you're planning on zipping about town, a Tageskarte day pass is better value than single tickets.

SALZBURG CITY CENTRE

★ HIGHLIGHTS
1 Festung Hohensalzburg

● SIGHTS
2 Friedhof St Sebastian
3 Mozart-Wohnhaus
4 Schloss Mirabell
5 Stift Nonnberg
6 Volksgarten
7 Würth Sculpture Garden
8 Zwerglgarten

● ACTIVITIES
9 Fräulein Maria's Bicycle Tours
10 Freibad Volksgarten
11 Mönchsberg
12 Salzburg Panorama Tours
13 Salzburg Sightseeing Tours
14 Segway Tours
15 Spielplatz Volksgarten

● SLEEPING
16 Arte Vida
17 Hotel Amadeus

● EATING
18 Bärenwirt
19 Bistro de Márquez
20 Esszimmer
21 Gelateria La Romana
22 Glass Garden
23 Green Garden
24 Heart of Joy
25 Imlauer Sky Bar
26 Johanneskeller
27 Organic Pizza Salzburg
28 Schranne

● DRINKING & NIGHTLIFE
29 220Grad
30 Augustiner Bräustübl
31 Die Weisse
32 Sacher

● ENTERTAINMENT
33 ARGEkultur
34 Mozarteum
35 Rockhouse
36 Salzburger Marionettentheater
37 Schlosskonzerte

● SHOPPING
38 Feinkost Stocker
39 Mayrische Musikalienhandlung

● TRANSPORT
40 aVelo

WHY I LOVE SALZBURG

Kerry Walker, Lonely Planet writer

I lost my heart to Salzburg when I first set foot on Austrian soil (well, snow...) more than 20 years ago – and I've been returning ever since as a Lonely Planet author. For me, Salzburg is Austria in microcosm, from the Altstadt, where alleys lead to baroque palaces, domes and a hilltop fortress freshly minted for a Disney fantasy, to the beautifully manicured gardens that unspool along the banks of the Salzach River, grand concert halls pumping out Mozart melodies and the ever-uplifting skyline of Alps. The city has a unique energy and spirit, bundling together high culture, art and a passion for the outdoors into one neat, beautifully wrapped package. It's a city that never fails to put a spring in my step.

Schloss Leopoldskron

Salzburg on High
Get a ringside city view

Salzburg is at its most entrancing from above, with domes, spires and rooftops spreading out before you and the turquoise Salzach River unfurling into the mountains. One of the most memorable ways to see the city away from the masses is to get out and stride. Puff up the Nonnbergstiege to Benedictine abbey **Stift Nonnberg** (p199), then continue your short but scenic walk along Hoher Weg and Festungsgasse to **Festung Hohensalzburg** (*festung-hohensalzburg.at; adult/child €13.60/5.20*). The city's crowning-glory fortress has dress-circle views of the baroque Altstadt. Time your walk for noon to hear bells ring out across the city.

You can easily devote an afternoon to wandering the 540m peak of **Mönchsberg**, the cliffs that give Salzburg its dramatic edge. Its sheer, wooded heights are crisscrossed by walking trails. A highly scenic hike leads 3km on from Festung Hohensalzburg, past the **Museum der Moderne** (*museumdermoderne.at; adult/child €14/free; see p190*) and through woods of beech, sycamore, linden and oak, to the jovial monastery-founded brewery **Augustiner Bräustübl** (*augustinerbier.at*).

EATING IN SALZBURG: TRADITIONAL FAVOURITES

Zirkelwirt: Jovial tucked-away inn with old-fashioned Austrian grub like crisp schnitzel and dumplings with sauerkraut. *11.30am-11pm* €€

Johanneskeller: Dig into hearty classics like Styrian pork roast in the cosy brick-vaulted cellar or arcaded inner courtyard. *5-11pm Tue-Sat* €€

Bärenwirt: Go for *Bierbraten* (beer roast) with dumplings, locally caught trout or organic wild-boar bratwurst at this rustic tavern, sizzling and stirring since 1663. *11am-11pm* €€

Paul Stube: Up the cobbled Herrengasse lies this warm, woody, old-world tavern, with a menu full of Austrian classics and a summer beer garden. *5pm-midnight Tue-Sat* €€

Here you can rest up with a cold foamy one under the chestnut trees in the beer garden.

A leap over the river to the Right Bank brings you to the forested, 640m-high hump of **Kapuzinerberg**, which frames the Altstadt like a postcard. Paths twist past Way of the Cross chapels to the Capuchin abbey at the top. Despite the glorious views, it's rarely busy – hence the reason it is still home to a colony of nimble-footed chamois, which you might spot if you're lucky (and quiet).

The Sound of Music Trail
The hills are alive

Ever since Hollywood box-office smash *The Sound of Music* hit big screens in 1965, Salzburg has been inseparable from the world's most famous singing nun. Channel your inner Julie Andrews by devising your own self-guided tour of the movie locations.

Start at the very beginning with a cable car ride to the summit of **Untersberg** *(untersbergbahn.at; return cable car adult/child €34/17)*, where Maria makes her twirling entrance through blooming alpine pastures and the Trapp family flee from the Nazis at the end.

At the foot of Mönchsberg's cliffs, the **Felsenreitschule** (p198) is the dramatic backdrop for the Salzburger Festspiele in the movie, where the Trapp Family Singers win the audience over with 'Edelweiss' and give the Nazis the slip with 'So Long, Farewell'. Close by is **Residenzplatz** (p194), where Maria belts out 'I Have Confidence' and playfully splashes the spouting horses of the **Residenzbrunnen** fountain. Hoof it uphill from here to Benedictine **Stift Nonnberg** (p199), where the nuns waltzed on their way to mass, including the ever-problematic Maria.

Palaces, you say? Romantically rococo **Schloss Leopoldskron** *(schloss-leopoldskron.com)*, a 15-minute stroll south of the centre, is where the lake scene was filmed. Its Venetian Room was the blueprint for the Trapps' opulent ballroom, where the von Trapp kids bid their heart-melting farewells. Now you can stay the night in its elegant hotel.

Back in town, the Pegasus fountain, gnomes and steps with fortress views in the **Schloss Mirabell** (p188) gardens might inspire a rendition of 'Do-Re-Mi' – especially if there's a drop of golden sun.

THE TRUTH BEHIND THE HOLLYWOOD LEGEND

While *The Sound of Music* is based on the real story of the Trapps, a singing family with a nun-turned-governess called Maria, fact and fiction blur in the movie, with directors adding a generous pinch of poetic licence. Did you know that in reality there were 10, not seven, Trapp children, the eldest of whom was Rupert and that (spoiler alert) there was no Liesl? Or that the captain was not stern and aloof, but rather a gentle, family-loving man? The real Maria, by contrast, was no soft touch. Unlike playful, warm-hearted Julie Andrews, she was devoutly religious, quick-tempered and strong willed. And during the Nazi annexation of Austria in 1938, the Trapp family left quietly by train to Italy then flew to the US instead of climbing every mountain to Switzerland.

 DRINKING IN SALZBURG: SKY-HIGH DRINKS

Steinterrasse: See the Altstadt lit up against the fortress at this 7th-floor terrace bar with champagne-sipping socialites. *7am-midnight Sun-Thu, to 1am Fri & Sat*

hu:goes14: The city looks tiny from this 14th-floor glass-walled bar and terrace at the arte Hotel. Get a signature mixed drink or classic cocktail. *4pm-midnight*

Imlauer Sky Bar: Salzburg spreads out in all its glory below this rooftop bar. It's spectacular after dark when the fortress lights up. *9am-1am*

Cool Mama Sky Terrace: Cocktails are served with the coolest of Salzburg views from this skyscraping hotel north of town. *noon-9pm Tue-Sat*

SALZBURG IN MOZART'S FOOTSTEPS

Get ready to rock like Amadeus with a spin of the historic centre.

START	END	LENGTH
Schloss Mirabell	Fürst	3.2km; 2hrs

Begin at baroque **1 Schloss Mirabell** (p188), where the resplendent Marmorsaal (Marble Hall) is the backdrop for chamber concerts of Mozart's music. Stroll south through fountain-dotted gardens, passing the angular **2 Mozarteum**, a foundation honouring Mozart, and the host of the Mozartwoche festival in January/February. Around the corner on Makartplatz is the 17th-century **3 Mozart-Wohnhaus** where you can see how the family lived and listen to rare recordings.

Amble north along Linzer Gasse to **4 Friedhof St Sebastian** (p190), the Italianate arcaded cemetery where Wolfgang's father Leopold and his wife Constanze lie buried. Retrace your steps towards the Salzach River, turning left onto medieval Steingasse, then through to Giselakai to cross the Art Nouveau **5 Mozartsteg** (Mozart Bridge).

On elegant **6 Mozartplatz**, a coiffed, pensive Mozart is put on a pedestal in bronze. The statue was unveiled in 1842 in the presence of Mozart's sons. Across the way is the **7 Residenz** (p194) palace where Mozart gave his first court concert. Beside it is the baroque **8 Salzburger Dom** (p198), where Mozart's parents were married in 1747 and little Wolfgang was baptised in 1756; Mozart later composed sacred music here and was cathedral organist.

Follow Franziskanergasse to the **9 Kollegienkirche** on Universitätsplatz, where Mozart's *Mass in D Minor* (K65) premiered in 1769. On Getreidegasse, contemplate the bright-yellow townhouse, birthplace of a genius in 1756, at **10 Mozarts Geburtshaus** and buy some chocolate *Mozartkugeln* (Mozart balls) at **11 Fürst** (p198).

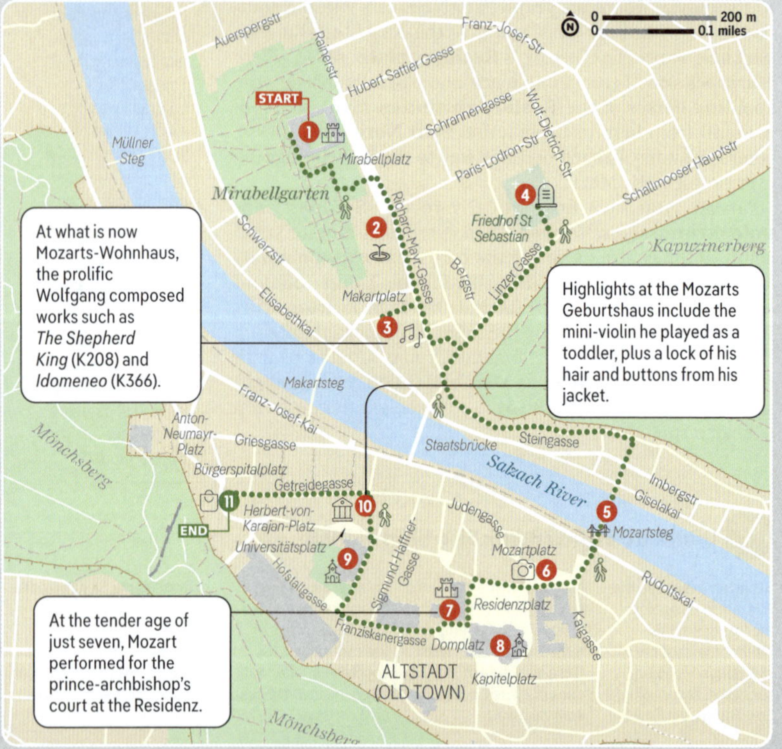

> At what is now Mozarts-Wohnhaus, the prolific Wolfgang composed works such as *The Shepherd King* (K208) and *Idomeneo* (K366).

> Highlights at the Mozarts Geburtshaus include the mini-violin he played as a toddler, plus a lock of his hair and buttons from his jacket.

> At the tender age of just seven, Mozart performed for the prince-archbishop's court at the Residenz.

Café Tomaselli (p188)

The Sound of Music By Bike
Sing as you pedal

You don't have to be a die-hard *The Sound of Music* fan or even be able to hit the high notes like Julie Andrews to want to hop into a bicycle saddle and belt out a few songs as you pedal between the film locations with **Fräulein Maria's Bicycle Tours** (*mariasbicycletours.com; tours adult/child €45/20*). Comfortable cruiser bikes whisk you through key backdrops to the movie, with plenty of fresh air, fun, quirky commentary and uplifting views thrown into the bargain.

'Do-Re-Mi', 'Sixteen Going on Seventeen', 'So Long, Farewell' – all the classics are in the mix on this half-day bike tour that rolls from palace to plaza, park to abbey. Kicking off at Mirabellplatz (just left of the entrance to the palace), tours run at 9.30am from April to October in all kinds of weather – get in quick in summer as the tours are crazily popular. From June to August, there are additional tours at 4.30pm if you prefer an early evening pedal.

Kaffeehaus Culture
Full of beans

Swinging open the heavy wooden doors of one of Salzburg's *Kaffeehäuser* (coffee houses) is your ticket to the city's soul. White-pinafored waitresses and bow-tied waiters whirl past with silver platters, the coffee list is long and elaborate, and more folk still chat and rustle newspapers than gaze blankly at smartphones. These unhurried micro-worlds remain largely immune to time and trends.

Vienna claims the coffee-house crown, but Salzburg can rival the Austrian capital with some highly *gemütlich*

SALZBURG CARD

If you're planning on doing lots of sightseeing, it's wise to invest in the money-saving **Salzburg Card** *(1-/2-/3-day card €34/41/47)*. The card gets you entry to all of the major sights, galleries, museums and attractions, unlimited use of public transport (including cable cars), and numerous discounts on tours and events. It also allows you to skip the queue at a number of attractions. The card is half-price for children and €3 cheaper in the low season.

The card can be purchased at the airport, the tourist office and most hotels. Or buy the digital version online at *salzburg.info* and use it immediately on your smartphone.

MORE SOUND OF MUSIC

Just south of the city, **Schlosspark Hellbrunn** (p202) hides the loved-up pavilion of 'Sixteen Going on Seventeen' fame, where you can act out those 'Oh, Liesl'…'Oh, Rolf…' fantasies.

BEST OF MOZART MAGIC

Mozart was the ultimate musical prodigy: he identified a pig's squeal as G-sharp aged two, began to compose at five and first performed for Empress Maria Theresa aged six. His symphonies, sonatas and concertos live on in Salzburg.

Mozarteum: Opened in 1880 and revered for its supreme acoustics, the Mozarteum highlights the life and works of Mozart through chamber music (October to June), concerts and opera. *mozarteum.at*

Mozart Week: The annual highlight is Mozart Week in late January, when much-lauded orchestras, conductors and soloists celebrate Mozart's birthday with an 11-day music feast.

Schlosskonzerte: A fantasy of coloured marble, stucco and frescos, the baroque Marmorsaal (Marble Hall) at Schloss Mirabell is the exquisite setting for Schlosskonzerte, chamber-music concerts *(adult/child from €42/28)* where renowned soloists and ensembles perform works from well-known composers such as Mozart, Haydn and Chopin. *schlosskonzerte-salzburg.at*

(cosy) cafes. Rococo and boho, trendy and touristy, grand and grungy – each *Kaffeehaus* has its own distinctive personality.

For full-on nostalgia, head to Alter Markt and **Café Tomaselli** *(tomaselli.at)*, founded in 1700. Mozart once hung out at this Salzburg institution, where magnificent cakes – including seasonal strudels that flake just so – grace marble-topped tables. Or dig a dainty fork into *Sacher Torte* (dark-chocolate sponge, iced and layered with apricot jam) at chandelier-lit **Café Sacher** *(sacher.com)* by the river. Its artsy neighbour **Café Bazar** *(cafe-bazar.at)* is a 1909 time warp of chandeliers and polished wood. Here locals enjoy the same river views over breakfast, cake and intelligent conversation as Marlene Dietrich did in 1936.

There are third-wave newcomers on the scene, naturally. Blink and you'll miss speciality coffee bar **Kaffee Alchemie** *(@kaffeealchemie)*. Headed up by a barista trainer, this retro riverfront cafe knows its beans and makes a cracking espresso. A step south of the Altstadt, post-industrial cool **220Grad** *(220grad.com)* wins for its freshly roasted coffee. Its name alludes to the perfect temperature for roasting beans. Its barista-made single-origin espressos and house blends pair brilliantly with delicious breakfasts and cakes.

Down by the River
Fun ways to see the sights

AW*(schifffahrtsalzburg.at; city cruise adult/child €18/9)* is a leisurely way to pick out Salzburg's sights. Forty-minute cruises depart from Makartsteg bridge, with some of them chugging on to Schloss Hellbrunn. Or swap ordinary boats in favour of **Amphibious Splash Tours** *(amphibious-splash-tours.at; adult/child €41/26)*, a novel combination of boat and floating bus. Tours last roughly 1½ hours, with several departures daily.

If you prefer to stay on dry land, guided **Segway Tours** *(segway-salzburg.at; tours from €59)* roll past the big sights by zippy battery-powered scooter. Trundle through the city before heading up to Mönchsberg on a 1½-hour ride, or tick off the trophy sights before speeding across to Schloss Leopoldskron for incredible views of the Altstadt and Alps on a two-hour spin. Kids in tow? Tours are suitable for children aged 12 and over.

Green Salzburg
Gardens, lido swims and cycling trails

With the turquoise Salzach River dashing through its heart and Alps hogging the horizon, Salzburg delivers a big hit of nature.

For a central picnic and stroll, head to **Schloss Mirabell** *(salzburg.info; free)*. Prince-Archbishop Wolf Dietrich built this lavish baroque palace in 1606 to woo his mistress Salome Alt, but it's the gardens that really shine. Here green-fingered Archbishop Johann Ernst von Thun added fountains, muses, parterres, rose gardens and the *Tänzerin* (dancer) sculpture, perfectly framing the view of high-on-a-hill Festung Hohensalzburg. The gardens seem familiar? Some scenes of *The Sound of Music* were filmed here. Cue the Pegasus statue, the

Salzach river with a view of Festung Hohensalzburg (p184)

steps and the gnomes of the **Zwerglgarten** (Dwarf Garden), where the Trapp kids learned to sing 'Do-Re-Mi'.

Unfurling from meadow to mountain, the banks of the **Salzach River** are a joy to cycle. Hire a bike or e-bike from **aVelo** *(bike rental per day €25)* at Staatsbrücke to pedal off past the Altstadt's domes and spires, perhaps stopping in the park at the **Volksgarten** for a picnic and swim in the **Freibad Volksgarten** *(adult/child €6/3.60)*, or rolling on south to **Waldbad Anif** *(waldbadanif.at; adult/child €9/7)* for a refreshing dip in a forest-rimmed lake. In summer, notch up the action with canoeing, SUPing or wakeboarding.

Make a Splash in the Almkanal

Swim and surf in the Almkanal

Flowing through the city since the Middle Ages, Salzburg's **Almkanal** provides a splash of history, with its network of hidden underground waterways. In summer, you can cycle or walk to **Schloss Leopoldskron** (p185) – the backdrop for the lake scene in *The Sound of Music* – for a bracing swim in the canal's chilly turquoise waters, floating towards the Altstadt before climbing the tree-lined banks and leaping in again.

Should you happen to have a board handy, join surfers to ride the canal's artificial wave, the **Surfwelle am Almkanal**,

CYCLE SALZBURG

There's no better way to see Salzburg than with your bum in a saddle, some say. And right they are. Salzburg is one of Austria's most bike-friendly cities and its vast, 180km-long network of cycling trails, heading off in all directions, including along the banks of the scenic Salzach River, is a two-wheel dream.

Renting a bike or e-bike (for instance from centrally located aVelo) is your backstage pass to a side to the city few get to see. While you can easily piece together your own itinerary, a good starting point is the **Instagrammable Salzburg Cycle Route**, a 23.6km, 10-stop ride beyond the Altstadt, stitching together photogenic churches, palaces, gardens and viewpoints. The website *salzburg. info* has details, or download a self-guided tour at *smart-guide.org*.

 EATING IN SALZBURG: ICE CREAM

Icezeit: Grab a cone at this Altstadt parlour, where flavours include salted peanut, caramel and passion fruit. *noon-8pm* €

Fabi's Frozen Yoghurt: Fabi is the whizz behind the frozen yoghurt here, including chocolate and fruit toppings. Organic and delicious. *noon-8pm* €

Eisl Eis: Cool off on Getreidegasse with organic sheep's-milk ice cream made at a 500-year-old farm on Wolfgangsee. *noon-6pm* €

Gelateria La Romana: Freshly made, properly authentic Italian gelato in flavours from cinnamon to blood orange. *11am-9pm Mon-Thu, to 10pm Fri-Sun* €

ESCAPE THE CROWDS IN SALZBURG

Hildegard Strohmeyer, an official Salzburg city and hiking guide, divulges her favourite spots for giving the crowds the slip. *hildastroh.com*

Friedhof St Sebastian: Mozart's father Leopold and wife Constanze are buried in this cemetery on Linzer Gasse, established in 1600 as an Italian 'campo santo'. Its centrepiece is the mausoleum of Prince-Archbishop Wolf-Dietrich of Raitenau. It's a haven of peace.

Bürgerspitalkirche St Blasius: The civic hospital church near Getreidegasse has an inner courtyard with Renaissance arcades. A Gothic church with 12th-century roots, it impresses with its vault, stained-glass windows and mystical interior.

Waldbad Anif: Rent a bike to pedal south along the Salzach River to this emerald-green lake, perfect in summer. It's like diving into a mountain lake – the water is cool and crystal clear.

---

for free, just north of Weidenstrasse bridge. Year-round it's surfable for all levels, from beginners to experts. Boards are available for hire from **Wuux** *(per half/full day €30/50)*. To reach the wave, take bus 5 to Salzburg Weidenstrasse.

Salzburg's Twin Peaks
Climb ev'ry mountain

Where Austria slams into Germany, the 1973m peak of **Untersberg** (p185) *(untersbergbahn.at; cable car return adult/child €34/17)* propels you into the mountains right on the city's southern fringes. A cable car hauls you up the craggy summit, which enthrals with front-row views of Salzburg, the Rositten Valley and the Austrian and Bavarian Alps. Paragliders launch themselves from the peak in summer (listen for the whoosh), while in winter, there's gentle skiing up here.

From the cable car top station, you can ramble along gentle trails through meadows to lookouts like **Geiereck** (1805m) and **Salzburg Hochthron** (1853m), or hike for a couple of hours across a wild karst plateau to the **Schellenberg Ice Cave** just over the border in Bavaria. Temperatures are significantly cooler up here than down in the valley, so bring a fleece or jacket and solid footwear. To reach the cable car valley station, take bus 25 from Salzburg's Hauptbahnhof or Mirabellplatz.

The rival peak is 1287m **Gaisberg**, puckering up east of the city. Here arresting views of the Salzburg Valley, the Salzkammergut lakes, the limestone Tennengebirge range and neighbouring Bavaria unravel. The best way to appreciate all of this is on the 6km, one to 1½-hour round-the-mountain **circular trail** (route 13a), starting at Zistelalm. Salzburgers head up here for mountain biking in summer, cross-country skiing in winter and sunsets that pop year-round. To reach the peak, take bus 151 from Mirabellplatz to Gaisberg.

Modern Art Talking
A brush with Salzburg's creative side

Though Salzburg generally moves to a historic beat, the **Museum der Moderne** *(see also p184; museumdermoderne.at; adult/child €14/free, with lift €16/free)*, perched atop Mönchsberg's cliffs, goes off-piste, pushing boundaries with its engrossing exhibitions of mixed-media 20th- and 21st-century art. The spotlight is on both emerging and established artists. Reached by a lift, the glass-and-white-marble, oblong-shaped gallery is the architectural antithesis to Festung Hohensalzburg on the other side of the hill. While you're up here, pop into **m32** *(m32.at)* for a coffee with a far-reaching view over Salzburg.

In the Altstadt, its sister gallery, covered by the same ticket, is the **Rupertinum**, which zooms in largely on graphic works and photography. Zany Austrian artist Friedensreich Hundertwasser left his mark on the inner courtyard in the form of glittering *Zungenbärte* ('tongue beards').

Museum der Moderne

But art isn't just confined to museums here. Bridging the gap between culture and the outdoors, there is public art sprinkled all over town that won't cost you a cent to admire. Top billing goes to the **Walk of Modern Art,** specially commissioned installations and sculptures that have Salzburg's cultural identity as a common thread. Here attention-grabbers include James Turrell's **Blue Pearl – Skyspace** (go at dawn or at dusk for the full-on bluesy effect) at Mönchsberg; Stephan Balkenhol's giant man-on-a-golden-globe **Sphaera** on Kapitelplatz; and Anselm Kiefer's 4m-high winged book stack, **The Language of Birds**, in Chiemseehof.

In summer, step south of town to Schloss Arenberg. Built for the lordly prince-archbishops in the 14th century, the palace's beautiful grounds conceal the **Würth Sculpture Garden**, brimming with contemporary, thought-provoking artworks.

Explore Salzburg's Altstadt
Royal bling and baroque in overdrive

For a city of dinky proportions, Salzburg packs an enormous amount of culture into its alley-woven historic centre. For

continued on p194

SALZBURG'S BEST TOURS

Salzburg City Guides: Pro guides lead insightful walking tours zooming in on everything from architecture to art and the city by night.

Panorama Tours: The 'original *Sound of Music* Tour', ticking off film-set biggies from Schloss Mirabell to Nonnberg, Hellbrunn and Mondsee.

Bob's Special Tours: Minibus tours to *The Sound of Music* locations, the Alps and Hallstatt, plus private biking and walking tours.

Rikschatours: Whizz around Salzburg by rickshaw with a clued-up guide. Tours range from a 40-minute spin of the historic centre to a three-hour 'Round of Music'.

Salzburg Sightseeing Tours: A multilingual hop-on, hop-off bus tour of the city's trophy sights and *The Sound of Music* locations, plus day trips further afield.

 EATING IN SALZBURG: ROMANTIC RESTAURANTS

| **Gasthof Schloss Aigen:** This 15th-century country manor does Austrian home cooking with panache. Try Wiener Melange, Pinzgauer beef and roast potatoes. *5.30-10pm Thu, 11.30am-10pm Fri-Sun* €€ | **Blaue Gans Restaurant:** In 650-year-old vaults, this restaurant riffs creatively on regional cuisine in seasonal dishes like saddle of venison with asparagus, celery and dandelion. *noon-midnight Mon-Sat* €€ | **Glass Garden:** Chef Simon Wagner serves sensations like tender Pinzgauer lamb with radish and wild garlic at Hotel Schloss Mönchstein's Michelin-starred restaurant. *noon-10pm Thu-Mon* €€€ | **Esszimmer:** Andreas Kaiblinger puts an innovative spin on market-driven French cuisine at this art-slung, Michelin-starred stunner. *noon-10pm Tue-Sat* €€€ |

SALZBURG ALTSTADT

★ HIGHLIGHTS
1. DomQuartier
2. Residenz

● SIGHTS
3. Blue Pearl – Skyspace
4. Bürgerspitalkirche St Blasius
5. Christmas Museum
6. Domplatz
7. Friedhof St Peter
8. Haus der Natur
9. Katakomben
10. Mozartplatz
11. Mozarts Geburtshaus
12. Museum der Moderne
13. Plaque to Joseph Mohr
14. Residenzbrunnen
15. Residenzplatz
16. Rupertinum
17. Salzburger Dom
18. Sphaera
19. Spielzeugmuseum
20. Steingasse
21. Stift St Peter
22. Stiftskirche St Peter
23. The Language of Birds

● ACTIVITIES
24. Amphibious Splash Tours
25. Bob's Special Tours
26. Kapuzinerberg
27. Rikschatours
28. Salzburg City Guides
29. Schifffahrt Salzburg

● SLEEPING
30. Arthotel Blaue Gans
31. Goldener Hirsch
32. Hotel am Dom

● EATING
33. Afro Café
34. Bäckerei Holztrattner

Blaue Gans Restaurant	**45** Stiftsbäckerei St Peter
Eisl Eis	**46** Uncle Van
Fabi's Frozen Bio Yogurt	**47** Zirkelwirt
Grünmarkt	● **DRINKING &**
Humboldt	**NIGHTLIFE**
Icezeit	**48** Café Bazar
Kajetanerplatz	**49** Café Tomaselli
M32	**50** Kaffee Alchemie
Paul Stube	**51** Steinterrasse
Salzburger Grill Imbiss	**52** Sternbräu

53 StieglKeller	**60** Fürst
● **ENTERTAINMENT**	**61** Kaslöchl
54 Felsenreitschule	**62** Klosterladen St Peter
55 Festspiele Ticket Office	**63** Salzburg Salz
56 Grosses Festspielhaus	**64** Salzburger Heimatwerk
57 Haus für Mozart	**65** Spirituosen Sporer
58 StageBar	**66** Wenger
● **SHOPPING**	● **TRANSPORT**
59 Drechslerei Lackner	**67** aVelo

OVERTOURISM IN SALZBURG

During peak holiday times (Christmas, Easter, July and August), Salzburg is chock-a-block and you can barely move for the heaving crowds pounding the narrow streets of the compact Altstadt, all in search of a little Mozart and Maria magic.

With 3.14 million overnight stays in Salzburg in 2024 (compared with a population of just 153,000), overtourism is a very real issue here, which is why it makes sense, if you can, to dodge the busiest times. Opt for the calmer shoulder seasons of spring and autumn and you won't have to face such colossal crowds and queues. Other tips for a more sustainable stay: venture out to quieter corners of the city beyond the historic centre and plan a longer trip. With its fantastic public transport network, Salzburg can easily be used as a base for exploring the wider Salzburgerland region.

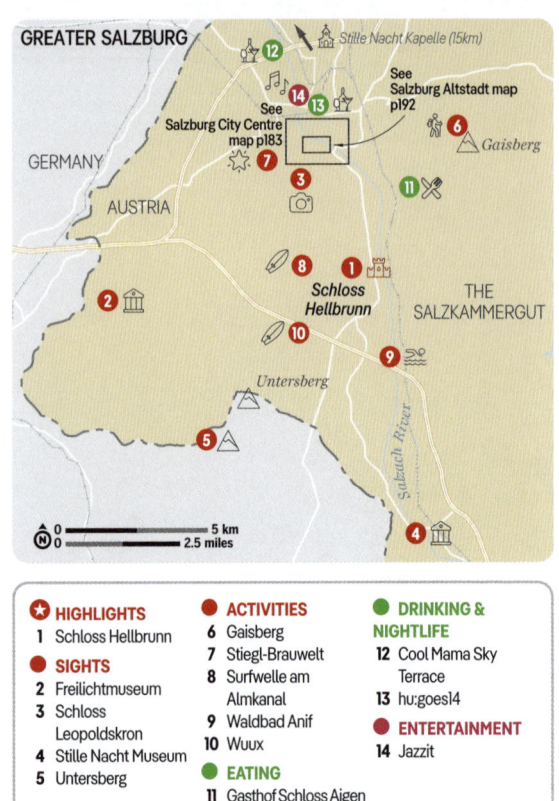

★ HIGHLIGHTS
1 Schloss Hellbrunn

● SIGHTS
2 Freilichtmuseum
3 Schloss Leopoldskron
4 Stille Nacht Museum
5 Untersberg

● ACTIVITIES
6 Gaisberg
7 Stiegl-Brauwelt
8 Surfwelle am Almkanal
9 Waldbad Anif
10 Wuux

● EATING
11 Gasthof Schloss Aigen

● DRINKING & NIGHTLIFE
12 Cool Mama Sky Terrace
13 hu:goes14

● ENTERTAINMENT
14 Jazzit

continued from p191

centuries, the ruling prince-archbishops frantically built castles, palaces, churches, domes and abbeys here. And nowhere is the pomp and circumstance of Salzburg more tangible than in the baroque Altstadt, a UNESCO World Heritage Site, with stately squares and museums to keep you absorbed for hours. Rise early to see them at their quiet, crowd-free best.

Begin with an eye-opening spin of Salzburg's baroque heart in the **DomQuartier** *(domquartier.at; adult/child €15/5)*. One ticket covers multiple sights. The showstopper is the **Salzburger Dom** (p198), the lavishly stuccoed and frescoed cathedral where Mozart was baptised. You'll also get entry to the **Residenz** palace. A man of grand designs, Wolf Dietrich von Raitenau, prince-archbishop of Salzburg from 1587 to 1612, gave the go-ahead to plonk this baroque palace on the site of an 11th-century bishop's residence. A tour races through exuberant state rooms adorned with tapestries, Johann Michael Rottmayr frescoes, and its gallery, rammed with Old Master paintings of the Rembrandt and Rubens ilk.

Out front, *Fiaker* (horse-drawn carriages) clip-clop across grand **Residenzplatz**, a late-16th-century vision inspired

Christmas market, Salzburg

by Rome and masterminded by Italian architect Vincenzo Scamozzi. Its centrepiece is the **Residenzbrunnen** (p185), an enormous marble fountain ringed by four water-spouting horses and topped by Triton bearing a conch shell.

Christmas in Salzburg

Concerts, carols and markets

Salzburg is a city with Christmas in its bones. It's particularly bewitching in December, when trees twinkle, carollers sing and the cinnamon-clove scent of gingerbread and *Glühwein* drift through the Altstadt's alleyways. The backdrop is a ready-made Christmas card, with the castle-topped baroque skyline lifting the gaze to the snow-dusted Alps.

You'll feel the wide-eyed wonder of a child at the **Christkindlmarkt** (*christkindlmarkt.co.at*) on **Domplatz** and **Residenzplatz** (p194), which shimmer gold from late November to New Year's Day. Here carollers sing angelically, brass bands play and huts sell chestnuts and *Glühwein*, candied almonds and beautifully carved nativity figurines and nutcrackers.

Go for a twirl on the ice rink on nearby **Mozartplatz**, or else head to the insanely romantic Christmas market at **Schloss Hellbrunn** (p201) (*hellbrunneradventzauber.at*). The palace is transformed into a giant Advent calendar (with each

BEST SHOPPING IN SALZBURG: GIFTS

Klosterladen St Peter: This monastery shop has it all from hand-carved angels to gentian syrup and monastic beer.

Salzburger Heimatwerk: This old-school emporium knocks fabric into beautiful Dirndls, and does a fine line in handicrafts, books and music.

Lackner: Hand-carved nutcrackers, nativity figurines, filigree Christmas stars and cuckoo clocks are the real deal at this traditional craft shop.

Mayrische Musikalienhandlung: An institution since it opened in the 16th century, this glorious shop stocks a fabulous array of music, sheet music, scores and books.

Wenger: Pick up Lederhosen, Dirndls, shawls, scarves and hats at this Getreidegasse classic.

 EATING IN SALZBURG: LUNCH SPOTS

Afro Café: Go for fair-trade coffees, lavish brunches and creative day specials at this Afro-chic cafe. *9am-8pm Mon-Sat* €

Green Garden: Tapping into plant power, this vegan cafe rustles up tasty Buddha bowls, brunches and superfood salads. *1-9pm Wed-Fri, 10am-9pm Sat & Sun* €

Heart of Joy: Ayurveda-inspired cafe with a vegetarian, part-vegan and mostly organic menu. Bagels, salads, homemade cakes, juices, and more. *8am-7pm* €

Humboldt: Like a blast of nouveau alpine chic, the vibe is cool yet cosy. A good buzz and all-organic, season-driven menu. *10.30am-11pm* €€

SALZBURG'S BEST LIVE MUSIC

Jazzit: Regular concerts, from tango to electro, plus workshops, club nights and free Tuesday-night jam sessions in the Jazzit bar.

ARGEkultur: Alternative arts centre. Concerts, cabaret, DJ nights, dance, poetry slams and world music traverse the arts spectrum.

Rockhouse: Salzburg's hottest live-music venue presents first-rate rock, pop, jazz, folk, metal and reggae concerts.

StageBar: Black-and-white photos of music legends plaster the walls of this Altstadt bar, where live music and karaoke are paired with cocktails.

Schloss Mirabell: Internationally renowned soloists and ensembles perform works by Mozart and other well-known composers such as Haydn and Chopin in a sublime palace setting.

window representing a door) and its gardens are illuminated by trick fountains and 700 glittering trees.

Music? Christmas brings a flurry of concerts, from carols and Mozart symphonies echoing through the medieval halls of **Festung Hohensalzburg** (p184) to Advent concerts at the **Grosses Festspielhaus**.

If you wish it could be Christmas every day, swing on over to Salzburg's **Christmas Museum** *(salzburger-weihnachtsmuseum.at; adult/child €9/5)*. The private collection brings year-round festive sparkle with Advent calendars, hand-carved cribs, baubles and nutcrackers.

All is Calm, All is Bright

Pilgrimage to Oberndorf

Nothing gives you that warm, fuzzy, festive feeling more than making the pilgrimage to **Oberndorf**, a serene town snug against the Bavarian border, a 25-minute train ride northwest from Salzburg.

If the flakes fall, pad through the snow to the **Stille Nacht Kapelle**, where Joseph Mohr was once pastor. He penned the six-stanza poem 'Silent Night' (Stille Nacht), handed it over to parish organist, Franz Xaver Gruber, and asked him to compose the melody. The peaceful carol debuted on 24 December 1818, with the pair singing it in front of the nativity scene. Hearing it sung here on a frosty Christmas Eve, more than two centuries down the line, is spine-tingling stuff.

Translated into 300 different languages, 'Silent Night' has become the world's most famous and best-loved carol.

Festung Hohensalzburg seen from the Schloss Mirabell gardens (p188)

Festival Time
All Salzburg's a stage

When the curtain rises on the **Salzburger Festspiele** *(Salzburg Festival; salzburgerfestspiele.at)* on a summer's evening and locals glide through the baroque streets dressed to the nines in *Tracht* (traditional costume), it's as if the city has been touched by magic. The first stars pinprick a deep-blue sky, the city's domes, churches and castle glow gold, audiences fall silent in squares, and concert halls reverberate with the sound of opera and orchestras.

In 1920, dream trio Hugo von Hofmannsthal, Max Reinhardt and Richard Strauss combined their creative forces, and the Salzburg Festival was born. Opera, drama and classical concerts of the highest calibre have propelled the five-week summer festival to international renown, attracting some of the world's best conductors, directors, orchestras and singers.

SAVE ON STAYS

Rocking up in peak summer season and expecting to find a deal is wishful thinking in Salzburg. In high-season months, hotels in the Altstadt can be eye-wateringly expensive, with prices leaping to double what they are in the low season. Note that high-season prices jack up another 10% to 20% during the Salzburg Festival. December is also primetime, with everyone flocking to the city's twinkling Christmas markets.

Finding reasonably priced accommodation is possible, however, if you're willing to go the extra mile, staying in private rooms and simple, family-run B&Bs. There's a cluster of these along Moosstrasse, which can be reached from the city centre in around 15 minutes on bus 21. If Salzburg is booked solid, consider staying in Hallein or across the border in Bavaria.

 EATING IN SALZBURG: STREET FOOD

Bistro de Márquez: Piedad brings Colombia to this wallet-friendly bistro, with *arepas* (filled maize crêpes) and *pandebono* (cheese bread). *11.30am-7pm Wed-Sat* €

Uncle Van: Hip Vietnamese spot on Steingasse. Authentic takes on ramen noodles, curries, summer rolls and pho. *11.30am-9pm Mon-Fri, noon-9pm Sat & Sun* €

Organic Pizza Salzburg: Good-natured staff, cool music and pizza with super-fresh, organic ingredients. *5-10pm Tue-Fri, noon-10pm Sat, noon-9pm Sun* €

Salzburger Grill Imbiss: Raymond is the wurst whizz at this sausage stand behind the Kollegienkirche. Go for a *Bosna* (pork bratwurst) topped with onions and mustard. *11am-5pm* €

Come festival time, Salzburg crackles with excitement, as a quarter of a million visitors descend on the city for some 200 productions. Theatre premieres, avant-garde works and the summer-resident Vienna Philharmonic performing works by Mozart are all in the mix. The **Festival District** on Hofstallgasse has a spectacular backdrop, framed by Mönchsberg's cliffs. Most performances are held in the cavernous **Grosses Festspielhaus** (p196), which accommodates 2179 theatregoers, the **Haus für Mozart** in the former royal stables, and the baroque **Felsenreitschule**.

If you plan to visit the festival, don't leave anything to chance – book your flights, hotel and tickets months in advance. Sometimes last-minute tickets are available at the **Festspiele Ticket Office** on Wiener-Philharmoniker-Gasse, but they're like gold dust, especially for the biggest crowd-puller – Hofmannsthal's soul-stirring morality play, *Jedermann* (Everyman), on Domplatz.

Spiritual Salzburg

In high spirits

Wander Salzburg's baroque Altstadt at the change of hour and fall silent as the city rings with tolling bells and chimes like a giant glockenspiel. It's the most uplifting of sights and sounds.

To tune into Salzburg's spiritual side, begin where the city did: **Stift St Peter** *(stift-stpeter.at)*, the oldest abbey in the German-speaking world, founded by a Frankish missionary named Rupert in 700. Its showpiece is an overwhelmingly baroque **church**, richly embellished with stucco and altar paintings by Martin Johann Schmidt. Composer Michael Haydn (1737–1806), opera singer Richard Mayr (1877–1935) and renowned Salzburg confectioner Paul Fürst (1856–1941) are buried among the sea of filigree wrought-iron crosses in the **cemetery** here. Most atmospheric of all are the **catacombs** *(adult/child €2/1.50)* – cave-like chapels and crypts carved into the sheer cliff face of Mönchsberg.

Close by, the baroque **Salzburger Dom** *(salzburger-dom.at; adult/child €5/free)* is gracefully crowned by a bulbous copper cupola and twin spires. Bronze portals symbolising faith, hope and charity lead into the cathedral. In the nave, Arsenio Mascagni's ceiling frescoes recounting the Passion of Christ guide the eye to the polychrome dome. To experience the cathedral at its captivating best, catch one of the half-hour lunchtime **organ concerts**, which begin just after the bells ring at 12.04pm.

All the more enchanting for being away from the tourist

BEST SHOPPING IN SALZBURG: A TASTE OF SALZBURG

Fürst: The pistachio, nougat and dark-chocolate Mozartkugeln (Mozart balls) are handmade to the original 1890 recipe.

Kaslöchl: Mouse-sized cheese shop, crammed with creamy alpine varieties, holey Emmenthal and fresh cheese with herbs.

Sporer: In Getreidegasse's narrowest house, Sporer has sold Austrian wines, herbal liqueurs and Vogelbeer schnapps since 1903.

Salzburg Salz: Pop into this Altstadt emporium to buy pure salt from the Alps of Salzburgerland, salts flavoured with flowers and herbs, and salt chocolate.

Feinkost Stocker: This old butcher's shop in Nonntal is a delight for the finest charcuterie, sausages and wines from the surrounding region.

SHOPPING IN SALZBURG: PICNIC FIXINGS

Grünmarkt: Picnic stop on Universitätsplatz. Stalls laden with regional cheeses, ham, fruit, bread and huge pretzels. *7am-5pm Mon-Fri, 6am-3pm Sat* €

Salzburg Schranne: Farmers set up at 5am Thursday in front of Andräkirche. Produce and flowers from Salzburg and its rural surrounds. *5am-1pm Thu* €

Kajetanerplatz: Locals flock to this organic farmers' market on Fridays for fresh produce, meat, cheese and baked treats. *6am-2pm Fri* €

Bäckerei Holztrattner: Pick up fresh-baked loaves, rolls, fruit bread and pastries from this bakery going strong since 1350. *6am-6pm Mon-Fri, to noon Sat* €

Salzburger Marionettentheater

crowds, Benedictine **Stift Nonnberg** *(nonnberg.at; free)* is a short, stiff uphill hike. Climb up to its rib-vaulted church to glimpse beautifully faded Romanesque frescoes and – if you're an early riser – hear the abbey's nuns singing Gregorian chorales at 6.45am.

Daily Bread
Buy a loaf at Salzburg's oldest bakery

A watermill still turns at **Stiftsbäckerei St Peter** *(stifts baeckerei.at)*. Part of the historic abbey complex, this vaulted, 700-year-old bakery is still blessed by locals for its daily bread. The bakery churns out Salzburg's finest loaves, lovingly kneaded by hand, made from freshly milled rye and wheat flour and natural sourdough, and baked until crunchy in a wood-fired oven. The bread keeps well, making it perfect for stashing in a backpack for a picnic up in the hills or down by the river. You can also pick up other goodies such as *Gewürzweckerl* (spiced rolls), plaited yeast buns and brioche here, too.

It's all brilliantly sustainable: the bakery is powered with wood from the monastery's forest and its own hydropower from the Almkanal.

Marionette Magic
Like a puppet on a string

Not only children are filled with wonder at the UNESCO World Heritage Site **Salzburger Marionettentheater** *(marionetten. at; adult €33-43, child €15)*, where the red curtain has risen on a miniature stage since 1913. The theatre is just as grand and intricate as a full-size one, with stucco embellishments and chandeliers. The level of detail that goes into the costumes and backdrops is extraordinary and the puppeteers are incredibly talented – you'll barely notice the strings as the marionettes dance, swoop and fly through the air.

BEST PLACES FOR KIDS IN SALZBURG

Haus der Natur: This hands-on museum dives deep into natural history. The clincher is the aquarium, with its clownfish and sharks. See archerfish, moray eels and piranhas being fed at 10.30am.

Spielzeugmuseum: Salzburg's very own toy story, this rambling attic of toys old and new even has 'adult parking areas' where grown-ups can hang out while kids play.

Freilichtmuseum: This huge open-air museum whisks you through Austrian farming life, with animals to pet, crafts to explore and a big adventure playground to romp around in.

Schloss Hellbrunn: On hot days, kids have a blast splashing in the trick fountains at this fairy tale palace just out of town.

Spielplatz Volksgarten: Let tots burn off excess energy, play with water and dig in the sand at one of the best adventure playgrounds in town.

SALZBURG DIARY DATES

As a high-spirited, music-loving, culture-mad city, Salzburg has a jam-packed events calendar, some of which are free.

Salzburger Festspiele: Can't snag Salzburg Festival tickets? In summer, **Kapitelplatz** gets crowds into the swing of the Salzburger Festspiele showing opera for free on a big screen.

Sternenkino: Kapitelplatz is also the castle-crowned backdrop for free arthouse movie nights at Sternenkino, held over 10 days from late June to early July. Films begin at 8.30pm. Bring along your own picnic or grab drinks and street food on the square. *sternenkino-salzburg.at*

Jazz & the City: Mid October brings Jazz & the City, with jazz acts – from rising stars to big names – hitting venues all over the city, from baroque churches to beer halls.

Stille Nacht Kapelle (p196)

The repertoire star is *The Sound of Music,* with a life-sized Mother Superior and a marionette-packed finale. Other enchanting productions include Mozart's *The Magic Flute*, Tchaikovsky's *The Nutcracker* and Beethoven's *Fidelio*. Performances (with multilingual subtitles) last around two hours. Or for a taste of the theatre's greatest hits, book the 35-minute **highlights show** *(adult/child €28/15).*

Silent Nights on Steingasse
Slip back to the Middle Ages

Slip away from the Altstadt's crowds and back to the Middle Ages on **Steingasse**. Hugging the banks of the Salzach River, the lane might not look like a major thoroughfare today, but it was once the main north–south route between the city and Italy, its cobbles worn smooth by many a horse's hoof and wagon wheel. Salt from nearby mines was transported from here to Europe and beyond.

The street is a beauty, with a curve of medieval townhouses in soft pastel colours, which are at their photogenic best in the morning sunlight or when lantern-lit in the blue dusk. Look out for the **plaque** at No 9 dedicated to famous past resident Joseph Mohr, who wrote the lyrics to that all-time classic carol 'Silent Night' (p196) in 1816, just after the end of the Napoleonic Wars.

MORE SILENT NIGHTS

In Hallein, visit the **Stille Nacht Museum** (p203), housed in the former residence of Franz Xaver Gruber.

Beyond
Salzburg

Salzburg is the curtain-raiser to Alps that will make your heart soar and cinematic backdrops that will prompt you to yodel out loud.

Within minutes of central Salzburg you can be swanning around the fountain-splashed gardens of exuberant baroque summer palace Schloss Hellbrunn, or brushing up on Celtic history and delving deep into medieval salt mines in Hallein.

And the further you venture, the better it gets. For a memorable day trip, take the quick train ride to Werfen, which thrills with a show-stopping medieval castle and the world's biggest ice caves, Eisriesenwelt. Here cliff-skimming trails thread through the rugged peaks of the limestone Tennengebirge, where eagles wheel, winds blow and silence reigns. Further south still, Filzmoos, hemmed in by saw-edged peaks, wings you away from the crowds and back to nature with hiking, skiing and snowshoeing in the Dachstein massif.

Places
Hellbrunn p201
Hallein p202
Werfen p203
Filzmoos p205
Liechtensteinklamm p206

Hellbrunn   TIME FROM SALZBURG: **15-20MINS**

Stomping Ground of the Prince-Archbishops

Many of Salzburg's prince-archbishops were absorbed in matters of a more religious nature, but not Markus Sittikus, Prince-Archbishop of Salzburg from 1612 to 1619. Markus had a frivolous streak, a wicked sense of humour and a love of drunken, hedonistic parties. So he had lavish, lemon-fronted Italianate palace **Schloss Hellbrunn** *(hellbrunn.at; adult/child €15/6.50)* built to escape his divine duties, inviting the clergy over to feast, drink and make merry in exotic gardens full of citrus trees, muses and fountains.

While Schloss Hellbrunn's whimsical interior is fabulous, especially the **Chinese Room** and frescoed **Festsaal**, it's the eccentric **Wasserspiele** (trick fountains) that are the big draw in summer. Be prepared to get soaked in the mock Roman theatre, shell-clad Neptune Grotto and the twittering Bird Grotto. No statue here is as it seems, including the emblematic tongue-poking-out Germaul mask (Sittikus' answer to his critics). The tour rounds out at the 18th-century water-powered **Mechanical Theatre**, where 200 limewood figurines depict life in a baroque city.

GETTING AROUND

Much of the region beyond Salzburg is brilliantly accessible by public transport (bus and train), removing the need to hire a car unless you crave the independence of having your own wheels. There are regional and S-Bahn trains running frequently from Salzburg to Hallein (15 minutes) and Werfen (40 minutes). The two-hour journey to Filzmoos is a little bit trickier, involving a train (to Bischoshofen) and two buses.

Don't dash off after seeing the palace. The **gardens** *(admission free)* are a brilliant spot for a picnic, stroll or run, with tree-shaded avenues, ponds and sculptures. Here you'll find the pavilion of *The Sound of Music* 'Sixteen Going on Seventeen' fame.

To reach Hellbrunn, it's a 20-minute bike ride (mostly along the Salzach River) from the city centre, or a 15-minute ride on bus 25, which departs from Mozartsteg/Rudolfskai in the Altstadt.

Ride Along the River to Hellbrunn

By far the most scenic way to reach Schloss Hellbrunn from Salzburg is by getting on your bike for the 20-minute roll south. Rent wheels at **aVelo** (p189; *bike rental per day €25*) by Staatsbrücke and leave the crowds of the Altstadt behind.

You'll pedal through the historic Kaiviertel district and avant-garde Unipark Nonntal before emerging on Mühlbacherhofweg. It's then a straightforward trundle through meadows, passing **Schloss Freisaal**, a dinky medieval castle rimmed by a lake, which backs onto the **Universität Salzburg Botanical Garden** *(salzburg.info; admission free)*. From here, you'll hook onto Hellbrunner Allee, a grand, straight-as-a-die avenue lined by ancient chestnut trees. Keep an eye out, too, for butter-yellow **Schloss Frohnburg**, a 17th-century summer palace that had a cameo role in *The Sound of Music* as the Von Trapp Villa.

Hallein

TIME FROM SALZBURG: **15MINS**

Trip Back to Medieval Times

But a pretzel-throw from Bavaria, the town of Hallein has medieval looks and a riveting mountain backdrop, yet somehow it has managed to dodge the tourist radar. Just a 15-minute train trundle south of Salzburg, it makes a terrific day trip. History here runs deep – in every possible sense of the expression.

During Salzburg's princely heyday, the sale of salt filled its coffers. Dive into the past at cavernous **Salzwelten** *(salzwelten.at; adult child €43/19.50)*, where 'white gold' was mined for 2600 years. Slip into a boiler suit for a tour deep underground, which takes you through a maze of claustrophobic passageways, across an atmospherically lit salt lake, over the border to Germany and down a miner's slide – don't brake, lift your legs and ask the guide to wax the slide for extra speed!

Or tune into Celtic heritage with a romp around the riverside **Keltenmuseum** *(keltenmuseum.at; adult/child*

ROMAN RULE

In the Holy Roman Empire, prince-archbishops ruled the roost in Salzburg from 1278 to 1803. Markus Sittikus loved pomp and play at Schloss Hellbrunn, but it was his predecessor and successor that made the history books big time.

Wolf Dietrich von Raitenau, prince-archbishop from 1587 to 1612, spearheaded the total baroque makeover of the city, commissioning many of its most beautiful churches, palaces and gardens. He fell from power after losing a fierce dispute over the salt trade with powerful Bavarian rulers, and died a prisoner.

Seizing the reins from Markus Sittikus in 1619 and in power until 1653, Trentino-born Paris von Lodron was stern and ambitious. He founded the Universität Salzburg in 1622 and managed to keep the principality out of the Europe-wide Thirty Years' War.

EATING & DRINKING IN HALLEIN: OUR PICKS

El'risa: Vaulted cafe with a relaxed vibe. Creative breakfasts, healthy vegan lunches and Austrian speciality coffees. *9am-2pm Mon-Wed & Fri, to 5pm Sat & Sun* €

Eckzimmer: Laid-back cafe for brunch, great coffee, light lunches and to-go picnic boxes. Sit on the garden terrace when the sun's out. *9am-6pm Wed-Sun* €

Hammerwirt: Austro-Italian dishes, such as *Backhendl* (crispy breaded chicken), and a chestnut-tree-canopied garden. *5-10pm Wed-Fri, 11.30am-10pm Sat & Sun* €€

Aarons Genusskrämerei: Regional produce is finessed into imaginative dishes served with flair and local wines at the town's oldest inn. *4-11pm Tue-Fri, 10am-11pm Sat* €€

Schloss Hellbrunn (p201)

€9.50/4.50). Overlooking the Salzach, the glass-fronted museum zips chronologically through the region's heritage. The beautifully vaulted rooms showcase a priceless stash of Celtic artefacts, from Bronze Age helmets to Celtic gold torques and the 'Mannes im Salz', the mummified remains of a prehistoric salt-miner.

Hallein's more festive claim to fame is as the one-time home of Franz Xaver Gruber (1787–1863), who composed the carol 'Silent Night' ('Stille Nacht'). Joseph Mohr penned the poem and Gruber, a schoolteacher at the time, came up with the melody on his guitar in 1818. The fabled guitar takes pride of place in the **Stille Nacht Museum** *(adult/child €5/2.50)*, lodged in Gruber's former residence, which recounts the story of the carol through documents and personal belongings.

Werfen

TIME FROM SALZBURG: **40MINS**  OR **1HR**

Cue the World's Biggest Ice Caves

High above Werfen, the pointed peaks of the Tennengebirge rise like a theatre curtain of solid limestone above the river-woven Salzach Valley. Take the cable car, then hoof it up the steep, scree-strewn trail to **Eisriesenwelt** *(eisriesenwelt.at; adult/child €42/21)*, the world's biggest accessible ice cave, open from May to October. Stepping through the huge 20m-wide

CENT SAVERS

All ÖBB train stations in the region sell the money-saving **Salt Worlds Salzburg** *(adult/child €38.30/15.50)* ticket. This covers a bus transfer to Bad Dürrnberg, plus entry to the Salzwelten salt mines, the Kelten Erlebnis Berg (Celtic Mountain) themed playground, where kids can take a playful dive into a prehistoric world, the Salina Celtic village, shining a light on the Ice Age settlement, and the Salt Worlds app, which brings Celtic objects to life in 3D.

Stay overnight in Hallein or Bad Dürrnberg and you will automatically receive the **TennengauPLUS-Card** *(tennengau.com)*, which gives you free travel on buses and trains (all the way to Salzburg) and discounted entry to local sights, museums and attractions.

 EATING IN WERFEN: OUR PICKS

Pizzeria im Markt: Pizzas fly out of the oven perfectly thin and crisp at this cosy pick in Werfen's heart. *10am-10pm* €

Oedlhaus: At Eisriesenwelt, this 1574m woodsy hut fortifies walkers with grub like Gröstl (meat and potato hash) and mountain views. *8am-4pm* €€

Stiege No 1: Venison, asparagus, wild garlic – the menu here sings of the seasons. In summer, sit in the lantern-lit garden. *11am-10pm Wed-Sun* €€

Obauer: At this Michelin-starred restaurant, the Obauer brothers make alpine, homegrown and foraged ingredients sing on the plate. *6-9pm Wed, noon-9pm Thu-Sun* €€€

GET A GUIDE

A one-stop shop for outdoor activities, **Filzmoos Aktiv** *(filzmoos-aktiv.at)* arranges everything from themed mountain and glacier hikes to e-bike tours, climbing courses, challenging summit ascents and multiday hut-to-hut treks taking you deeper into the Alps of Salzburgerland, including a three-day trek around the iconic Bischofsmütze.

In winter, slip on snowshoes to crunch through the fresh powder snow and twinkling forests in quiet exhilaration. Guided snowshoeing tours range from a 2½-hour stomp at Rossbrand mountain to a two-day tour at the foot of Bischofsmütze and a heart-pumping five-day snowshoeing expedition on the frozen Dachstein plateau, never lovelier than in its winter mantle of white.

---

gash in the rock, feeling the frosty blast of 0°C air and seeing the ice twinkle is like pushing through the wardrobe into Narnia.

A 1¼-hour guided tour by old-fashioned carbide lamp illuminates your passage through this pitch-black, glittering underworld of frozen tunnels and passageways, where you will be blown away by the scale and beauty of the ice. The clifftop location and elevation at 1641m mean electric lighting has never been installed here, so to walk in these caves today is to feel like an early explorer.

In the soft glow, formations appear from the shadows: there are wavy walls of ice rippled through like marble, frozen waterfalls and stalactites as delicate as cut crystal, and a steep ice mountain that you climb via a flight of wooden steps (watch your footing). Guides hold a flare up to ice sculptures shaped like elephants and polar bears. Most impressive of all, however, is the echoing, cathedral-like **Eispalast** (Ice Palace), with icicles as big as organ pipes and ice-veined walls shimmering from pearl white to sapphire blue.

Passing back through the hole, you emerge in dazzling daylight and back into the mountains that kept these ice caves and their giants a secret for so long.

Big Views & Birds of Prey at Burg Hohenwerfen

Slung high on a wooded clifftop and cowering below the gnarly peaks of the Tennengebirge, **Burg Hohenwerfen** *(burg-hohenwerfen.at; adult/child incl lift €17.90/6.10, with guided tour €20.90/7.60)* is visible from afar. For 900 years this turreted beauty of a castle has guarded the Salzach Valley. You'll be mostly captivated by the mountain views from the 16th-century belfry, but the dingy dungeons (displaying the usual nasties such as the iron maiden and thumb screw) are equally worth a look.

Time your visit to catch the stunning **falconry show** (11.15am and 3.15pm daily) in the grounds, where falconers in medieval costume release eagles, owls, falcons and vultures to wheel in front of the ramparts. The brisk walk up from Werfen takes 20 minutes, or you can cheat by catching the lift.

Sing like Maria

Werfen looks like something that a romantically inclined film director has dreamed up, with its soaring Tennengebirge rising like fantasy fortifications and whopping medieval castle – and indeed it was the backdrop for the picnic scene in 1965 Hollywood blockbuster *The Sound of Music*. It was here that Julie Andrews (aka Maria the singing nun) played her guitar to teach the von Trapp kids 'Do-Re-Mi'.

Unspooling through wildflower-freckled meadows and hills, the 1.4km, hour-long **Sound of Music Trail** follows in the footsteps of the Trapp family, from the town centre to the Gschwandtanger viewpoint, with cinematic views over the Salzach Valley. Begin your walk at Werfen tourist office. The trail is well signposted and information panels along the way give insights into the different film locations. Oh, and don't forget your picnic (and guitar!).

Entrance to Eisriesenwelt (p203)

Hut-to-Hut Hiking on the Salzburger Almenweg

Peak bagging is all well and good, but there's more to Salzburgerland than simply aiming for the cloud-shredding summits. The **Salzburger Almenweg** (Pfarrwerfen to the Gastein Valley) is a mood-lifting, 350km, 25-stage, moderately demanding romp through the region's lush, flower-spotted, cow-nibbled alpine pastures. Many scenes from *The Sound of Music* were shot right here – think Julie Andrews twirling to 'The Hills Are Alive'.

Marked with a blue gentian flower and running mostly above the treeline, the hut-to-hut trek starts and ends in Pfarrwerfen at the foot of the Tennengebirge's limestone spires, then climbs up and over meadows and deeply riven valleys to the wild, waterfall-splashed Gastein Valley and beyond. The views of the glacier-capped Hohe Tauern peaks are out of this world. Sections 9 to 11 are particularly striking, diving deep into the Gastein Valley, with its crashing falls, giddy heights and forgotten valleys.

Filzmoos

TIME FROM SALZBURG: 1¼HRS

Long-Distance Hikes & Heady Views

The summits of the Dachstein massif fling up like the fortifications of a fantasy fortress above rolling pastures and placid lakes. Crowned by the knobbly Bischofsmütze (Bishop's Mitre), Filzmoos is every inch the mountain dream. And with its tucked-away location, the village has preserved its rural, low-key charm, too.

The tug of the trail is strong here. Bring boots for long-distance stomps like the eight-day, 126km **Dachstein Circuit** (Dachsteinrunde in German) through the jagged limestone Dachstein range. The walk takes in the entire spectrum of alpine landscapes, from glaciers and lofty mountains to forests, karst plateaus, fast-flowing rivers and pretty meadows.

REACHING EISRIESENWELT

Everyone wants to see Eisriesenwelt, but if you're day tripping from Salzburg or want to tie the ice caves in with a visit to Burg Hohenwerfen, you'll need to get your timings right with careful pre-planning.

Minibuses *(return adult/child €10/8)* run at 8.18am, 10.18am, 12.18pm and 2.18pm from Werfen train station to Eisriesenwelt car park, which is a 20-minute walk from the bottom station of the cable car. Cable cars run at least half hourly and the journey to the top takes just three minutes. The last return bus departs at 5.32pm. Allow roughly three hours for the return trip (including the tour). You can walk the whole route, but it's a challenging, exposed four-hour ascent, rising 1100m above the village.

THE CHIMNEY EFFECT

Eisriesenwelt is a paradox. Even in the face of climate change, with rapidly retreating glaciers and melting icecaps, ice growth here remains stable. Ironically, recent hot dry summers caused the ice to grow, where rain would have made it melt. Warm winters are bad news, though, as the temperatures need to be cold for the subzero freeze to happen. With ever-warmer winters on the horizon due to global warming, the future of the caves remains uncertain.

Geologically speaking, Eisriesenwelt blows hot and cold – a phenomenon scientifically known as the 'chimney effect'. When temperatures are lower outside than in, warm air rises out of the top of the cave through fissures in the limestone rock, while cold air is drawn in through the entrance, causing the first few kilometres of the cave to freeze and the ice to grow.

Helix staircase, Liechtensteinklamm

For a shorter but no less spectacular walk, hook onto the two-day, 23km **Gosaukamm Circuit**, which dives into the ragged Gosaukamm range, sometimes dubbed 'Salzburg's Dolomites' because they are similar in size and scale. The highlight is the 2012m **Steigl Pass**, an exposed, fixed-cable route that involves some scrambling. Pick up trail maps at the tourist office.

Liechtensteinklamm

TIME FROM SALZBURG: **1HR**

A Gorge Fit for a Prince

One of the deepest, longest gorges in the Alps, the **Liechtensteinklamm** *(josalzburg.com; adult/child €15/8.50)* near St Johann in Pongau is full-on drama, with vertical 300m-high cliffs thrusting above a foaming turquoise river, rainbow-kissed falls and mossy boulders. The ravine is named after Johann II, Prince of Liechtenstein, who took a fancy to it in 1875 and bankrolled the trail, with bridges, galleries and tunnels hacked into slate cliffs veined with white granite.

Arrive first thing in the morning or in the early evening for the dreamiest light and fewest crowds. Most photogenic of all is the **Helix**, a weathered steel spiral staircase corkscrewing 30m into the depths of the gorge.

Places We Love to Stay

€ Budget €€ Midrange €€€ Top End

Salzburg Altstadt
MAP p183 and p192

Hotel am Dom €€ Antique meets boutique at an Altstadt hotel in an 800-year-old building. Original vaults and beams contrast with sharp design.

Arte Vida €€ With the boho-chic feel of a Moroccan riad, this colourful pick has generously sized apartments big enough to accommodate families.

Hotel Amadeus €€ Centrally situated on the right bank, this 500-year-old hotel has a boutique feel, with bespoke touches such as chandeliers and four-poster beds.

Goldener Hirsch €€€ A skylight illuminates the arcaded inner courtyard of this 600-year-old Altstadt pile, where famous past guests include Queen Elizabeth II and Pavarotti.

Arthotel Blaue Gans €€€ Welcoming folk since 1350, this art hotel blends avant-garde design with original vaulting, beams and floors.

Beyond Salzburg Altstadt

YoHo € Backpacker dream: comfy bunks, cheap beer and *The Sound of Music* movie screenings daily at 8pm. Staff can arrange bike hire.

A&O Salzburg Hauptbahnhof € Modern hostel in a revamped factory near the Hauptbahnhof. Airy dorms and rooms among the city's cheapest.

Haus am Moos € An alpine-style chalet offering a slice of rural calm. Rooms have gorgeous mountain views and there's an outdoor pool.

Hotel & Villa Auersperg €€ Fuses late-19th-century flair with contemporary. Relax in the vine-swaddled garden or rooftop spa with Kapuzinerberg views.

Cool Mama €€ This ultra-modern skyscraper is a burst of urban cool near the Salzburg Exhibition Centre. Glass-walled rooms perfectly frame views of the city and Alps.

Hotel Rosenvilla €€ This bijou hotel goes the extra mile with its sharp-styled contemporary rooms, faultless service and incredible breakfasts.

Schloss Mönchstein €€€ On a fairy tale perch atop Mönchsberg and set in hectares of wooded grounds, this 16th-century castle is honeymoon (and second mortgage) material.

Hallein

Kranzbichlhof €€ In serene gardens, this Bad Dürrnberg chalet has spacious rooms, a natural pool and a spa with Ayurvedic treatments.

Pension Sommerauer €€ Housed in a 300-year-old farmhouse on the fringes of Hallein, this welcoming guesthouse has rustic rooms, a heated pool and kids' playground.

Werfen

Weisses Rössl € In the village centre, this good-value pension has great views of the fortress and the Tennengebirge from its rooftop terrace.

Landgasthof Reitsamerhof €€ Rousing views of the Tennengebirge peaks at a sunny yellow, geranium-bedecked chalet just south of Werfen.

Söldenhütte € Above Werfen, this woody 1531m hut is a cracking base for Tennengebirge hiking. The restaurant rolls out hearty dumplings, goulash and homemade cakes.

Filzmoos

Naturhotel Hammerhof €€ Ecofriendly hotel in a 400-year-old farmhouse in Filzmoos with light-bathed rooms, a herbal bath and horses to saddle.

Hotel Alpenblick €€ Right on the doorstep of the slopes and hiking trails, this smart chalet has a petite spa, restaurant, sun terrace and kids' playground.

For places to stay in Stuttgart & the Black Forest, see p266

Above: Titisee Lake (p237); Right: Blackforestline suspension bridge (p234), Todtnau

THE MAIN AREAS

STUTTGART
Industrious wine capital. **p214**

FREIBURG
Gateway to the Black Forest. **p226**

THE BLACK FOREST
Enchanting fairy tale forest. **p234**

Researched by
Kat Barber

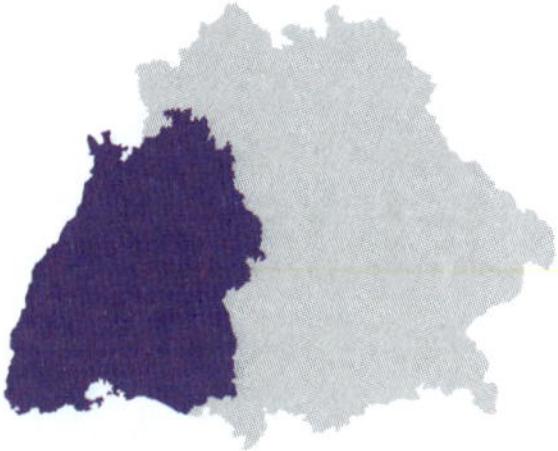

Stuttgart & the Black Forest

FORESTS, LAKES, SPAS AND AUTOMOBILES

Beyond the urban appeal of Stuttgart lies a region ripe for exploration.

Welcome to the southwest, known as the sunniest region in Germany. You're in the state of Baden-Württemberg, where locals are renowned for their inventiveness, hard work and prosperity. But they also love a good *Feierabend* (end-of-work) drink with friends, and with so much of the region covered in vineyards, it's not hard to find a decent drop.

Stuttgart, the region's capital, boasts a proud history of engineering that has given the world the automobile, spark plugs and the pretzel. From here, it's like a *Choose Your Own Adventure* novel. Head west if you want to indulge in the good-good life in spa capital Baden-Baden. Venture east to explore Ulm, with its record-breaking church steeple and crooked house in charming Fischerviertel. To the south, you'll find yourself in the European summer playground of Lake Constance, the meeting point of Germany, Austria and Switzerland. A destination for all things water sports, its lakeside towns are surprisingly full of charm and history. And in the southwestern corner, Freiburg is the gateway to exploring the depths of the Black Forest (Schwarzwald). Whether you want to break a sweat on the forest trails, scream your lungs out on a rollercoaster or simply indulge in the sweet taste of Black Forest cake, this is the destination for you.

With the scent of Swabian specialities following you down cobbled alleyways and across leafy courtyards, you'll also be well fed everywhere you go.

BADEN-BADEN
Refined spa town. **p241**

LAKE CONSTANCE
European summer playground. **p251**

ULM
Towering church and crooked houses. **p258**

Find Your Way

Covering the southwest corner of the country, the state of Baden-Württemberg is well connected by train, bus and autobahn. Trains run regularly and are your best option for getting around, and towns are best explored on foot.

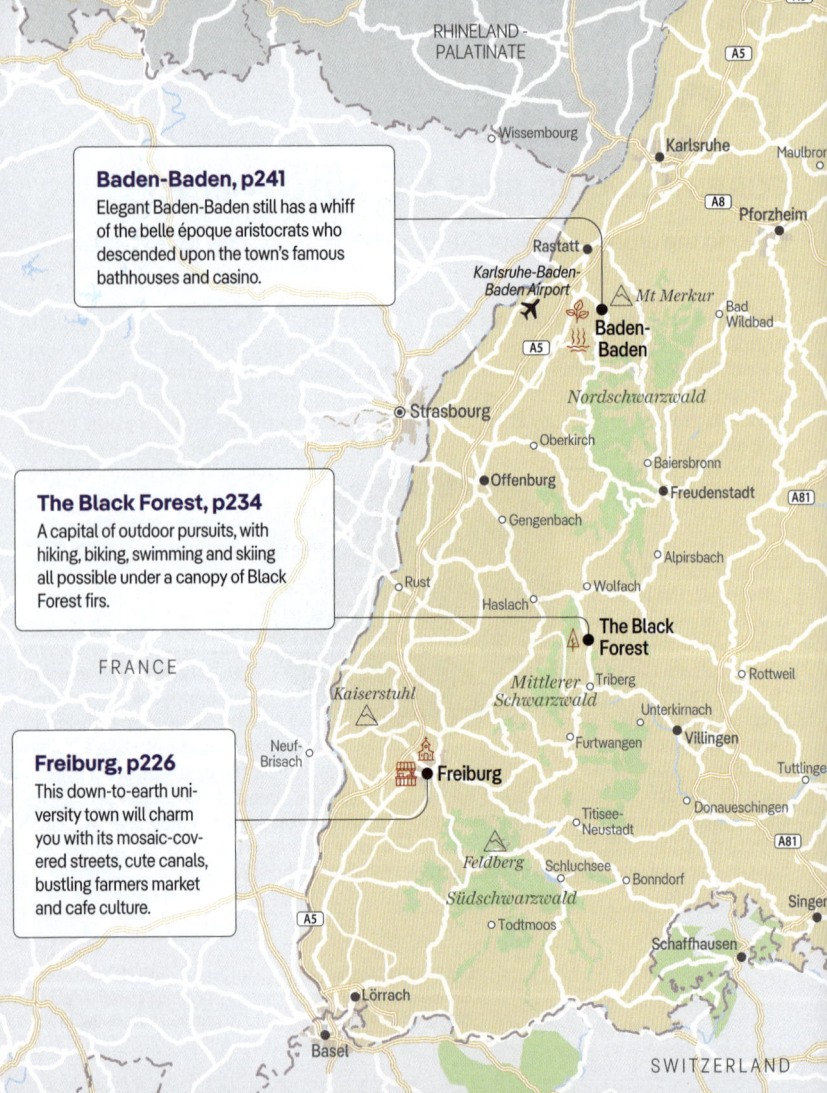

Baden-Baden, p241
Elegant Baden-Baden still has a whiff of the belle époque aristocrats who descended upon the town's famous bathhouses and casino.

The Black Forest, p234
A capital of outdoor pursuits, with hiking, biking, swimming and skiing all possible under a canopy of Black Forest firs.

Freiburg, p226
This down-to-earth university town will charm you with its mosaic-covered streets, cute canals, bustling farmers market and cafe culture.

Stuttgart, p214

While cars are likely what put Stuttgart on your radar, there's plenty more to discover in this Swabian city.

Ulm, p258

Set on the banks of the flowing Danube, Ulm is a hub for cyclists; visit its towering church and wander the charming Altstadt.

Lake Constance, p251

Cruise across the calm waters or cycle the shoreline, stopping in at medieval lakeside towns along this lake, which shares a border with Austria and Switzerland.

CAR

A car allows you to see more and do more. The autobahn connects the major cities, and small winding roads take you to picturesque villages, scenic viewpoints and lovely lakes.

TRAIN

Trains here are clean, fast and efficient. Not only are they the more sustainable choice, but trains also allow you to take the slow road and soak up the scenery along the way.

BICYCLE

Cyclists will find dedicated bike paths in even the smallest of towns. However, navigating long distances on two wheels may see you riding in the slip lane a fair bit. Bike routes such as the Lake Constance Cycle Path are good options.

Plan Your Time

Cities and villages, forests and valleys – it's all possible here. Plan ahead to ensure you get to taste all the flavours of the region.

Freiburg (p226)

If You Only Do One Thing

● It's a tough choice, but we'd probably recommend heading straight to **Freiburg** (p226). This lively university town in the far south is known as the 'Green City' thanks to its position in the middle of the Black Forest, as well as its sustainable credentials.

● Soak up the medieval **Altstadt** (p228), climb the towering **Freiburger Münster** (p229), eat your way around its daily **produce market** (p228) and sip local wine in the lively **bars** (p229). At sundown, venture uphill to take in the stunning views of downtown and the thick forest surrounds from the top of **Schlossberg** (p229).

Seasonal Highlights

The best time to visit is from April to June. Warmer days are perfect for hiking and cycling, and the tulips are blooming.

JANUARY
Fastnacht is celebrated a little differently in the Black Forest, with scary costumes and parades to expel bad winter spirits.

APRIL
Warm weather and blooming tulips bring locals out of hibernation to celebrate **Frühlingsfes** (p219), a spring beer festival in Stuttgart.

MAY
This is peak **Spargelzeit** (p233), the season when the beloved white asparagus pops up on menus everywhere.

A Long Weekend

● **Baden-Baden** (p241) is the ultimate destination for a luxurious long weekend. Arrive on a Friday and head straight to the **thermal spas** (p241) to get your mind and body into holiday mode.

● The next two days can then be spent wandering the town's wide boulevards, boutiques and museums, before enjoying a memorable dinner in one of the superb **gourmet restaurants** (p243). See out the weekend with a leisurely drive along the scenic **Black Forest High Road** (p248), travelling to **Freudenstadt** (p247) via **Mummelsee** (p248).

● If you're keen to explore a little further afield, border-hop via the train to **Strasbourg** (p246) and get a taste of France as you cruise along the waterways, wander through narrow cobbled streets and colourful half-timbered houses, and enjoy Alsatian cuisine.

A Weeklong Stay

● A weeklong road trip will give you enough time to cover the biggest hits of the south. Start your trip with a visit to Stuttgart's impressive **Porsche and Mercedes-Benz museums** (p214) before heading south to the **Black Forest** (p234).

● Base yourself in **Freiburg** (p226) and soak up the university town's youthful vibes and cafe culture, taking day trips to **Triberg** (p238), to see the thundering waterfalls and chirping cuckoo clocks, and **Todtnau** (p234), to fly down Germany's longest toboggan run. Take a day hike with a stop in a typical German **mountain hut for lunch** (p235).

● Then follow Lake Constance's shoreline from quaint **Meersburg** (p253) to lovely **Lindau** (p255), with a cruise across the lake to **Konstanz** (p251) to round out the week.

JULY
It's a non-stop party when the **Jazz Open** (p219) takes over Stuttgart, with international acts featuring over two big weeks.

SEPTEMBER
Rivalling Munich's Oktoberfest, Stuttgart's **Cannstatter Wasen** (p219) is a 17-day extravaganza of beer tents, carnival rides and Lederhosen.

OCTOBER
This is the perfect time for a wine hike as the vineyards change into a beautiful kaleidoscope of autumn colours across the region.

DECEMBER
Christmas markets (p225, 236) brighten up winter with a jumble of *Glühwein* (mulled wine) stands, craft stalls and gluttonous serves of food.

Stuttgart

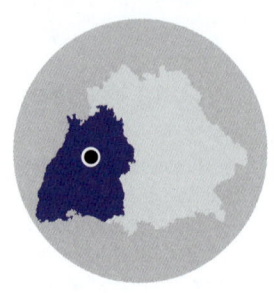

AUTOMOBILE HISTORY | WINE | CITY HIKES

GETTING AROUND

The train from the airport is easy and cheap, and only takes 30 minutes to reach the Hauptbahnhof. You don't need a car to get around Stuttgart and you probably won't want one, as parking can be tricky. Instead explore the city by foot, S-Bahn (train) and U-Bahn (tram). Get your tickets at ticket machines or download the DB or SSB app to purchase tickets online.

☑ TOP TIP

Grab a StuttCard for free entry to 30 attractions and discounts at over 20 more. Plus get unlimited travel on public transport if you choose the '+PT' version. It's great value, especially if you're planning on visiting both the Mercedes-Benz and Porsche Museum in one or two days.

Stuttgart often finds itself left off European itineraries, but this industrious southern German city, home to the hard-working Swabians, offers more than meets the eye, if you know where to look.

Transformed from a winegrowing capital to an industrial city in the 19th century, Stuttgart now has its roots firmly in the automobile industry. With Karl Benz and Gottlieb Daimler – the inventors of the modern automobile – hailing from here, and Ferdinand Porsche building his empire from a site in the city's north, it's a proud history that can be explored at two world-class car museums. Beyond the cars, you'll find a city that loves wine almost as much as beer, art and architecture, plus a basin topography that has created a system of hidden stairways leading to charming squares, hilltop beer gardens and stunning views.

Schedule a visit to the capital of Baden-Württemberg, then linger a little longer to get a taste of the Swabian countryside.

Rev Your Engines
Paradise for car lovers

There's nothing more synonymous with Stuttgart than Porsche. If you take a close look at the badge, you'll even see the name Stuttgart printed across its shield. The luxury car manufacturer still operates from its original site in Zuffenhausen, just 15 minutes out of town by train, and draws pilgrims from around the world to its dedicated **Porsche Museum** *(porsche.com/germany/aboutporsche/porschemuseum; adult/child €12/6)*. Alongside almost 100 Porsche vehicles on display, there are kids exhibits, a racing simulator and a comprehensive audio tour. If you've got cash to splash, you can even rent a Porsche for the day from the ticket desk.

Across town in Bad Cannstatt, the **Mercedes-Benz Museum** *(mercedes-benz.com/en/art-and-culture/museum; adult/child €16/8)* celebrates the evolution of the car over 135 years through the context of world history. From Gottlieb Daimler's first internal combustion engine to Bertha Benz'

STUTTGART

★ HIGHLIGHTS
1 Staatsgalerie

● SIGHTS
2 Eugensplatz
3 Fernsehturm
4 Grabkapelle auf dem Württemberg
5 Haus der Geschichte Baden-Württemberg
6 Karlshöhe
7 Landesmuseum Württemberg
8 Mercedes-Benz Museum
9 Neues Schloss
10 Porsche Museum
11 Rathaus
12 Schloss Solitude
13 Schweinemuseum
14 Stadtbibliothek
15 Stadtpalais
16 Weinbaumuseum
17 Weissenhof Estate

● ACTIVITIES
18 Stuttgarter Weinwanderweg

● SLEEPING
19 a&o Stuttgart City
20 Attimo Hotel Stuttgart
21 EmiLu Design Hotel
22 Hostel Alex 30
23 Maritim Hotel

● EATING
24 Brauhaus Schönbuch
25 Gasthaus Bären
26 Netzer
27 Ochs'n'Willi
28 Restaurant Tauberquelle

see 13 Schlachthof Stuttgart
29 The Nosh

● DRINKING & NIGHTLIFE
30 Biergarten im Schlossgarten
31 Misch Misch
32 Palast der Republik
33 TATTI
34 Tschechen & Söhne
35 Weingut Schwarz
36 Weinmanufaktur Untertürkheim

Staatsgalerie

BEST STUTTGART VIEWPOINTS

Eugensplatz: Grab an ice cream from **Eis Pinguin** and share the views with the scantily clad Galatea fountain.

Fernsehturm: The world's first TV tower delivers 360-degree views from the 153m-high observation platform. Head up just before sundown.

Stadtbibliothek: Enjoy impressive views of the futuristic interior from level 7, then head to the rooftop for city views.

Grabkapelle auf dem Württemberg: This burial chapel built to honour the young Queen Katharina is the ultimate spot for a romantic picnic thanks to its sweeping views over vine-covered hills.

Karlshöhe: Hidden atop the Oscar-Heiler-Staffel stairway you'll discover a laid-back beer garden with impressive downtown views.

history-making 104km long-distance road trip in 1888, through to the Silver Arrows sports car hall of fame, the collection is as impressive as it is vast. Other highlights include the Popemobile, the Mercedes-Benz once owned by Princess Diana and the world's most expensive car – the 300 SLR Uhlenhaut Coupé. The museum itself is an architectural marvel with its double-helix design, earning an entry in the Guinness World Records for the world's biggest artificial tornado – a feature in the atrium designed to quickly suck out smoke in case of fire.

The Cultural Mile

Art and architecture

Stuttgart's cultural mile runs along the main thoroughfare Hauptstatter Strasse and is home to many of the city's museums and galleries. Start at the **Haus der Geschichte Baden-Württemberg** *(History Museum of Baden-Württemberg; hdgbw.de; adult/child from €5/free)* to learn about 200 years of state history.

The **Stadtpalais** *(stadtpalais-stuttgart.de; free)* focuses on Stuttgart's history, with a huge collection of items and artefacts that seek to answer the question 'Who is Stuttgart?' It also has a free kids' construction playzone in the basement.

For art lovers, the **Staatsgalerie** *(staatsgalerie.de/en; adult/child from €10/free)* is a must-visit. This contemporary art gallery packs a punch, with modernist works by Monet and Picasso, and classics dating back to the 14th century. Entry is free on Wednesdays.

DRINKING IN STUTTGART: BEST COFFEE

Netzer: A popular brunch spot with healthy, vegan and gluten-free options and fantastic coffee. *8am-3pm Mon, & Wed-Fri, 9am-4pm Sat & Sun*

Misch Misch: Nestled among trendy cafes and bars on a bike highway, it serves strong coffee and snacks. *hours vary, closed Sun*

The Nosh: Fuel up with a coffee, then stroll Calwer Strasse, one of Stuttgart's most beautiful streets. *8am-10pm Mon-Fri, 9am-10.30pm Sat, to 4.30pm Sun*

TATTI: Artisanal coffee, yummy pastries and a large, sunny courtyard at this chic central spot. *7.30am-late Mon-Fri, hours vary Sat & Sun*

Further along, the **Rathaus** is an example of both brutalist and Art Deco architecture, and is home to one of Stuttgart's quirkiest secret treasures. The paternoster (vintage lift) operates on a continuous loop and there are no doors on the cabins, so you can just step in and out at the floor you need. Head through the Rathaus lobby to find it on the left. Visit on weekdays between 8am and 5pm.

Form Follows Function
Bauhaus beauty

While much of Stuttgart's city architecture is dominated by post-WWII brutalist buildings, a great example of Germany's Bauhaus movement, which eschewed ornament for blocky, functional forms, can be found in the **Weissenhof Estate** *(weissenhofmuseum.de; adult/child from €6.5/3)*. The exhibition homes were built in 1927 as prototypes for workers' housing. Eleven of the 21 buildings remain, and two designed by Le Corbusier have been awarded UNESCO World Heritage status in recognition of their contribution to modernism, and are open to the public.

Step Into History
Stories behind the sights

For a self-paced jaunt into Stuttgart's heart, download the Stuttgart tour on the **Lausch app** *(lauschtour.de)* and pop in your headphones for a free one-hour walking tour. This audioguided route takes you from Marktplatz, along the shopping street Königstrasse, and past the Altes Schloss and Neues Schloss, while delivering engaging stories about the famous landmarks and their rich history.

If you prefer an in-person guided tour, check out the tip-based **Can You Handle It walking tour** *(cyhitours.com)* led by engaging locals. Two-hour English language tours run on Saturdays and Sundays at 11am, and Mondays at 5pm. Highlights include a visit to the inner courtyard of the Altes Schloss (p219) and the Stauffenberg memorial dedicated to Claus von Stauffenberg and other members of the German resistance movement involved in the failed 20 July 1944 assassination attempt on Hitler.

King of the Castle
Kingdoms of the past

One of the few remaining 18th-century structures in town, **Neues Schloss** (New Palace) was restored to its former glory after a

---

WHY I LOVE STUTTGART

Kat Barber, Lonely Planet writer

I lived in Stuttgart for a number of years and it's certainly a city that grows on you the longer you spend here. At the beginning, I couldn't cope when everything was closed on Sundays, but I grew to love spending these days hiking or bike riding and capping it off with a drink in a leafy beer garden.

My three must-dos in Stuttgart are to take a ride in the vintage doorless lift in the Rathaus, check out the ultra-modern library and soak up the romantic views over the vines at the Grabkapelle auf dem Württemberg. And if you time it right, don't miss the Frühlingsfest beer festival in spring, Cannstatter Wasen in autumn and the enchanting Christmas markets in December.

🍸 DRINKING IN STUTTGART: BEST BEER GARDENS

Biergarten im Schlossgarten: This Schlossgarten parklands beer garden has cheap meals, a playground and live music on Sundays. *11am-11pm*

Tschechen & Söhne: Casual Karlshöhe spot serving beer, wine, coffee and snacks with impressive downtown views. *11am-midnight Apr-Oct in dry weather*

Palast der Republik: Don't let the fact that it used to be a public toilet put you off – there's no cooler place to grab a cheap beer. *11am-2am Mon-Sat, from 3pm Sun*

Schlachthof Stuttgart: Pause for a drink in this huge beer garden after a visit to the quirky Schweinemuseum. *noon-2.30pm & 5-11pm*

HIKE STUTTGART'S HIDDEN STAIRWAYS

This city hike covers seven of Stuttgart's most beautiful *Stäffele* stairways through charming districts with rewarding views.

START	END	LENGTH
Marienplatz	Santiago-de-Chile-Platz	4km; 1½ hrs

Originally built by vintners to access their hillside vines, today around 500 *Stäffele* provide fast access to upper suburbia. Starting at ❶ **Marienplatz**, stroll north, turning left at Arminstrasse, where you'll meet your first stairway, ❷ **Else-Himmelheber-Staffeln**.

At the top, head left until you reach ❸ **Friedrich-E-Vogt-Stäffele**. Climb past some of Stuttgart's most expensive Art Deco homes and leafy bourgeois villas. Take in the panoramic views before continuing in the same direction to ❹ **Oscar-Heiler-Staffel**. This short stairway will take you up to ❺ **Karlshöhe** (p216), a former quarry-turned-playground. Meander down Stuttgart's longest stairway, ❻ **Willy-Reichert-Staffel**, until you reach Tübinger Strasse.

Head back to Marienplatz and cross it to reach ❼ **Liststaffel**. March those tired legs to the top, turn left, then follow Zellerstrasse up until you get to Am Lehenweg. At the top you'll find ❽ **Fritz-Münch-Staffel**. Enjoy expansive views over the Alte Weinsteige (old vineyards) district.

Cross the road and join ❾ **Haigststaffel**. At the end, turn left and head uphill until you see the Weinsteige U-Bahn stop. Soak up the view from ❿ **Santiago-de-Chile-Platz**, before riding the tram back to the city centre.

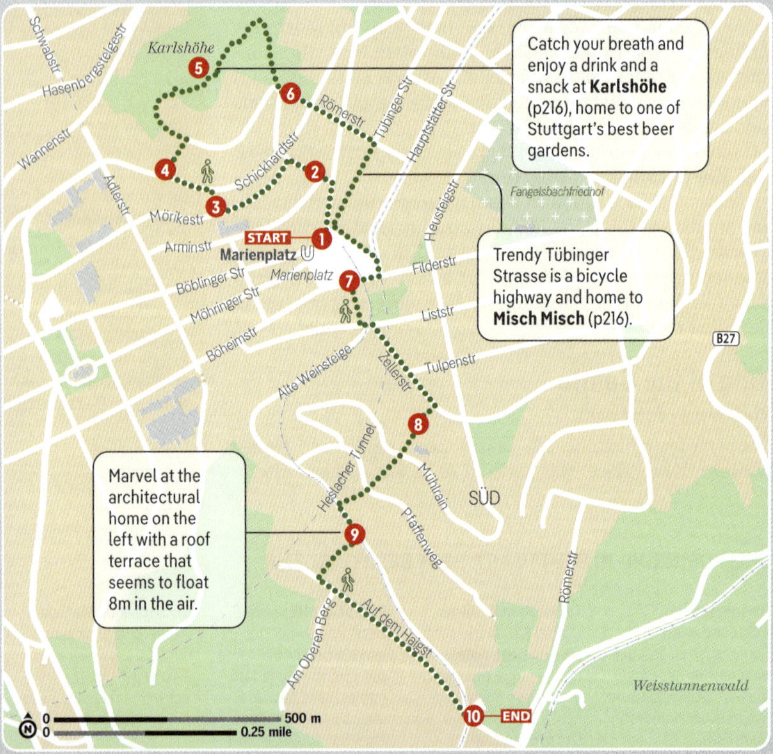

> Catch your breath and enjoy a drink and a snack at **Karlshöhe** (p216), home to one of Stuttgart's best beer gardens.

> Trendy Tübinger Strasse is a bicycle highway and home to **Misch Misch** (p216).

> Marvel at the architectural home on the left with a roof terrace that seems to float 8m in the air.

public referendum in 1957 narrowly rejected turning it into a hotel after it was badly damaged by WWII bombing. Flanking the entire length of the central Schlossplatz, the current state ministry office is unfortunately closed to visitors. Its predecessor, the nearby **Altes Schloss** (Old Palace), which was deemed too small in 1746 by the young Duke Carl Eugen of Württemberg, now houses the **Landesmuseum Württemberg** *(landesmuseum-stuttgart. de; adult/child €8/free)*, chronicling the cultural history of the region. Marvel at one of the world's most primitive instruments, a 35,000-year-old flute, or head underground to the royal crypt to learn about the legacy of the five royals buried here. You can visit the courtyard without a ticket and check out the stairway with shallow, wide steps built for horses to transport guests, and the rams that butt heads every hour atop the clocktower.

Located outside Stuttgart are the summer and winter residences of the old House of Württemberg (German royals who ruled the region from 1081 to 1918). These two baroque beauties impress with their history and architectural flourishes. On the western side of town, Duke Carl Eugen erected the **Schloss Solitude** *(schloss-solitude.de; adult/child €7/3.50)* in the late 1700s as a hunting lodge and status symbol. Its lavish interiors include the Weisse Sal, a white oval ballroom with a painted ceiling depicting allegorical figures. A 10km public pathway links it to Residenzschloss Ludwigsburg (p221), known as the Versailles of Swabia.

Time to Wine Down
Exploring the vineyards

In a hop-happy country, Stuttgart is especially proud of its viniculture. Vintners have been producing wine on the steep slopes encircling Stuttgart since the 12th century. Wine consumption here is twice as much per capita as any other part of Germany. Best known for producing light reds, the fruity Trollinger, crisp Lemberger and Spätburgunder (Pinot noir) dominate the 430 hectares of city vineyards today.

The 10km circular **Stuttgarter Weinwanderweg** is a great way to explore the city's vineyards on foot. Ride the train from town 15 minutes towards Obertürkheim train station, then follow the signs through the winegrowing village towards Uhlbach. Stop in at the **Weinbaumuseum** to learn more about local winegrowing and sample some local drops. The museum hosts wine-tasting events every Friday night, where a sommelier guides you through three local wines.

Continue up towards the Grabkapelle auf dem Württemberg (p216), the burial chapel built by King Wilhelm I von Württemberg in honour of his beloved wife Katharina, who died at just 30 years of age. The ornate sandstone temple is one of the best viewpoints in Stuttgart: from here, you can see just how much winegrowing still dominates the region.

Afterwards, meander through the vineyards once again towards Untertürkheim, where **Weinmanufaktur Untertürkheim** and **Weingut Schwarz** both make great options for a final wine tasting before heading back to the train thoroughly content.

FESTIVAL CITY

In April, locals come out of hibernation to celebrate **Frühlingsfest**, a joyful spring beer festival held over two long weeks in Bad Cannstatt. By the time summer rolls around, Stuttgart's events calendar is fully booked: the **Jazz Open**, **Winedorf**, **Hamburger Fischmarkt** and **Christopher Street Day** gay and lesbian parade take over the city. Rivalling Munich's Oktoberfest, the **Cannstatter Wasen** – 17 days of beer tents, music, carnival rides and Lederhosen-wearing revellers – is held in late September. And as winter sets in, the **Christmas markets** sprinkle joy right across the city throughout December.

WINEMAKING IN STUTTGART

Jack Murfett, local winemaker
wogv.de

Stuttgart has a rich history of winemaking. The centuries-old traditions still heavily influence the culture of the region. The cool climate, clay soil and steep basin topography create perfect growing conditions. Crisp white Riesling is a popular variety produced in the region. There's also Trollinger (a light red grape variety unique to the region), Pinot noir and Grauburgunder. A *Weinwanderung* (wine walk) is a great way to experience this culture. Many wine districts run scheduled walks throughout the year, or you can simply bring your own glass and wander through the vines and stop in at a *Weingut* (cellar door) for a tasting.

Weinmanufaktur Untertürkheim (p219)

Behind the Broom
Sweep into a Besenwirtschaft

Don't miss paying a visit to a *Besenwirtschaft* – a pop-up wine tavern. A special law allows small-batch wine producers to set up shop for up to 16 weeks a year in their homes, garages or barns to sell their latest harvest alongside simple home-cooked fare. The atmosphere is friendly and homey, with shared tables, generous pours and live music. Don't worry if you can't understand your new friends (most locals speak the Swabish dialect) – a smile and a *Prost!* (Cheers!) will do. A broom hung out the front signifies 'We're open'; otherwise plan your visit with the calendar at *besen-stuttgart.de/termine*.

Pig Out on Culture
50,000 pigs went to a museum

The quirky **Schweinemuseum** *(Pig Museum; schweinemuseum. de; adult/child €5.90/3)* is a collection of over 50,000 pig ornaments, decorations and toys, curated by passionate collector Erika Wilhelmer over more than 40 years. Housed in an old slaughterhouse, it's spread over two levels and features 27 themed rooms including pigs in mythology, pigs gambling and pigs in sexuality. Don't miss the final room dedicated to the collector to learn more about her eccentric life. The on-site restaurant and beer garden is also renowned for its suckling pig and pork knuckle.

EATING IN STUTTGART: SWABIAN FOOD

Gasthaus Bären: Try a bit of everything at this city restaurant dishing up Swabian tapas and delicious cocktails. *noon-midnight Mon-Sat* €€

Brauhaus Schönbuch: Enjoy a stein of the local brew alongside a plate of regional specialities in this huge, central brewery. *11am-midnight* €€

Ochs'n'Willi: A cosy tavern serving Swabian fare alongside German classics such as pork knuckle and schnitzel. *11.30am-10.30pm Sun-Thu, to 11.30pm Fri & Sat* €€

Restaurant Tauberquelle: With a heated rear courtyard, this tavern serves the classics and offers lunch specials weekdays. *11.30am-midnight Mon-Sat* €

Beyond Stuttgart

If Stuttgart's big-city vibes don't float your boat, its picture-perfect neighbours sure will.

Stuttgart's central position makes it the perfect jumping-off point for some of Germany's most beautiful small towns, with half-timbered houses and flower box–lined windows, winding cobblestone streets, hearty regional dishes and centuries-old traditions all waiting to be discovered.

Day trips to Esslingen, Ludwigsburg and Tübingen are made easy with train travel and offer a lovely respite from Stuttgart's hectic city environment. The mountain tops are covered with well-preserved neo-revival castles with equally impressive views, and there are endless hiking opportunities throughout the region. So whether you're into history, nature, architecture or food, it'll be worth your while spending a few days exploring this lesser-known German region.

Places
Ludwigsburg p221
Esslingen p221
Tübingen p222
Burg Hohenzollern p224
Schloss Lichtenstein p224
Metzingen p224
Bad Urach p225

Ludwigsburg
TIME FROM STUTTGART: **20 MINS** S
Baroque Ludwigsburg: the Swabian Versailles
Schloss Ludwigsburg (schloss-ludwigsburg.de; adult/child €10/5), a 452-room baroque palace, is the main attraction in this small town north of Stuttgart. Built by Duke Eberhard Ludwig in the early 18th century, the palace served as a secondary royal seat, and its construction saw the town of Ludwigsburg bloom around it. The capital of Württemberg swapped back and forth between Stuttgart and Ludwigsburg over the next century, and it was only in 1798 that Ludwigsburg settled into its 'summer residence' function.

Guided tours of the grandiose interior are offered in English twice a day between April and October.

The real highlight? The **pumpkin festival** held here every autumn, featuring pumpkin canoe races, pumpkin carving, pumpkin-weighing competitions and pumpkin dishes of every kind.

Esslingen
TIME FROM STUTTGART: **15 MINS** S
Alluring half-timbered village
Although it's just a quick S-Bahn ride away, you'll certainly notice the change of pace as you approach Esslingen's **Altstadt**. With a long history rooted in viticulture and trade, the town's centuries-old architecture was thankfully spared during WWII, attracting tourists today. On your walk in, gaze up at **Schelztor**, a gate tower from the 13th century that now

GETTING AROUND

The train is your best best for exploring the region beyond Stuttgart. Trains run from Stuttgart's Hauptbahnhof regularly and most towns can be reached in an hour or less. Check out multiday offers on bwtarif.info. When the city's new train station, project Stuttgart21, is completed in late 2026, the tracks will be brought underground, making travel through the region even quicker.

DECODING SWABIAN FOOD

Swabian food is simple, hearty and seasonal. Look out for these typical dishes.

Maultaschen: These meat-filled pasta pockets are like giant ravioli. They are served fried or in a broth, and typically filled with pork and onions or spinach.

Käsespätzle: A German version of mac and cheese, these thick, doughy noodles are topped with cheese and caramelised onions and baked in the oven.

Zwiebelrostbraten: A large piece of roast beef served with a rich caramelised onion gravy and *Spätzle* (egg noodles) or potatoes.

Linsen & Spätzle: A simple winter warmer: boiled lentils served over *Spätzle* alongside two long sausages.

Butterbretzel: A pretzel with butter slathered on it. Simple. Delicious.

holds up the *Skywalker* sculpture, one of the most famous images of the city.

Esslingen lays claim to Germany's oldest half-timbered house, dating back to 1267, at Webergasse 8, plus the oldest row of half-timbered houses (1328–31) at Hafenmarkt 4–10, as well as the oldest sparkling-wine producer, Kessler Sekt, established here in 1826.

When the hunger pains kick in, get off the main drag and relax at one of the cute cafes on Unterer Metzgerbach or along 'Little Venice' – the small canals running along the Altstadt.

Esslingen's defender

Perched above the town, **Esslinger Burg** never served as a royal residence, but was used to defend the town from attacks. A short but steep walk up through the vineyards will take you to the main gun tower and from here you can visit the castle gardens. Follow the covered fortified wall on the way down as you take in stunning views over the town, its church spires and vine-covered hills.

Saddle up

Follow the Neckar River along the **Neckar Cycle Path** from Stuttgart to Esslingen. This 17km stretch is fairly flat and wide, making it ideal for cyclists of all levels. The path winds through picturesque landscapes, including vineyards and historic towns, away from busy roads. There are city bikes docks all around Stuttgart; download the RegioRadStuttgart app to rent one. If you don't feel like riding back, you can take your bike on the train: just remember to pay for a bike ticket too.

Tübingen

TIME FROM STUTTGART: **50 MINS**

Tübingen for young and old

Tübingen's colourful half-timbered houses, bustling Marktplatz, canal-lined cobbled streets, overflowing floral baskets and Stocherkähne canoes punting silently up and down the Neckar river are straight out of a fairy tale. It also has an incredibly rich history, first mentioned in 1078. The ornately decorated **Rathaus** dates back to 1435, and its astronomical clock tracking the moon, sun and zodiac was added in 1511. Combined with its numerous pavement cafes, bars and boutiques, it's easy to see why Tübingen is considered one of Germany's most beautiful towns.

With a prestigious university drawing thousands of students

EATING IN LUDWIGSBURG: OUR PICKS

Wok on Fire: Decent Asian dishes with vegan options at reasonable prices located on the Marktplatz. The pad thai is a crowd favourite. *11am-10pm* €

Blauer Engel: A popular gastropub dishing up generously portioned German fare, with a huge alfresco area. *10am-11pm Sun-Thu, to 1am Fri & Sat* €€

Die Blaue Agave: A vibrant Mexican restaurant with delicious cocktails and guacamole near the train station. *5pm-midnight Sun-Thu, to 2am Fri & Sat* €€

Cafe Soufflé: Japanese-inspired cafe behind the Marktplatz serving healthy brunches and artisanal coffees. *8.30am-9pm Tue-Sat, 9.30am-9pm Sun* €

Tübingen

to study here, it's often been said, 'Tübingen doesn't have a university; Tübingen is a university'.

The university lays claim to no fewer than nine Nobel laureates, as well as scientific breakthroughs including the discovery of DNA. Explore some of these discoveries at the museum of the **Schloss Hohentübingen** (*unimuseum.uni-tuebingen.de; adult/child €5/3*), which also hosts the **Museum Alte Kulturen** (Ancient Culture Museum), with the world's oldest musical instrument and largest wine barrel (it can hold an impressive 84,000L).

Step through history

As part of Germany's dedication to honouring the victims of the Nazi regime through education, **Der Geschichtspfad zum Nationalsozialismus** (The History Path to National Socialism) is a 16-stop walking tour that recognises major sites of the victims and perpetrators of the Holocaust. The signage boards are in German, but you can scan the QR code to get the English version or you can pick up a map from the tourist office.

You can also sign up for English-language **walking tours** at the Tübingen tourist office on Saturdays at 11am from April to October.

HALF-TIMBERED HOUSES

A beloved feature throughout Germany, half-timbered houses *(Fachwerk)* have striking wooden beams and colourful clay or brick inlay. This building method is extremely ecological, economical and aesthetically pleasing. While the architectural style was used in other countries, it was nowhere near as prolific as it was in Germany, where around 2.5 million half-timbered houses exist. Today, their kaleidoscope of colourful facades and wonky frames make for stunning photos.

If you're a fan of the architectural style, the **Deutsche Fachwerkstrasse** *(deutsche-fachwerk strasse.de)* is a 3000km multisection route that passes by some of the best half-timbered villages across the country, each with their own distinctive style.

EATING & DRINKING IN ESSLINGEN: OUR PICKS

Cafe Findelkind: A cosy cafe serving delicious waffles, brunch bowls and artisanal coffee. *9am-5pm, from 10am Sun* €

L'Osteria: Offering one of the best views over the canals, this Italian chain serves huge pizzas and lunch specials. *11.30am-11pm* €€

Weinkeller Einhorn: This cavernous tavern dishes up tasty Swabian dishes and local wine and beer in its cellar. *11.30am-2pm & 5-11pm Tue-Sat* €€

Kessler Sekt: Don't miss taking a sip of Kessler Sekt, Germany's oldest sparkling wine, at its very own bar. *11.30am-8pm Tue-Fri, from 10am Sat* €

Burg Hohenzollern

TIME FROM STUTTGART: **1 HR**

Adventures in castle land

Burg Hohenzollern *(burg-hohenzollern.com/de; adult/child €26/14)* is the ancestral seat of the House of Hohenzollern, the former German royal dynasty that ruled until Emperor Wilhelm II renounced the throne in 1918 at the end of WWI. The current castle is the third iteration to have stood on the site, and was built between 1846 and 1867. While it has never been permanently occupied by members of the royal family, it was extravagantly decorated as befitting royalty in the 19th century. Just 30km south of Stuttgart, it's an easy day trip by car or train. After a 15-minute walk up from the car park, or a five-minute ride on the free shuttle bus, you'll reach the castle drawbridge and its dramatic winding bastion. After marvelling at the sweeping views, enter the main square, where you can tour the treasure trove of family jewels, swords and armour, the underground casemates, the king and queen's private chambers, and the ornate library and halls. And keep an eye out for the 'Lady in White', a ghost rumoured to be haunting the halls after murdering her children in a desperate act of love.

Schloss Lichtenstein

TIME FROM STUTTGART: **50 MINS**

Castle hopping

Schloss Lichtenstein *(schloss-lichtenstein.de; adult €5-14, child €3-8)* is a neo-Gothic private castle built in 1840. Commonly known as Cinderella's Castle, it's delicately perched on the edge of an escarpment above the Echaz valley. Built by Count Wilhelm of Württemberg, Duke of Urach, the private castle's Gothic-revival turrets and drawbridges pay homage to the Middle Ages. Today, it is still privately owned by Count Wilhelm's great-grandchildren, and visitors can tour the gardens or join a 30-minute guided tour through some of the castle rooms.

Metzingen

TIME FROM STUTTGART: **1 HR**

Bargain hunting

Outletcity Metzingen *(outletcity.com/en/metzingen)* is Europe's largest outlet mall, with more than 150 premium and luxury brands including Burberry, Nike, Gucci and BOSS offering huge discounts on clothes, shoes and accessories. It's a sprawling space that dominates the small village of

---

TÜBINGEN'S WACKY BOAT RACE

The **Stocherkahnrennen**, Tübingen's traditional punting-boat race, is a hilariously colourful day hosted each year in May or June (it's held on the Feast of Corpus Christi) by student fraternities. The event has grown since 1956 and now draws thousands of spectators who flank the river to watch the spectacle.

Over 40 teams dress in outrageous costumes as they race down the Neckar, navigating tricky turns and a chaotic ducking obstacle. The losing team is punished with skolling half a litre of cod oil and given the arduous task of organising the following year's event, while winners enjoy a keg of beer and a trophy. It's Tübingen at its quirky, youthful best.

 DRINKING IN TÜBINGEN: BEST COFFEE

Cafe Hanseatica: 'Hanse' is a beloved local haunt that's been serving a large selection of coffee, tea and pastries for over 60 years. *8am-6.30pm Mon-Sat*

SUEDHANG: A speciality third-wave coffee roastery with cosy bay-window seats and a laid-back Scandi vibe. *8am-6pm Mon-Fri, from 9am Sat, from 10am Sun*

Katesch: Great coffee, cake and epic brunches at student prices make this place a winner. *9am-4pm Mon-Sat*

GenussArt: South of town near the train station, this good-value brunch spot has great coffee and weekly specials. *8.30am-6pm Mon-Fri, from 10am Sat & Sun*

Schloss Lichtenstein

Metzingen, just under an hour south of Stuttgart. Plenty of parking is available on-site, or you can catch the train or dedicated shuttle bus from Stuttgart Airport or Hauptbahnhof on Mondays, Thursdays, Fridays and Saturdays.

Bad Urach

TIME FROM STUTTGART: **40 MINS**

Chasing waterfalls

The easy (but slippery) **Wasserfallsteig** in the spa town of Bad Urach takes you from the picturesque town square to the top of its 37m-high **waterfall**.

Once out of town, the trail follows a gentle stream through lush meadows and woodlands, leading to the base of the 37m-high cascade. The initial path is flat and family-friendly, making it suitable for all ages and even strollers. For more of a challenge, continue up a series of steps alongside the waterfall for panoramic views from the top. The total hike is around 5.7km and takes about two hours to complete. The trail is open year-round, and is especially charming in winter, when icicles form in the cascades.

Soak it up

Unwind in Bad Urach's **AlbThermen** *(albthermen.com; from €14.90)*, a thermal spa complex fed by mineral-rich waters from 770m underground. The spa features six indoor and outdoor pools with temperatures ranging from 32°C to 38°C, and entry is for those eight years and above. Swim in the pools, relax on bubble loungers or soothe tired muscles on the jets. There is also a number of clothing-free saunas.

BEST CHRISTMAS MARKETS AROUND STUTTGART

Esslingen: A unique medieval Christmas market where traders in costume sell traditional handicrafts under candlelight.

Ludwigsburg: Illuminated golden angel wings and charming wooden chalet stalls in Ludwigsburg's Marktplatz.

Tübingen: Held over one long weekend in mid-December with over 300 twinkling stalls selling handmade items.

Burg Hohenzollern: From late November, the Royal Winter Magic Festival brightens the castle with illuminations and elaborate decorations.

Stuttgart: Glühwein stalls, craft and toy stands, an ice skating rink and miniature train rides.

THE FESTIVE SPIRIT

Can't get enough of the Christmas markets? Check out Strasbourg, the **Capital of Christmas** (p247), and the **Black Forest's best Christmas markets** (p236).

Freiburg

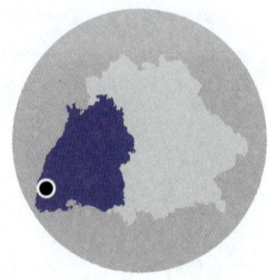

WALKABLE OLD TOWN | CUTE CANALS | GREEN CITY

GETTING AROUND

Freiburg is an extremely walkable city, so the only reason you'd need a car is if you plan on exploring the Black Forest from here. Pick up a €27 three-day WelcomeCard from the **Freiburg Tourist Office**, which gets you unlimited travel on the bus, train and cable-car network, as well as entry to all city museums. Or better yet, explore this bicycle-friendly city on two wheels.

Nestled near the border of Switzerland, France and Germany, and surrounded by the intensity of the Black Forest, this sunny city in the southwest celebrated its 900th birthday in 2020. There's a certain vibe in Freiburg that's hard to capture with words. Is it the youthful energy from the large student population? The international joie de vivre filtering in from its neighbours? Its reputation as a green destination in both sustainability and landscape, or its centuries old Bächle, the flowing water canals running along every street? Whatever it is, it's a feeling you won't find anywhere else in Germany. In fact, it was this youthful, relaxed vibe and pioneering environmental movement that earned Freiburg a spot on our *Best in Travel* list in 2022. Discover this down-to-earth beauty for yourself, but be careful not to set foot in its waters, as legend has it you may never want to leave.

Green City Freiburg

On the road to sustainability

Freiburg's sustainable roots can be traced back to 1975 when thousands of protestors successfully halted the construction of the proposed Wyhl nuclear power plant, just 30km north of Freiburg. This citizen-led activism flourished into a green movement, which today sees Freiburg as a world-leading 'green city'.

The district of **Vauban** is a great example of an intentionally planned sustainable community. Residents here are famously more green, more alternative and more social than elsewhere in the city. Civic involvement goes hand in hand with 'collective building' – where citizens buy a piece of land and share the building and development costs together. Houses are low-energy and solar-powered, food-sharing pantries and co-op supermarkets are common, and bicycles are favoured over cars.

With 400km of bike paths and twice as many bikes as cars, Freiburg is a cyclist's paradise. Rent a city 'Frelo' bike and pedal along the FR1, a dedicated bike highway that follows

☑ TOP TIP

Visiting in summer? Do as the locals do: grab a bottle of wine, gather some friends, and find a spot along the charming Bächle city canals. Kick off your shoes, dip your toes in the cool water, and soak up the laid-back, sun-soaked vibe that defines the city in warmer months.

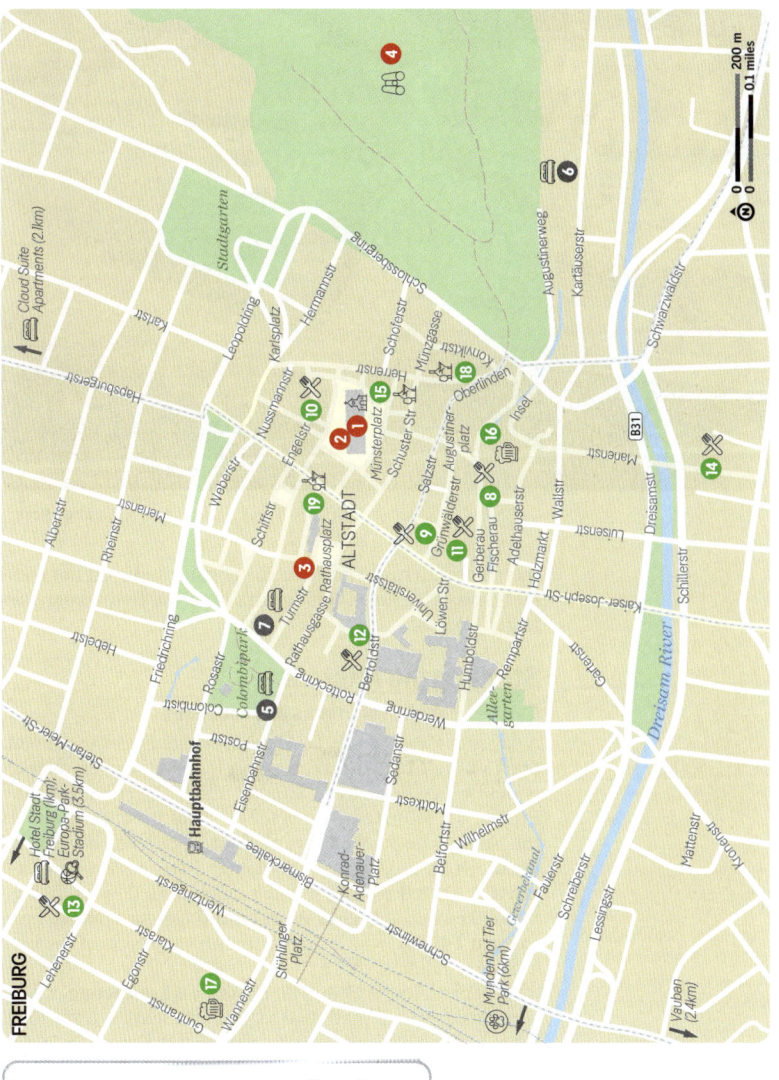

FREIBURG

SIGHTS
1. Freiburger Münster
2. Marktplatz
3. Rathaus
4. Schlossberg

SLEEPING
5. Best Western Premier Hotel Victoria
6. Black Forest Hostel
7. Colombi Hotel

EATING
8. Adelhaus
9. Grosser Meyerhof
10. Heiliggeist
11. Marktplatz Stüble
see 11 Martin's Bräu
12. Schmidt
13. Walee
14. Zuka Solicafe

DRINKING & NIGHTLIFE
15. Alte Wache
16. Hausbrauerei Feierling
17. Heimliche Kneipe
18. Rädle Feine Kost
19. SKAJO

INFORMATION
see 3 Freiburg Tourist Office

Lange Rote

the Dreisam river. The river is the place to be on hot summer days, with large boulders inviting you to dip your toes in and cool off.

Strolling the Altstadt

Canals, mosaics, churches and sausages

A day spent wandering the Altstadt brings a week of content. Start at the **Marktplatz**, where a bustling farmers market is held every day except Sunday under the shadow of the Freiburger Münster. Restricted to local producers, this is the place to stock up on organic fruit, vegetables, cheese and bread. Don't miss sampling a Lange Rote, a 35cm-long red sausage, served with or without onions and doused in mustard or ketchup at **Lichts Wurststand**. Vegetarians can head to **Tofu Taifun**, which serves up its own version of the long sausage – made of tofu.

The longest line is always for **Stefan's Käsekuchen**, a local cheesecake vendor that's had a spot at the market since 2002. From humble beginnings, it's earned a cult following far beyond Freiburg and often sells out before noon. If you do miss out, there's a 24/7 cheesecake vending machine at the Freiburg Hauptbahnhof.

 EATING IN FREIBURG: LOCAL CUISINE

Grosser Meyerhof: This tavern in the Altstadt specialises in local Badish dishes such as *Maultaschen, Leberwurst* and *Schäufele*. *11.30am-11pm* €€

Heiliggeist Stüble: Dine on local specialities with the sound of church bells filling the air at this stylish tavern under the Münster. *11.30am-11pm* €€

Martin's Bräu: Homebrewed ales and meaty snacks such as ox-tongue salad, bratwurst and pork knuckle. *11am-11pm Sun-Thu, to midnight Fri & Sat* €€

Schmidt: This is the best place to enjoy a fluffy, rich Black Forest cake and coffee. A big breakfast menu too. *9am-6pm Mon-Sat* €

Before you leave, pick up sunset picnic supplies: perhaps a locally produced Riesling or Prosecco, or swing past **Alles Käs** stand to try a Hübschentäler Bergkäse, an intense Valley Mountain Cheese produced 40km away in Hübschental.

Work off the cake by climbing the 333 spiral steps of the lacy spire of **Freiburger Münster**. From here you'll be rewarded with views of the red tiled rooftops and surrounding forested hills. Remarkably, the church was spared from any major damage during WWII, and has witnessed over 800 years of history. Its soft sandstone bricks are in constant need of maintenance, so expect to see the church with scaffolding cladding on at least one of its sides. In fact, the only time the scaffolding came down was when Pope Benedict XVI came to town in 2011.

As you're wandering around, don't forget to look down. Mosaics made from coloured stone from the Rhine have decorated the city's streets since the 19th century. They often depict business emblems or cultural motifs, so you might find a pretzel at the entrance to a bakery. Don't miss paying a visit to the **Rathaus**, where you'll find the coats of arms of Freiburg's 12 sister cities at the entrance.

Sunsets at Schlossberg
Hip hilltop hangout

There's no better spot to take in Freiburg's warmth than from the top of forested **Schlossberg** – although it's more of a hill than a mountain. The walk starts at Schwabentor and is a gentle 30-minute uphill climb, or you can take the easy option and ride the Schlossberg cable car from downtown.

As the sun goes down, the hill swarms with couples and groups of friends soaking up the last rays of the day. Join them with a beer under the chestnut trees in the beer garden, or check out the views from the 360-degree viewing tower.

Catch a Match
Cheer on SC Freiburg

If you time it right and you're in town when football (soccer) club SC Freiburg has a home game at **Europa-Park-Stadium**, try to snag tickets. This proud club has a very passionate supporter base, and is currently playing in the Bundesliga (Germany's top football league). If you miss out on tickets, don a red scarf and head along to sports pub **Heimliche Kneipe** to watch a game with local fans.

A FREIBURG LOCAL'S FAVOURITES

Lena Hug A local photographer shares her most beautiful streets in Freiburg. @freiburg.streets

Konviktstrasse: A very photogenic street in the city centre with boutiques and concept stores.

Adelhauser Klosterplatz: A beautiful oasis of calm in the bustling city centre.

Schneckenvorstadt: The area known as Little Venice is beautiful and the pretty, narrow cobblestone streets are filled with wonderful small cafes and shops.

Buttergasse: I love taking photos on this small street with a view of the Münster. It has a cool vintage sign from one of Freiburg's oldest shops, Rapp.

Wilhelmstrasse: There's always something interesting to capture. Plus, the cafe Wilhelm Moltke makes excellent coffee.

 DRINKING IN FREIBURG: OUR PICKS

| **Rädle Feine Kost**: In warm weather, dip your toes in the canal as you sip on a wine and nibble on cheese. *11am-6pm Wed & Thu, to 7.30pm Sat & Sun* | **Hausbrauerei Feierling**: A proudly local brewery serving snacks in the beer garden in summer and hearty meals in winter. *11am-midnight* | **SKAJO**: A bar and restaurant slinging delicious cocktails, with a chic rooftop terrace overlooking the city. *11am-10pm Mon-Thu, to midnight Fri & Sat* | **Alte Wache**: A popular wine bar in the shadow of the Münster. In summer, try the speciality 'Kalte Sophie', an ice slushy wine. *10am-9pm Mon-Sat* |

WHAT ARE THE BÄCHLE?

Running along the streets of the Altstadt, the *Bächle* water canals are as iconic for Freiburg as the Münster spire. They used to serve as canals for firefighting in the Middle Ages, when most homes were made of wood and fires were a common occurrence. Today, you'll likely find kids tugging sailboats along them, dogs taking a refreshing drink, or locals dipping their toes in over afternoon drinks. Two full-time *Bächle* cleaners have the important job of keeping the canals free of rubbish and debris year-round.

Watch your step: according to the local legend, if you set foot in a canal, may never leave.

Europa-Park-Stadium (p229)

The 37,000-seat stadium has impressive eco-credentials: it's decked out with enough solar panels to provide all the energy required to heat the stadium, as well as thousands of bike-parking spots and e-vehicle charging, with the aim of becoming climate neutral in the near future. It became the men's team's home ground in 2021, after it outgrew the beloved Dreisamstadion, which was infamous for its short, sloping pitch. Dreisamstadion is now home to the SC Freiburg women's team.

Paws & Claws

Explore Freiburg's free zoo

Mundenhof Tier Park (*mundenhof.de; free*) is just a short bike or tram ride out of town and has over 30 species of domestic and farm animals from around the world across its 38 hectares. Meet camels, yaks, llamas, meerkats, gibbons and bears, explore the aquarium housing both saltwater and freshwater species, and visit the bird aviary. You can join the keepers on their daily feeding round from March to October at 2.30pm every day except Fridays. Best of all, it's open daily and always free of charge. There are a number of playgrounds, several snack kiosks and a restaurant too.

EATING IN FREIBURG: BEST VEGETARIAN EATS

Adelhaus: A buffet-style vegetarian restaurant offering a huge selection of salads, dips, soups and curries. *11am-5pm Mon-Thu, to 10pm Sat & Sun* €€

Zuka Solicafe: Enjoy a vegetarian meal prepared by refugees on a pay-as-you-can basis on weekdays at this social enterprise. *noon-2pm Mon-Fri* €

Walee: One of the best falafel joints in town, this stand on Agnesenstrasse serves up cheap and filling falafel wraps and burgers. *10am-8pm Mon-Sat* €

Markthalle: You'll be spoilt for choice here with an array of international food stands and bars inside a covered market. *8am-8pm Mon-Thu, to midnight Fri & Sat* €€

Beyond Freiburg

Freiburg is known as the gateway to the Black Forest and with just one step outside the city, you'll find yourself surrounded by greenery.

The winters here are mild and sunny days plentiful, so whether you're looking for thrills or chills, fun in the sun or snowy escapades, you're in the right place. The mountains and lakes around the city offer a wide range of activities year-round, and cosy taverns are the best place to try regional dishes and local produce. Thrill-seekers young and old will feel at home at the Europa Park theme park and its waterpark Rulantica, both just a short drive away. An easy trip from the city centre, Schauinsland is Freiburg's tallest peak and offers epic views. So if you're pressed for time, these day trips from Freiburg will give you a taste of the Black Forest without having to repack your suitcase.

Europa-Park

TIME FROM FREIBURG: **30 MINS**

Get your pulse racing

Europa-Park *(europapark.de; adult/child from €52/44)* is one of Europe's biggest and best theme parks, located in the border town of Rust. With 13 high-adrenaline roller-coasters, shows running all day and a huge fairy tale children's world for the littlest adventurers, you can easily spend a whole day here and not see it all. The Icelandic-themed Blue Fire Megacoaster blasts you from 0 to 100km/h in just 2.5 seconds, while crowd-favourite Silver Star delivers enormous G-force as it shoots down from 73m high. Many attractions offer fast-track single-rider lines and child-swapping queues for parents.

For those who prefer to stay at ground level, you can wander the 16 authentically designed regions inspired by different European countries, which are a sight unto themselves. You can get a croissant in a Parisian brasserie, Nordic smoked salmon or a gyros in a Greek taverna.

If you've got anything left in the tank, **Rulantica** *(europapark. de/en/rulantica; adult/child €39/36.50)* is Europa-Park's dedicated waterpark, situated just across the road. It's vast, loud and hot inside, purposely designed so it can remain open year-round. Highlights include a family-friendly tubing river, 17 high-speed waterslides (including the vertical free-fall Vildfål for the brave), a wave pool, swim-up bars, fast-food restaurants and plenty of cabanas and loungers.

Places

Europa-Park p231
Schauinsland p232
Ravennaschlucht p232

GETTING AROUND

Exploring Freiburg's immediate surrounds is fairly easy using the well-connected train, tram and bus network. If you want to explore some of the smaller villages around Freiburg, considering renting a bicycle and exploring at your leisure. With thousands of kilometres of bike paths it's a great way to get around.

Stay in one of the themed hotels to get discounted entry tickets and early access to both parks.

Schauinsland

TIME FROM FREIBURG: **30 MINS**

Freiburg's highest point

Soar high in Germany's longest loop cable car, the **Schauinslandbahn**, to the top of this former silver mine. It reaches an elevation of 1284m in 20 minutes, so you'll have plenty of time to take in the views and plan your day. The main attractions of **Schauinsland Peak** (meaning 'look into the country') are the sweeping views and the walking and cycling trails. From the top of the viewing tower you can see the Vosges mountain range in France, the depths of the Black Forest and the peaks of the Swiss Alps on a clear day.

If you're up for an adventure, try out Europe's longest **scooter track**. Book at *schauinsland.de/rollerstrecke* and bounce down 8km of off-road track through coniferous forest on two wheels. Scooter rental and protective gear are included in the booking fee, and closed-toe shoes and long pants and sleeves are required. Open Sundays and public holidays in May and June, and Saturdays from July to October.

It's also a popular year-round hiking region, and in winter attracts cross-country skiers to its glistening ski trails and toboggan runs. If you've ever wanted to try snowshoeing, this is the place to give it a go. Half-day guided tours are bookable at *schauinslandbahn.de* and include snowshoe rental, cable-car tickets and some heartwarming schnapps and tea.

Magical family fun

Buried deep in the forest just 7km from Schauinsland, nature-based **Steinwasen Park** *(steinwasen-park.de; adult/child €28/24)* is a big hit with families. Follow a walking trail through animal enclosures with wild boar, ibex and marmots. Or take in the views from the 218m-long suspension bridge. It's also got a chair lift, rides galore, and a toboggan run to keep the young and young-at-heart entertained all day. Open daily from early April to early November.

Ravennaschlucht

TIME FROM FREIBURG: **35 MINS**

Scenic hikes in deep canyons

Melting ice from the end of the last Ice Age helped carve out numerous steep gorges in the region. These lush gorges are abundant with flora and fauna and offer unforgettable hiking

BEST SWIMMING SPOTS NEAR FREIBURG

Dreisam River: The shallow Dreisam river is the perfect spot to dip your toes into the cool water. You'll find locals reading, picnicking and relaxing on the boulders all along the river's length.

Panorama-Freibad Glottertal: Framed by tall forest trees, this is one of the region's most beautiful outdoor swimming pools.

Opfinger See: Two neighbouring lakes offer refreshing water, spacious lawns, BBQs and kiosks, and are easily accessible by bus from Freiburg.

Tunisee: Ever wanted to try water-skiing or wakeboarding? You can at the Tunisee wake park.

Keidel Mineral-Thermalbad: Unwind in the warm waters at this large thermal bath, with both indoor and outdoor pools.

EATING BEYOND FREIBURG: OUR PICKS

Die Bergstation: This restaurant atop Schauinsland whips up a fantastic brunch platter on a terrace with stunning panoramic views. *9.30am-5pm* €€

Gaststätte Griestal-Strausse: Try seasonal ingredients such as white asparagus at this tavern in wine village Tuniberg. *5-11.30pm Mon-Sat, from noon Sun* €€

Das Blümchen Restaurant: Enjoy Black Forest cuisine with a twist, with a menu of delicious tapas-style dishes. *5-11pm daily, noon-3pm Sat & Sun* €€€

Sonne: Treat yourself to classic, regional cuisine at this eco-friendly farm-to-table restaurant and hotel in Sankt Peter. *noon-2pm & 6-8.30pm* €€€

Ravenna Viaduct

opportunities. **Ravennaschlucht** is a narrow gorge cutting its way through mossy overgrowth and waterfalls in the Hollental valley, just 30 minutes from Freiburg by car. Step under the impressive towering arches of the Ravenna Viaduct at the trailhead, then follow the winding path, narrow bridges and steep steps along its 3km length

Slightly further afield, a one-hour drive east from Freiburg, **Wutachschlucht** is one of the most popular hikes in the central Black Forest. The craggy canyons, original forests, fossils and a large native butterfly population create a truly unique landscape. As it's an out-and-back trail, a shuttle bus takes hikers back to the parking area between April and October.

SPARGELZEIT

It might sound crazy that the humble asparagus has its own season, called *Spargelzeit*, but in Germany this vegetable has developed something of a cult status. The white variety, known as *Spargel*, has a short growing season from mid-April to late June, making it even more sought-after.

During *Spargelzeit* expect to see asparagus on menus, supermarket shelves and at roadside stalls everywhere. The best *Spargel* stems are firm yet plump, and have a lovely velvety sheen and an intact tip.

In the asparagus strongholds around Freiburg, they are often served with *Kratzete* (pancake strips) or simply with ham, hollandaise sauce and potatoes, so as not to overwhelm the delicate flavour.

The Black Forest

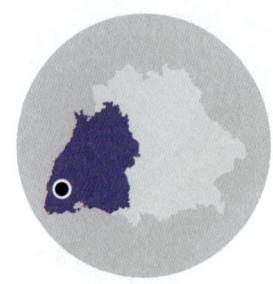

HIKING | LAKES | SNOWFIELDS

Places
Todtnau p234
Bernau p236
Feldberg p237
Titisee p237
Schluchsee p237
Triberg p238
Wolfach p239
Black Forest National Park p239

GETTING AROUND

To explore the Black Forest's nooks and crannies, a car will be helpful. The main towns are well connected by train, but the sheer size of the Black Forest means getting around will not be linear. Check timetables ahead of time as some smaller towns are not regularly serviced. The Konus card (offered to all visitors staying in hotels in the region) gives you access to free public transport across the entire Black Forest.

The Black Forest (Schwarzwald) is a sprawling mass of spruce trees, tight-knit villages and pocket-sized lakes, stretching 160km from top to bottom. It's a place that both adventure seekers and slow travellers will be captivated by, and with plenty to keep the kids entertained, it's also a great place for an outdoor family holiday. The name itself casts a mysterious spell over the region, and you wouldn't be blamed for expecting to see a wicked witch straight out of a Brothers Grimm fairy tale cackling in the sky. But with one step into the undergrowth, you'll soon discover the only mystery here is how they make such a delicious cake. Sure, check out the giant cuckoo clocks and misty waterfalls, but don't miss the chance to hit the trails and explore some off-the-radar corners to get a complete picture of this enchanting neck of the woods. A word of warning: the weather changes very quickly here, so check the weather forecast each day and pack accordingly. A waterproof jacket and boots will be your best friend.

Todtnau

TIME FROM FREIBURG: **35 MINS**

Swing through the trees

The **Blackforestline suspension bridge** *(blackforestline.de; adult/child €12/9)* in Todtnau is an exhilarating experience, stretching 450m over the dense forest and soaring 120m off the ground. Opened in 2023, this engineering marvel gives you a bird's-eye view of the **Todtnauer Wasserfall** below. As sturdy as it is, be prepared for some sway as you cross. A combined ticket gets you entry into both the bridge and the waterfall, with a 2.4km circular walk connecting the two. The spectacular waterfall tumbles 97m over multiple tiers, making it one of the highest natural waterfalls in Germany. The falls are especially impressive in spring and after heavy rains. Snap the best photo from the wooden viewing platform at the bottom as the cool mist fills the air. Free parking is available at the western entrance.

THE BLACK FOREST

THE BEST BLACK FOREST CAKE

If you're on a quest to find the region's best Black Forest cake *(Schwarzwälder Kirschtorte)*, your search will be long. Every cafe, bakery and restaurant in every town claims to have the best, so it's up to you to decide. Look out for freshness, juicy cherries, plenty of fresh cream and dark chocolate shavings on top. German cherry liqueur is what gives the cake its punch, and an EU rule states that it must be added to any cake calling itself Black Forest cake.

Learn to make your own at **Cafe Zimmermann** in Todtmoos. It offers workshops every Tuesday at 3pm on how to make this decadent dessert.

Get your heart racing

Just 6km down the road, the **Hasenhorn Rodelbahn** (*hasenhorn-rodelbahn.de*; adult/child €14.50/12.50) is an epic 2.9km downhill toboggan run that operates year-round. Ride the chairlift up, then buckle into your sled fixed to the looping metal track. Don't forget to test your brakes, because before you know it, you'll be flying around those tight curves at top speed.

Hiking the Belchensteig

Just 10 minutes south of Todtnau, this 15km circular hike up to the summit of the **Belchen** is *the* hike to do if you only have time for one. It's got it all: sweeping views, friendly animals, photo

 EATING IN THE BLACK FOREST: COSY PICKS

Raimartihof – Gasthaus zum Feldsee: This family-run mountain hut serves snacks, soups and drinks. *10am-5pm Tue-Thu, to 6pm Fri-Sun* €

St Wilhelmer Hütte: Every hike requires a short break: this rustic hut on the way to Feldberg's summit is just the spot. *10am-5pm Thu-Mon* €

Krunkelbachhütte: Sit down for a sausage, potato salad, soup or cake along the Bernauer Hochtal Steig hiking trail. *10.30am-6pm* €

Löwen Patisserie: This cafe south of Triberg makes incredible cakes, as well as breakfast and lunch options. *11am-6pm Mon-Thu, 9-6pm Fri-Sun* €

BEST CHRISTMAS MARKETS IN THE BLACK FOREST

Ravennaschlucht: Set under the illuminated arches of the Ravenna viaduct, this magical Christmas market is held on the four weekends before Christmas.

Freiburg: Be enchanted by the atmospheric Christmas market that takes over Freiburg's charming squares.

Bad Wildbad: Running for just 10 days in December, these markets boast a less commercial, small-town atmosphere.

Gengenbach: Visit the World's Largest Advent Calendar, where each evening in December, a new window of the town hall is illuminated with festive artwork.

Triberg: Stroll through enchanting stalls and millions of twinkling lights illuminating the Triberg Waterfalls.

Snowshoeing, Feldberg

opportunities, lush rainforest, restaurants and even a cable car halfway up if you need to call it quits. The hike is a fairly moderate uphill for the first half, then an easy downhill after the epic views from the summit. It's well-signed, suitable in all weather, and you can leave your car in the car park at the bottom or catch the regional bus from Münstertal or Titisee train station.

Bernau

TIME FROM TODTNAU: **20 MINS**

Embrace your wanderlust

The 15km **Bernauer Hochtal Steig** is a well-signed, enchanting hike through lush pastures and forests with a rewarding view of the surrounding mountains and valleys, including the French Alps. The hike was nominated for the most beautiful hike in 2025 by Germany's *Wandern* magazine. Starting just outside the town of Bernau, the initial 6km follows a steep uphill climb. At the top, check out the Viscope – a telescope that automatically shows the mountains' names as you sweep over them. Another 1.5km along is the **Krunkelbachhütte** *(krunkelbach.de),* so relax over a sausage, potato salad, soup or cake and a beer. There's also a hot tub on the deck to rest weary legs, which must be pre-booked by calling the hut.

DRINKING IN THE BLACK FOREST: LOCAL TIPPLES

Rothaus: Visit the Black Forest brewery in Grafenhausen to taste what makes their cult beer, the Tannenzapfle, so special. *11am-6pm*

Alpirsbacher Klosterbrau: This family-owned brewery in Alpirsbach has been crafting award-winning brews since 1880. Tours available. *hours vary*

Black Forest Distillers: Pre-book a distillery tour in Lossburg to try Monkey 47, an award-winning dry gin made using 47 botanicals. *noon & 2pm Sat*

Emil Scheibel Schwarzwald-Brennerei: Learn to make great fruit schnapps at this distillery in Kappelrodeck. *9am-5pm Mon-Fri, 10am-1pm Sat*

Feldberg

TIME FROM TODTNAU: **15 MINS**

'Tis the ski-son

While the Black Forest is not renowned as a winter destination, its higher parts do see snow over winter. The freshest powder is usually in mid-January, creating fantastic skiing, tobogganing, winter hiking and cross-country ski runs.

Feldberg, the Black Forest's highest peak at 1493m, is the place to go. One lift pass will get you access to 28 lifts and 63km of ski piste winding through the Black Forest mountains. It's family-friendly, with ski runs catering for beginner to intermediate levels, and ski hire is available on the mountain. Cross-country skiing is also a popular winter pursuit in the area, with 120km of marked trails winding through enchanting winter scenery.

Non-skiers might want to give snowshoeing a try. **Schneebrett Feldberg** has snowshoe rental and offers lessons and guided tours. And for the kids, tobogganing provides hours of entertainment on the dedicated *Rodeln* runs.

After a long day on the slopes, the ski resorts of Todtnauberg, Todtnau, Feldberg and Altglashütten all have cosy après-ski bars to cap off the day.

KEEN FOR MORE WINTER ADVENTURES?

Check out the ski resorts of **Garmisch-Partenkirchen** (p145) in Bavaria.

Titisee

TIME FROM FELDBERG: **15 MINS**

Make a splash

The **Badeparadies Schwarzwald** (*badeparadies-schwarzwald.de; adult/child from €23/19*) indoor pool complex in Titisee is an oasis in the forest, come rain, hail or shine. Unwind in the warm waters under real swaying palm trees and enjoy views over the dense Black Forest. As thick steam rises off the outdoor pool, lay back and let thunderous jets pummel every aching muscle. Once you've had enough downtime, step into the Galaxy playground with 23 thrilling water slides, a huge wave pool, loungers and snack bars.

The scenic **Titisee lake** has a quaint tourist village on its shores. This alpine lake comes alive in summer, when pedal boats, pleasure cruises, inflatables and stand-up paddleboards (SUPs) cruise along its calm surface. A walk around the 7km shoreline takes around 90 minutes, and you'll pass plenty of quieter swimming spots along the way. The low-key town has a number of good restaurants and boutiques if you want to shop for souvenirs.

Get a grip!

Swing from the trees at **Action Forest Kletterwald** (*action-forest.com/kletterwald-schwarzwald; adult/child from €27/17*), a challenging high-ropes course in Titisee. With varying difficulty levels from easy-peasy to almost impossible, it's an action-packed activity for adventure seekers.

Schluchsee

TIME FROM TITISEE: **15 MINS**

Lake life

Just 20km from Titisee, **Schluchsee** is a summer hot spot with boat rental, playgrounds and lots of hidden swimming

WHAT IS THE REINHEITSGEBOT?

'Thou shalt use no other piece than barley, hops and water for making beer', decreed Wilhelm IV, Duke of Bavaria, in 1516. This beer purity law, known as the *Reinheitsgebot,* was originally created to save grain and wheat for bread-making, and to keep out anything that might disguise a rotten beer.

Apart from the addition of yeast (undiscovered at the time), the law has remained largely unchanged for 500 years, and has helped the German beer industry gain an international reputation for quality and flavour. Look for the *'Reinheitsgebot'* label on beer bottles to ensure the brewer adheres to this beer purity law. For more on the law see p300.

BLACK FOREST HAM

The tradition of smoking meat dates from the Middle Ages, and *Schwarzwälder Schinken* (Black Forest ham) still uses traditional methods today. This dry-cured, cold-smoked ham is known for its smoky aroma, dark outer crust, and tender, salty-sweet interior. The process begins with pork leg, which is seasoned with salt, garlic, coriander, juniper and pepper, then cured for several weeks. It's smoked over fir and spruce wood before being air-dried at high altitudes, giving it its distinct character. Only ham made in the Black Forest region can carry this name, in an effort to ensure it's made using traditional methods and authentic regional ingredients. It's often enjoyed with thick slices of bread or added to *Flammkuchen* (Alsatian pizza).

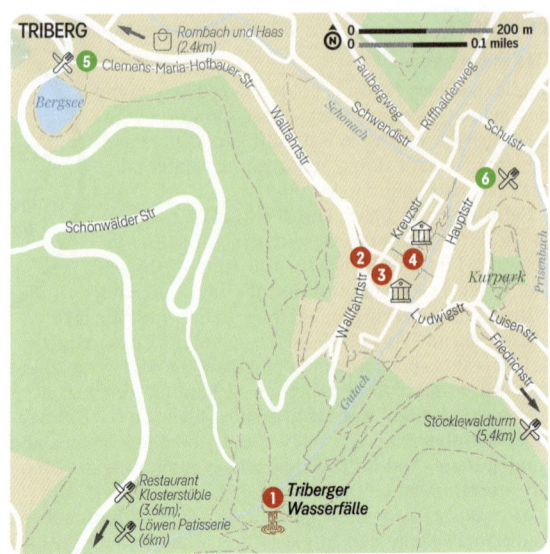

★ HIGHLIGHTS
1 Triberger Wasserfälle

● SIGHTS
2 Oli's Schnitzstube
3 Schwarzwaldmuseum
4 Triberg-Fantasy

● EATING
5 Restaurant & Café Bergseestüble
6 Restaurant Tresor

spots. The reservoir lake's cool water promises welcome relief on hot days, and boat tours around the lake are the best way to take in its beauty.

Triberg

TIME FROM SCHLUCHSEE: **55 MINS**

Germany's highest falls

Triberg is a busy little tourist town in the middle of the Black Forest, where cuckoo clocks outnumber inhabitants and Black Forest cake is a staple. Its main street is both charming and kitsch, with souvenir shops overflowing with wooden ornaments and clocks. But that's not to say it's not worth a visit.

The **Triberger Wasserfälle** (*triberg.de; adult/child €8/7.50*) is Germany's highest waterfall at 163m, and an entry ticket gets you access to over 2km of winding boardwalks and trails with beautiful vantage points the entire way. Your ticket also

 EATING IN & AROUND TRIBERG: OUR PICKS

Restaurant Tresor: A cosy tavern on Triberg's main street with large portions and an extensive menu of German classics. Cash only. *11am-10pm Thu-Mon* €€

Stöcklewaldturm: The woodsy summit cafe at Stöcklewaldturm is an inviting spot for a beer and snack or, in winter, hot chocolate. *11am-7pm Wed-Sun* €

Restaurant & Café Bergseestüble: Friendly staff and a spacious terrace overlooking the lake, plus a kids playground. *noon-9pm Fri-Tue* €€

Restaurant Klosterstüble: Has served delicious German specialities since 1993 in a cosy tavern in Schönwald. *4-9pm Wed-Fri, from 11am Sat & Sun* €€

gets you free entry into the **Schwarzwaldmuseum** (Black Forest Museum) and the museum dedicated to Instagram selfies, **Triberg-Fantasy**.

Going cuckoo over the Black Forest
Cuckoo-clock production started in the Black Forest in the mid-1700s as a side hustle for farmers in between harvests and gradually became a thriving industry thanks to an unlimited supply of wood. Cheap imports have seen a number of clock workshops close down over the years, but **Oli's Schnitzstube** in Triberg still produces hand-crafted, locally made clocks. Look for the black tick of authenticity to ensure you are getting a genuine product.

If you prefer modern timepieces, stop in at **Rombach und Haas** clock shop in Schonach, where a collection of ultra-modern cuckoo clocks are on display and you can see the clockmakers at work through the street-level workshop. Just out of town, two enormous cuckoo clocks compete for the title of 'World's Biggest', with both clocks chirping every half-hour.

Wolfach
TIME FROM TRIBERG: **30 MINS**

A journey through glassmaking
Glass production flourished in the Black Forest from the 12th century onwards thanks to an abundance of key resources: silica sand, beech wood and water. Locally produced glass has a slightly green tinge due to the high iron content in the local sand. Today, the industry is on the decline, so take the time to visit a glass manufacturer and appreciate this traditional craft. At the **Dorotheenhütte** glass factory in Wolfach you can try your hand at glass-blowing and help create your very own vase or bauble in a matter of minutes. The shop has a big selection of glass ornaments and Christmas decorations, plus a short history tour.

Six hundred years of living history
The **Vogtsbauernhof Schwarzwälder Freilichtmuseum** *(Black Forest Open Air Museum; vogtsbauernhof.de; adult/child €13/7)* might be a mouthful to say, but don't let that put you off. Across a spacious field, and fuelled by one man's dedication to preserving Black Forest history, lie 26 real homes from the past 600 years. While only one of these homes, the Vogtsbauernhof, stands in its original location, the others have been delicately dismantled, transported here from all over the Black Forest, and then faithfully rebuilt.

You can walk through all of the homes and get a fascinating insight into rural life in centuries past. There are plenty of hands-on activities and farm animals to keep the kids happy, demonstrations from artisans, an on-site restaurant serving up authentic Black Forest cuisine, and guided tours in English (daily in July and August).

Black Forest National Park
TIME FROM WOLFACH: **45 MIN**

A wild adventure
The **Nationalpark Schwarzwald** *(nationalpark-schwarz wald.de)* was designated a protected national park in 2014,

---

BLACK FOREST CARD

If you're staying in the area for a few days, consider grabbing a **SchwarzwaldCard** *(Black Forest Card; schwarzwaldcard. shop/en; adult/child from €51/35)*. It's the best way to explore the Black Forest while saving money. This discount pass offers free or reduced entry to over 200 attractions, including cable cars, museums, adventure parks and swimming pools. Popular inclusions are the Triberger Wasserfälle, the Vogtsbauernhof Schwarzwälder Freilichtmuseum, Europa-Park (p231) and scenic train rides. The card is valid on any three days over a year, giving you the flexibility to explore at your own pace. Cards can be bought online at or at tourist offices across the region.

LEARN MORE ABOUT THE REINHEITSGEBOT

Beer afficionado? See **Germany's Beer Purity Law** (p300) to discover more about the history and philosophy of the *Reinheitsgebot*.

meaning the majority of the 10,000-hectare area is protected from human intervention to let nature rewild. The visitors centre at **Ruhestein** offers maps and an exhibition on the project.

The best way to experience the beauty of the park is on foot. As you walk, the magic of the forest and its flora and fauna comesto life. For a real adventure, you can even stay a night in the wilderness at a secret nature camp only accessible on foot. Each of the 22 camps scattered throughout the national park offer nothing more than a bush toilet, a campfire and space for three tents. You'll need to bring your own tent, water and supplies, and take away all rubbish, leaving no trace the next day. Camps aren't signposted, but you'll be sent directions and a map 24 hours in advance via email. Many sites are within walking distance of each other, so you can build your own multi-day hike. Bookings are open from May to October at *trekking-schwarzwald.de* and cost €15 per tent.

BEST SHORT HIKES IN THE BLACK FOREST

Uhrwaldpfad Rohrhardsberg: This 8km circular hike through dense forest features over 30 cuckoo clocks along the path from April to October.

Mummelsee to Hornisgrinde: Starting at picturesque Mummelsee, this 4km loop ascends to Hornisgrinde, the highest peak in the northern Black Forest.

Allerheiligen Wasserfälle: This trail near Oppenau leads hikers 4.2km through a series of stunning waterfalls nestled within a lush forest.

Gauchach Gorge Gourmet Trail: This challenging 5.6km trail leads through the wild Gauchach Gorge with its many waterfalls.

Muggenbrunn Barefoot Path: Feel spruce cones, bark mulch and fresh mountain water underfoot on this 600m-long trail. Great for kids.

Nationalpark Schwarzwald (p239)

Baden-Baden

SOOTHING SPAS | RITZY CASINO | GOURMET FOOD

Baden-Baden is elegance personified. With a soundscape of bubbling water and midday bells tolling across the hills, it attracts retirees, millionaires and weary travellers looking for a change of pace. The whiff of the belle époque aristocrats who descended upon the curative spa town in the 19th century still lingers. The dazzling casino, with its dress code and roulette tables, harks back to a bygone era, and the horse-drawn carriages that trot along leafy Lichtentaler Allee imbue the town with a certain charm that makes you want to dress a little more nicely and stand a little taller.

With five-star hotels, luxury shops, world-class art galleries and Michelin-starred restaurants, this is one place to really enjoy a taste of the high life. For those on a backpacker budget, the walkable city and surrounding hiking trails are worth exploring. A vibrant music and arts scene means there's always something going on in the concert halls and outdoor stages.

Great Spa Town of Europe
Rejuvenation and relaxation

Baden-Baden has been recognised by UNESCO as a 'Great Spa Town of Europe', so this is the best place to begin your explorations of this town. Every day more than 800,000L of thermal water bubbles up from the Earth's core. For travellers seeking wellness and rejuvenation, the historic bath house **Friedrichsbad** *(friedrichsbad.eu; adult €38)* and the modern **Caracalla Spa** *(caracalla.de; adult & child from €20)* promise just that with their curative thermal waters. With medicinal minerals such as sodium, chloride and fluorine, a long soak can reputedly help improve blood circulation, metabolic disorders and respiratory diseases.

Temple-like Friedrichsbad is the more traditional of the two, with a 17-stage bathing regime that includes hot and cold baths, massages, saunas and steam rooms. Oh, and it's

GETTING AROUND

Karlsruhe/Baden-Baden Airport often has cheap connections on budget airlines to major European cities. International airport Frankfurt am Main is only 90 minutes away by high-speed train. With the train station on the outskirts of the city, buses are the best way to get anywhere that can't be reached on foot. Taxis are often waiting at the train station, and some only take cash.

☑ TOP TIP

The train station is a little way out of town, so bring some cash so you can catch a taxi to your hotel in Baden-Baden if you're arriving here early or late.

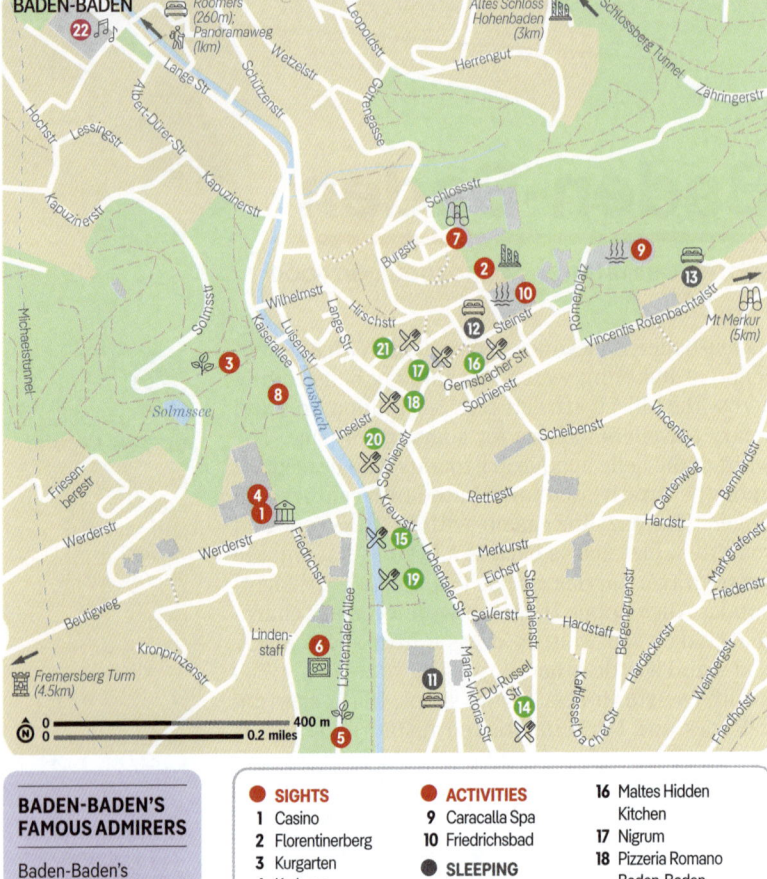

BADEN-BADEN'S FAMOUS ADMIRERS

Baden-Baden's fans include Roman emperors, French aristocrats, Russian authors and American celebrities. Marlene Dietrich called Baden-Baden 'the most beautiful casino in the world'. Russian novelist Fyodor Dostoevsky was inspired by Baden-Baden's roulette tables to write *The Gambler*, while US novelist Mark Twain claimed Baden-Baden's waters cured his rheumatism and washed away his worries.

● SIGHTS
1. Casino
2. Florentinerberg
3. Kurgarten
4. Kurhaus
5. Lichtentaler Allee
6. Museum Frieder Burda
7. Panorama Baden-Baden
8. Trinkhalle

● ACTIVITIES
9. Caracalla Spa
10. Friedrichsbad

● SLEEPING
11. Brenners Park Hotel
12. Hotel am Markt
13. TRIBE Baden-Baden

● EATING
14. Fantastic Kebap Pizza
15. Le Jardin de France
16. Maltes Hidden Kitchen
17. Nigrum
18. Pizzeria Romano Baden-Baden
19. Rizzi
20. Wall Street im Hamilton
21. Weinstube im Baldreit

● ENTERTAINMENT
22. Festspielhau

all done completely naked. Children over 14 are permitted with an adult.

For those wanting to keep their kit on, you might want to head next door to Caracalla. Here, a huge expanse of indoor and outdoor pools, whirlpools and steam rooms invite you to linger a little longer. Water temperatures reach 38°C, making it a perfect year-round activity, and children aged seven years and above are welcome. Upstairs, a naked sauna area has more than 10 themed saunas where you can sweat it out for an additional fee.

The Good-Good Life
Exploring the casino and Altstadt

Stretching from the middle of town, **Lichtentaler Allee** takes you from grand hotels and museums to even grander theatres and festival halls. It's home to magnificent mature trees, ornate bridges and a flowing creek – take a stroll along the park's 2.3km length and soak up the tranquillity.

Stop in at the bright jewel in the park, **Museum Frieder Burda** *(museum-frieder-burda.de; adult/child €16/6)*, a private collector's gallery featuring over 1000 exemplary artworks from the 20th and 21st centuries.

For 11 months of the year, the hum of classical music reverberates through **Festspielhaus** (Festival Hall), a neoclassical opera hall celebrated for its amazing acoustics. Kids will love Toccarion, a children's music world inside the hall with a giant piano and various activities and instruments to play with.

Don't miss the **Trinkhalle**, a striking 90m-long building originally built to pump curative drinking water. Unfortunately, the water is no longer suitable for drinking owing to minuscule amounts of arsenic. Instead, marvel at the murals that flank the open walkway depicting the northern Black Forest. From here step into the **Kurgarten** and **Kurhaus**, the crown jewels of this belle époque town. It's here that Baden-Baden's Christmas markets brighten up winter, with festively decorated wooden huts selling handicrafts, choir performances and an ice rink from early December until early January.

Next up, visit the famed **Casino Baden-Baden** *(casino-baden-baden.de; adult €5)*. If you're picturing the raucousness of the Las Vegas strip, you couldn't be more wrong. With its ornate ceilings, exquisite French silk–lined walls, tiered chandeliers and hushed tones, this casino is an example of old-world charm. Roulette, blackjack and poker are the main games here, with slot machines tucked away in the basement. A formal dress code requires a suit for men, and passports must be presented at the ticket desk. Join a guided tour in English, daily in June and August, to learn more about the casino's secrets, and you'll receive a free entry pass to return to play in the evening.

Hiking the Panorama Trail
Take the scenic route

The Baden-Baden **Panoramaweg** is consistently voted one of Germany's most beautiful trails. Its 45km broken up into four

WHAT'S BEHIND THE NAME?

Baden-Baden traces its origins back over 2000 years to Roman times. The Romans named their settlement Aquae, Latin for 'waters', in honour of the thermal springs they discovered here. In the Middle Ages, the town was simply known as Baden, meaning 'baths'.

To distinguish it from other European towns with the same name (Baden in Switzerland and Baden near Vienna), the double name Baden-Baden was adopted as early as the 16th century. However, it was only in 1931 that Baden-Baden became the official name of the spa town that is now known throughout the world.

The name reflects the town's spa culture and history, and reinforces its reputation as a curative spa destination.

EATING IN BADEN-BADEN: GOURMET BITES

Maltes Hidden Kitchen: A cafe by day, by night this is a gourmet restaurant hidden behind a sliding door offering modern cuisine. *7pm-midnight Wed-Sat €€€*

Rizzi: Attracting a glam crowd, this lively riverside restaurant is modern Asian fusion at its best. *noon-11pm €€€*

Nigrum: A *Michelin Guide* restaurant at the top of town, with a moody interior and modern international set menus. *6-11pm Wed-Sat €€€*

Le Jardin de France: Creative French tasting menus and Black Forest wines in an elegant dining room with a glass ceiling. *lunch Tue-Fri €€€*

BEST VIEWS IN BADEN-BADEN

Mt Merkur: The 360-degree views stretch all the way to the Rhine Valley on a clear day.

Panorama Baden-Baden: This small balcony offers superb views over the city, and it's just a short climb up the steps behind Friedrichsbad.

Altes Schloss Hohenbaden: Explore these old castle ruins and take in the sweeping views and soft notes of the 4m-tall wind harp.

Fremersberg Turm: Climb the 144 tower steps to the observation deck to be rewarded with views of the Black Forest mountains, the Rhine plains and the Vosges.

Florentinerberg: Just a short walk from the Trinkhalle and Kurhaus, Florentine Hill offers a lovely perspective over the old town.

Mt Merkur

shorter stages, offering beautiful views, breathtaking nature and culinary delights. Highlights include old castle ruins, Mt Merkur, Geroldsauer waterfall and Lichtental Abbey. Experienced hikers could combine the stages to finish it in just two days, with an overnight stay in one of the hotels in Geroldsau. Alternatively, bus connections make it easy to tackle any of the individual stages on a day hike. The route is well signposted, but make sure you grab an up-to-date map from the Baden-Baden tourist office before you set out.

Baden-Baden's Highest Point

Aboard the Merkur funicular

Mt Merkur, Baden-Baden's tallest peak, is an easy 15-minute bus ride from town. Reach the top aboard the *Merkurbergbahn,* one of Europe's steepest funiculars, that'll have you oohing and aahing as the track gets insanely steep near the top. From here, visit Rapunzel's tower for breathtaking views over the Rhine Valley and the Black Forest, or catch some rays on the sun loungers.

The **Merkurstüble** restaurant is a lovely spot to grab a beer or an ice cream while watching the paragliders take off from the hillside launch site in good weather.

 EATING IN BADEN-BADEN: OUR PICKS

| **Fantastic Kebap Pizza**: If you're on a budget, fill up on huge kebabs or pizza for under €10 at this central spot. *11am-11pm Tue-Sun* € | **Pizzeria Romano Baden-Baden**: One of the best Italian joints in town, with huge pizzas generously topped with quality ingredients. *11am-9.30pm Thu-Mon* €€ | **Wall Street im Hamilton**: A leafy patio tucked off the main street with big breakfasts, lunch specials and a huge cocktail list. *9am-11pm* €€ | **Weinstube im Baldreit**: An atmospheric hidden-courtyard wine bar serving delicious meals. Bookings essential. *5-10pm Tue-Fri, 11am-3pm Sat* €€ |

Beyond Baden-Baden

This region is a great base for exciting excursions in every direction.

Located at the northern tip of the Black Forest, Baden-Baden's neighbouring countryside and towns offer fascinating day trips to suit every interest in every direction. The region is one of Germany's best Riesling-growing districts and a must-visit for connoisseurs of good wine.

Head north to liberal Karlsruhe, a large city dominated by its grand palace, or venture west and cross the border into France and admire Strasbourg, the capital of Christmas.

Get behind the wheel and follow the Black Forest High Road in either direction between Baden-Baden and Freudenstadt, stopping to admire the lakes, views and waterfalls along the way. Or head to the east, where Bad Wildbad's Sommerberg mountain is an adventurer's playground.

Folk fest, wine fest or music fest, there's always something going on. Check the tourist office website *(baden.baden.com)* to find out what's on.

Karlsruhe
TIME FROM BADEN-BADEN: **20 MINS**

Big fan of Karlsruhe
This large progressive town is a hub of science and technology, media and the arts. While it has the requisite grand palace occupying prime position, it is lacking the medieval Altstadt that's common among its neighbours. That's because Karlsruhe is a relatively young city, purpose-built in 1715 after a dispute forced Margrave Karl III Wilhelm of Baden-Durlach to abandon his previous capital, Durlach. The design, with the ornate **Schloss** *(landesmuseum.de/schloss; adult/child €8/free)* at its centre and 32 avenues radiating away from it like a fan, has become a city emblem.

You can take the 158 steps up the palace tower to get a bird's-eye view of the area. Inside, the rooms have been turned into the **Badisches Landesmuseum** *(landesmuseum.de/museum; adult/child €8/free)*, which exhibits European cultural artefacts, from ancient war and hunting weapons to Ottoman Empire handicrafts. The exhibitions are all in German, so it might be worth saving your pennies if you don't understand the language, or visit on Friday after 2pm when entry is free.

Places
Karlsruhe p245
Strasbourg p246
Freudenstadt p247
Oberkirch p249
Bad Wildbad p249

GETTING AROUND

A car is your best option for getting around, especially if you want to drive along the Black Forest High Road. Some car-rental companies charge extra to drive across borders, so if you plan on visiting Strasbourg, consider leaving your car in the Park & Ride at Kehl Bahnhof and catching the tram across to France. While there is no official border control, you should still take your passport with you.

Furry and feathered locals

The centrally located **Zoological Gardens Karlsruhe** *(zoo-karlsruhe.de; adult/child €14/6)* is not your average zoo. It features 22 hectares of expansive green lawns and themed gardens, 450 animal species, boat rides on the carp-filled lake and numerous restaurants and playgrounds.

Go tech-heavy at ZKM

Don't miss the **Zentrum für Kunst und Medientechnologie** *(ZKM, Centre for Art and Media; zkm.de; adult/child €14/6)*, set in a historic munitions factory, with its dynamic exhibitions on electronic media, tech and video games that'll be sure to impress even the most apathetic museum-goer.

Strasbourg

TIME FROM BADEN-BADEN: 1 HR

Border-hop to France

Nip across the border to get a taste of France in Strasbourg. Less than an hour by train or car from Baden-Baden, this charming Alsatian town is the perfect day trip when you need a break from schnitzels and sauerkraut.

The city of Strasbourg has bounced back and forth between Germany and France five times since the 17th century. Today, a dual Franco-German culture is reflected in its Alsatian language, cuisine and architecture.

As a European capital, and with the Grande-Île and Neustadt districts inscribed on UNESCO's World Heritage List, it's no surprise Strasbourg draws huge crowds.

The pink sandstone of Strasbourg's leading lady, **Cathédrale Notre-Dame**, has cast a long shadow over this prosperous town since the 11th century. The beauty of imperfection reigns supreme here, as you'll quickly notice its quite lopsided. A number of drawings exist proving there was a plan to build a second spire on the south side, but it seems the death of architect Hans Hültz in 1449 and a serious fire a decade later meant the project was never completed. The cathedral is free to enter, so plan to visit early to avoid the queues.

If you've got time, check out **Parc de l'Orangerie**, a city park that's famous as a successful stork-breeding ground. Over 800 of the once-endangered birds have been born here since the 1970s.

Tours on land or water

Wandering through the cobbled alleys, quaint canals and narrow streets, it may feel like you've stepped onto a Disney movie set. The half-timbered houses that hang over narrow

---

THE INSPIRATION FOR WASHINGTON DC

Karlsruhe is famous for its unique fan-shaped city layout, designed in 1715 by Margrave Karl Wilhelm. At its heart stands Karlsruhe Palace, from which 32 streets radiate outward like sunbeams, giving the city its nickname, *Fächerstadt* (fan city). This Enlightenment-era design was meant to reflect order, clarity and rational urban planning, in striking contrast to the narrow, crooked alleyways of medieval cities of the time. The concept was so innovative that it inspired city planners far beyond Germany. Most notably, Pierre L'Enfant, the French-born architect of Washington DC, drew direct influence from Karlsruhe's radial design when mapping out the US capital.

 EATING IN KARLSRUHE: OUR PICKS

Alte Bank: A shady terrace for nibbles and drinks opposite a kids playground. *9am-midnight Sun-Thu, to 1am Fri & Sat* €

Schwarzer Kater: This casual corner pub with friendly staff has a wide selection of main meals, beer and whisky. *hours vary* €€

Passagehof: A centrally located outdoor food court offering a variety of international restaurants from Indian to Mexican. *hours vary* €€

My Heart Beats Vegan: A cosy cafe offering vegan burgers, wraps, salads, cake and coffee. Gluten-free options too. *5-10pm Mon-Fri, from noon Sat & Sun* €

Cathédrale Notre-Dame

canals in **La Petite France**, the cascading floral baskets and the drawbridges and lochs are all part of the city's charm. With so much history, it's worth joining a tour to get your bearings. Walking tours depart from the Cathedral square most days and are tip-based, so bring cash.

Alternatively, **Batorama** offers one-hour boat tours that lap the main island, or you can don your captain's hat and rent your own mini electric boat from Captain Bretzel or Strasboat.

Freudenstadt

TIME FROM BADEN-BADEN: **70 MINS**

The Freudenstadt miracle

A town of only 23,000 inhabitants, Freudenstadt is home to Germany's largest **Marktplatz**, a space laid out for a castle in the 16th century that never materialised. Most of the town was burnt to the ground just weeks before the end of WWII, then completely rebuilt just nine years later in its current form. Locals call it the 'Freudenstadt Miracle', and the sculpture of Venus next to the dancing fountains honours this history. Unsurprisingly, the square is the backdrop for a beautiful Christmas market every year.

THE CAPITAL OF CHRISTMAS

Given that Strasbourg is the self-proclaimed 'Capital of Christmas', expectations are high for the city's Christmas markets. And they do not disappoint. From late November, the entire city is transformed into a magical wonderland, with twinkling lights, giant Christmas trees, wooden stalls, nativity scenes and festive decorations adorning every street.

Must-do activities include ice-skating under the gleaming 30m-high Christmas tree in Place Kléber, wandering the city at night under the twinkling lights, and sampling all the varieties of *Bredle* (Alsatian Christmas cookies). Plan ahead and book early if you want to stay in town; otherwise, you can visit Strasbourg on a day trip from Baden-Baden or Freiburg.

 EATING IN STRASBOURG: FRENCH CLASSICS

Caupona Taverne: Huge burgers and crisp *Flammkuchen* are dished up in a laid-back atmosphere with all-day dining and a terrace. *8am-1.30am €€*

La Hache: This bistro delivers French classics such as beef tartare, escargot and crème brûlée that will not disappoint. *noon-1.30am €€*

Bistrot Coco: Give the chef 'carte blanche' and be surprised with an inspiring modern French tasting menu and matched wines. *noon-1.30pm & 7-9pm Tue-Sat €€€*

La Crepe Gourmande: Delicious, filling, sweet and savoury crepes at fair prices near the Cathedral. *noon-2pm & 6.30-9.30pm Mon-Sat, 11.30am-4pm Sun €*

DRIVING THE BLACK FOREST HIGH ROAD

Follow the gentle curves along the *Schwarzwaldhochstrasse* (B500) between Freudenstadt and Baden-Baden at the top of the Black Forest.

START	END	LENGTH
Freudenstadt	Baden-Baden	60km; 2 hrs

Grab a coffee in ❶ **Freudenstadt** or do a spot of shopping in Germany's biggest Marktplatz before you hit the road.

First up, detour through the tiny village of Kniebis for the ❷ **Ellbachsee viewing platform** to see the rapidly disappearing cirque lake far below. Continue on to ❸ **Lotharpfad**, a series of interconnected boardwalks built after Hurricane Lothar tore through the forest in 1999.

Next up, stretch your legs at ❹ **Mummelsee**. Take in the scenery on a 20-minute walk around the lake, hit the water in a pedal boat, or grab lunch and souvenirs from Berghotel Mummelsee.

Continue towards the village of Geroldsauer, taking a sharp left to pay a visit to the peaceful ❺ **Geroldsauer Wasserfälle**. Just a couple of minutes down the road is one of the region's best beer gardens, ❻ **Wirtshaus zur Geroldsauer Mühle**, and its 150-year-old waterwheel. The hearty German meals, large outdoor patio and kids playground will keep everyone happy.

From here, it's just a short drive to the splendour of ❼ **Baden-Baden**. Park in one of the underground car parks then stretch your legs on a wander through town, or even take a soak in a curative thermal bath.

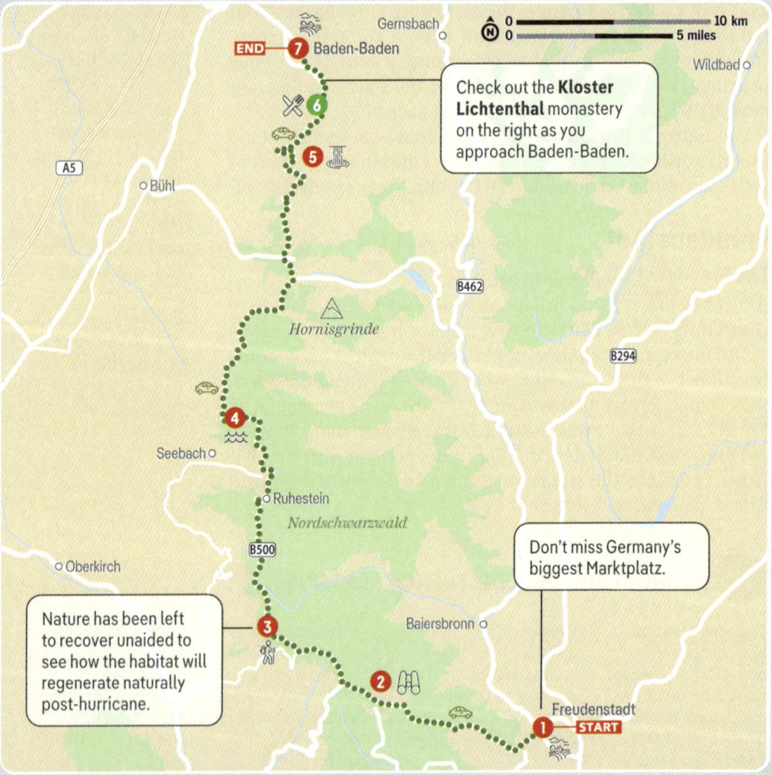

Check out the **Kloster Lichtenthal** monastery on the right as you approach Baden-Baden.

Don't miss Germany's biggest Marktplatz.

Nature has been left to recover unaided to see how the habitat will regenerate naturally post-hurricane.

Take a wander

A short 2.5km walk from town will take you to **Berghütte Lauterbad**, a scenic mountain hut that dishes up delicious coffee and cake, *Flammkuchen* and cocktails year-round. Pay a visit to **Herzog-Friedrich Turm** on the way, a scenic view tower built in 1899 with the help of a citizen crowd-funding campaign.

Oberkirch
TIME FROM BADEN-BADEN: **40 MINS**

Save water – drink schnapps

Oberkirch is the unofficial heartland of schnapps thanks to its abundance of fruit orchards. Apple, plums, pears and more are grown in this fruitful region. What do you do with excess fruit? Turn it into delicious schnapps. And you can sample plenty of these sweet spirits on the **Oberkircher Brennersteig**, a 14km Schnapps Circuit. The route kicks off in Oberkirch and takes you past small *Brennereis* (distilleries) offering little schnapps fountains for you to sample along the way. Little pools of flowing water and cabins keep the liquors cool, and tins are left out for donations, so bring cash. So all you have to do is take a sip…or two.

Bad Wildbad
TIME FROM BADEN-BADEN: **1 HR**

Therapeutic waters

The idyllic locale of Bad Wildbad has plenty to keep you busy for a day or two. This historic spa town boasts two thermal spas, **Vital Therme** (*vitaltherme-wildbad.de; adult/child €14/7*) and **Palais Thermal** (*palais-thermal.de; adult/child over 12 from €17*), both promising to cure your ailments with their therapeutic waters. The **Kurpark** (Spa Gardens) are some of the most beautiful in Germany, with walking and cycling trails, a children's playground, resident swans and a stunning rose garden.

Adventure awaits

The **Sommerbergbahn** (*bad-wildbad.de/sommerbergbahn; adult/child €5.50/3.50*) funicular connects the town centre to the top of Sommerberg in a matter of minutes. From the top, it's just a short walk to the main attractions. Start at **Baumwimpfelpfad**, a treetop boardwalk that stretches over 1km through forest canopy before reaching the highlight – an enormous spiral viewing tower. Its clever ramp design means the ascent has a maximum 6% incline, making it an

THE SPIRIT OF TRADITION

Oberkirch's schnapps-making tradition goes back to the Middle Ages, when farmers turned surplus fruit into schnapps for medicinal purposes. Today, the region boasts over 900 small-scale distilleries, many of them family-run and still using the same centuries-old copper stills. Cherries, plums, raspberries and pears from local orchards remain the star ingredients. So too, *Zibärtle*, a wild plum found only here near the Black Forest, that's harvested after the first frost and has marzipan notes. Unlike sugary versions drunk elsewhere, German schnapps are dry, clear and seriously strong – crafted from all-natural fruit with no artificial flavours. Strict laws govern purity and strength, with ABVs ranging from 15% to a heady 80%.

 EATING IN BAIERSBRONN: MICHELIN-STARRED RESTAURANTS

| **Schwarzwaldstube**: Quality local ingredients and wild flavours foraged from the surrounding forest. Three stars. *7-10pm Wed-Sun & noon-2pm Sat & Sun* €€€ | **Restaurant Bareiss**: Classic French haute cuisine, and epic cheese and dessert trolleys. Three stars. *noon-2pm & 7-11pm Thu-Sun* €€€ | **Gourmetrestaurant Schlossberg**: A culinary institution, Jörg and Nico Sackmann offer a modern international set menu. One star. *6-9pm Wed-Sun* €€€ | **1789**: A warm, modern interior, attentive service and sophisticated Asian-fusion cuisine. One star. *6.30-10pm Tue-Sat* €€€ |

Wildline

A BOISTEROUS & CREEPY CARNIVAL

The Swabian-Alemannic **Fasnacht** is a 500-year-old pre-Lenten folk festival celebrated in southwestern Germany to banish winter. Starting on Epiphany and reaching a crescendo the week before Ash Wednesday, this is a darker and more mystical rite than Cologne's Karneval. Each town has its own rituals and elaborate handmade wooden masks that are worn by wild, creepy figures known as *Narren*, who storm through town chasing away winter spirits (and scaring unsuspecting children) during street parades. While the most traditional and atmospheric celebrations can be found at Rottweil, Villingen-Schwenningen and Gengenbach, every town in the region stages its own colourful procession.

easy path for wheelchairs and prams alike. Admire the views of the upper Black Forest landscape, the Swabian Alps and even Stuttgart's TV tower on clear days from the wooden platform. Between April and November you can whizz back down on the 55m-long slide.

Continue the fun at **Abenteuerwald** (Adventure Forest), a ticketed forest playground with zip lines, a jumping pillow and a low rope course that will keep the kids happy for hours. Lastly, follow the signs to **Wildline**. With a span of 380m, this suspension bridge deep in the forest is not for the faint-hearted or acrophobic, especially if the wind picks up. While 60m above the ground you can eyeball the tops of the 100-year-old fir trees. The bridge is open year-round, with reduced opening hours from December to March.

Lake Constance

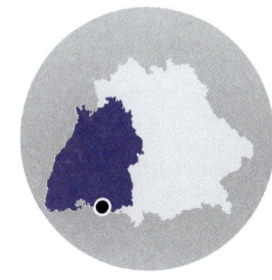

AVIATION GOLDEN AGE | CRUISIN' | FLORAL ISLAND

Nestled between Germany, Austria and Switzerland, Lake Constance is a dazzling summer playground. Stretching across 536 sq km, it's Europe's third-largest lake and a hub for alpine and water sports. Quaint villages dot the edges, each flaunting its own history. Castles weathered by time stand tall, Stone Age pile dwellings hug the water's edge, charming seaside promenades recall a simpler time and verdant gardens flourish.

Paradise for sailors, sun-bakers, cyclists and seniors, here there's a distinct rhythm to the days, and it's not fast. If you're on the streets by 9am you won't find much open. By 10am the cafe terraces begin to fill up and boat wakes begin to paint the lake's surface. In warm weather, the lido lawns are full and the pedalos are booked out. In bad weather, the fascinating museums are the places to shelter. Lake Constance invites visitors to dive into its crystal-clear water, cycle its shoreline, hike its peaks or simply unwind and switch off.

Places
Konstanz p251
Mainau Island p252
Meersburg p253
Friedrichshafen p254
Lindau p255
Bregenz p256
Ravensburg p257

GETTING AROUND

The best way to explore the lake is by ferry *(bsb.de)*. Konstanz is the main hub, but Meersburg and Friedrichshafen also connect to other towns. Most towns except Meersburg have a train station. In summer, ErlebnisBusse runs two routes every hour along the German shore: between Salem and Oberuhldingen and between Uhldingen and Meersburg. A car-ferry connects Meersburg with Konstanz.

Konstanz

TIME FROM MEERSBURG: **30 MINS**

History and tranquillity

Touching the Swiss border and surrounded by the snow-capped Alps, Konstanz enjoys a delightful blend of history, culture, shopping and scenery. Its proximity to neutral Switzerland in WWII mercifully saved it from destruction, so the rich layers of history in this ancient town can be appreciated today.

On a wander through the **Altstadt**, you will be charmed by the narrow cobbled streets and boutiques. The **Niederburg** district is where you'll want to go if you are an antiques addict, while the avenues closer to the water's edge are the place to go for a wardrobe update. Continue your promenade along the harbour, stopping in at **Rheintorturm**, an ancient city-gate tower, to marvel at the panoramic views from its upper level.

Learn about the town's Roman roots by paying a visit to the **Römersiedlung**. The glass pyramid houses the remains of

KONSTANZ

- **SIGHTS**
  1. Niederburg
  2. Rheintorturm
  3. Römersiedlung
  4. Sea Life
- **SLEEPING**
  5. Steigenberger Inselhotel
- **EATING**
  6. Constanzer Wirtshaus
  7. Das Voglhaus
  8. San Martino Gourmet
  9. Tolle Knolle

FOUR COUNTRIES IN ONE DAY

Where else can you embrace the novelty of visiting four countries in one day and still get home in time for dinner? Grab a pretzel for breakfast in Germany, take the ferry to Switzerland for a lunch of fondue, cross over to Bregenz in Austria for afternoon tea and then jump on a train and get your souvenir passport stamp from the Vaduz tourist office in the capital of teeny tiny Liechtenstein. This enclave has been a principality under the rule of the Liechtenstein family since 1719, and has prospered through banking and industry. Don't miss walking the **Old Rhine Bridge**, a 135m-long rustic wooden footbridge linking Switerzland and Liechtenstein.

the Roman fort Constantia from 300 CE, and tours will take you down a staircase into the ruins below.

If you've got kids in tow, **Sea Life** *(visitsealife.com/konstanz; adult/child €22/14.40)* aquarium's diverse marine life and interactive exhibits will keep them happy for a couple of hours.

Circle the lake on two wheels

The **Bodensee Radweg** (Lake Constance Cycle Path) is a popular 273km bike path that loops the entire shore of Lake Constance. You'll cruise past vineyards, fruit orchards, wetlands and farmland on this well-marked bitumen route. Allow a week to take it at a leisurely pace, or, if you only have a weekend, make use of the ferry between Friedrichshafen and Konstanz to shave off some time.

Many hotels around the lake cater to cyclists, with bike-friendly amenities such as storage rooms, bike pumps and repair kits, as well as spas to soothe aching muscles. You can hire bicycles from shops in most towns.

Mainau Island
TIME FROM KONSTANZ: **35 MINS**

Garden of Eden

Explore the island of **Mainau** *(mainau.de; adult/child from €26.90/free)* on Lake Constance. This privately owned island was purchased by Grand Duke Friedrich I of Baden in 1853, and he immediately set to work transforming it into the botanical paradise it is today. The doors were opened to the public in the early 20th century, and the 'Island of Flowers' has been delighting botanists ever since. Highlights include the botanical gardens, the butterfly house, the arboretum and the thousands of roses that bloom throughout summer.

Tickets aren't cheap, so make a day of it to get your money's worth. Save money by buying online or with your ferry ticket. Between June and September, afternoon discounted tickets are available from 5pm till sunset. You can access the island by ferry from Konstanz or Meersburg, or by bike from Konstanz.

Meersburg

TIME FROM MAINAU: 25 MINS

Old and new castles

With so many lakeside towns vying for your attention, under-the-radar Meersburg, a patchwork of hillside vines, perky turrets, cobbled alleys and swimming spots, invites you to savour its storybook atmosphere.

Dating back to the 7th century, **Burg Meersburg** *(burg-meersburg.de; adult/child €12.80/8)* takes centre stage here, with its historical re-creations in each room providing insight into the castle's history. Tour the elegantly adorned rooms, long halls, dungeons and torture chamber. The information boards in German paint a picture of castle life.

Snap some photos of the panoramic lake views from the terrace of the **Neues Schloss**, then meander down to the **Seepromenade** where you'll find boat hire, the satirical *Magische Säule* (Magic Column) sculpture, lakeside lidos and inviting *Weinstuben* (wine taverns).

Discover the sunken village

It is known that people lived on the lake well before the Romans, thanks to the discovery of prehistoric pile dwellings. Small communities who lived on the lake built these stilt houses to adapt to the changing lake height throughout the seasons. The faithfully reconstructed stilt dwellings form the **Pfahlbauten** *(pfahlbauten.de; adult/child €14/8.50)*, a UNESCO World Heritage Site located just 5km from Meersburg. This site transports you back to life in the Stone Age, and guided tours are offered regularly in German, or you can pick up an English-language information booklet from the ticket window. There are also hands-on activities to entertain little ones, such as digging for treasure and wood carving.

BEST SWIM SPOTS AROUND THE LAKE

Strandbad Meersburg: A private swimming pool and beach with shady spots, a jumping platform and lake-access ramps.

Strandbad Bregenz: This central lido has a lakeside beach, outdoor pools with waterslides, and activities including volleyball and table tennis.

Strandbad Friedrichshafen: A short stroll from town, this fenced-off beach area has sprawling lawns, water sports, kiosks and kiddie pools.

Strandbad Horn: A Konstanz favourite with spacious lawns, sandy beaches and lake access. It's free, family-friendly and great for picnics.

Lindenhofbad: Outdoor pool with free access to the lake, west of Lindau. Sunbathing lawn with plenty of shade, canoe and stand-up paddleboard (SUP) board rental.

 EATING IN KONSTANZ: OUR PICKS

Tolle Knolle: Potatoes take a starring role on the creative menu at this longtime Konstanz classic on Bodanplatz. *11am-10pm* €€

Das Voglhaus: The 'birdhouse' has plenty of cosy nooks for enjoying a coffee or slice of cake. *8am-7pm Mon-Sat, 9am-6pm Sun* €

Constanzer Wirtshaus: A relaxed brewpub serving German classics and vegetarian options with lovely lake views from the terrace. *11am-11pm* €€

San Martino Gourmet: If you're looking to treat yourself, this 16-seat Michelin-starred restaurant will do the trick. *11.30am-2pm & 5.30-10.30pm* €€€

THE ZEPPELIN

The zeppelin, named after its inventor Count Ferdinand von Zeppelin, has a storied history as an iconic airship. When it first took to the skies in 1900 it was a huge step forward in aviation. The blimp was in vogue for wealthy travellers crossing the Atlantic thanks to its spacious passenger cabins and in-flight service.

Unfortunately, the *Hindenburg* disaster that claimed the lives of 35 people spelled the end of the zeppelin's glory days. These days, blimps are mainly used for advertising and reconnaissance missions. And of course, scenic flights over Lake Constance. Take a ride yourself on one of the flights leaving from Friedrichshafen airport.

Take a whiff

Check out the **Vineum** *(vineum-bodensee.de; adult/child €7/5)*, a fascinating museum that celebrates the town's long history of viticulture. Here, you can immerse yourself in the world of wine, learning about local winemaking traditions, grape varieties and regional terroirs. Test your nose by sniffing 16 common wine aromas before heading to the bar downstairs for a tasting.

Monkeying around

The **Affenberg Salem** *(affenberg-salem.de; adult/child €12.50/8.50)*, 12km north of Meersburg, is a conservation area where over 200 endangered Barbary macaques happily roam a 20-hectare woodland. The monkeys are divided into three larger family groups numbering 60 to 80 each, so you can expect to see some territorial fighting as you enter through the gates. Park rangers are on hand to answer questions and protect the wellbeing of the primates, while feedings every hour give you a chance to witness their playful antics up close.

The park is also home to storks, who have taken up residence on many of the rooftops, as well as a herd of fallow deer.

Friedrichshafen TIME FROM MEERSBURG: 20 MINS 🚗 + 1 HR ⛴

Don your aviators

In contrast to Lake Constance's other quaint towns, Friedrichshafen has more of an industrial feel. As a key WWII arms manufacturer, the town was a major target for the Allies and was completely devastated during the war. Unfortunately, the speed and limited funds available when it came time to rebuild left it looking less beautiful than some of its neighbours. But its important aviation history still makes it worth a visit.

Friedrichshafen's main claim to fame is as the birthplace of the zeppelin blimp. The **Zeppelin Museum** *(zeppelin-museum.de; adult/child €14.50/8)* has a central location at the harbour, and charts the history of the airship's creation and its rapid demise. The museum even has a life-size Bauhaus-style zeppelin replica, with aluminium-framed furniture in a lovely retro orange hue. The lounge room and bunk beds are certainly an improvement on economy class.

Aviation buffs can continue on at the **Dornier Museum** *(dorniermuseum.de; adult/child €13.50/8)*, which showcases the history of aviation and aerospace engineering in a large hangar. Most of the planes are open, so you can climb into the cockpit and re-create your very own *Top Gun* moment. Combined tickets are available for both the Dornier and Zeppelin Museums.

EATING & DRINKING IN LINDAU: OUR PICKS

Al Porto Risto Kiosk: The view over the port and cheap cocktails make this Italian bar a winner for a quick bite or aperitif. *10.30am–midnight* €

Grosstadt: Relaxed bar-restaurant dishing up all-day breakfasts, bagels and wraps. A variety of gluten-free and vegan options. *11.30am–10pm Wed–Sun* €

Wissingers im Schlechterbräu: If you've got a hankering for hearty German food, head out the back to this beer garden. *noon–2pm & 6–10pm Wed–Sun* €€

Valentin: Romance and warmth at this fine-dining restaurant serving French and international flavours. Optional matched wines. *noon–11pm Thu–Sun, from 4pm Tue & Wed* €€€

CHOOSING WHERE TO STAY

With so many lakeside towns, it can be hard to pick one. This quick guide should help and see Places We Love to Stay (p266) for more options.

Friedrichshafen: Affordable options and good road connections, but the town is less attractive.

Lindau: Great if you want to be in a bustling town, although it is considerably quieter at night when the day-trippers depart.

Konstanz: There are more options here at the higher end of the budget, and more shopping, nightlife and restaurants. It's also the place to stay if you want easy access to Switzerland.

Meersburg: Has great swimming spots and is a very charming city. It also has a ferry connection directly to Mainau and Konstanz.

SIGHTS
1 Altes Rathaus
2 Diebsturm
3 Mangturm

ACTIVITIES
4 Bootsverleih Hodrius

SLEEPING
5 Hotel Anker
6 Hotel Engel

EATING
7 Grosstadt
8 Valentin

DRINKING & NIGHTLIFE
9 Al Porto Risto Kiosk
10 Wissingers im Schlechterbräu

Lindau

TIME FROM FRIEDRICHSHAFEN: **30 MINS** 🚗 + 1½ HR ⛴

The Bavarian Riviera

Aah, ain't she lovely? From the lush gardens to the lion proudly perched on the end of the sheltered port, Lindau is a city that has been called the Bavarian Riviera. While that might be a bit of a leap, Lindau is certainly the prettiest town along Lake Constance's shores.

During the warmer months, every speck of pavement is given over to outdoor wining and dining. If you want to hit the water, boat rental is available from the northern edge, with **Bootsverleih Hodrius** offering pedalos and small motorboats by the hour – just enough time to do a circuit of the island in the latter.

THE BODENSEE CARD PLUS

The Bodensee Card PLUS is one of the better tourist cards going around. It gives you free entry to 160 attractions in all the countries around Lake Constance, plus free ferry rides. You can get a three- or seven-day pass, and the days don't have to be consecutive. With the card, you could ride the Pfänderbahn in Bregenz, see the monkeys at Affenberg Salem (p254), check out the Pfahlbauten Museum (p253) in Unteruhldingen, tour the Zeppelin Museum (p254) in Friedrichshafen, head 2500m up on the Säntis cable car and take a moped tour in Taufen, Switzerland. Prices start at €78.

SINA ETTMER PHOTOGRAPHY/SHUTTERSTOCK

A signposted 5km walking tour takes you on a lap of the island's main sights, including the harbour, the tower **Mangturm**, the turreted **Diebsturm** and the **Altes Rathaus**, with its ornately decorated facade.

Bregenz

TIME FROM LINDAU: **10 MINS** + **15 MINS**

The sound of music

Step across the border into Bregenz, the Austrian city famed for its summer opera programme and mountain-top playground.

Held in July, the **Bregenzer Festspiele** *(bregenzerfestspiele.com/de)* is an open-air opera event that attracts music fans from around the world. The floating stages are true works of art, and create an overwhelming audio and visual feast under the night sky. A stroll along Bregenz' promenade will take you to the 7000-seat lakeside **Seebühne** amphitheatre, which you can freely wander when the opera is not in town.

View from the top

Prefer fresh mountain air? Cruise up to the top of Bregenz by cable car in just six minutes on the **Pfänderbahn** *(pfaenderbahn.at; adult/child €18/9)*. Awaiting you at the top is a veritable Disneyland of attractions. Take in the incredible panoramic views from a number of viewpoints, say 'hi' to the red deer, boars and alpine ibexes who live at the **Alpine Game Park Pfänder**, or grab lunch in a mountain hut.

If you want a bit of peace and quiet, hit one of the hiking trails. The **Käsewanderweg** (Cheese Trail) is an easy 8 km over dairy pastures dotted with small farmers' huts selling cheese and sausage direct to hungry hikers.

Ravensburg

Ravensburg

Get playful

TIME FROM FRIEDRICHSHAFEN:
10 MINS 🚗 **+ 15 MINS** ⛴

In contrast to Friedrichshafen, Ravensburg is a well-maintained example of a fortified German town, with half-timbered, canal-lined streets and old town walls. Made famous by its puzzles and games company Ravensburg, it's worth exploring this history at the **Museum Ravensburger** *(museum-ravensburger.de; adult/child €13/10)*. The board-game exhibitions, reading rooms and puzzle rooms allow you to release your inner child. If you're visiting in September, don't miss **Ravensburg Spielt** (Ravensburg Plays), a weekend-long festival where the city turns into a giant game board, complete with giant puzzles and city quests.

Continue the fun at **Spieleland** *(spieleland.de; adult/child €39)*, a theme park with rides, a petting zoo and live-action shows, located 10km south of town.

A town of wowers

Take a wander through the **Altstadt** and you'll come across charming squares, shops and cafes, and narrow streets lined with canals. Affectionately known as the 'city of towers and gates', Ravensburg has no fewer than 10 towers. The oldest, **Obertor**, houses 'the poor sinner's bell', which used to be rung during executions. You can enjoy the views from atop two: **Blaserturm**, in the centre of town, and the bright-white **Mehlsack** (flour sack), the beloved city symbol, at the southern end of town.

Ulm

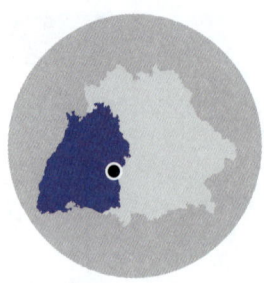

SOARING SPIRE | CYCLE PARADISE | CHARMING OLD TOWN

GETTING AROUND

Ulm is pretty small, so it's easily explored on foot or by bicycle if you want to go a little further afield. It's situated roughly halfway between Stuttgart and Munich, with regular high-speed train connections with both cities. The UlmCard gets you free entry to the Münster tower, most city museums, pools and the zoo, as well as offers at a number of restaurants for 24 or 48 hours.

☑ TOP TIP

Stand back near the fountain in the Marktplatz for the best shot of the entire Münster soaring above the square. Switch your perspective and take the 768 steps to the spire's highest viewing platform. Your reward is an unbeatable panoramic view of the city. Don't forget your water bottle for the climb!

Ulm is an attractive city divided by the Danube, surrounded by old city walls and medieval half-timbered houses on one side, and modernity on the other in Neu-Ulm. This best-of-both-worlds approach came about after much of the Altstadt was destroyed during WWII, and allows the city to honour both its history and future, as well as its Bavarian and Swabian sides.

The Ulm Münster dominates the city – a beacon of hope that has remained unscathed throughout the centuries. Ulm's busy square hosts a weekly farmers market that showcases the region's rich agriculture, and the picturesque Fischerviertel recalls a past centred on fishing and leather making. For a small town it packs in some of the country's biggest, oldest and crookedest sights, yet still manages to fly under the radar. Around one hour from Stuttgart by train, Ulm makes an easy day trip or stopover on the way to Munich. On the way, try attempting the tongue twister: 'In Ulm, um Ulm, und um Ulm herum' ('In Ulm, around Ulm and all around Ulm').

A Captivating Cityscape

Ulm's architectural wonders

For centuries, the **Ulmer Münster** has shaped this beautiful city. This goliath of cathedrals took a staggering 500 years to build, and was financed entirely by Ulm's citizens. When more than 80% of the city was destroyed on one fateful day in December 1944, the church was barely touched. Home to the highest church tower in the world, the Gothic masterpiece stretches 161.5m high, taller than the Sydney Harbour Bridge and more than double the height of the Taj Mahal. Step inside and admire the stained-glass windows and vaulted ceilings before braving the 768 narrow spiral steps to the uppermost viewing platform. From this vantage point, shoppers in the Marktplatz look like ants scurrying along the cobblestone alleys, and on clear days you can see Zugspitze, Germany's highest mountain peak. The church hosts free organ concerts on weekdays.

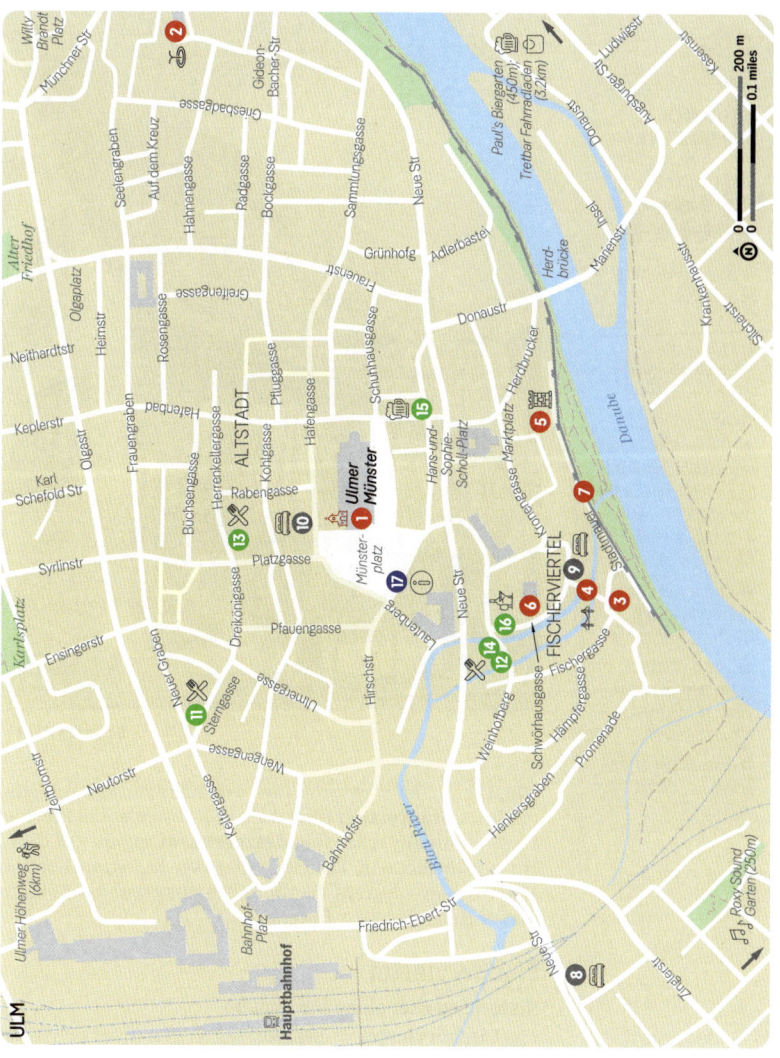

ULM

🟠 HIGHLIGHTS
1 Ulmer Münster

🔴 SIGHTS
2 Einstein Fountain & Monument
3 Fischerviertel
4 Häuslesbrücke
5 Metzgerturm
6 Schwörhaus
7 Stadtmauer

⚫ SLEEPING
8 B&B Hotel Ulm
9 Schiefes Haus

10 Ulmer Münster Hotel

🟢 EATING
11 Da Franco
12 Gerberhaus
13 Herrenkeller
14 Tanivera

🟢 DRINKING & NIGHTLIFE
15 Barfüsser
16 Zur Zill

🔵 INFORMATION
17 Ulm Tourist Office

A TOWN OF SUPERLATIVES

Ulm's sights are often spoken about in superlatives. It features:
- The crookedest house, at Schwörhausgasse 6.
- One of the narrowest hotels, just 4.5m wide, at Fischergasse 27.
- The world's oldest zoomorphic sculpture, Löwenmensch, dating back 30,000 years. It can be seen at the Ulm Museum.
- The world's tallest cathedral tower, reaching 161.5m high.
- The birthplace of the world's most famous scientist, Albert Einstein.
- The oldest bridge in the city dates back to 1316.

Schiefes Haus

Just south, for views over the riverbanks you can walk the red-brick **Stadtmauer** (City Wall) as it straddles the Danube. You'll eventually reach the **Metzgerturm**, another of Ulm's crooked attractions. The city gate tower has an inclination of more than 3 degrees thanks to swampy ground, similar to that of Italy's Leaning Tower of Pisa.

Fischerviertel

Historic quarter along the Danube

The **Fischerviertel** (Fishermen's Quarter) is a real gem of the Altstadt. Since the 800s, its proximity to the flowing Danube has made the area popular with fishers, leather artisans and

 EATING IN ULM: OUR PICKS

Tanivera: In the Fischerviertel, grab a table by the water and enjoy the wood-fired pizza. *11am-11pm* €€

Herrenkeller: Well-priced German restaurant with an outdoor patio and cosy timber booths serving classics such as schnitzel. *11am-10.30pm Mon-Sat* €€

Gerberhaus: This inviting woodcutter's cottage hits the mark with its delicious mix of Swabian and Italian dishes. *11.30am-2.30pm & 5.30-11pm* €€

Da Franco: Affordable, delicious fresh pasta and pizza in this off-the-beaten-track Italian restaurant with friendly staff. *11am-2.30pm & 5.30-11pm Tue-Sun* €€

shipbuilders. Today, lovingly restored half-timbered houses lean over babbling brooks, and inviting taverns and cafes occupy cosy courtyards. It's here you can spot the **Schiefes Haus** (Crookedest House) and the **Häuslesbrücke**, the city's oldest bridge (dating from 1316).

Saddle Up
Exploring on two wheels

Wandering along the riverside with streams of Lycra-clad cyclists whizzing past, you'll quickly realise that Ulm is a bike town.

Not only is it the starting point for the popular Danube–Lake Constance cycling path, running 156km to Lake Constance, but it's also a main stop on the 357km Oberschwaben–Allgäu circular route.

If those distances sound a bit intimidating, you may want to start with the easy 12km **StadtRadRoute**. You'll pedal past Ulm's major attractions, including the Münster, **Einstein's Fountain & Monument**, the greenery of the **Tiergarten**, the flowing Donau river, the Bavarian Neu-Ulm district and the romantic Fischerviertel and Altstadt.

Bike rental is available from **Tretbar Fahrradladen**, or jump on one of the TIER e-bikes scattered around town and pay by the minute. Who knows, you might even have a stroke of genius like Ulm's most famous son, Albert Einstein, who once said, 'It occurred to me while I was riding my bicycle'.

Trailblazing Above the City
Hiking up high

The impressive **Ulmer Höhenweg** hiking trail tracks 12km of footpath high above the city of Ulm. The hills of the Swabian Alps fade into the Danube valleys and the background is silhouetted by the peaks of the Bavarian mountains. You'll have the city sights on one side and natural landscapes on the other as you pass botanical gardens, the Wilhelmsburg stone fortress and the Albeck Fort.

Well-marked yellow arrows signpost the route, and you can also grab a map from the **Ulm Tourist Office**. You can walk in either direction, with tramline 2 taking you to Eselsberg at the western end of the trail, or tramline 1 to Böfingen at the eastern end.

WHAT IS SCHWÖRMONTAG?

Each year, on the penultimate Monday in July (known as Schwörmontag), the mayor takes an oath from the Imperial City Constitution of 1397, vowing 'to be a common man to rich and poor in all equal' from the balcony of the **Schwörhaus** (Oath House), a traditional dating back to 1345. After the hour-long speech, locals flock to the river and the city carnival begins. Hundreds of rafts, inflatable boats and revellers party on the Danube in what's known as *Nabada* (roughly translating to 'swim down'). If you prefer to stay dry, grab a spot on the bank and enjoy the colourful procession, or enjoy some live music at the various stages set up around town.

DRINKING IN ULM: BEST BEER GARDENS

Paul's Biergarten: Tarte flambée, schnitzel, cold beer and live music make this a winner. Has a huge outdoor patio right on the river in Neu-Ulm. *3-10pm Thu-Sun*

Roxy Sound Garten: In the charming Fischerviertel, this lively music venue features local and international acts and DJs. Entry is free. *5pm-late Wed-Sat*

Barfüsser: A large brewpub in the main pedestrian area drawing locals. Grab a tasting paddle to try three brews. Bookings recommended. *11am-midnight*

Zur Zill: Join locals and tourists at this riverside restaurant with a sprawling terrace and vaulted cavernous interior. *10am-midnight*

Beyond Ulm

Intrepid travellers will enjoy discovering these lesser-known gems and peaceful surrounds.

Places
Blaubeuren p262
Wiblingen Abbey p263
Donaueschingen p264

GETTING AROUND

Trains run regularly from Ulm to Blaubeuren, and bus 4 will get you from town to Wiblingen Abbey in 10 minutes. If you want to explore the caves and hikes in the Swabian Alps, a car will be helpful.

A day in Ulm is enough to see its main sights, but if you have some more time, the surrounding region has a multitude of excursions. From the deep-blue lake in the under-the-radar Swabian Alps to the UNESCO-listed Ice Age caves, and then onto the world's most beautiful library – everything is within reach. If you've got two wheels, exploring the region by bike on the Danube Cycle Path gives you a chance to take the slow road and discover the many villages, castles and abbeys along the route. You are well off the tourist trail here, so relax and enjoy the peace and quiet.

Blaubeuren
TIME FROM ULM: **10 MINS**

A blue pearl in the Swabian Alps

The **Blautopf** (meaning 'Blue Pot') is a striking lake with a vibrant deep-blue hue that could rival Ol' Blue Eyes himself. Nestled in the medieval town of Blaubeuren, this fascinating natural site is only a 20km drive from Ulm. The water here surfaces from Germany's largest underground spring and exits from a cave. As it mixes with limestone sediments, it takes on a rich blue colour. In the morning when the weather is clear, the water is at its brightest. Circling the spring only takes 20 minutes, and gives you plenty of beautiful vantage points.

Continue on to explore **Blaubeuren** itself, with a self-guided 1.5km walking tour directing you to the town's historical courtyards, buildings, monastery and Rathaus.

UNESCO-listed caves

Around 200 million years ago, the Swabian Alps region had more volcanoes than anywhere else in the world. This geology created a smattering of caves and sinkholes all across the area.

EATING & DRINKING: BEST COUNTRY PUBS

Barfüsser (p261): A lovely atmosphere, great food and a kids playground in Glacis Park on the outskirts of town. *11am-8pm* €€

Wirtshaus im Butzental: Surrounded by forests and meadows, enjoy a breathtaking view in one of Ulm's highest beer gardens. *2-8pm Wed-Sat, from 11am Sun* €

Wirtshaus Silberwald: A large beer garden and cosy interior make this a great option after a visit to Wiblingen Abbey. *11am-11pm Tue-Sun* €€

Brauerei Schwanen: Try the fresh ales at this fifth-generation family-run brewery and guesthouse in the small town of Echingen. *11am-2pm & 5-11pm Mon-Sat* €€

Wiblingen Abbey

Three of these caves, **Geissenklösterle**, **Sirgenstein Höhle** and **Hohle Fels**, earned UNESCO World Heritage status in 2017 after Ice Age finds, including bone flutes, figurines and mammoth ivory, were excavated from within. Many of these finds are now on display in the **Blaubeuren Prehistoric Museum** (Urgeschichtliches Museum Blaubeuren).

The **Ice Age hiking trail** connects all three caves from Blaubeuren. The first cave, Geissenklösterle, is at the 1km mark, then cross the road and continue another 3km to Sirgenstein Höhle. Both of these caves are currently closed to visitors due to ongoing excavations. However, if you continue a further 2.5km, you can explore Hohle Fels Friday to Sunday from May to October. Guided tours are offered in German on Saturdays.

Wiblingen Abbey

TIME FROM ULM: **10 MINS**

The world's most beautiful library

Wiblingen Abbey (kloster-wiblingen.de; adult/child €6/3) is a large Benedictine monastery not far from Ulm's city centre. The baroque church with its delicate ceiling paintings dates from the 18th century; today, many of the buildings are used by the town's university.

 EATING IN BLAUBEUREN: OUR PICKS

Blautopfhaus: Set on the water's edge overlooking the lake, this homey cafe serves up light meals and homemade cakes. *10am-5pm* €

Il Gusto: This charming cafe in town has great coffee, a huge range of gelato and sweet treats. *9.30am-5.30pm Mon-Sat, 1-5.30pm Sun* €

Pizzeria Vesuvio: A great little Italian joint by the train station serving delicious wood-fired pizzas and pasta. *11.30am-2pm & 5-10pm Tue-Sun* €€

Gasthof Blautopf - Das Steakhaus: Large servings of rump steak, fish, burgers and more at this intimate restaurant. *5-9pm Tue-Fri, 11.30am-9pm Sat & Sun* €€

IMPORTANT FINDS IN THE SWABIAN ALPS

In 2017, UNESCO declared six caves in the Swabian Jura a World Heritage Site. In these caves some 40,000 years ago, Ice Age people carved very lifelike figures of mammoths, wild horses, cave lions and other animals from mammoth ivory. Some of the most important finds include:

● Venus vom Hohle Fels, the oldest figurative representation of a human being found in Hohle Fels.

● The mammoth-ivory Lion Man, a figurine of a half-human, half-lion hybrid.

● The world's oldest musical instruments: flutes made from bird bones, proving that people were making music over 40,000 years ago.

FLORIAN AUGUSTIN/SHUTTERSTOCK

But the real reason to visit is for the library, which is considered one of the world's most beautiful thanks to its seriously over-the-top rococo design, with ornate marble pillars, intricate gold stucco and stunning curved balustrades. It was designed to be a space that would inspire the monks to learn. Unfortunately, the vintage books are kept safely behind caged bookshelves, so if you're inspired to learn yourself, pick up an audioguide on your way in. The library and its surrounding museum is only open on weekends in winter, and from Tuesday to Sunday from March to October.

Donaueschingen

TIME FROM ULM: 2¼ HR

Long-distance cycling routes

The **Danube Cycle Path** was one of Europe's original river-cycling routes and is still one of the most popular thanks to its beautiful scenery and lack of hills, making it a perfect choice for families and casual cyclists. It follows the meandering Danube for about 1200km from Donaueschingen in the Black Forest to the Hungarian capital of Budapest, passing through Ulm.

Danube Cycle Path

You can easily pick up the trail in Ulm or take the train to **Donaueschingen** and start at the river's source. You'll cycle past magical castles, palaces and abbeys, the striking blue lake at Blaubeuren (p262), then Ulm (p258), before arriving at the final stop on this 315km section, the charming village of **Donauwörth**. With plenty of bike-friendly hotels and guesthouses lining the route, it's easy to break the trip up into multiple shorter sections, or join a fully guided tour and simply enjoy the ride.

Alternatively, you can venture south from Ulm's towering spire to the peaceful shores of Lake Constance (p251) on the 156km Danube–Lake Constance Cycle Path. It's a slightly hillier ride than the Danube Cycle Path, but the views are a just reward after the steep ascents. Soothe aching muscles in the **Waldsee** thermal baths on the way, and pay a visit to **Wangen**'s Altstadt, before beginning your descent through fruitful orchards towards **Kressbronn** on the lake. From here you can spend some time exploring the lake's beautiful towns or jump on the train with your bike back to Ulm.

BLAUTOPF'S MYTHICAL MERMAID

The *Schöne Lau* is a beloved local legend connected to the mystical Blautopf lake (p262). According to the 19th-century tale written by Eduard Mörike, the *Schöne Lau* was a water spirit or mermaid who lived in the depths of the Blautopf. She had been banished there by her husband, the Danube King, because she could not laugh and had lost several children at birth.

To break her curse and return home, she was told she had to laugh five times. The townspeople of Blaubeuren helped her rediscover joy through kindness, stories and everyday life. Eventually, her laughter bubbled up from the spring itself, restoring her happiness and making the Blautopf a place of local magic ever since.

Places We Love to Stay

€ Budget €€ Midrange €€€ Top End

Stuttgart
MAP p215

Hostel Alex 30 € A relaxed, social hostel in the city centre with a mix of dorms and private rooms, a communal kitchen, and a friendly atmosphere.

a&o Stuttgart City € With affordable private rooms, dorms and easy access to public transport, this is a great budget option.

Maritim Hotel €€ The enormous buffet breakfast, indoor pool, spacious rooms and central location make up for the slightly dated interior.

Attimo Hotel Stuttgart €€ Conveniently located near the Bad Cannstatt S-Bahn station, this no-nonsense hotel offers comfortable rooms, good value, and easy access to the city's main attractions.

EmiLu Design Hotel €€€ Smack bang in the centre of town, this trendy hotel offers stylish rooms, a rooftop bar and a fab breakfast buffet.

Freiburg
MAP p227

Black Forest Hostel € A 20-minute walk from the main station, this down-to-earth hostel has dorms, private rooms and a large common room.

Cloud Suite Apartments €€ If you need a bit more space, these stylish modern apartments just out of town offer great value and on-site parking.

Best Western Premier Hotel Victoria €€ An eco-conscious hotel near the Altstadt and train station, and directly opposite Colombi park.

Hotel Stadt Freiburg €€ A solid choice with spacious rooms and a top-notch restaurant, close to the university hospital, football stadiums and conference centre.

Colombi Hotel €€€ An elegant five-star hotel in the Altstadt with classically designed, spacious rooms and a friendly concierge desk.

The Black Forest

Haberjockelshof €€ Enjoy breathtaking views, a wellness area, alpaca walks and large apartments at this farm stay near Titisee.

Gasthof Linde €€ A cosy, family-run inn in the heart of the Black Forest, offering hearty local dishes and a warm welcome. Ideal for hikers and nature lovers.

Hotel Schlehdorn €€€ This alpine-style four-star hotel with a pool and spa in tiny Altglashütten is perfect for summer or winter escapes.

Baden-Baden
MAP p242

TRIBE Baden-Baden €€ A great-value stay in the heart of Baden-Baden, this hotel offers trendy, colourful rooms and friendly service.

Hotel am Markt €€ A small family-run hotel offering package stays in the bathhouse district. Ask for a room with a view.

Roomers €€€ A rooftop pool and bar, an Asian restaurant and a spa complex are all offered at this swanky hotel.

Brenners Park Hotel €€€ If your pockets are deep, there's no better place for a luxury spa getaway than this grand dame.

Karlsruhe

Spacehotel Karlsruhe € Spend the night in space at this capsule hotel right in the centre of town. Common areas offer a kitchen, desks and wi-fi.

Leonardo Hotel €€ Located directly across from City Park, this modern midrange hotel offers sleek rooms, a hearty breakfast buffet and a convenient location.

Hotel Santo €€ The perfect central spot for a Karlsruhe overnight stay, with spacious rooms, a cocktail bar and free rooftop parking.

Freudenstadt

Hotel Schwarzwald Freudenstadt €€ Set on the edge of town, this relaxed hotel offers classic rooms and a wellness area with a pool and sauna at reasonable rates.

Hotel Grüner Wald €€€ In a stunning rural locale only 2km out of Freudenstadt, this eco-conscious spa hotel invites relaxation.

Fritz Lauterbad €€€ A sophisticated four-star hotel in Freudenstadt with expansive forest views from all rooms and the outdoor pool.

Black Forest High Road

Berghotel Mummelsee €€€ Set on the shores of the mystical Mummelsee along the Black Forest High Road, guests can enjoy lake views from every room.

Wellness & Nationalpark-Hotel Schliffkopf €€€ In the wooded heart of the Black Forest National Park, this hilltop hotel has spacious, warm-toned rooms (some big enough to accommodate families), a spa, a sauna and an outdoor pool.

Lake Constance MAP p255

Hotel Zum Schiff €€ Occupying prime position on Meersburg's foreshore, this three-star hotel offers good-value lake-view rooms and a huge buffet breakfast.

Hotel Engel €€ Take in the Lindau views from the rooftop terrace and unwind in the spacious, stylish rooms in this 1390 guesthouse right near the harbour.

Hotel Anker €€ Shiny parquet floors, citrus colours and artwork have spruced up the charming and peaceful rooms at this central guesthouse, tucked down a cobbled lane in Lindau. Rates include a hearty breakfast.

Konstanz MAP p252

Ko'Ono Hotel €€ A laid-back, tropical-themed hotel just outside Konstanz, known for its colourful design, relaxed vibe, and great Hawaiian-inspired restaurant.

Steigenberger Inselhotel €€€ Housed in a former monastery on its own private island, this grand hotel offers elegant rooms, a fine-dining restaurant and spectacular views over Lake Constance.

Ulm MAP p259

B&B Hotel Ulm € Good-value rooms near the centre with underground parking and a sound breakfast.

Ulmer Münster Hotel €€ This relaxed central hotel by the cathedral offers bike rental, hearty breakfasts and sunny terraces.

Schiefes Haus (p260) **€€€** For a truly unique stay, book a night in Ulm's crookedest house and sleep under the historic wood-lined ceilings.

Hotel Engel

Konstanz harbor (p251), Lake Constance
VIACHESLAV LOPATIN/SHUTTERSTOCK

TOOLKIT

The chapters in this section cover the most important topics you'll need to know about in Munich, Bavaria & the Black Forest. They're full of nuts-and-bolts information and valuable insights to help you understand and navigate Munich, Bavaria & the Black Forest and get the most out of your trip.

Arriving
p270

Money
p271

Getting Around
p272

Travel by Train
p273

Accommodation
p274

Family Travel
p275

Health & Safe Travel
p276

LGBTIQ+ Travellers
p277

Food, Drink & Nightlife
p278

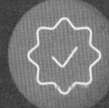
Responsible Travel
p280

Accessible Travel
p282

Nuts & Bolts
p283

Language
p284

Arriving

Munich Airport is the primary point of entry for some international travellers, though many land in Frankfurt and enter Bavaria and Baden-Württemberg by land. Munich's main train station, the Hauptbahnhof, is another common arrivals point with services from neighbouring countries and beyond.

Visas
The vast majority of visitors from Western countries do not need a visa. Those arriving from Schengen countries have no entry formalities to complete but should still have their passport or ID card with them.

SIM Cards
Local SIM cards are available from a few mobile phone operators at Munich Airport and from newsstands at the Hauptbahnhof. However, these days an e-SIM is a much more convenient way of connecting.

Arriving at Munich Hauptbahnhof
The Hauptbahnhof lies on the western edge of the city centre, within walking distance of the Marienplatz, and is served by all of Munich's transport systems.

Wi-Fi
Wi-fi is called WLAN in Germany. There is free access at the airport, though you must register your e-mail address to do so.

Transport from Munich Airport to City Centre

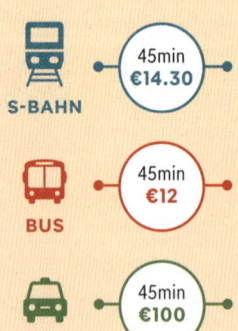

S-BAHN — 45min €14.30

BUS — 45min €12

TAXI — 45min €100

BAVARIA'S BORDERS

Bavaria is bordered by the German states of Thüringen, Hessen, Sachsen and Baden-Württemberg to the north and west, Czechia to the east and Austria to the south. Although ringed by German territory or Schengen countries, in recent years the Bavarian authorities have intermittently imposed ad hoc border checks on travellers coming from Czechia and sometimes Austria. This means taking ID is always a good idea. Otherwise you can be detained until the authorities ascertain who you are.

Money

CURRENCY: EURO (€)

Cards

Card is now king, as are payments with smartphones and smartwatches. Some venues such as the Olympiapark are now entirely cash-free and this is likely to prove a growing trend. In theory, you could get through an entire stay in Munich or Nuremberg without seeing a euro.

ATMs

An ATM or cash machine is never difficult to find even in small towns. Even the odd village has one, though never rely on that. ATMs are mostly installed on the facades of bank buildings but sometimes you might need your card to open the door to access one inside.

Exchanging Cash

Withdrawing funds from southern Germany's many ATMs is usually preferable to exchanging cash, but if you do need to, reputable banks are the most trustworthy sources of euros. Exchanging cash in rural areas can be tricky.

Cash

You will still need cash for most public toilets and luggage lockers, and for a small deposit on reusable cups and bottles.

HOW MUCH FOR...

Museum entry
€5–10

Munich-Nuremberg ICE train ticket
€65

Return Königssee boat ticket
€22.80

Toll charge on Germany's motorways
€0

TO... Rounding up the bill to the nearest €5 or €10 will probably satisfy most waiters and taxi drivers. Tipping is not generally expected across Germany's south and adding 10% to restaurant and bar bills will bring looks of bemused joy to those in the service industries. Naturally, only tip if you are actually satisfied with the service.

LOCAL TIP
It's perfectly acceptable to picnic at beer gardens and just order a beer. Just don't sit at tables with tablecloths or cutlery.

SAVING MONEY

- Visit Munich's Kunstareal on a Sunday when the main venues charge only €1 admission.
- Avoid Munich in late September and early October when Oktoberfest sends accommodation costs sky high.
- Purchase day tickets on public transport.
- Some big attractions such as BMW Welt, the English Garden and most churches are free to enter.
- Eat out at lunch when many restaurants do affordable menus for local office workers.
- Take a picnic into the Alps instead of eating at now wickedly expensive huts and chalets.

Getting Around

Although having your own car in southern Germany will make any trip go more smoothly, Germany's excellent public transport system means this isn't necessarily a must.

TRAVEL COSTS

Car rental
Per day from €50

Petrol
Per litre approx €1.70

Train tickets
Bayern-Ticket €32

Bicycle rental
From €20 per day

Car Hire

Vehicles can be hired at all of the region's airports and in downtown Munich. Hire costs are higher than they once were and the fuel price is now higher in Germany than in surrounding countries. Drivers should have a valid licence and a credit or debit card. Some rental agencies require a minimum age of 21.

LOCAL TRANSPORT

Large towns and cities have efficient public transport systems. The big cities integrate buses, trams, and U-Bahn (underground) and S-Bahn (suburban) trains into a single network. Tickets are bought from ticket machines before boarding any mode of transport and must be stamped before or upon boarding in order to be valid, though city transport apps now save a lot of hassle. *Tageskarten* (day passes) generally offer better value than single-ride tickets.

TIP
The websites *blablacar.de* and *drive2day.de* are local online rideshare boards. Advertise a ride yourself or link up with a driver going your way.

Road Conditions

Southern Germany has excellent roads and toll-free *autobahns* (motorways) with rest areas every 40km to 60km. Be aware that speed restrictions do apply on motorways and only certain sections are unlimited. Even where there is no speed restriction, limits do apply in certain weather conditions. Snow is quickly cleared in the Alps but be careful of icy conditions across the region.

Train

Germany's south has a dense network of efficient railway lines. Regional tickets (Baden-Württemberg-Ticket and Bayern-Ticket) give a whole day of unlimited state-wide travel, and the bigger the group of passengers, the cheaper. They are not valid on high-speed services. For further details, see the Deutsche Bahn *(bahn.de)* website.

Bus

You'll need to swap rail for road in the Alps and in the Bavarian Forest, where train services peter out. RVO is the main operator in the Alps. They mostly meet the needs of schoolkids and commuters and are quieter at weekends. Fast coaches, mostly Flixbus, connect the big cities, including Munich, Stuttgart and Nuremberg.

Boat

Southern Bavaria is a land of lakes and often the only way to get around them is by boat. Bayerische Seenschifffahrt operates most services, including on the Königssee. Sailing the Danube on a cruise boat from Regensburg and Passau is an enjoyably slow way of moving around the state.

DRIVING ESSENTIALS

Drive on the right

Speed limit on A roads is 100kmph

.05
Blood alcohol limit is 0.05%

Travel by Train

Unless you are staying put in one city or have a hire car for the entirety of your trip, sooner or later you are very likely to find yourself aboard a train.

Regional Tickets

The Bayern-Ticket and Baden-Württemberg-Ticket are special regional passes valid on all public transport (except ICE, IC and EC trains) within the given area. You can only use them after 9am until 3am the next day. The Bayern-Ticket costs €32 for one person with every further traveller (up to five in total) adding another €10. It is valid as far as Salzburg but not to any station in neighbouring Czechia. The Baden-Württemberg-Ticket is €27 for one person with every further traveller (up to five in total) adding €9. This regional ticket is valid as far as Basel in Switzerland. Three children between the ages of six and 14 travel free of charge on both tickets.

Deutschland-Ticket

This much-talked-about nationwide pass gives a month's travel on all public transport across the entire country (except ICE, IC and EC trains) for €58. However, unlike regional tickets, this is per person – you cannot add travellers. It's a superb deal for lone travellers who intend on making several journeys in a month. It's not the right pass for a group who might only be travelling two or three times by train. You must have a smartphone to buy it and travellers should be aware that this is actually a monthly subscription that you will need to cancel by the 10th day of the following month.

Train Companies

The vast majority of rail services are operated by Deutsche Bahn *(bahn.de)* which, to say the least, does not enjoy the best of reputations across Germany. They also operates the S-Bahn systems in large cities. Other regional companies include Vogtlandbahn, Agilis and Alex. You may even find yourself aboard a train belonging to one of Germany's neighbours such as České dráhy (Czechia), ÖBB (Austria) or SBB (Switzerland).

Ticket Offices & Machines

Large train stations have a *Reisezentrum* (travel centre) where staff sell tickets and can help plan itineraries, but note that a €2 surcharge is added when buying regional tickets from a ticket office. Smaller stations may only have a few ticket windows or no staff at all, which means you might have no choice but to buy your ticket from a vending machine. These are plentiful at staffed and unstaffed stations and convenient if you don't want to queue at a counter. Instructions are in English, but although some simplification has been implemented, these can still completely bamboozle the uninitiated. You must buy a ticket before boarding.

Station Facilities

In Nuremberg, Munich and Stuttgart stations bustle with passengers, bakeries, fast food joints and retail outlets as trains from across Europe glide to a halt at packed platforms. Staff are plentiful and help is always on hand from strategically located kiosks. The contrast with stations out in the sticks is stark – all you might find is a baffling ticket machine and a deserted Perspex shelter. Toilets are always paid at stations that have them but they are largely a thing of the past. Left luggage lockers are handy if just jumping off a train to take a quick look round a town – you can check whether a station has them on the Deutsche Bahn website.

Train Classes

German trains have 1st- and 2nd-class cars, both modern and comfortable. Seating is in open-plan carriages with panoramic windows, though you might still encounter some corridor trains. Trains almost always have wi-fi, WC, a trolley service and often plugs. High-speed ICE and IC trains offer the best services between big cities. These are fully air-conditioned and have a restaurant or self-service bistro. EC trains are international services and vary enormously in standards and facilities depending on the operator. Seat reservations are highly recommended for busy times, especially if travelling in a group. Lower down the rail food chain are the RE class regional expresses and RB trains, the slowest services that stop at every station. S-Bahn trains start out in the sticks, head into a large city centre and then back out into the countryside in a different direction.

Accommodation

Short-Term Rentals

Southern Germany seems to have avoided the short-term rental woes that have afflicted cities like Prague and Budapest, with short-term rental properties highly regulated in places like Munich. Excellent city transport networks mean you can easily reach the centre from even far-flung locations.

Hostels

Germany's south has many hostels of both the independent and youth *(DJH; jugendherberge.de)* varieties, though with the rise of short-term rentals, the number has waned in recent years. The advantage of bagging a dorm room in downtown Munich is that it puts you in a central location. The disadvantage of these often large hostels are that they attract people intent on partying.

Pensions & Guesthouses

Pensionen (guesthouses) and *Gasthöfe* or *Gasthäuser* (inns) are smaller, less formal and cheaper than hotels; the latter usually have a restaurant. Expect clean rooms but only minimal amenities – a very small TV and slow wi-fi. Facilities may even be shared. What rooms lack in amenities, they often make up for in charm, authenticity and retro quirkiness.

Hotels

Germany's south has everything from charming, family-run hotels to huge luxury establishments for hundreds of euros a night. At the lower end of the market, prices have skyrocketed in recent years and even midrange hotels can now present a challenge to budgets. Facilities vary from grotty to opulent, though the vast majority of hotels maintain decent standards.

HOW MUCH FOR A NIGHT IN A...

Hostel dorm
€27

Double in a midrange hotel
€150

Single in a guesthouse
€80

Camping

Almost every town in southern Germany has a camping ground a short bus ride away. German camping grounds are normally well maintained and offer a wide range of facilities. The core season runs from May to September with only a few campsites open year-round. Another option is **Nomady** *(mycabin.eu)* where farmers and other people with land offer field and garden space.

ALPINE HUTS

One place in Bavaria where your accommodation becomes the experience is the Alps, where you can stay in a hut high up in the mountains. These are often used by hikers to overnight before heading for a peak and then descending, but anyone can book a stay. Facilities range from midrange standard doubles to a bothy room where you can roll out a camping mat. Booking months ahead through the **Deutscher Alpenverein** *(alpenverein.de)* is pretty much essential if you want a room. It's often enough just to call ahead on the day to bag floor space.

CLOCKWISE FROM TOP LEFT: PIXEL-SHOT/SHUTTERSTOCK,
ROLF G WACKENBERG/SHUTTERSTOCK, NEW AFRICA/SHUTTERSTOCK,

Family Travel

With its beer halls, Lederhosen and tipsy oompah ensembles, you'd be excused for regarding southern Germany as a wholly unsuitable place to bring little 'uns. But you'd be wrong. The region's cities have lots of tot-focused activities. In fact, having kids on board can bring you closer to the locals than lager ever could.

Discounts

Family tickets are available at the vast majority of sights. It's always worth asking if there's a discount, even if none is advertised. On trains, children up to five years of age travel free without a ticket. Between six and 14 there's no charge but a ticket is required. It's always good to carry ID for teenagers who might look older than they are.

Feeding Time

When it comes to feeding the pack, Germany's south is one of Europe's easier destinations. Most restaurants welcome young diners with smaller portions, special menus and perhaps even a free balloon. Kids are welcome in beer gardens as long as accompanied by an adult. Schnitzel, sausages, sweet dumplings and strudel are traditional menu items kids will love. Breastfeeding in public is perfectly acceptable.

Experience Bavaria

The tourist website *erlebe.bayern* has countless tips and articles on things to do with children across the Free State. Tourist offices across the region can advise on kid-friendly activities, attractions and suitable places to eat.

Nuremberg

The capital of Franconia is arguably the most child-friendly city in all of central Europe. The city has more child-focused attractions than any other, including Playmobil FunPark, the Deutsche Bahn Museum and the Children & Young People's Museum.

KID-FRIENDLY PICKS

Playmobil FunPark
Headquartered in Zindorf just outside Nuremberg, the adjoining fun park is one of the region's best family attractions.

Deutsche Bahn Museum
Germany's top railway museum in Nuremberg has a huge interactive section for choo-choo enthusiasts.

Partnachklamm
Looking to introduce the kids to hiking? This very easy and highly dramatic gorge trail in Garmisch-Partenkirchen will have them hooked for life.

BMW Welt (p80)
Kids can grip the wheel of BMW's latest models and wish they were old enough to have a driving licence.

QUIRKY KIDS' ACTIVITIES

There really is lots to get kids' minds racing in southern Germany. In Rothenburg ob der Tauber, the most popular stop on the Romantic Road, you can explore the Christmas Museum and festive bauble superstore before biting into a snowball year-round. In Baden-Württemberg, some kids will burst into tears at the sight of a titchy bird lurching out of a Triburg-made clock, others will go cuckoo at the very thought. In Munich, don't worry about young ones not understanding the script of a puppet show – if they've never seen one before, they're sure to beg you for a repeat performance.

Health & Safe Travel

INSURANCE

Insurance is not compulsory when travelling to Germany, but it is, of course, recommended. Consider policies that cover both health emergencies and flight cancellation. EU citizens should have their European Health Insurance Card (EHIC) with them; this covers medical costs when outside your home country, even those associated with long-term conditions.

Crime

Bavaria is a very low-crime destination and your chances of becoming a victim of criminal activity are relatively slim. However, Oktoberfest sees a spike in pickpocketing, criminal damage and general ne'er-do-welling. The streets around Munich's Hauptbahnhof can have a slightly seedy feel, as can a late Saturday night ride on the S-Bahn.

Ticks

The most dangerous creature out in the forests of southern Germany? Bears, wolves, lynx? No, the tiny tick which can potentially give you Lyme disease and, in the worst case, tick-borne encephalitis. Check yourself at the end of every day in the woods and avoid walking through long grass in the summer. If you are really concerned, consider vaccination against tick-borne encephalitis.

TAP WATER

Tap water is perfectly safe to drink across southern Germany, even in big cities like Munich and Stuttgart.

SKI SLOPE SIGNS IN EUROPE

| New skier/child | Beginner | Intermediate | Advanced | Expert | Advanced expert |

Pharmacies

Like every central European city, Munich, Stuttgart and Nuremberg have many pharmacies that can provide advice and sell over-the-counter medication. They also advise when more specialised help is required and point you in the right direction. If you need medicines for long-term conditions, you may be able to get them using prescriptions from other EU countries, though you'll pay the full amount.

WINTER MOTORING

If travelling to southern Germany by car, you must have winter tyres fitted between November and March, and carry chains if you are heading anywhere near the Alps. Spiked tyres are banned. Anti-freeze coolant and proper screenwash are also essential. Slow down when conditions are icy and snowy, especially on motorways where special speed limits often apply in bad weather.

LGBTIQ+ Travellers

Homosexuality is widely accepted in Bavaria, but the scene, even in Munich and Stuttgart, is small compared to, say, Berlin or Cologne. LGBTIQ+ travellers should experience no hostility though. All cities have a relaxed attitude to the LGBTIQ+ community, but in rural areas, especially the more conservative Alps, queer people tend to keep a slightly lower profile.

Glockenbachviertel

Munich's gay quarter is without doubt the Glockenbachviertel, an area south of the Altstadt. It's here you'll find the majority of gay and lesbian clubs, cafes, hotels and organisations, though they have dispersed slightly over the last decade. The Glockenbachviertel is the place to come to meet like-minded individuals with Wednesdays declared gay day by almost all local businesses. Freddie Mercury was once a regular around here and quite incredibly some of the clubs and bars have been open since the late 1960s.

CHRISTOPHER STREET DAYS

Christopher Street Day *(csdmuenchen.de)* is the name by which Gay Pride is often referred to in southern Germany, Austria and Switzerland. Usually taking place in June, Munich's CSD is a huge event that now takes over almost the entire city with many businesses and attractions getting in on the act. Straight or gay, it's a colourful and reassuring time to be in the Bavarian capital.

Help & Assistance

The Sub *(subonline.org)*, based at Müllerstrasse 14 just south of the Altstadt, is a one-stop-shop for the LGBTIQ+ community for advice and assistance. There's a superb cafe on the premises, too.

GAY TOURIST INFO

Munich's official tourist information portal is one of the best places to go for LGBTIQ+-specific tourist information. The LGBTIQ+ section has a comprehensive overview in English of things to do, specific venues and other snippets for the community all gathered together in one place.

Gay Outdoor Club München

A section of the **Deutsche Alpenverein** *(Germany Alpine Club; dav-goc.de)* organises hikes and climbs in the Alps for members of the LGBTIQ+ community. Activities are open to non-members, too, though you may need some German.

GAY OKTOBERFEST

The world's biggest booze-up has for years included events aimed specifically at the gay community. The first Sunday of Oktoberfest is unofficially known as Gay Sunday with the action centered on the Bräurosl beer tent. The first Monday sees another gay gathering and some LGBTIQ+ businesses have a presence at the festival. There are virtually no reports of hostility during the festivities.

Food, Drink & Nightlife

When to Eat

Frühstuck (6–8am) Germans take breakfast seriously, as you are likely to witness in hotels that offer morning buffets.

Mittagessen (noon–2pm) Lunch can range from a light sandwich and soup to a full-blown meat and dumplings combo.

Abendessen (Abendbrot) (6–9pm) Now often the main meal of the day, restaurants and beer halls offer everything from vegan burgers to Michelin-blessed tasting menus.

Where to Eat

Restaurants Germany's south has everything from Michelin-starred French fine dining to Turkish kebab joints.

Beer halls & pubs These are often the best places to source hearty local cuisine.

Cafes These range from coffee and cake shops to light lunch halts.

Beer gardens The food at these outdoor places is usually very good and relatively cheap.

Fast food Sausages on the run are the fast food of choice in Bavaria, available almost everywhere.

MENU DECODER

Speisekarte Menu, though you'll often see just 'Menu' these days

Gericht Dish

Vorspeise Starter

Kleines Gericht Literally a 'small dish' if you are not that hungry

Suppe Soup

Brotzeiten Open sandwiches (often as starters or to go with beer)

Hauptgericht Main course

Warme Küche Warm meals/starters

Wurstspezialitäten Sausage specialities/dishes

Vegetarisch Vegetarian

Glutenfrei Gluten-free

Vegan Vegan

Fleisch Meat

Schweinefleisch Pork

Rindfleisch Beef

Hühnchen Chicken

Gebraten Fried

Gekocht Boiled

Geröstet Roasted

Getränke Drinks

Rotwein/Weisswein Red wine/white wine

Bier Beer; often there are several types on offer

Wasser Water

Flasche Bottle

Nachtisch Dessert. This literally translates as 'after-table.' The range of desserts is often very limited

Spirituosen Spirits

Kaffee Coffee

Die Rechnung The bill

Trinkgeld Tip

HOW TO... Pay Your Bill

Settling up at the end of a meal is no minefield of finely-tuned etiquette in the taverns and inns of southern Germany. But the process might differ from what you are used to back home. Attracting the waiter's attention might be your first hurdle – clicking fingers and calling 'waiter' (or worse) is likely to get you ignored. The relevant staff member having arrived at your tableside (this may be the head waiter, the only one trusted to take payments), there are two decisions to be made – pay all together, and cash or card. This is probably late in the day to ask whether that chalet at 2000m up a mountain with no mobile reception takes plastic, but most other eateries now do. To tip, either round up the bill with notes or ask the waiter to add something to the card transaction.

HOW MUCH FOR...

Coffee
€3.50

Half-litre of beer
€4-5

Weisswurst breakfast
€12

Half-litre bottle of water
€2

Glass of wine
€6

Strudel with vanilla sauce
€8

Six Nürnberger Bratwurst
€11

HOW TO... Enjoy a Beer Garden

Other cities such as Pilsen and Brussels occasionally launch weak bids, but none can rival Munich when it comes to claiming the title of 'beer capital of the world'. In the summer months there's no better place to enjoy Bavaria's beers than in a beer garden. They originate in Munich – the first one was established at the Hofbräukeller in the late 19th century. If you plan on spending an evening at a beer garden such as the Chinesischer Turm or the monster Hirschgarten, there are some things you might need to know beforehand. Most traditional beer gardens have common features – fairy lights strung between the chestnut trees that shade drinkers from the sun and, for a time at least, summer drizzle. Chairs are slatted and foldable, as are the tables. The ground is normally gravel that soaks up spilled suds best! Table reservations may be possible but don't count on it – it's the luck of the draw where you sit. Steer clear of the *Stammtisch* area; this is reserved for regulars. There's rarely waiter service; instead order your food and drink at central points (separate counters at large beer gardens). You pay a *Pfand* (deposit; normally €2) for your glass. Carry everything back to the table yourself, and when you want more beer, take your tankard back to the serving point.

Fast Fact

Despite often excessive alcohol consumption, public drunkenness and disorder (among locals at least) is rarely seen, and most beer halls and gardens are encouragingly family friendly, with kids' playgrounds and specially gauged food portions.

BAVARIA'S BAMBOOZLING BEERS

Some 40 different types of beer are brewed in Bavaria. Add to that specials and craft beers and the list can become a confusing list of strange-sounding concoctions. Here we bring you a beer menu decipherer for informed drinking:

Bier Generic term that will meet with confused looks from almost every waiter across the land if you order it.

Helles Usually the most common beer in restaurants – the name simply means 'light'.

Dunkel Caramelly dark lager produced by all of Munich's breweries but not always available on tap.

Weissbier (aka Weizen) Wheat beer is a Bavarian classic and pleasingly less sweet than, say, the Belgian types. The Erding brewery specialises in this rather fruity type of beer.

Bock Lightly hopped, smooth and very strong lager served in a small glass.

Doppelbock Malty, strong version of a Bock with a darkish hue.

Rauchbier Found mostly in Bamberg, the smokey flavour of this lager comes from the roasting process applied to the barley.

Märzen Amber lager closely associated with Oktoberfest as it was brewed in March (März means March in German) and drunk in autumn.

Dunkelweizen A cross between a Dunkel and a Weissbier – a dark wheat beer.

Weizenbock Something between a wheat beer and a Doppelbock.

Lager/Pilsner Generic name for this style of beer.

Oktoberfestbier The beers brewed specially for Oktoberfest are often very strong, as much as 6% proof.

Rotbier Translates as Red Beer and is typical for Nuremberg. Top-fermented and malty and best sampled at source in Nuremberg's taverns.

Responsible Travel

Climate Change & Travel

It's impossible to ignore the impact we have when travelling; Lonely Planet urges all travellers to engage with their travel carbon footprint, which will mainly come from air travel. While there often isn't an alternative, travellers can look to minimise the number of flights they take, opt for newer aircrafts and use cleaner ground transport, such as trains. One proposed solution—purchasing carbon offsets—unfortunately does not cancel out the impact of individual flights. While most destinations will depend on air travel for the foreseeable future, for now, pursuing ground-based travel where possible is the best course of action.

The **UN Carbon Offset Calculator** shows how flying impacts a household's emissions

The **ICAO's carbon emissions calculator** allows visitors to analyse the CO2 generated by point-to-point journeys

BISS is a specially produced magazine that provides an income for people living on the streets or in temporary accommodation around Munich. Buy it to help them out a bit.

Take a reusable bottle to fill up at your accommodation and public taps instead of buying water in plastic bottles – Munich's tap water is tasty, free and completely safe to drink.

Green Fashion Tour

Take a tour of Munich's vintage and sustainable clothing boutiques with *cosh.eco*, the antidote to throwaway fashion. The website has the full list if you want to go it alone.

City Driving

Munich, Nuremberg and Stuttgart city centres are low-emission zones (Umweltzone) where you'll need to pay for a special windscreen sticker (Feinstaubplakette). These are available at *tuev-nord.de*.

MOTORWAY MADNESS

Ignore the BMWs driving at 250kmph on the autobahn and stick to the standard 130. Germans' green credentials go out of the window as soon as they get behind the wheel, but yours don't have to.

ORGANIC IN THE GARDEN

When in the English Garden, seek out Milchhäusl *(milchhaeusl.bio)* which serves exclusively organic food made with produce from Bavaria. It even has a Bio-Biergarten.

Roecklplatz in Munich

Superb restaurant **Roecklplatz** *(roecklplatz.de)* in the Isartalstrasse trains up socially disadvantaged young people to be chefs, with one place always going to a refugee. You can support their work by eating here or donating.

Train Travel

Southern Germany has one of Europe's densest and most efficient rail networks so ditch the hire car for the restaurant and take the train.

Tourist Tax

Many visitors, especially to the Alps, are sometimes irked at having to pay the tourist tax, often in cash, on top of their room rate. However, this pays for all the facilities you use as a tourist.

Returnables

You pay a deposit (Pfand) on almost all bottles in Germany, including plastic ones. You can return them to shops or leave them out for someone collecting bottles – but never put them in the bin!

Stay Green

On the Germany tourism website *(germany.travel)* you can check the green credentials of almost 400 accommodation providers across Bavaria and Baden-Württemberg. These are hotels with Green Sign certification or other sustainability awards.

RECUP and REBOWL *(recup.de)* is a popular way of returning takeaway containers after use.

Support initiatives helping Ukrainian and other refugees, who have arrived in southern Germany in their thousands, through *aktion-deutschland-hilft.de*.

Those with a deeper interest in Munich's commitment to a sustainable future should arrange a visit to the **Ökologisches Bildungszentrum** *(Ecological Education Centre; oebz.de)* in the Bogenhausen district of the city.

RESOURCES

wwf.de
Germany's WWF website has lots of info and volunteering opportunities.

aktion-deutschland-hilft.de
Find out how you can help refugees in southern Germany.

munich.travel
Has a large sustainable travel section.

Accessible Travel

Generally speaking, Munich and southern Germany cater well for the needs of those with disabilities. EU accessibility regulations are actually implemented here with public transport made increasingly easy to use and public buildings and spaces open to all.

Train Travel

All Deutsche Bahn trains are now fully accessible to all, though those belonging to other operators may not be. The revamped Hauptbahnhof will be fully barrier-free.

Airport

All airports in the region come up to and possibly beyond EU standards for accessibility with assistance services, stair-free access and many other services you may (or may not) be used to back home.

Accommodation

Upper-end and most midrange hotels are completely barrier free though may have only a couple of rooms for wheelchair users. Beware short-term rentals with eight flights of stairs to the door.

BEER GARDENS

The region's beer gardens are some of the best places for those with disabilities to eat and drink as they are by their nature open and barrier-free.

Hotel Search

The accommodation section of the Munich tourist office website has a search facility for finding suitably accessible accommodation in the capital. Other cities are not so well set up.

City Transport

You should be able to get a wheelchair even onto a village bus in the Alps, never mind the trams, metros and buses of cities such as Munich, Stuttgart and Nuremberg.

RENTAL & EQUIPMENT

For wheelchair and scooter rental plus any other equipment you may need, the most central point to turn to is **Von Schlieben** (vonschlieben.de) at Karlsplatz/Stachus, who offer a full service.

RESOURCES

Deutsche Bahn Mobility Service Centre (bahn.com) Train-access information and route-planning assistance.

Simply Munich (munich.travel) The official tourism website has a comprehensive section for travellers with disabilities to enjoy Munich to the full.

Natko (natko.de) Central clearing house for enquiries about barrier-free travel in all of Germany.

Munich Accessible Culture (kultur-barrierefrei-muenchen.de) Website dedicated to helping those with disabilities enjoy culture in the Bavarian capital.

The **Munich tourist office** (munich.travel) arranges barrier-free guided tours of the city centre for travellers with disabilities. These last between two and three hours and can be booked by calling the office. Prices are relatively high.

Nuts & Bolts

OPENING HOURS

Opening hours are similar to the rest of central Europe. Exceptions include supermarkets, which are closed on Sundays, and some city-centre shops which might stay open on a Saturday afternoon. The day generally begins earlier in southern Germany than it does in the rest of Western Europe.

Toilets

Public toilets are rarely free in Germany. Rather irritating Sanifair paid toilets are even being installed in shopping centres and train stations (these give a voucher for use in the location where they are situated).

Weights & Measures

All of Germany uses the metric system in everyday life.

Smoking

Smoking in public places is banned, besides some smoking areas in airports and train stations.

GOOD TO KNOW

Time zone
GMT+1

Country calling code
+49

Emergency number
112

Population
24.7 million

Electricity
Type F; 230V/50Hz

PUBLIC HOLIDAYS

Businesses and offices are closed on the following public holidays:

Neujahrstag (New Year's Day) 1 January

Heilige Drei Könige (Epiphany) 6 January

Ostern (Easter) March/April Good Friday, Easter Sunday and Easter Monday

Maifeiertag (Labour Day) 1 May

Christi Himmelfahrt (Ascension Day) 40 days after Easter

Pfingsten (Whitsun/Pentecost) mid-May to mid-June – Whit Sunday and Whit Monday

Fronleichnam (Corpus Christi) 10 days after Pentecost

Mariä Himmelfahrt (Assumption Day, Bavaria only) 15 August

Tag der Deutschen Einheit (Day of German Unity) 3 October

Weihnachtstag (Christmas Day) 25 December

Zweiter Weihnachtstag (Second Day of Christmas) 26 December

Language

German belongs to the West Germanic language family, with English and Dutch as close relatives.

Basics
Hello. Guten Tag. *goo·ten tahk*
Goodbye. Auf Wiedersehen. *owf vee·der·zay·en*
Yes. Ja. *yah*
No. Nein. *nain*
Please. Bitte. *bi·te*
Thank you. Danke. *dang·ke*
Excuse me. Entschuldigung. *ent·shul·di·gung*
Sorry. Entschuldigung. *ent·shul·di·gung*
What's your name?
Wie ist Ihr Name? (pol) *vee ist eer nah·me*
Wie heißt du? (inf) *vee haist doo*
My name is...
Mein Name ist... (pol) *main nah·me ist...*
Ich heiße... (inf) *ikh hai·se...*
Do you speak English?
Sprechen Sie Englisch? (pol) *shpre·khen zee eng·lish*
Sprichst du Englisch? (inf) *shprikhst doo eng·lish*
I don't understand. Ich verstehe nicht. *ikh fer·shtay·e nikht*

Directions
Where's (the station)?
Wo ist (der Bahnhof). *vo ist (der bahn·hawf)*
What's the address?
Wie ist die Adresse? *vee ist dee a·dre·se*
Could you please write it down?
Könnten Sie das bitte aufschreiben? *kern·ten zee das bi·te owf·shrai·ben*
Can you show me (on the map)?
Können Sie es mir (auf der Karte) zeige *ker·nen zee es meer (owf dair kar·te) tsai·gen*

Signs
Ausgang Exit
Eingang Entrance
Damen Women
Herren Men
Heiß Hot
Kalt Cold
Offen Open
Geschlossen Closed
Kein Zutritt No Entry
Rauchen Verboten No Smoking
Verboten Prohibited

Time
What time is it? Wie spät ist es? *vee shpayt ist es*
It's (10) o'clock. Es ist (zehn) Uhr. *es ist (tsayn) oor*
morning Morgen *mor·gen*
afternoon Nachmittag *nahkh·mi·tahk*
evening Abend *ah·bent*
yesterday gestern *ges·tern*
today heute *hoy·te*
tomorrow morgen *mor·gen*

Emergencies
Help! Hilfe! *hil·fe*
Go away! Gehen Sie weg! *gay·en zee vek*
I'm ill. Ich bin krank. *ikh bin krangk*
Call the police! Rufen Sie die Polizei! *roo·fen zee dee po·li·tsai*
Call a doctor! Rufen Sie einen Arzt! *roo·fen zee ai·nen artst*

NUMBERS

1 **eins** *ains*
2 **zwei** *tsvai*
3 **drei** *drai*
4 **vier** *feer*
5 **fünf** *fünf*
6 **sechs** *zeks*
7 **sieben** *zee·ben*
8 **acht** *akht*
9 **neun** *noyn*
10 **zehn** *tsayn*

DONATIONS TO ENGLISH

Numerous – you may recognise kindergarten, kitsch, waltz, hamburger, poodle

DISTINCTIVE SOUNDS

The ü (pronounced as 'e' with rounded lips), plus the throaty kh (like in the Scottish loch or the name Bach) and r (a bit like gargling).

Sound Like a Local

Hey! Hey! *hei*
Great! Toll! *tol*
Cool! Spitze! *shpi·tse*
No problem. Kein Problem. *kain pro·blaym*
Sure. Klar! *klahr*
Maybe. Vielleicht. *fi·laikht*
No way! Auf keinen Fall! *owf kai·nen fal*
It's OK. Alles klar. *a·les klahr*
What a pity! Schade! *shah·de*
Doesn't matter. Macht Nichts. *makht nikhts*

False Friends

Warning: many German words look like English words but have a different meaning altogether, eg *Chef* is boss, not chef (which is *Koch* in German).

Must-know Grammar

German words can have a number of different endings, depending on their role in the sentence. There's also a formal and informal word for 'you' (*Sie* and *du* respectively).

Why Bother

Don't be put off by the fact that German tends to join words together to express a single notion – it's not hard to tell parts of words, and you'll have fun recognising 'the Football World Cup qualifying match' hidden within *Fussballweltmeisterschaftsqualifikationsspiel*.

German in the World

It's not usually described as romantic, but its role in science has long been recognised, and the German language lays claim to some of the most famous works ever printed – just think of the influence of Goethe, Nietzsche, Freud and Einstein.

WHO SPEAKS GERMAN?

German is the official or co-official language of Germany, Austria, Liechtenstein, Belgium, Switzerland and Luxembourg, and a recognised language in Namibia.

STORYBOOK

THE MUNICH, BAVARIA & THE BLACK FOREST

STORYBOOK

Our writers delve deep into different aspects of Munich, Bavaria & the Black Forest life

History of Munich, Bavaria & the Black Forest in 15 Places

From war, revolution and mad dictators to prosperity.

Marc Di Duca

p288

Ludwig II

Deposed and derided as mad in his lifetime, Bavaria's most famous monarch left behind an incomparable legacy.

Marc Di Duca

p292

Germany's Wild South

The battle to preserve one of Europe's most beautiful corners.

Anthony Ham

p295

Brands & Inventions of Southern Germany

From clocks that go cuckoo to snazzy trainers, Bavaria has given the world some of its most truly iconic brands.

Marc Di Duca

p298

Germany's Beer Purity Law

The *Reinheitsgebot*, testament to the artistry and dedication that Germans hold towards their beloved beverage.

Kat Barber

p300

Hofbräuhaus exterior (p49), Munich

A HISTORY OF MUNICH, BAVARIA & THE BLACK FOREST IN
15 PLACES

One of Europe's oldest states, Bavaria has enjoyed a long and eventful past, populated by a weird-and-wunderbar cast of Roman emperors, oddball kings and infamous Nazis. Despite war and revolution, mad dictators and the destruction of WWII, all's well that ends well, with southern Germany now one of the world's most prosperous places.

SOUTHERN GERMANY'S DOCUMENTED story goes back to Roman times when much of the region was part of the Roman Empire. In fact, for the Romans, Eastern Bavaria was the edge of the known world; beyond lurked only a scarily forested land of barbarian nomads.

Having served as the epicentre of the Holy Roman Empire and passed through Europe's medieval religious strife with many a scar to show for it, Bavaria entered the 19th century as a powerful state under the Wittelsbachs who rebuilt Munich then, under Ludwig II, set about creating a set of castles that accidentally launched the region's tourist industry.

Not long after Ludwig, Sissi and other notable royals left the stage of history and the region found itself on the wrong side in WWI, a fact that led to the rise of Hitler and the Nazis who used Bavarian imagery and tradition as the blueprint for how Germans should look and behave. Hitler moved on to Berlin and Poland, but Bavaria, most notably Würzburg, bore the brunt of Germany's defeat.

Few other places so eloquently tell the story of Germany's postwar revival and economic miracle than Munich, with its 1974 Olympic venues, high-tech BMW plant and first-rate city infrastructure.

1. Kastell Boiotro
PASSAU'S ROMAN HERITAGE
Located on the southern bank of the River Inn in Passau, no other Roman site in Bavaria has given up so much information about Bavaria's centuries under Roman rule. The Roman fortress stood here for 150 years until around 400 CE, guarding the strategic confluence of three rivers, though it was used more as a customs post as Passau was a border town between two customs territories. More Roman heritage can be found heading northeast up the Danube (Donau) at Regensburg where the oversize Porta Praetoria is still used as an access gate to the cathedral.

For more on Kastell Boiotro, see p169.

2. Weltenburg Monastery
POWER OF THE MONASTERIES
On a particularly tight bend in the Danube near the town of Kelheim, the Benedictine Weltenburg Monastery is a symbol of the key role religion once played in central Europe. Founded around the year 617 by Scottish missionaries, it's probably the oldest monastery in Bavaria. It was later given a makeover into a baroque residence, the Assam brothers kitting out the monastery church. Southern Germany is pep-

pered with similar grand edifices that illustrate the power and wealth of the Catholic Church in the Middle Ages, influence that led to religious wars and the deaths of large numbers of the southern German population.

For more on Weltenburg Monastery, see p165.

3. Kaiserburg
SAFEBOX OF THE HOLY ROMAN EMPIRE
Rising high above Nuremberg, the Kaiserburg was once an important location within the Holy Roman Empire as it was where Emperor Charles IV kept the imperial crown jewels. The Holy Roman Empire was a Christian continuation of the Western Roman Empire but was nothing to do with Rome. It was dominated by the kingdoms and states of Germany, putting German rulers at the top of a power structure that dominated medieval Europe. The local Hohenstaufen and Wittelsbach dynasties both provided several emperors, but it was an Austrian Habsburg who eventually dissolved the empire in 1806 after a millennium in existence.

For more on the Kaiserburg, see p102.

4. Munich Residence
HOME OF THE WITTELSBACHS
No rundown of Bavarian history is complete without a mention of the House of Wittelsbach, a dynasty that ruled the state for over eight centuries. Their winter home was the Residenz in the very heart of Munich, now a major tourist attraction. The two kings who shaped the state as far as architecture is concerned were Ludwig I, who attempted to rebuild Munich as 'Athens on the Isar', adding the neo-Classical attractions around the Königsplatz, and his grandson Ludwig II who famously emptied his private coffers constructing castles and palaces.

For more on the Munich Residenz, see p54.

5. Baden-Baden
EMBODIMENT OF 19TH-CENTURY LEISURE
In 2021 UNESCO recognised the importance of Europe's spa industry when it handed World Cultural Heritage status to 11 European spa towns, one of them Baden-Baden. Arguably Europe's most famous place to take the waters, Baden-Baden was once the most fashionable place in Europe, attracting the Forbes list of the 19th century. These spa towns remain as symbols of a major change in 19th-century society – the rise of leisure, a concept that hadn't really existed until that time. Baden-Baden's grand spa hotels continue to exemplify the notion of leisure, once the preserve of the very rich but now accessible to all.

For more on Baden-Baden, see p241.

6. Schloss Neuschwanstein
LUDWIG II AND ALL THAT
The Ludwig II chapter in Bavaria's history is a chapter unto itself, though you could see his flights of fancy in the shape of fairy tale castles as representing a movement at the time away from the squalor and pollution of the Industrial Revolution back to a more idyllic, mythical past. Ludwig frittered away his wealth and borrowed heavily to fund three megalomanic projects, including the dreamy Neuschwanstein. Bavaria's most famous monarch probably

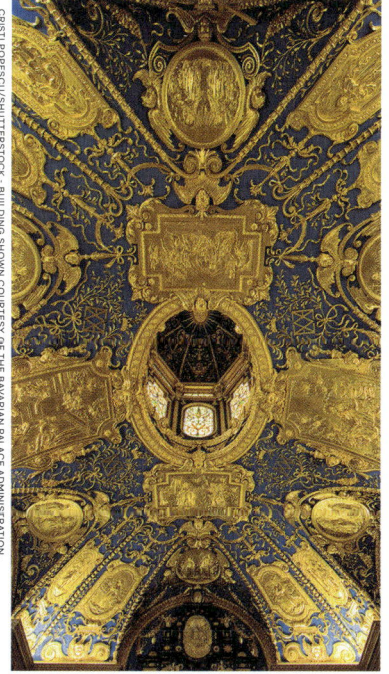

Residenz (p54), Munich

paid for his fixation on folly construction with his life, an event that remains one of the greatest historical mysteries in Germany's south.

For more on Schloss Neuschwanstein, see p142.

7. Mercedes-Benz Museum, Stuttgart
MOTORING THROUGH HISTORY

Not only did Stuttgart give the world its best car brand, Mercedes (other car brands are available), Gottlieb Daimler of Schorndorf near the city was the man who actually invented the internal combustion engine in the first place, paving the way for Germany's future as a top automobile producer. Bertha Benz, the pioneering woman who drove a car 104km in 1888, thus becoming the first person to travel a long distance in a vehicle, hailed from Pforzheim, 50km to the northwest. Southern Germany and cars – historically there's just always been a spark(plug) between them, and no other place in Baden-Württemberg celebrates the fact better than Stuttgart's Mercedes-Benz Museum

For more on Stuttgart's Mercedes-Benz Museum, see p214.

8. Burg Hohenzollern
LAST DAYS OF IMPERIAL GERMANY

Hohenzollern Castle is a historically important place as it served as the ancestral seat of the House of Hohenzollern, the German royal dynasty that ruled until 1918. The last of the Hohenzollerns, Emperor Wilhelm II, gave up the throne at the end of WWI, bringing to an end the dynasty's illustrious rule and 50 years of a united Germany's days under an emperor. The castle itself is the third to sit atop the wooded Zollerberg; today's incarnation is a rebuild by the dynasty dating from the mid-19th century as a neo-Gothic showpiece. None of the four Hohenzollern emperors of Germany ever lived there.

For more on Burg Hohenzollern, see p224.

9. Reichsparteitagsgelände
THE RISE OF THE NAZIS

A working-class railway town greatly affected by Germany's post-WWI woes, Nuremberg was fertile ground for the Nazis' rabble rousing. With that in mind, it comes as little surprise that the infamous footage of a a shrieking Hitler whipping up a mass frenzy was often shot at Nuremberg's Reichsparteitagsgelände, a huge open space to the southeast of the city centre. The Dokumentationszentrum (Documentation Centre) there looks at Nuremberg's role in the Nazi episode. Nuremberg also played its part after the war when the international court charged with prosecuting prominent Nazis sat in the city for the Nuremberg Trials.

For more on Reichsparteitagsgelände, see p104.

10. Hitler's Eagle's Nest
BIRTHPLACE OF A DICTATORSHIP

All that remains of the residences and compounds the Nazis built around Berchtesgaden (most of it was either bombed by the RAF or dynamited by the postwar government), the Eagle's Nest has come to represent the arrogance of an out-of-touch dictator, lost, a little like Ludwig II before him, in a Wagnerian Alpine fantasy where he played the lead role. Eva Braun liked to sunbathe here, but Hitler spent most of his time at the nearby compound where some of the biggest decisions before and during WWII were made. The Eagle's Nest is now a restaurant, and hard-to-reach one at that, but the views are out of this world.

For more on the Eagle's Nest, see p155.

11. Dachau Concentration Camp
THE NAZIS' FIRST CAMP

An incredibly significant site just outside Munich, Dachau was the first concentration camp set up by the Nazis as early as 1933. Some of the practices here would be copied across Eastern Europe in horrific death camps such as Auschwitz and Treblinka. No one knows exactly how many people died here, but 41,500 deaths were documented in the 12 years it served as a concentration camp. Interestingly, the camp only closed in 1960. In the immediate aftermath of WWII it was used as a prison for SS soldiers, then to house Sudeten Germans expelled from Czechoslovakia, and lastly as a US Cold War military base.

For more on the Dachau Concentration Camp, see p90.

Mercedes-Benz Museum (p214), Stuttgart

12. Weisse Rose Monument
ACT OF WARTIME RESISTENCE

Few acts of wartime resistance to the Nazis are more moving than the story of the Weisse Rose. Three of the members of the White Rose Movement, students Christoph Probst, Sophie Scholl and Hans Scholl, were beheaded by the Gestapo in February 1943 for distributing leaflets at Munich University. A space has been set aside in the uni building to pay tribute to this futile attempt to turn the tide of Nazism. Few others during the years of Nazi rule were brave enough to resist, a fact that makes the students' story all the more disturbing.

For more on the Weisse Rose Monument, see p63.

13. Olympiapark
SYMBOL OF POSTWAR RESURRECTION

There's no greater symbol in Bavaria of the resurrection Germany experienced in the postwar years than Munich's Olympiapark. Just 29 years after the end of WWII, the city that spawned the Nazis and Hitler was hosting a celebration of international cooperation and peace, though the games were marred by a terrorist attack on members of the Israeli team. Today, the once impressively space-age structures that the 1974 summer games bequeathed still stand as a reminder of Germany's rehabilitation to a Western democracy and continue, unlike some Olympic sites, to be fully used to this day.

For more on Olympiapark, see p77.

14. Wyhl
THE SEEDS OF GERMANY'S GREEN MOVEMENT

In the early 1970s, the village of Wyhl, 35km to the north of Freiburg and on the border with France, was slated as the site of a new nuclear power station. Local demonstrations against the decision were brutally mishandled by the police and this inadvertently sparked a debate about the place of nuclear power in Germany's electricity producing mix. In 1975, planning permission was revoked, but the incident left Freiburg as the centre of a sprouting green movement which has now become mainstream across Germany, and even influences decision-making at an EU level.

For more on Wyhl, see p226.

15. BMW Welt
FORWARD-LOOKING E-FUTURE

Nowhere else in Bavaria is the future on show as much as at BMW's gleaming BMW Welt (BMW World), a free attraction showcasing BMW's latest models as well as other aspects of the company's output. That future, according to BMW, is electric, a far cry from the Teutonic gas-guzzlers of but a decade or so ago. While many green activists may frown at the idea of mass car ownership going forward into a sustainable future, BMW would seek to disagree.

For more on BMW Welt, see p80.

Portrait of Ludwig II (1865), painted by Ferdinand II Piloty
DEA/A. DAGLI ORTI/GETTY IMAGES

THE STORY & LEGACY OF LUDWIG II

Deposed and derided as mad in his lifetime, Bavaria's most famous monarch left behind an incomparable legacy. By Marc Di Duca.

SPEND MORE THAN a day in southern Bavaria and sooner or later you are sure to hear the name, or see an image, of King Ludwig II. But just who was this most celebrated and often ridiculed Bavarian monarch – the Swan King, Mad King Ludwig – a man who inadvertently did so much to influence the tourist offerings of Munich and Upper Bavaria?

Early Life

Ludwig Otto Friedrich Wilhelm von Wittelsbach was born at Nymphenburg Palace on 25 August 1845 (the bed on which he first saw the light of day still stands in the palace) to Crown Prince Maximilian II and Princess Marie of Prussia, his folks becoming king and queen when Ludwig was three. Prince Ludwig's childhood was mostly spent at Schloss Hohenschwangau and Lake Starnberg, but it doesn't appear to have been a happy one. In keeping with the norms of the day (King Edward VII of England was born four years earlier and suffered similarly), Ludwig was constantly reminded of his burden to rule, but showed little interest in this or the affairs of state. The people closest to him were his grandfather Ludwig I and cousin Elizabeth, or the famous 'Sisi', who later became Empress of Austria. His parents became distant.

Ludwig's Reign

Ludwig was crowned Bavarian king in 1864 at just 18, an introverted young lover of art and Wagner and really not monarch material at all. Handsome, enigmatic and one of the wealthiest men in central Europe, the freshly hatched ruler was popular with his subjects, but not with the Bavarian government or court. He despised all public functions, took almost no part in running state affairs and shunned Munich for the Bavarian countryside. Despite being engaged to his cousin, Ludwig was most certainly homosexual and did not father an heir. As his reign progressed, his fixations with the works of Richard Wagner, summoned to the Bavarian court soon after Ludwig was crowned, and his reclusiveness grew ever stronger. Meanwhile, the most important event during Ludwig's reign was the unification of Germany under Bismarck and King Wilhelm I of Prussia, which saw Bavaria essentially lose its position as a sovereign state.

Wagner Obsession

Ludwig had first heard Wagner's operas as an impressionable teenager, his imagination fed by the composer's world of myth and fantasy. Wagner had special status at the Munich court, premiering his later operas at the Royal Court Theatre (today's Bavarian State Opera) and even asking for 100,000 thalers to build his Festspielhaus in Bayreuth (now the venue for the world's premier annual Wagner Festival). The king also commissioned a residence for the composer (who was notoriously 'bad with money'), Villa Wahnfried in Bayreuth, behind which the composer was laid to rest in 1883. Wagner's works heavily influenced the design of Ludwig's famous castles, especially Schloss Neuschwanstein.

Castles

Patronage of Wagner aside, Ludwig II is remembered most for what he bequeathed to the state of Bavaria in bricks, mortar and imagination – his castles. It's often claimed that the king bankrupted the state coffers to construct these flights of fancy, but that's simply not true as he actually used his own personal wealth. Inspired by Versailles, Wartburg Castle in Thuringia and several other medieval piles, he set about designing a legacy that would live on well beyond his years and inadvertently lay the foundations of the Bavarian tourist industry. Neuschwanstein, with its most romantic of Alpine locations and Wagnerian frescoes, would have been enough on its own, but Versailles-esque Herrenchiemsee and mini Schloss Linderhof, lost in the Alps, sealed Ludwig's place in history.

Costing millions of marks and employing thousands, these castles are testament to his imagination. If Ludwig had lived past the modest age of 42, the ground would have been broken on at least three more mega-projects. As it was, none of his palaces was ever fully finished.

Mysterious Death

Though not directly funded by the Bavarian state, by 1885 Ludwig was borrowing heavily to pay for his ill-advised construction projects. Harrassed by officials and told to economise, Ludwig was just about to dismiss the whole government when the ministers got in the first blow. They declared the king insane and invited Ludwig's uncle, Prince Luitpold, to take the reins of power. However, Luitpold wanted to see some proof of Ludwig's mental state, so over the next two months a famous report was concocted on his mental health. A web of hearsay, anecdotal evidence and gossip, the report was dismissed by Bismarck, but this didn't stop four head psychiatrists signing it off in June 1886. Ludwig had essentially been deposed by a government that disliked his odd behaviour and disdain for state affairs. After a stand-off and disturbances in Munich, the king was taken into custody at Neuschwanstein Castle and transferred to Berg Castle on Lake Starnberg along with one of the psychiatrists, Bernhard von Gudden, head of the Munich Mental Asylum.

The next day, 13 June 1886, with von Gudden having spent time with the king and already expressing doubts about the diagnosis, the two men went for an evening stroll by the shores of the lake. They never returned. From the moment they were found dead in the water, conspiracy theories abounded as to what happened to the king and psychiatrist. The official autopsy found no injuries on the bodies, but some believe the king was shot trying to escape from Berg Castle and the murder was covered up by the state that had deposed him. The Museum of Bavarian History in Regensburg even claims to have the 'murder weapon'. A large, dark cross stands in the shallow water of Lake Starnberg where Ludwig's body was discovered. He is buried in St Michael's Church in Munich's Altstadt.

Mad King Ludwig?

On hearing of Ludwig's demise, his cousin Sisi is said to have claimed, 'The King was not insane – he was just an eccentric living in a dream world'. But mud sticks and Ludwig will eternally be the victim of a 19th-century disinformation campaign. A creative, dreamy and sensitive soul, Ludwig was simply unfit for the cut-throat politics of a newly unified Germany, preferring instead to lose himself in Alpine make-believe to a soundtrack of Teutonic fantasy.

GERMANY'S WILD SOUTH

Welcome to wild Germany at its best, a thrilling, complicated story of the ongoing battle to preserve and protect one of Europe's most beautiful corners. By Anthony Ham

GERMANY'S SOUTH IS one of Europe's most dramatic wild realms, home as it is to much-loved natural wonders: the Black Forest; the Danube and Rhine; and the Alps in all their very different glories, including Zugspitze (2962m), Germany's highest peak. These provide the backdrop to a fascinating story.

The Natural World

It is impossible to talk about the natural world in these parts without first speaking about the canvas upon which that story is written. Take Bavaria, for example, whose 70,555 sq km alone makes up one-fifth of Germany – it's larger than Ireland, Portugal or Denmark. Lake Constance, which Bavaria shares with Baden-Württemberg, is Germany's largest lake. And then there's the Black Forest, which represents 10% of all German forests.

The Alps are another of the south's natural epics. While appearing as one range to the uninitiated, the Alps include the Bavarian Alps (created by tectonic uplift 770 million years ago), the limestone Allgäuer Alps, or the glaciated Wetterstein/Karwendel Alps (including the Zugspitze at 2962m) and the Berchtesgaden Alps.

Germany has 17 UNESCO Biosphere Reserves, and in the country's south, most occur in Alpine regions, including the Bavarian Forest, the Berchtesgaden Alps and the Swabian Alb.

Titisee Lake (p237)

Forests

The Black Forest straddles the Continental Divide. Waters flowing down off the heights and out from the forest either drain into the north-flowing Rhine, which empties into the North Sea, or into the east-flowing Danube, which empties into the Black Sea. And it's not just the geography that gives the Black Forest its allure – the forest is a storied quilt that includes waterfalls, rolling hills, sparkling lakes, lush vineyards, and oak, pine and beech forests in one mystique-laden package. Not surprisingly, legends have always attached themselves to the Schwarzwald. The Romans found the forest to be so dark and mysterious that they were the first to give it the name. And the wonder of this place became a thing of worldwide renown, thanks to the fairy tales and dark magic of the Brothers Grimm.

The protection of these and other forests is by no means guaranteed. Across the state border in Bavaria, close to 58% of forests are privately owned, and less than one-third is subject to some form of official protection.

Wildlife

Like much of Europe, the story of the south's wildlife is a history of growing human populations and shrinking wildlife numbers, followed by more recent attempts to bring back many of the species that had been lost.

Sometimes that has been a success. Beavers, for example, were once coveted for their pelts and as a food source, and nearly became extinct in the 19th century. Reintroduced in the 1960s, beavers are again thriving – your best chance of seeing them is along the Danube, between Ingolstadt and Kelheim, and its tributaries.

Attempts to rehabilitate other species has been more problematic, especially predators and larger mammals such as the European brown bear. In 2006, a bear nicknamed Bruno crossed the border from Austria and was believed to be the first brown bear to set foot on German soil in 170 years. After much media coverage, Bruno was shot in southern Bavaria after he began feeding on domestic pets and livestock; there is no resident brown bear population in Germany, although individuals occasional turn up.

The Eurasian lynx, a predator that is widespread across central Europe, disappeared from Germany in the 19th century and plans to reintroduce the species have met with fierce opposition from farmers. Occasional sightings in the Bavarian Forest and around Feldberg in the southern Black Forest may be individuals who have crossed the border from a reintroduced population in Czechia's Bohemian Forest.

According to a study by the International Wolf Center *(wolf.org)*, there were around 1600 wolves in Germany in early 2024. Other estimates suggest that this population is growing by an impressive 25% each year. Most wolves are in Germany's northeast, but sightings are increasing in the south. That may change after the German government, under pressure from farmers and the powerful hunting lobby, in 2024 voted in favour of an EU law to downgrade the protection of wolves, making it easier for governments to permit the shooting of wolves to protect livestock. Surprisingly, the move was approved by then-Environment Minister Steffi Lemke, a member of the Green Party.

Berchtesgaden National Park (p154)

Species that you might see in southern Germany include red deer, fox, wild boar, Alpine marmot, wild goat and snow hare. More than 400 bird species have been recorded in southern Germany.

National Parks & the Political Context

Southern Germany has Germany's oldest national park (Bavarian Forest National Park, which was founded in 1970) and its newest (Black Forest National Park, established in Baden-Württemberg in 2014). Of 16 national parks in the country, only one other is in the south: Berchtesgaden National Park on the Austrian border is a ravishing mountainscape of big-shouldered Alps and jewel-coloured, fjordlike lakes.

In addition to the national parks, the Black Forest also has two nature parks, which enjoy a lower degree of environmental protection and are essentially outdoor playgrounds. These are sprawling rural landscapes criss-crossed by roads and dotted with villages. Selective logging (no clear-cutting) and agriculture here is done in a controlled and environmentally friendly fashion.

Behind these statements, however, lies a whole world of complication. Logging companies, two of the state's big political parties, the CDU and the FDP, and many locals opposed the creation of Black Forest National Park. The resulting park was a compromise: at 100 sq km, it's a small area split into two parts roughly 3.5km apart, and represents just 0.7% of Baden-Württemberg's considerable forest cover.

These modern environmental battlegrounds – the creation of national parks, the reintroduction of predators – reflects the small foothold that the Greens hold in Bavaria. At the time of writing, the Greens held just 32 seats in the 203-seat Bavarian parliament after winning 14.4% of the popular vote in the 2023 election. They fared much better in Baden-Württemberg, sweeping one-third of the popular vote and emerging as the largest party in the Landtag with 58 seats out of 154 in 2021. At the time of writing, they formed part of the ruling coalition in the state.

BRANDS & INVENTIONS
OF SOUTHERN GERMANY

From clocks that go cuckoo to snazzy trainers, indestructible trucks to blue jeans, Bavaria has given the world some of its most truly iconic brands. By Marc Di Duca.

THE INHABITANTS OF southern Germany have always been an industrious lot, even centuries before the first M3 trundled off the production line or Röntgen took a rather odd picture of his wife's hand. But the stories behind some of the world's most famous brands and inventions may come as a surprise to many.

Luxury Cars & More

There's only one place to start when it comes to the items southern Germany makes – cars. BMW, Audi, Mercedes and Porsche are all based in the region, their instantly recognisable badges having become synonymous with Germany's postwar economic revival and the country's engineering prowess. BMW is the top name in the Bavarian motoring world and has even branched out into best-selling motorbikes. So successful has the Bayerische Motoren Werke been that the company now owns iconic 'British' brands such as Rolls Royce and Mini. BMW's museum and statement showroom for many constitute the world's top motoring tourist attractions. Audi is a bit of a newcomer to the south, having started life in Saxony. It also has a company museum in Ingolstadt, as does Mercedes in Stuttgart.

Pictured clockwise from top left: Bosch Parkhaus; Playmobil dolls; Röntgen Memorial (p120), Würzburg; Cuckoo clock

But southern Germany doesn't just produce sleek saloons and raunchy roadsters. Bavaria-based MAN is one of the leading makers of lorries while indestructible Unimog trucks can be found across the globe cleaning streets, ploughing snow and providing an on-the-road home for overlanders. While Fendt is a brand of agricultural machinery you will see across central and Eastern Europe, its massive harvesters and balers roaming vast acreages from Kazakhstan to the Alps.

Icons of the Fashion World

Sons of a local shoemaker, Adolf 'Adi' Dassler and brother Rudolf founded a small but innovative sports shoe factory in the small Bavarian town of Herzogenaurach in the 1920s, their greatest joint success coming at the 1936 Berlin Olympics when Jesse Owens famously claimed four gold medals in their trainers as Hitler looked on. A postwar fallout led to the foundation of Germany's two greatest sports shoe brands: Adi's Adidas and Rudolf's Puma. Over the years, Adidas hasn't just dressed the world's youth in three stripes, it has also been at the forefront of sports shoe development, introducing the screw-in boot studs that helped West Germany win the 1954 World Cup and producing some of the road running shoes that are currently on the feet of elite marathon winners across the world.

Buttenheim is a sleepy little place between Bamberg and Forchheim, but this affluent community indirectly gave the world one of its most common items of clothing – jeans. Levi Strauss was born there in 1829 but by mid-century was in San Francisco making a fortune producing workwear during the Gold Rush. In 1873, a Nevada tailor called Davis came up with the idea of adding strength to garments with copper rivets and the Levi Strauss brand was born.

Everyday Objects

Have a Bosch drill, a Siemens fridge or a Stihl chainsaw at home? Then you own something designed and developed (though probably not now made) in Germany's southern states. Skiers will certainly know the Fischer brand, a company founded near Salzburg that makes both downhill and cross-country skis. Some are still manufactured in the region, though most now come off a production line in Mukacheve in Ukraine's west. Playmobil is one of the best-loved play things in the world and a global toy industry success story. The figures were designed in Zirndorf near Nuremberg in the early 1970s by toymaker and carpenter Hans Beck. The company now operates a themed fun park near the original factory that attracts almost a million visitors a year.

Imagine a World Without...

...the X-ray machine, a concept developed by Wilhelm Röntgen in 1895 in Würzburg. You can visit the lab where he worked at Würzburg University – for his efforts he was awarded the first ever Nobel Prize for Physics in 1901. Later, Munich-based Max von Laue built on Röntgen's work with his X-ray crystallography.

The world would come to a virtual standstill without the diesel engine, invented in Augsburg by Rudolf Diesel in the 1890s (making this arguably the greatest case of eponymy since the Earl of Sandwich put his beef cuts between two slices of bread). Despite its polluting effects, Diesel's invention is so efficient that it will certainly see its 200th anniversary.

Who Knew?

The historical industrial output of southern Germany isn't all about big machines and blue jeans. In the mid-18th century someone in the Black Forest had the idea to make a clock whose chime would involve a small wooden bird popping out of a tiny door on the hour – the cuckoo clock was born.

Ever seen footage of the early years of The Beatles? Those odd-shaped guitars Paul and John are strumming are Höfners, made in Bubenreuth, a small town in Bavaria. The Höfners were violin makers in the small Czech town of Luby but were expelled as Sudeten Germans in 1945. They set up shop in Bubenreuth and the rest is Fab Four history. The Sudetendeutsches Museum in Munich has an original Höfner guitar and Paul McCartney still plays his.

Another musical connection emanated from the intriguingly named Fraunhofer Institute for Integrated Circuits in Erlangen where as early as the mid-1980s local boffins were storing music in MP3 format. It's still the file of choice for digital music across the globe.

GERMANY'S BEER PURITY LAW

In Bavaria, where the hills are covered with barley fields and the scent of hops fills the air, a brewing decree was born. By Kat Barber

THE REINHEITSGEBOT (LITERALLY 'purity decree'), known as the Beer Purity Law, emerged as a testament to the artistry and dedication that Germans hold towards their beloved beverage.

In the Middle Ages, beer was more than just a drink – it was sustenance, culture and a cornerstone of communal life. Alongside wine, it was often the safest drinking option, as water commonly carried disease. In an effort to protect the important brew, Wilhelm IV, Duke of Bavaria, decreed in 1516, 'Thou shalt use no other piece than barley, hops, and water for making beer'. This simple statement laid the foundation for the unparalleled purity and quality that has helped German beer gain its reputation, which still holds today.

By creating the law, Duke Wilhelm IV hoped to solve three problems. At the time, bread was a major source of sustenance, so it was essential that barley supplies were protected for bread making. Secondly, brewmasters had started randomly adding a chaotic blend of additives to their brews to disguise the taste of rotten beer that left many people sick, and the essence of brewing under attack. And lastly, he wanted to keep beer affordable. In fact, the majority of the law deals with pricing, and it now falls within a tax code ensuring the government takes a cut of brewer profits.

Over time, the law slowly spread beyond Bavaria and, eventually, Kaiser Wilhelm II made it mandatory for all brewers throughout Germany in 1906. Today it has morphed into more than just a law; it has become a statement of identity and a testament to a nation's dedication to its traditions. Breweries, large and small, continue to uphold its principles, ensuring that each sip of beer is as good as the last. It's this commitment to quality that has made a German beer tour a bucket-list item for beer lovers around the world.

Since 1516, some tweaks have been made to the law. Wheat and yeast, the latter of which was only fully understood in the 19th century, were added, and then barley was replaced with malted grains to give brewers a few more options. Recently, regulators also allowed the use of natural sugar in top-fermented beers. For example, if a brewery brews a lighter beer, it is allowed to add a beer concentrate to make it darker. While this sounds like it goes against the law's principles, it is all above board according to the current *Reinheitsgebot* definition.

There is no mandatory tick of approval, although many breweries do choose to label their beers with the word Reinheitsgebot as a marketing tactic. To keep the industry honest, inspectors regularly visit breweries and take samples for lab testing. Beers with additives such as chocolate or sugar can only be called 'beer mixed drinks'. And in Bavaria, it's not unheard of for beers like milk stouts to be destroyed if they are deemed to be 'misleading' consumers.

Bavaria's Oktoberfest (p31) is easily the most famous beer festival in the world. So are all those five million litres of beer served every year brewed according to the Beer Purity Law? They sure are. The rules dictate that all beers served at Oktoberfest must adhere to this law, and they must be brewed within Munich's city limits.

With beer experimentation on the rise through craft brewing, some brewers are calling for more flexibility in the law. But fifth-generation brewer Michael Miller from Brauerei Schwanen in Ehingen says it's not the law that needs changing, but the approach. 'We have over 70 types of malt, over 300 types of hops, over 150 different types of yeast, and all the different small steps in the brewing process – temperature, time, amount and ratios. So if you can't manage to brew your own unique beer, you shouldn't be a brewer.'

Take, for example, the Weizen (wheat beer), popular in Bavarian breweries such as the world's oldest continuously operating brewery, Weihenstephan. With its bouquet of coriander, clove and banana notes, you would rightly wonder how it's possible to achieve these flavours within the limits of its ingredients.

Lagers such as pilsner, helles and bock are some of the most widely drunk beers. Elsewhere in Germany, distinct beer styles, such Kölsch in Cologne and Rauchbier in Bamberg, are firm favourites. Then you've got the Roggen rye beer, Schwarzbier and Dunkel for lovers of darker styles.

An unfiltered, unpasteurised Kellerbier, such as Zwickelbier and Landbier served in Franconia, is loaded with both subtlety and complexity. On the other hand, Altbiers are favoured in the brewpubs of Düsseldorf, where some of the best top-fermented beers in the world are produced. In fact, there are well over 7000 varieties of beer in Germany, and close to 1300 breweries, with beers as diverse as they are rich in flavours.

Even outside Germany, brewers such as Red Oak Brewery in North Carolina, USA, Rocks Brewing Co in Sydney, Australia, and Namibia Breweries in Windhoek, Namibia, choose to adopt the Beer Purity Law as part of their brewing processes. Some see it as a marketing strategy, others as a surefire way to brew a delicious German-style brew.

The *Reinheitsgebot* is more than just a marketing ploy or a relic of the past – it's a living philosophy. So whether you're taking a sip of a traditional Weissbier in a lively beer hall in Munich or enjoying an ice-cold Stange (narrrow glass) of Kölsch at a pub in Cologne, you're also tasting a piece of history and the collective wisdom of generations. *Prost!*

INDEX

A

accessible travel 282
accommodation 24, 274, *see also* camping *individual locations*
activities 13, 36-7, **38-9**, *see also individual activities*
airports 270
alpine ibexes 256
Alps 18-19, **18-19**, *see also* mountains & rock formations
Alter Simp 63
Altstadt (Esslingen) 221
Altstadt (Munich) 48-59, **50-1**
Altstadt (Nuremberg) 105, **105**
Altstadt (Ravensburg) 257
Altstadt (Salzburg) 191-5, **192-3**
amusement parks
  Abenteuerwald 250
  BMW Welt 275, 291
  Europa-Park 231-2
  Playmobil FunPark 106-7, 275
  Rulantica 231
  Spieleland 257
aquariums
  Sea Life (Konstanz) 252
  Sea Life (Munich) 79
archaeological sites & museums
  Blaubeuren Prehistoric Museum 263
  Jura-Museum 111
  Würzburg 121
architecture
  Bauhaus 217
  Brutalist 217
  Jugendstil 60
  Postmodern 77, 291
art, *see* art galleries, public art, statues, sculptures & monuments
art galleries
  Ahnengallery 54
  Alte Pinakothek 68-9
  Antiquarium 54-5
  Dom Mariä Heimsuchung 135-6
  Glyptothek 70-1
  Haus der Kunst 62
  Kunstareal 68-9
  Kunstbau 71
  Kunstsammlungen 116
  Lenbachhaus 71
  Museum Brandhorst 69
  Museum Moderner Kunst 171
  Pinakothek der Moderne 70
  Rupertinum 190
  Schönheitsgalerie 83
  Staatsgalerie (Füssen) 138
  Staatsgalerie (Stuttgart) 216
  Städtische Gemäldegalerie 138
  Umschreibung 75
ATMs 271
Augsburg 132, 134-7, **135**
  accommodation 177
  food 137
  travel within Augsburg 134
  walking tours 136, **136**
Augustiner Bräustuben 74

B

Baden-Baden 241-4, 289, **242**
  accommodation 266
  beyond Baden-Baden 245-50
  food 243, 244
  travel within Baden-Baden 241
Bad Urach 225
Bad Wildbad 249-50
Bamberg 22, 112-15, **113**
  accommodation 176
  beyond Bamberg 116-17
  food 115
  travel within Bamberg 112
  walking tours 114, **114**, 115
Barbary macaques 254
baseball 37
bathrooms 283
Bavaria 94-177, **96-7**
  accommodation 176-7
  festivals & events 23, 98, 99
  itineraries 18-19, 22-3, 98-9, **18-19**, **22-3**
  navigation 96-7
  tourist offices 151
  travel seasons 98-9
  travel within Bavaria 97
  weather 98-9
Bavarian Forest 172-5, **173**
  accommodation 177
  food 175
  travel within Bavarian Forest 172
Bavarian Riviera 255-6
Bayreuth 23, 117
beer 8-9, 28, 29, 278, 279, 300-1, *see also* Oktoberfest
  Augustiner Bräustübl 184
  Bier & Oktoberfestmuseum 59
  BierSchmecker tour 115
  Franconian 108
  Fränkisches Brauereimuseum 113
  glossary 49
  Reinheitsgebot 108, 237, 300-1
beer festivals
  Cannstatter Wasen 29, 219
  Dachau Folk Festival 74
  Frühlingsfest (Bad Cannstatt) 219
  Frühlingsfest (Munich) 74
  Gäubodenfest 29, 166
  Herbstfest Erding 29, 74
  Oktoberfest 29, 31-3, 72-3, 277
  Munich 74
  Starkbierzeit 29, 74
beer halls & gardens 8-9, 271, 278, 279
  Augustiner Bräustuben 74
  Augustiner Bräustübl 184-5
  Augustiner Keller 66
  Augustiner Stammhaus 56
  Barfüsser 261
  Biergarten im Schlossgarten 217
  Biergarten Muffatwerk 88
  Bräustübl 155
  Chineser Turm 63, 64
  Die Kneipe 80 66
  English Garden 64, 87
  Gaststätte St Bartholomä 152
  Karlshöhe 216, 218
  Hausbrauerei Feierling 229
  Hirschau 64
  Hirschgarten 84
  Hofbräuhaus 49, 52
  Hofbräukeller 87, 89
  Kellerwald 109-10
  Klosterschenke Weltenburg 166
  La Vecchia Masseria 75
  Lechgarten 132
  Löwenbräukeller 66
  Neue Galerie Das MO 167
  Palast der Republik 217
  Park Cafe 66
  Paul Stube 184
  Paul's Biergarten 261
  Posthotel Traube 130
  Roxy Sound Garten 261
  Schlachthof Stuttgart 217
  Schlossberg 229
  Schneider Bräuhaus 56
  Schweinemuseum 220
  Tschechen & Söhne 217
  Viktualienmarkt 57
  WeissbräuHaus 167
  Willibaldsburg 111
  Wirtshaus im Butzental 262
  Wirtshaus Silberwald 262
  Wirtshaus zur Geroldsauer Mühle 248

Wissingers im
   Schlechterbräu 254
Zur Zill 261
Berchtesgaden 19, 152-6, **153**
   accommodation 177
   festivals & events 155
   food 155
   travel within Berchtesgaden 152
Bernau 236
bicycle travel, see cycling
birds
   falcons 204
   storks 246
Black Forest 234-40, **235**
   accommodation 266-7
   drinking 236
   driving tours 248, **248**
   food 235, 238
   travel within the Black Forest 234
Black Forest National Park 239-40
Blaubeuren 262-3
   food 263
Blautopf 262
BMW Plant 81
boar 256
boat travel 272
boat trips
   Danube 164-6
   Forggensee 140-1
   Königssee 152-4
   Lindau 255
   Meersburg 253
   Munich 64, 79
   Zoological Gardens Karlsruhe 246
books 27
   Frankenstein 165
border crossings 270
Brecht, Bertolt 136
Bregenz 256
breweries
   Augustiner 32
   Augustiner Bräustübl 184
   Franconian Switzerland 109
   Hacker-Pschorr 32
   Hofbräu-München 32
   Klosterbräu 115
   Kloster Ettal 150
   Löwenbräu 32
   Paulaner 32
   Spatenbräu 32
bridges
   Augsburger Strasse Bridge 124
   Blackforestline suspension bridge 234
   Doppelbrücke 127
   Greyerswörthbrücke 113
   Häuslesbrücke 261
Marienbrücke 124, 143
Mozartsteg 186
Old Rhine Bridge 252
Ravenna Viaduct 233
Steinerne Brücke 163
Stone Bridge 124
bus travel 272, see also road trips & bus tours
business hours, 283
bushwalking, see hiking

cable cars
   Eibsee-Seilbahn 147
   Jennerbahn am Königssee 154
   Laber-Bergbahn 150
   Pfänderbahn 256
   Schauinslandbahn 232
   Schlossberg 229
   Tegelbergbahn 140
   Untersberg 185, 190
camping 274
   Black Forest 240
car museums
   Audi Factory 167
   Audi Museum Mobile 167
   BMW Experience 80-1
   BMW Museum 81, 275, 291
   BMW Welt 80-1
   Deutsches Museum- Verkehrszentrum 74
   Mercedes-Benz Museum 214, 216, 290
   Porsche Museum 214
car rental 272
car travel 272
   winter 276
cash 271
Casino Baden-Baden 243
castles & palaces 10-11
   Altes Schloss 219
   Burg Hohenwerfen 204
   Burg Hohenzollern 224, 290
   Burg Meersburg 253
   Burg Trausnitz 166
   Eispalast 204
   Festung Hohensalzburg 184, 196
   Festung Marienberg 121, 132
   Fürstbischöfliche Residenz 110
   Hohes Schloss 138
   Kaiserburg 102-3, 289
   Karlsruhe Schloss 245
   Kastell Boiotro 288
   Munich Residenz 54-5, 289
   Neue Residenz (Bamberg) 114
Neues Schloss (Meersburg) 253
Neues Schloss (Stuttgart) 217-18
Residenz (Salzburg) 194-5
Schloss Berg 158
Schloss Ehrenburg 116
Schloss Freisaal 202
Schloss Frohnburg 202
Schloss Harburg 131, 132
Schloss Hellbrunn 195-6, 201
Schloss Herrenchiemsee 157
Schloss Hohenschwangau 132, 143-4
Schloss Hohentübingen 223
Schloss Leopoldskron 185, 189
Schloss Lichtenstein 224
Schloss Linderhof 150-1
Schloss Ludwigsburg 221
Schloss Mirabell 185, 186, 188
Schloss Neuschwanstein 19, 132, 289-90
Schloss Nymphenburg 82
Schloss Solitude 219
Schloss Thurn und Taxis 159
Schloss Weikersheim 124, 132
Veste Coburg 116
Walhalla 164-5
Willibaldsburg 111
Würzburg Residenz 118-19
cathedrals, see churches & cathedrals
caves, see mines & caves
cell phones 270
cemeteries
   Friedhof St Sebastian 186, 190
   Stift St Peter 198
   St-Johannis Cemetery 19, 103
Chiemsee 19, 157-8, **158**
   travel within Chiemsee 157
children, travel with, see family travel
christmas markets 25
   Bamberg 115
   Black Forest 236
   Freudenstadt 247
   Käthe Wohlfahrt Christmas shops 107, 115
   Käthe Wohlfahrt Weihnachtsdorf 127-8
   Munich 58
Nuremberg 101-2
Regensburg 161
Salzburg 195-6
Strasbourg 247
Stuttgart & around 219, 225
Christmas Village 25, 127-8
churches & cathedrals
   All Saints' Church 55
   Asamkirche 52
   Asamkirche Maria de Victoria 167
   Bamberger Dom 114
   Bürgerspitalkirche St Blasius 190
   Cathédrale Notre-Dame 246
   Church of St Coloman 141
   Dom Mariä Heimsuchung 135-6
   Dom St Kilian (Würzburg Cathedral) 120
   Dom St Peter 161
   Dom St Stephan 170
   Eichstätt Dom 110
   Frauenkirche 53, 56
   Frauenwörth Abbey 158
   Freiburger Münster 229
   Gaststätte St Bartholomä 152
   Heilig-Kreuz-Kirche 133
   Hofkirche 119
   Jakobskirche 127
   Johanniskirche 133
   Klosterkirche St Anna im Lehel 89
   Kollegienkirche 186
   Lorenzkirche 105
   Ludwigskirche 63
   Michaelskirche 53
   Münster St Georg 129
   Ost-West Friedenskirche 77
   Pfarrkirche Unsere Liebe Frau 105
   Salzburger Dom 186, 194, 198
   Schottenkirche St Jakob 161
   St Anna Kirche 135
   St Martin Church 167
   St Nikolaikirche 89
   St Peterskirche 52
   St Sebalduskirche 105
   Stadt-pfarrkirche Mariä Himmelfahrt 133
   Stift St Peter 198
   Stille Nacht Kapelle 196
   Theatinerkirche 58-9
   Ulmer Münster 258
   Wieskirche 141
city halls, see Rathäuser
city walls, see fortifications & city walls

climate 24-5
climate change 280-1
Coburg 22, 116-17
composers, *see also* Mozart, Wolfgang Amadeus
　Gruber, Franz Xaver 196, 203-4
　Mohr, Joseph 196, 200, 203-4
　Wagner, Richard 23, 117, 144
concentration camps 90-1, 290
concert halls, *see* theatres & concert halls
convents, *see* monasteries & convents
costs 271
　accommodation 274
　food & drinks 279
　travel 272
credit cards 271
cricket 37
crime 276
cross-country skiing *see* skiing & snowboarding
cuckoo clocks 239
currency 271
Cuvilliés, François de 55
cycle hire
　Munich 88
　Salzburg 189, 202
　Ulm 261
cycling 37, 38-9, **38-9**
　Bad Wildbad 249
　Bavarian Forest National Park 172-3
　Bodensee Radweg 252
　Chiemsee 158
　Danube Cycle Path 264-5
　Danube-Lake Constance cycling path 261
　Freiburg 226
　Munich 88
　Neckar Cycle Path 222
　Nuremberg 106
　Oberschwaben-Allgäu circular 261
　Regensburg 159
　Salzach River 189
　Salzburg 189, 190
　Schauinsland 232
　StadtRadRoute 261
　Ulm 261

Dachau Concentration Camp 90-1, 290
Danube Gorge 165-6
Der Geschichtspfad zum Nationalsozialismus 223
Dinkelsbühl 128-30, **129**
　accommodation 176
　festivals & events 128
　food 128
directions, language 284
disabilities, travellers with, 282
discount cards & passes
　Bodensee Card PLUS 256
　Deutschland-Ticket 273
　DomQuartier 194
　Salzburg Card 187
　SchwarzwaldCard 239
　StuttCard 214
　Top Snow Card 145
documentaries 27
Donaueschingen 264-5
Donauwörth (Romantic Road) 131-2
Donauwörth (Ulm) 265
　food 130
Dreiflusseck 168-9
drinking 278-9, *see also individual locations*
drinks, *see also* beer, water, wine
　Ettaler Klosterlikör 150
　schnapps 249
drinks festivals 29, *see also* beer festivals
driving, *see* car travel, road trips & bus tours 272
Dürer, Albrecht 102-3

Eagle's Nest 155, 290
Eichstätt 110-11
electricity 283
emergencies 283
　language 284
English Garden 64
Esslingen 221-2
　drinking 223
　food 223
Ettal 150
Ettal Monastery 18, 150
Europa-Park 231-2
Europa-Park-Stadium 229
events, *see* festivals & events

Map Pages **000**

Fachwerk, *see* half-timbered buildings
family travel 14, 37, 275
　Muggenbrunn Barefoot Path 240
　Munich 86, 87
　Nuremberg 106-7
　Salzburg 199
　Steinwasen Park 232
Feldberg 237
festivals & events 25, 29, 31-3, *see also* beer festivals
　Africa Festival 25, 121
　Almabtrieb 155
　AlpenTestival 37, 146
　Bregenzer Festspiele 256
　Buttnmandl 155
　Christopher Street Day 219
　Dult 161
　Fasnacht 250
　Hamburger Fischmarkt 219
　Heimatwochen 146
　Hofgarten Wine Festival 121
　Jazz Open 219
　Kinderzeche 128
　Landshuter Hochzeit 167
　Mozart Fest 25, 121
　Munich Pride 57
　Palm Sunday 155
　Ravensburg Spielt 257
　Salzburger Festspiele 25, 197
　Schellenberger Dult 155
　St John's Day 155
　Stocherkahnrennen 224
　Stramu 121
　traditional Alpine 155
　Wagner Festival 23, 25, 117
　Weinfest im Hofgarten 121
　Winedorf 219
films 27, *see also* Sound of Music, The
Filzmoos 205-6
　accommodation 207
Fischerviertel (Ulm) 260-1
food 15, 28-30, 278-9, *see also* Michelin-starred food, *individual locations*
　Black Forest gateau 15, 20, 28, 235, 238
　desserts 29-30
　Mozartkugeln 186, 198
　pastries 29-30
　recipes 27
　Sacher Torte 188
　sausages 15, 28, 29, 30, 52, 107
　Schneeball 15, 35, 127
　seasonal 30
　Spargelzeit 15, 233
　Swabian 222
　Weisswurst 52
football
　FC Nürnberg 107
　SC Freiburg 229
Forchheim 109-10
fortifications & city walls
　Bavaria 133
　Dinkelsbühl 128-9, 133
　Esslinger Burg 222
　Kastell Boiotro 169
　Landsberg am Lech 132-3, 133
　Metzgerturm 260
　Nördlingen 130, 133
　Nuremberg 133
　Porta Praetoria 163
　Regensburg 163
　Rothenburg ob der Tauber 126-7, 133
　Ulm 260
　Veste Oberhaus 171
France 246-7
Franconian Switzerland 110
Frauenau 174-5
Fraueninsel 158
Freiburg 226-30, **227**
　accommodation 266
　beyond Freiburg 231-3
　drinking 229
　food 228, 230
　travel within Freiburg 226
Freudenstadt 247, 248, 249
　accommodation 266
Friedrichshafen 254, 255
Fugger, Jakob 134-5
Fuggerei 134-5
Fünf-seen-Land (Five Lakes District) 158
Fürth 109
Füssen 19, 133, 138-44, **139**
　accommodation 177
　food 141
　travel within Füssen 138

gardens, *see* parks & gardens
Garmisch-Partenkirchen 18, 37, 145-7, **146**
　accommodation 177
　beyond Garmisch-Partenkirchen 148-51
　festivals & events 146
　food 146
　travel within Garmisch-Partenkirchen 145

gay traveller, see LGBTIQ+ travellers
German language 284
glass-making
　Dorotheenhütte 239
　Glasmuseum Passau 170-1
　Glasstrasse 174-5
Glasstrasse 174-5
Glockenbachviertel (Munich) 277
Glockenspiel 49
Grimm Brothers 148-9
guesthouses 274

half-timbered buildings
　Altes Rathaus (Bamberg) 112
　Deutsche Fachwerkstrasse 223
　Dinkelsbühl 128-9
　Esslingen 221-2
　Hexenhäusle 104
　Hotel Elch 176
　Hotel Sankt Nepomuk 176
　Klein Venedig 115
　Petite France, La 246-7
　Pilatushaus 105
　Ravensburg 257
　Rothenburg ob der Tauber 125-7
　Strasbourg 246-7
　Marktplatz (Tauberbischofsheim) 123
　Tübingen 222-3
　Ulm 260-1
　Weib's Brauhaus 128
Hallein 202-3
　accommodation 207
　drinking 202
　food 202
Harburg 131
　accommodation 176
health 276
Hellbrunn 201-2
Herrenchiemsee 19
Herreninsel 157
high ropes, see treetop walkways & high ropes
highlights 8-15
hiking 13, 36-9, **38-9**
　Allerheiligen Wasserfälle 240
　Alpsee 141
　Bad Wildbad 249
　Bavarian Forest National Park 172-3
　Belchensteig 235-6
　Berchtesgaden 154
　Bernauer Hochtal

　Steig 236
　Black Forest 240
　Dachstein Circuit 205
　Filzmoos 204
　Gauchach Gorge Gourmet Trail 240
　Gosaukamm Circuit 206
　Ice Age hiking trail 263
　Käsewanderweg 256
　Königssee 154
　Liechtensteinklamm 206
　Malerwinkelrundweg 154
　Mummelsee to Hornisgrinde 240
　Neuschwanstein Hill 141
　Nonnbergstiege 184
　Oberkircher Brennersteig 249
　Panoramaweg 243-8
　Partnachklamm 37, 145, 275
　Ravennaschlucht 232-3
　Salzburg 190
　Salzburger Almenweg 205
　Salzburgerland 204
　Schauinsland 232
　Sound of Music Trail 204
　Steigl Pass 206
　Stuttgarter Weinwanderweg 219
　Tellsteige trail 121
　Uhrwaldpfad Rohrhardsberg 240
　Ulmer Höhenweg 261
　Wasserfallsteig 37, 225
　Wutachschlucht 233
Hirschgarten 84
Historischer Kunstbunker 105
historic buildings & sites
　Albrecht-Dürer-Haus 103
　Brechthaus 136
　Falkenhaus 120
　Feldherrnhalle 57-8
　Festspielhaus 117
　Fürstbischöfliche Residenz 110
　Grafeneckart 120
　Kepler-Gedächtnishaus 163
　Knights' & Imperial Hall 103
　Königshaus am Schachen 145, 146
　Kurgarten 243
　Kurhaus 243
　Liebfrauenmünster 167
　Maximilianeum 89
　Mittelalterliche Lochgefängnisse 105
　Museum Villa Stuck 88
　Neue Residenz (Bamberg) 114

　Neumünster 120
　Pilatushaus 148
　Plönlein 126
　Sammlung Schack 89
　Schöner Brunnen 105
　Steingasse 200
　Stille Nacht Museum 203
　Trinkhalle 243
　Würzburg Residenz 118-19
history
　1972 Olympics 79
　aviation 254
　Baden-Baden 289
　BMW Welt 291
　Burg Hohenzoller 290
　Cold War 175
　Dachau Concentration Camp 90-1, 290
　Eagle's Nest 290
　history books 27
　Kaiserburg 289
　Kastell Boiotro 288
　Mercedes-Benz Museum 290
　Munich Residence 289
　Oktoberfest 31
　Olympiapark 291
　Reichsparteitagsgelände 290
　Roman 113, 169, 171, 202, 243
　Schloss Neuschwanstein 289-90
　Steingasse 200
　Teutonic 108, 164, 292-4, 298-9
　Thirty Years' War 128
　Weisse Rose Monument 63, 291
　Weltenburg Monastery 288
　WWII 27, 87, 103, 106, 119, 290
　Wyhl 291
Hitler, Adolf see also Nazism
　assassination attempt 217
　Beer Hall Putsch 58
　books about 27
　Eagle's Nest 155, 290
　family (Passau) 171
　headquarters (Berchtesgaden) 156
　imprisonment 58
Hofbräuhaus 49
holidays 283
hostels 274
hot springs, see spas & hot springs

ice skating 195

Ingolstadt 167
　drinking 167
　food 167
insurance 276
internet access 270
inventions 298-9
itineraries 18-23, **18-19**, **21**, **23**, see also individual locations

Jewish history & culture
　Document Neupfarrplatz 162
　Jüdisches Museum (Munich) 53
　Jüdisches Museum Augsburg Schwaben 136
　Jüdisches Museum Franken 109
　Munich 53

Kaethe Krus 132
Karlsruhe 245-6
　accommodation 266
　food 246
Käthe Wohlfahrt Christmas shops 107, 115
Käthe Wohlfahrt Weihnachtsdorf 127-8
kayaking 36
Kelheim 166
kitesurfing 38-9, **38-9**
Klein Venedig 115
Kleine Propyläen 67
Königssee 19, 152-4
Konstanz 251-2, **252**
　accommodation 255, 267
　food 253
Kressbronn 265
Kreuztor 167
Kunstareal 68-9

Lake Constance 251-7
　accommodation 255, 267
　travel around Lake Constance 251
lakes & water bodies 25
　Alpsee 141
　Blautopf 262
　Eibsee 147
　Forggensee 140-1
　Fünf-seen-Land (Five Lakes District) 158
　Kleinhesseloher See 64
　Königssee 19, 152-4

Lake Constance 251-7
Mummelsee 248
Olympiasee 79
Opfinger See 232
Schluchsee 237-8
Starnberger See 18, 158
Titisee 237
Tunisee 232
Waldbad Anif 189, 190
Landsberg am
 Lech 132-3, **133**
 accommodation 177
Landshut 166-7
 food 166
language 27, 284-5
LGBTIQ+ travellers 277
 Christopher Street Day
  219, 277
 Munich Pride 57
libraries
 Stadtbibliothek 216
 Wiblingen Abbey 263-4
Liebfrauenmünster 167
Liechtenstein 252
Liechtensteinklamm 206
Lindau 254-6
 food 254
Little Red Riding Hood
 House 148-9
Lotharpfad 248
Ludwig II 10-11, 27
Ludwig-Maximilians-
 Universität 63
Ludwigsburg 221
 food 222

Mainau Island 252-3
Marienplatz 48-9
markets, *see also*
 Christmas markets
 Viktualienmarkt 57
Max-Morlock-Stadion 107
Meersburg 253-4, 255
measures 283
memorials
 Dachau 91
 Erinnerungsort Olympia-
  Attentat 79
 Kepler
  Gedächtnishaus 163
 Memorium Nuremberg
  Trials 106

Röntgen-
 Gedächtnisstätte 120
Siegestor 63
Stauffenberg
 memorial 217
Walhalla 165
Weisse Rose 63
Memorium Nuremberg
 Trials 106
Metzingen 224-5
Michelin-starred food 28,
 30, 35
 Augsburg 137
 Baden-Baden 243
 Baiersbronn 249
 Berchtesgaden 155
 Dinkelsbühl 128
 Ingolstadt 167
 Konstanz 253
 Munich 53, 62
 Nördlingen 130
 Nuremberg 103
 Salzburg 191
 Werfen 203
mines & caves
 Eiskapelle 37, 152, 154
 Eisriesenwelt 203-4, 206
 Salzbergwerk 154-5
 Swabian Alps 262-3
 Salzwelten 202
mobile phones 270
monasteries & convents
 Capucin abbey 185
 Kloster Andechs 158
 Kloster Ettal 150
 Kloster Lichtenthal 248
 Kloster St Michael 114
 Kloster St Walburga 110-11
 Stift Nonnberg 184, 185,
  198-9
 Stift St Peter 198
 Weltenburg Monastery
  166, 288
 Wiblingen Abbey 263-4
money 271
Monopteros 64
monuments, *see* statues,
 sculptures & monuments
mountain biking,
 see cycling
mountaineering, *see* hiking
mountain huts 274
mountains & rock
 formations 13, 36-7
 Belchen 235-6
 Bischofsmütze 205
 Feldberg 237
 Kapuzinerberg 185
 Liechtensteinklamm 206
 Mönchberg 184
 Mt Grosser Arber 172-3
 Mt Lusen 172
 Mt Merkur 244
 Schlossberg 229

Swabian Alps 262-3
 Untersberg 185, 190
 Zugspitze 147
Mozart, Wolfgang
 Amadeus
 baptism location 194
 childhood 188
 festivals & concerts 121,
  188, 196, 198
 Mozarteum 188
 puppet theatre 137, 200
 walking tour (Salzburg)
  186, **186**
Munich 43-93, **44-5**
 accommodation 92-3
 Altstadt 48-59, **50-1**
 Au 85-91, **86**
 drinking 49, 52, 57, 63, 66,
  73-4, 84
 entertainment 57, 59, 88
 family travel 86, 87
 festivals & events 31-3,
  72-3, 74, 277
 food 52, 53, 56, 59, 62, 75,
  84, 87, 88
 Haidhausen 85-91, **86**
 itineraries 46-7
 Lehel 85-91, **86**
 LGBTIQ+ 57
 Maxvorstadt 65-71, **66**
 navigation 44-5
 Nymphenburg 82-4, **83**
 Olympiapark 76-81, **76**, **78**
 Schwabing 60-4, **61**
 shopping 53, 56-7, 58, 63
 Theresienwiese 72-5, **73**
 tours 59
 travel within Munich 44,
  48, 60, 65, 67, 72, 76,
  82, 85
 walking tours 75, 79,
  89, **89**
 Westend 72-5, **73**
museums 14, 25, *see also*
 archeological sites &
 museums, car museums
 Antikensammlungen 71
 Badisches
  Landesmuseum 245
 Bayerisches
  Eisenbahnmuseum 131
 Bayerisches
  Nationalmuseum 60
 Bier &
  Oktoberfestmuseum 59
 Children & Young
  People's Museum 107
 Christmas Museum 196
 Deutsche Bahn
  Museum 104, 275
 Deutsches Museum 85
 Deutsches
  Weihnachtsmuseum
  128

Document
 Neupfarrplatz 162
Dokumentation
 Obersalzberg 155
Dokumentationszentrum
 106
DomQuartier 194
Domschatzmuseum 110
Dornier Museum 254
Fränkisches
 Brauereimuseum 113
Fürstenbaumuseum 121
Germanisches
 Nationalmuseum 108
Glasmuseum
 (Frauenau) 174
Glasmuseum
 Passau 170-1
Golf Museum 163
Haus der Geschichte 129
Haus der Geschichte
 Baden-
 Württemberg 216
Historisches Museum 114
House of Bavarian
 History 161
Jüdisches Museum
 (Munich) 53
Jüdisches Museum
 Augsburg
 Schwaben 136
Jüdisches Museum
 Franken 109
Kaiserburg Museum 103
Käthe-Kruse-
 Puppenmuseum 132
Keltenmuseum 202-3
Landesmuseum
 Württemberg 219
Mainfränkisches
 Museum 121
Marstallmuseum 84
Maximilianmuseum 136
Mittelalterliches
 Kriminalmuseum 128
Mozarts Geburtshaus 186
Museum Alte
 Kulturen 223
Museum der Bayerischen
 Könige 144
Museum der
 Moderne 184, 190
Museum Frieder
 Burda 243
Museum Fünf
 Kontinente 87
Museum Mensch und
 Natur 84
Museum of the 3rd
 Dimension 130
Museum
 Ravensburger 257
Museumsdorf
 Bayerischer Wald 175

Map Pages **000**

306

Museum Villa Stuck 88
NS Dokuzentrum 65
Oberammergau Museum 149
Richard Wagner Museum 23, 117
RiesKrater Museum 130
Römermuseum 169
School Museum 107
Schwarzwaldmuseum 239
Schweinemuseum 220
Spielzeugmuseum 107
Stadtmauermuseum 131
Stadtmuseum (Nördlingen) 131
Stadtmuseum Fembohaus 105
Stadtpalais 216
State Museum of Egyptian Art 71
Stille Nacht Museum 203
Sudetendeutsches Museum 87
Tauberfränkisches Landschaftsmuseum 123
technology museums 14
Triberg-Fantasy 239
Vineum 254
Vogtsbauernhof Schwarzwälder Freilichtmuseum 239
Waldmuseum 175
Weinbaumuseum 219
Zentrum für Kunst und Medientechnologie 246
Zeppelin Museum 254
music 23, 27, see also composers
concerts 55, 127, 170, 188, 195-8, 256, 258
Mozart Fest 121
opera 117, 197
Silent Nights 196, 200, 203-4
Wagner Festival 23, 25, 117

national parks & reserves 38-9, 297, **38-9**
Bavarian Forest National Park 172-3
Berchtesgaden National Park 152-4
Black Forest National Park 239-40
Nationalpark Schwarzwald, see Black Forest National Park
nature preservation 295-7

nature reserves, see wildlife sanctuaries & nature reserves
Nazism 65, 104-6, 155, 156, 223, see also concentration camps
Neuschwanstein 19, 132, 289-90
nightlife 278-9
Nördlingen 130-1, **130**
accommodation 176
food 130
Nuremberg 22, 100-8, **101**
accommodation 176
beyond Nuremberg 109-11
cycling tours 106
drinking 104, 107
family travel 106-7
food 102, 103, 107
nightlife 107
shopping 107
travel within Nuremberg 100
walking tours 105, 106, **105**
Nuremberg Trials 103

Oberammergau 18, 148-50
accommodation 177
food 150
tours 149-50
Oberkirch 249
Oberndorf 196
Obersalzberg 155, 156
Oktoberfest 29, 31-3, 72-3, 277
accomodation 33
activities 32-3
history 31
practicalities 32-3
Olympiapark 77-9
Olympiastadion 77
opening hours 283
opera
Markgräfliches Opernhaus 117
Salzburger Festspiele 197
outdoor activities 13, 36-7, **38-9**, see also individual activities

Pagodenburg 83
palaces, see castles & palaces
parks & gardens
Alter Botanischer Garten 67
Altmühltal Nature Park 111

English Garden 64
Hofgarten 59, 119
Kurpark 249
Parc de l'Orangerie 246
Schloss Hellbrunn 201-2
Schloss Weikersheim 124
Steinwasen Park 232
Universität Salzburg Botanical Garden 202
Volksgarten 189
Würth Sculpture Garden 191
Zwerglgarten 189
Partnachklamm 18
Passau 168-71, **169**
food 170
travel within Passau 168
Passion Play 149
Perseusbrunnen 54
Pfahlbauten 253
pharmacies 276
planning
clothes 26
etiquette 26, 278-9
Oktoberfest 31-3
Munich, Bavaria & the Black Forest basics 26-7
Romantic Road 34-5
trains 273
plazas, see squares & plazas
public art 191
public holidays 283

Rathäuser
Altes Rathaus (Bamberg) 112
Altes Rathaus (Munich) 49
Altes Rathaus (Nuremberg) 105
Altes Rathaus (Passau) 171
Altes Rathaus (Regensburg) 163
Neues Rathaus (Munich) 48
Rathaus (Blaubeuren) 262
Rathaus (Donauwörth) 132
Rathaus (Freiburg) 229
Rathaus (Lindau) 256
Rathaus (Stuttgart) 217
Rathaus (Tauberbischofsheim) 123
Rathaus (Tübingen) 222

Ravennaschlucht 232-3
Ravensburg 257
recycling 280-1
Regensburg 159-63, **160**
beyond Regensburg 164-7
drinking 162
festivals & events 161
food 161
travel within Regensburg 159
walking tours 163, **163**
Reichsparteitagsgelände 106
Reinheitsgebot 108, 237, 300-1
Residenz, 54-5, 289
responsible travel 280-1
restaurants 15, 278-9, see also Michelin-starred food
ride shares 272
rivers
Danube 159, 164-6, 169, 264-5
Donau 261
Dreiflusseck 168
Dreisam 228, 232
Ilz 169
Inn 169
Neckar 222
Pegnitz 105
Regnitz 112-13
road trips & bus tours, see also itineraries
Black Forest 248, **248**
Deutsche Fachwerkstrasse 223
Romantic Road 123, 131, **123**
Rossfeld Scenic Road 156
rock formations, see mountains & rock formations
Romantic Road 34-5, 122-33, **123**
bus tours 131
castles 132
planning 35
travel along the Romantic Road 122
Romantische Strasse, see Romantic Road
Rothenburg ob der Tauber 124-8, **125**
accommodation 176
food 124, 127
Ruhestein 240
running 36-7
Bavarian Forest National Park 172-3
Munich Marathon 83
Zugspitz Ultratrail 146

S

safe travel 276
Salet 154
Salzburg 182-200
  accommodation 197, 207
  Altstadt 191-5, **192-3**
  beyond Salzburg 201-6
  drinking 185, 187-8
  entertainment 196, 197-8, 198, 200
  family travel 199
  festivals & events 197-8, 200
  food 184, 189, 191, 195, 197, 199
  planning 194
  shopping 195, 198
  tours 187, 188, 191
  travel within Salzburg 182, 187
  walking tours 186, **186**
Salzburg & around 178-207
  accomodation 207
  activities 181
  climate 181
  festivals & events 181
  itineraries 181
  navigation 180
  travel seasons 181
  travel within Salzburg & around 180
  weather 181
Salzburger Festspiele 25, 197
Schauinsland 232
Schiefes Haus 261
Schindler, Oskar 163
Schloss Neuschwanstein 19, 132, 289-90
Schluchsee 237-8
Schönau 154
Schwarzwald, see Black Forest
science 298-9
science experiences 14
scooting 232
sculptures, see statues, sculptures & monuments
Segway tours 188
Shelley, Mary 165
shopping, see also Christmas markets, markets

Map Pages **000**

Outletcity Metzingen 224-5
short-term rentals 274
Siegestor 63
SIM cards 270
skiing & snowboarding 13, 24, 37, 276, **38-9**
  Bavarian Forest 173-4
  Berchtesgaden 154
  Feldberg 237
  Gaisberg 190
  Garmisch-Partenkirchen 146-7
  Grosser Arber 173-4
  Hasenhorn Rodelbahn 235
  Jenner-Königssee 154
  Reit im Winkl 24
  Salzburg 190
  Schauinsland 232
  Tegelberg-Schwangau 140
  Untersberg 190
smoking 283
snowboarding, see skiing & snowboarding
Sound of Music, The 185, 187, 188-9, 199-200, 202, 204-5
spas & hot springs 36
  AlbThermen 225
  Bad Wildbad 249
  Baden-Baden 241-3, 289
  Badenburg 83-4
  Caracalla Spa 241
  Friedrichsbad 241-2
  Keidel Mineral-Thermalbad 232
  Palais Thermal 249
  Vital Therme 249
  Waldsee 265
squares & plazas
  Domplatz 195
  Hauptmarkt 105
  Kapitelplatz 191
  Marienplatz 218
  Marktplatz (Coburg) 116
  Marktplatz (Freiburg) 228
  Marktplatz (Freudenstadt) 247
  Marktplatz (Rothenburg ob der Tauber) 126
  Marktplatz (Tauberbischofsheim) 123
  Mirabellplatz 187
  Mozartplatz 186, 195
  Obstmarkt 114
  Rathausplatz (Augsburg) 136
  Rathausplatz (Passau) 171
  Residenzplatz 194
  Schlossplatz 123

St Bartholomä 152
Stäffele
  Stuttgart 218
Starnberger See 18, 158
statues, sculptures & monuments
  Albrecht Dürer Monument 103
  Bavaria statue 33, 73
  Einstein's Fountain & Monument 261
  Friedensengel 89
  Mozart 186
  Neptunbrunnen 67
  Oskar Schindler Plaque 163
  Pegasus 187
  Prince Albert 116
  Ruhmeshalle 73
  Würth Sculpture Garden 191
Stocherkahnrennen 224
Strasbourg 246-7
  food 247
  walking tours 247
Straubing 166
Stuttgart 214-20, **215**
  accommodation 266
  beyond Stuttgart 221-5
  drinking 216, 217
  festivals & events 219
  food 220
  travel within Stuttgart 214
  walking tours 217, 218, **218**
Stuttgart & the Black Forest 209-67, **210-11**
  accommodation 266-7
  festivals & events 212-13
  itineraries 20-1, 212-13, **21**
  navigation 210-11
  travel seasons 212-13
  travel within Stuttgart & the Black Forest 211
  weather 212-13
surfing 189
sustainabilty 280-1
swimming 13, 37
  Almkanal 189
  Badeparadies Schwarzwald 237
  Freiburg 232
  Freibad Volksgarten 189
  Lake Constance 253
  Müller'sches Volksbad 88
  Waldbad Anif

T

tap water 276
Tauberbischofsheim 122-3
technology 298-9
technology experiences 14
theatres & concert halls

ARGEkultur 196
Augsburger Puppenkiste 137
Cuvilliés-Theater 55, 59
Felsenreitschule 198
Festspielhaus 243
Grosses Festspielhaus 198
Haus für Mozart 198
Jazzit 196
Markgräfliches Opernhaus 117
Münchner Kammerspiele 59
Münchner Marionettentheater 59
Nationaltheater 57
Passion Play 149
Passionstheater 149
Prinzregententheater 88
Residenztheater 59
Rockhouse 196
Salzburger Marionettentheater 199-200
Seebühne 256
Staatstheater am Gärtnerplatz 59
StageBar 196
Theater im Marstall 59
Theresienwiese 31, 72-3
ticks 276
time 283
  language 284
tipping 271
Titisee 237
tobogganing
  Hasenhorn Rodelbahn 235
Todtnau 234-6
toilets 283
towers & viewpoints
  Altes Schloss Hohenbaden 244
  Church of St Coloman 141
  Eugensplatz 216
  Fernsehturm 216
  Florentinerberg 244
  Fremersberg Turm 244
  Grabkapelle auf dem Württemberg 216
  Greyerswörthbrücke 113
  Herzog-Friedrich Turm 249
  Kapuzinerberg 185
  Karlshöhe 216
  Königsblick 154
  Kreuztor 167
  Malerwinkel 154
  Mönchberg 184
  Mt Merkur 244
  Olympiaberg 78
  Olympiaturm 78

Panorama Baden-Baden 244
Perlachturm 136
Rathausturm 127
Ravensburg 257
Röderturm 127
Romantic Road 124
Schelztor 221
Schlossberg 229
Schmalzturm 133
Sinwell Tower 103
Stadtbibliothek 216
Tiergärtnertor 105
train travel 272-3
trains, tourist & scenic 14
  Bayerisches Eisenbahnmuseum 131
  Romantic Road 34-5
  Sommerbergbahn 249
  Zugspitzbahn 147
travelling with kids, see family travel
travel seasons 24-5, see also individual locations
travel to/from Munich, Bavaria & the Black Forest 270-3
travel within Munich, Bavaria & the Black Forest 272
treetop walkways & high ropes
  Abenteuerwald 250
  Action Forest Kletterwald 237
  Baumwimpfelpfad 249-50
  Blackforestline suspension bridge 234
  Wildline 250
trekking, see hiking
Triberg 238-9, **238**
  drinking 238
  food 238
Trödelmarktinsel 105
Tübingen 222-3
  drinking 224
  walking tours 223

Ulm 258-61, **259**
  accommodation 267
  beyond Ulm 262-5
  drinking 261
  food 260
  travel within Ulm 258
UNESCO World Heritage sites
  Altstadt (Salzburg) 191-5, **192-3**
  Baden-Baden 241-4, 289, **242**

Bamberg 112-15, **113**
Bavarian 162
Behaim Globe 108
Markgräfliches Opernhaus 117
Pfahlbauten 253
Regensburg 159-63, **160**
Salzburger Marionettentheater 199-200
Strasbourg 246-7
Swabian caves 262-3
Weissenhof Estate 217
Wieskirche 141
Würzburg Residenz 118-19

Vauban 226
vegetarian & vegan travellers 15, 28-30
viewpoints, see towers & viewpoints
vineyards
  Stuttgart 219, 220
  Weingut Schwarz 219
  Weinmanufaktur Untertürkheim 219
visas 270

Waldsee 265
Walhalla 164-5
walking, see hiking
walking tours
  Augsburg 136, **136**
  Bamberg 114, **114**
  Munich 75, 79, 89, **89**
  Nuremberg 105, 106, **106**
  Regensburg 163, **163**
  Salzburg 186, **186**
  Strasbourg 247
  Stuttgart 217, 218, **218**
  Tübingen 223
  Würzburg 120, **120**
Wangen 265
water, drinking 276
waterfalls
  Allerheiligen Wasserfälle 240
  Bad Urach 225
  Gauchach Gorge 240
  Geroldsauer Wasserfälle 248
  Todtnauer Wasserfall 234
  Triberger Wasserfälle 37, 238-9
water bodies, see lakes & water bodies

water sports, see kitesurfing, surfing, swimming, windsurfing
Way of Human Rights 106
weather 24-5, see also individual locations
weights 283
Weikersheim 123-4
Weissenhof Estate 217
Weisses Bräuhaus 53
Werfen 203-5
  accommodation 207
  food 203
Wiblingen Abbey 263-4
Wiener Platz 89
wildlife 296-7, see also alpine ibexes, Barbary macaques, boar
wildlife sanctuaries & nature reserves
  Affenberg Salem 254
  Alpine Game Park Pfänder 256
windsurfing 13, 38-9, **38-9**
wine 28-30
  Besenwirtschaft 220
  Hofgarten Wine Festival 121
  Stuttgarter Weinwanderweg 219
  Vineum 254
  Wein am Stein 121
  Weinbaumuseum 219
  Winedorf 219
  winemaking 220, 222, 254
Wolfach 239
Würzburg 23, 118-21, 122, **119**
  accommodation 176
  festivals & events 121
  food 119
  travel within Würzburg 118
  walking tours 120, **120**
WWII 27, 87, 103, 106, 119, 290

Zentrum für Kunst und Medientechnologie 246
Zeppelinfeld 106
zeppelins 254
zip lining
  Abenteuerwald 250
zoos
  Mundenhof Tier Park 230
  Spieleland 257
  Zoological Gardens Karlsruhe 246
Zugspitze 18, 37, 147
Zwiesel 174-5

"On a bend in the River Main, the northern terminus of the Romantic Road lies a busy city called Würzburg, known for wines, architecture and a miraculous rise from the ashes of WWII."

ANTHONY HAM

"Geography may have granted Germany a mere narrow strip of the Alps, but the Bavarians certainly know how to use it. Countless ski resorts scour the mountainsides and it would seem locals hike from babyhood."

MARC DI DUCA

FROM LEFT: BORIS STROUJKO/SHUTTERSTOCK, MOREIMAGES/SHUTTERSTOCK

All rights reserved. No part of this publication may be copied, stored in a retrieval system, or transmitted in any form by any means, electronic, mechanical, recording or otherwise, except brief extracts for the purpose of review, and no part of this publication may be sold or hired, without the written permission of the publisher. Lonely Planet and the Lonely Planet logo are trademarks of Lonely Planet and are registered in the US Patent and Trademark Office and in other countries. Lonely Planet does not allow its name or logo to be appropriated by commercial establishments, such as retailers, restaurants or hotels. Please let us know of any misuses: lonelyplanet.com/legal/intellectual-property.

Mapping data sources:
© Lonely Planet
© OpenStreetMap http://openstreetmap.org/copyright

THIS BOOK

The 9th edition of Lonely Planet's Munich, Bavaria & the Black Forest guidebook was written and researched by Marc Di Duca, Kat Barber, Anthony Ham and Kerry Walker. The previous edition was written by Marc Di Duca, Kat Barber and Kerry Walker. This guidebook was produced by the following:

Destination Editor
Sandie Kestell

Coordinating Editor
Gabrielle Innes

Production Editors
Jeremy Toynbee
Martijn Vos

Image Editor
Kat Marsh
Clara Monitto

Cartographer
Valentina Kremenchutskaya

Cover Researcher
Daisy Korpics

Thanks
Sofie Andersen, Natalie Butler, Peterjon Cresswell, Alison Killilea, Anne Mulvaney, Doc O'Connell, Charlotte Orr

Paper in this book is certified against the Forest Stewardship Council™ standards. FSC™ promotes environmentally responsible, socially beneficial and economically viable management of the world's forests.

Published by Lonely Planet Global Limited
CRN 554153
9th edition – Apr 2026
ISBN 978 1 83869 837 9 © Lonely Planet 2026
10 9 8 7 6 5 4 3 2 1
Printed in China

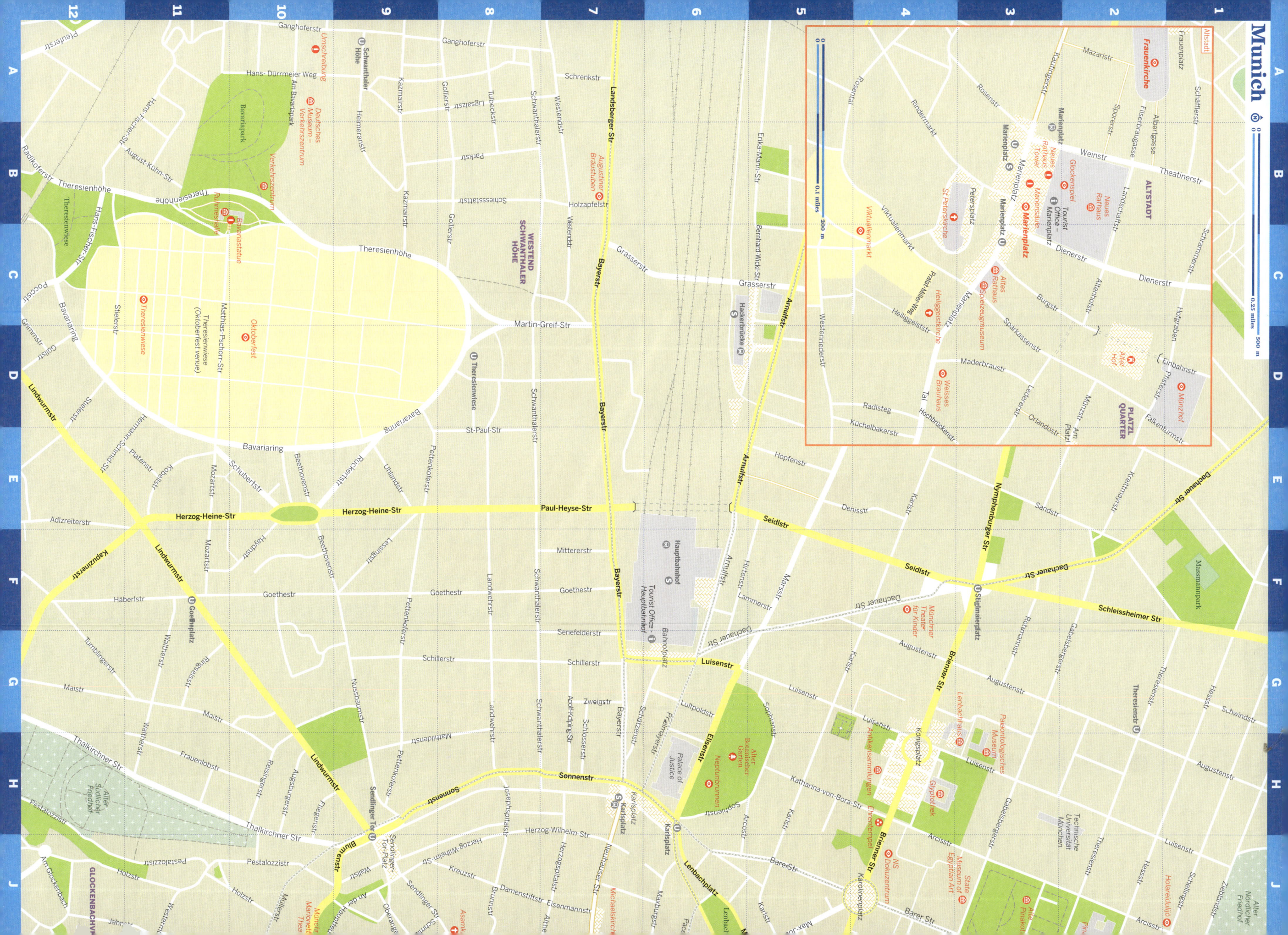

Greater Munich

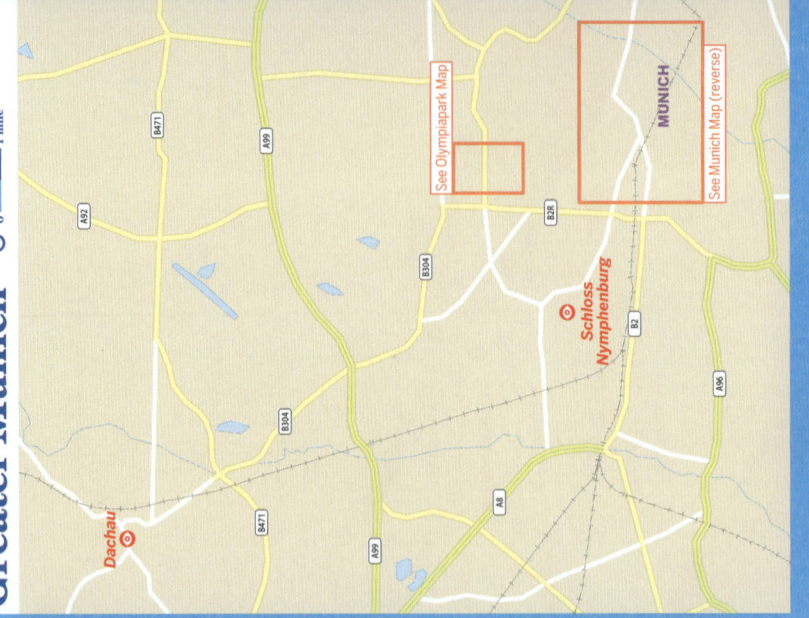

Olympiapark

GETTING AROUND

Munich has excellent public transport with the S-Bahn, the U-Bahn, trams and buses operated by MVV (mvv-muenchen.de) reaching every part of the city. The system is easy to navigate and relatively inexpensive. Other options include a superb network of cycling trails, ride shares or, of course, your own legs, often the best choice in the centre.

S-Bahn
Lines reach out into the suburbs and beyond. All S-Bahn trains follow the Stammstrecke (central line) through central Munich and services run almost 24 hours a day (approximately 4am to 1am). This is the most convenient mode of transport for getting to/from the airport, Dachau and Oberschleissheim.

U-Bahn
The modern underground system serves the city centre almost 24 hours a day. It's good for medium journeys such as to the Olympiapark and Haidhausen.

Tram
Munich's modern trams link the suburbs with the inner suburbs and are good for short and medium-length journeys. This is the best way to reach Nymphenburg and get around without heading underground.

Bike
Munich has one of the best networks of cycle lanes in Europe. Cycle hire is fairly easy to arrange. Bikes can be taken on the S-Bahn but not from 6am to 9am and 4pm to 6pm Monday to Friday (rush hours). All bikes need a ticket. Helmets are not legally required but are of course recommended.

WALK SCHWABING

Centred around the university and the Academy of Fine Arts, this bolthole for 19th- and early-20th-century artists and writers still has a bohemian feel, despite postwar gentrification. Join the students for a bite to eat, peruse vintage-clothes shops and admire the Art Nouveau architecture.

Start Ludwig-Maximilians-Universität
End Wedekind-Platz
Length 3km, 1¾ hours

1 Munich Uni
From morning till dusk the area around Ludwig-Maximilians-Universität bustles with students, many of whom tie up their rattling two-wheelers along Ludwigstrasse. The top attraction for visitors within the uni building is the DenkStätte Weisse Rose.

2 Cafes & Books
Alongside the uni, Schelling-strasse funnels students to various watering and feeding spots. In addition to its many cafes, it's also the location of Words' Worth Books, the city's best English bookstore, and the uni bookshop.

3 Lunch Spot
Running north–south, Amalien-strasse bustles with cafes, delis and restaurants that serve a multitude of cuisines. It's one of the best places for lunch, but gets very busy with hungry students.

4 Shops & Famed Drinking Hole
Make your way over to Türken-strasse, home to interesting shops, including many stocking antiques and vintage clothes. But the highlight here is Alter Simpl, one of Munich's most famous pubs, where Thomas Mann, Hermann Hesse and other Schwabing writers, poets and artists once drank.

5 Neighbourhood Park
Take a break at Leopoldpark, good for children with its large playground. It's a relaxing place to soak up the atmosphere.

6 Literary History
Schwabing becomes more gentrified the further north you stroll, but it wasn't that way when Wassily Kandinsky and Rainer Maria Rilke lived at Nos 36 and 34 respectively on Ainmiller-strasse. Seek out their brass plaques and admire the perfectly renovated Art Nouveau facades.

7 Neo-Renaissance Church
St Ursula's Church on Kaiserplatz is an impressive wedge of neo-Renaissance dating from 1897. The church is 100% original having suffered virtually no bomb damage in WWII.

8 Nightlife Hotspot
The area around Wedekind-Platz is a nightlife hotspot, with bars, cafes and quirky German-language comedy theatres. Look out for the crooked lamp post, the Schwabinger Laterne, once made famous by local chanson singer, Schwabinger Gisela.

HOW MUCH FOR

Adult museum entry €5–8
Central restaurant dinner €50
Double ensuite room €100–150
Cappuccino in a cafe €3–4
Opera ticket €60–100

MONEY

Currency euro (€)

Tipping It is fine just to round the bill up to the nearest €5 or €10 or not tip at all. Tip 10% in restaurants for very good service and round up in bars, pubs, and cafes. Don't leave cash on tables as you leave as this is considered slightly rude (by Bavarian servers at least). It is very unusual to tip hotel staff.

€1 Sundays Nine state-run museums charge only a single euro admission on Sundays. This includes several in the Kunstareal and the Bayerisches Nationalmuseum. However, be aware that this rarely includes special and temporary exhibitions.

Oktoberfest No cash changes hands within the beer tents. To get a beer, buy special metal tokens (Biermarken) from outside the tents. Bring lots of cash.

Sights

Olympiazentrum D2

Sights
BMW Museum D3
BMW Welt C3
Connollystrasse 31 B2
Erinnerungsort Olympia-Attentat B2
Olympia Schwimmhalle B4
Olympiaberg B5
Olympiasee C3
Olympiastadion A4
Olympiaturm C3
Olympic village B1
Ost-West Friedenskirche B5
Rock Museum C3
Sea Life C4

Streets
A Ackermannstr C5
G Georg-Brauchle-Ring A3
L Lerchenauer Str C1
Lillian-Board-Weg B4
R Rudolf-Harbig-Weg B5
S Spiridon-Louis-Ring A3

Water Features
Eisbach Creek P1
Isar L12-S2

Sights

Marienplatz B3
Maximilianeum R8
Michaelskirche K7
Monopteros P2
Monument to the Victims of National Socialism L5
Müller'sches Volksbad P10
Münchner Marionetten Theater K10
Münchner Theater für Kinder F4
Munich Residenz M6
Münzhof D1
Museum Brandhorst L3
Museum Reich der Kristalle K3
Museum Villa Stuck S6
Nationaltheater M6
Neptunbrunnen K2
Neue Pinakothek B2
Neues Rathaus L6
Neues Rathaus Tower B3
NS Dokuzentrum J4
Oktoberfest D10
Paläontologisches Museum H3
Pinakothek der Moderne K3
Residenz M6
Residenzmuseum M6

Ruhmeshalle B11
Sammlung Schack Q5
Siegestor N1
Spielzeugmuseum C3
St Peterskirche B4
Staatliches Museum für Völkerkunde O7
State Museum of Egyptian Art J3
Sudetendeutsches Museum P10
Theatinerkirche L6
Theresienwiese C11
Umschreibung A10
Verkehrszentrum B10
Viktualienmarkt C4
Weisses Brauhaus D4

Parks & Gardens
Alter Nördlicher Friedhof J1
Alter Südlicher Friedhof H12
Bavariapark A10
Englischer Garten P1, P4
Isarlorplatz N5
Lenbachplatz J6
Massmannpark F1
Maximiliananlagen R3, R7

Marienplatz B3, L8
Max-Weber-Platz S8
Neighbourhoods
Altstadt B2, L8
Glockenbachviertel J12
Haidhausen S10
Lehel P6
Maxvorstadt K4
P2, M7
Westend
Schwanthaler Höhe C8

Transportation
Hackerbrücke C6
Hauptbahnhof F6
Isartor N8
Karlsplatz H7
Rosenheimer Platz R11

Sights
Alte Pinakothek J3
Alter Botanischer Garten H6
Alter Hof D2
Alter Simpl L2
Altes Rathaus C3
Antikensammlungen H4
Asamkirche J8
Augustiner Bräustuben B7
Bavariastatue B10
Bayerisches Nationalmuseum Q5

Bier & Oktoberfestmuseum M8
Cuvilliés-Theater M6
DenkStätte Weisse Rose M2
Deutsches Museum N11
Theresienwiese D8
Universität N2

Railway Stations
Hackerbrücke D6
Hauptbahnhof F6
Isartor N8
Karlsplatz H7
Rosenheimer Platz R11

S-Bahn Stations
Hackerbrücke C6
Hauptbahnhof F6
Marienplatz B3, L8
Rosenheimer Platz R11

U-Bahn Stations
Fraunhoferstr L11
Goetheplatz F11
Karlsplatz H6
Lehel P6

Z
Zenneckbrücke O10
Zeppelinstr J1
Zieblandstr J1
Zweibrückenstr H12
Zweigstr G7

Plazas
Am Platz D2, M7
Bahnhofplatz S6
Europaplatz S6
Frauenplatz A1, K7
Gärnerplatzviertel L10
Geschwister-Scholl-Platz M2
Johannisplatz J4
Karlsplatz H7
Königsplatz G4
Max-Joseph-Platz
Odeonsplatz L5
Pauianerplatz O11
Petersplatz B3, L8
Professor-Huber-Platz N2
Rozenheimer Platz R11
Sebastiansplatz K9
St-Anna-Platz O6
St-Jakobs-Platz K9
Thierschplatz P7

Weissenburger Platz R11
Wiener Platz R9

Dienammerstr J9
Hofbräuhaus J3
Hofgarten M5
Holareiduljö J1
Jüdisches Museum K9
Klosterkirche St Anna im Lehel O6
Kulturzentrum Gasteig Q10
Kunstareal K3
Lion Statues M6
Ludwigskirche N3

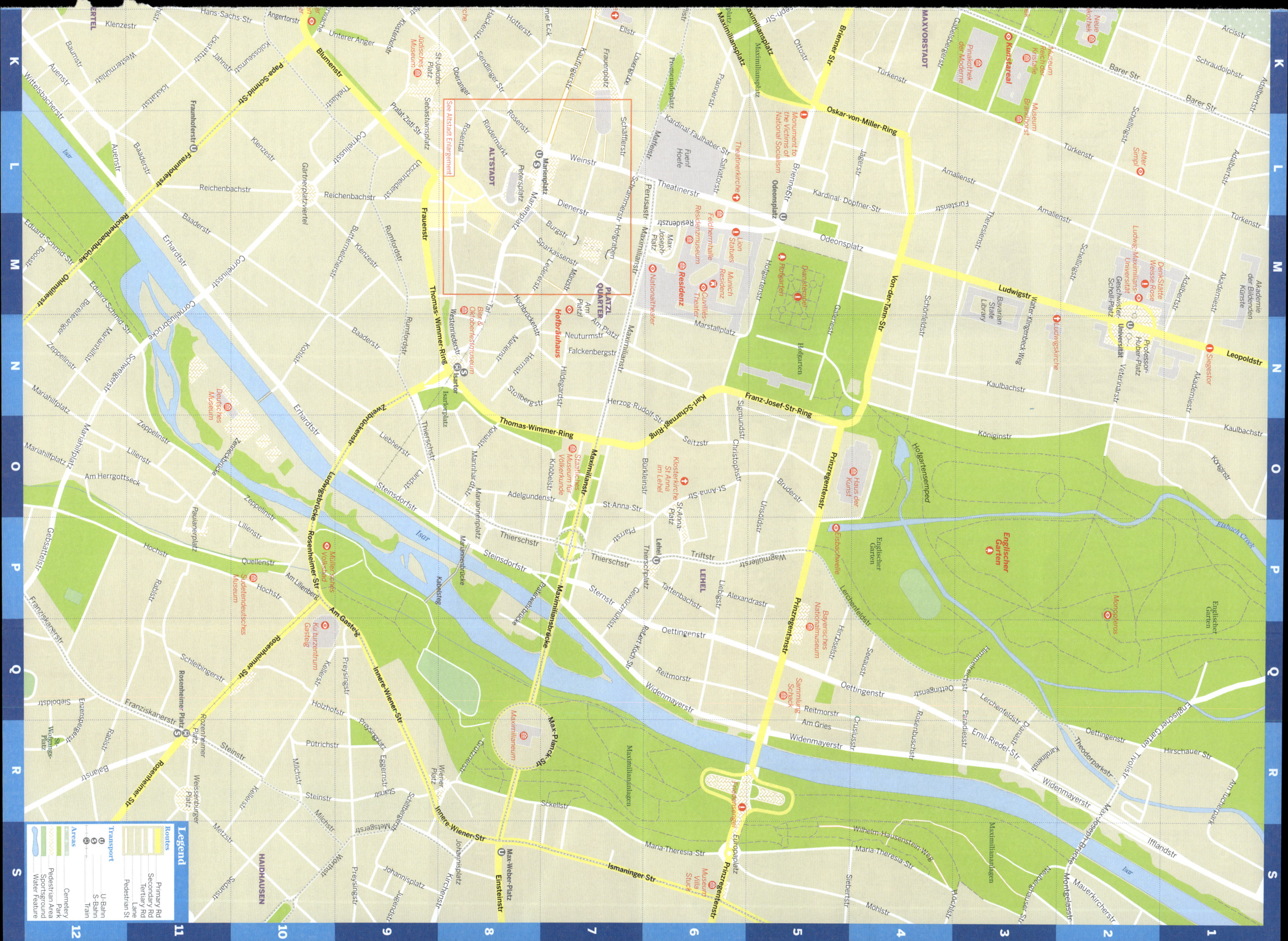

MUNICH CITY MAP

Lonely Planet

lonelyplanet.com

- Must-See Highlights
- Travel Tips
- Walking Tour

NEED TO KNOW

Opening Hours
Shops 9am–8pm Monday–Saturday
Bars 5pm–1am or later
Cafes 8am–8pm
Restaurants 11am–10pm
Supermarkets 8am–7pm Mon–Sat

Key information
Toilets Public toilets are rarely free. Rather irritating SaniFair barriered paid toilets are common. They cost up to €1 and aren't always in the best condition.
Emergency number 112

OUR PICKS

▲ Witness Munich and Bavaria's cultural and historical bull's-eye at the energetic **Marienplatz**, Munich's premier piazza. Munich B3

▲ Immerse yourself in southern Germany's finest art museums in the myriad of institutions at the Munich **Kunstareal**. Munich K3

▲ Admire the architectural styles preferred by a long list of Wittelsbach royals at Munich's top attraction, the **Residenz**. Munich M6

▲ Gaze up at the 100m-high towers of the **Frauenkirche** that dominate Munich's city-centre skyline. Munich A2

▲ Stroll the ornate hallways, chambers and chapels of **Schloss Nymphenburg**, the royal Wittelsbach family's erstwhile summer residence. Greater Munich

▲ Trek the paths and climb the hills of Munich's 1972 **Olympiapark** without parting with a single cent. The view from the Olympiaberg is captivating. Olympiapark C3

▲ Pay your respects and learn the story of the **Dachau Concentration Camp Memorial Site**, the first camp that set the evil standards for all future camps. Greater Munich

▲ Jog, cycle or just stroll the vast meadows of Munich's sprawling city park, **Englischer Garten** (English Garden). Munich P3

▲ Wonder at Bavaria's ability to make cars at the **BMW Museum**, where Elvis' 1950s cabriolet takes pride of place. Olympiapark D3

▲ Marvel at the mothership of all the world's beer halls, the **Hofbräuhaus**, a traditional tavern and tourist attraction rolled into one. Munich M7

MUNICH

Streets

A
Adalbertstr K1–M1
Adelgunderstr O8
Adzreiterstr E12
Adolf-Kolping-Str G7
Akademiestr M1–N1
Albertgasse A2
Alexanderstr P6
Altenhofstr C5
Altheimer Eck J7
Am Bavariapark A10
Am Gasteig P10
Am Glockenbach J12
Am Gries R5
Am Herrgottseck O12
Am Lilienberg P10
Am Platzl N7
Am Tucherpark R1
Amalienstr L3–L4
An der Hauptfeuerwache J9
Angertorstr K10
Arcisstr J2–K1
Arnulfstr C5–F6
Auenstr K12–L12
Augsburgerstr H10
Augustenstr G3–J6

B
August-Kühn-Str B11
Baaderstr L11–N9
Balanstr R12
Barer Str J4–K2
Baumstr K12
Bavariaring C12–E10
Bayerstr C7–G7
Beethovenstr E10–F10
Bereiteranger M12
Bernhard-Wicki-Str C5
Blumenstr J9–K10
Booststr M12
Brienner Str G4–L5
Broderstr O5
Brunnstr J8
Burgstr C3, M7
Bürkleinstr O7
Buttermelcherstr M9

C
Christophstr O6
Corneliusbrücke M11
Corneliusstr L11
Crusiusstr Q4

D
Dachauer Str E1–F5
Damenstiftstr J8
Denisstr E5
Dianastr Q3
Dienerstr C2, L7

E
Eduard-Schmid-Str M12
Eggenstr R9
Einbahnstr D2
Eisenmannstr S8
Eisenstr J7
Elisenstr K7
Ellstr K7
Emil-Riedel-Str R3
Englischer Garten Q1
Enzensbergerstr Q12
Erhardtstr M11–N10
Erika-Mann-Str B5

F
Falckenbergstr N7
Falkenturmstr D2
Fliserbraugasse A2
Fliegenstr H10
Franziskanerstr P12–Q12
Franz-Josef-Str-Ring N6
Frauenlobstr H11
Frauenstr L9
Fraunhoferstr L11
Fürstenstr L3

G
Gabelsbergerstr F2–K4
Galeriestr M5
Gangferstr A6–A10
Gebsattelstr P12
Gewürzmühlstr P7
Goethestr F7–F10
Gollierstr A8–B8
Grasserstr C6–C7
Grimmstr C12
Grützlerstr R8
Güllstr D12

H
Häberlstr F12
Hackenstr J8
Hans-Dürrmeier-Weg A10
Hans-Fischer-Str A11–B12
Hans-Sachs-Str K11
Haydnstr F10
Heiliggeiststr C4
Heimeranstr A9
Hermann-Schmid-Str D11
Hermstr N8
Herzog-Heinrich-Str E9–E11
Herzog-Rudolf-Str N7
Herzogspitalstr J7
Herzog-Wilhelm-Str H8–J8
Hesstr E1–J2
Hildegardstr N7
Himmelreichstr Q5
Hirschauer Str R1
Hirtenstr F6
Hochbrückenstr D4, M8
Höchstr S4
Hochstr P10–P11
Hofgartensemped M5
Hofgartenstr D1
Hofgraben C1, M7
Hofzapfelstr B7
Hofstatt Q10
Holzstr J10–J12
Hopfenstr E5
Hötterstr K8

I
Ickstattstr K11
Iffandstr S2
Innere-Wiener-Str E2
Ismaninger Str S7

J
Jägerstr L4
Landsberger Str A7
Johannisplatz S9
Josephspitalstr H8
Jugendstr S9

K
Kabelsteg P9
Kanalstr O8
Kapuzinerstr F12
Kardinal-Döpfner-Str L5
Kardinal-Faulhaber-Str L6
Karl-Scharnagl-Ring N6
Karlstr E4–J5
Karolinenstr R3
Katharina-von-Bora-Str H5
Kaufingerstr A3–K7
Kaufingerstr N3–O1
Kazmairstr A9–B9
Kellerstr Q10–R10
Kirchenstr S8
Klenzestr K12–M9
Klosterhofstr K9
Knöbelstr O7
Kobellstr N10
Kohlstr N10
Kolosseumstr K10
Königinstr O1–O3
Kreittmayrstr E2
Kreuzstr J8
Küchelbäckerstr D5

L
Lammerstr N6
Landsberger Str A7
Landschaftstr B2
Landstr O9
Landwehrstr D3, M7
Lederrerstr D3, M7
Leopoldstr N1
Lerchenfeldstr N6
Lessingstr F9
Liebherrstr O9
Liebigstr P6
Ligsalzstr A8
Liliensstr O11–P10
Lindwurmstr D12–H10

Löwengrube K7
Ludwigsbrücke O10
Ludwigstr M3
Luitpoldstr G6
Luisenstr G6–J1

M
Maderbraustl D3
Maffeistr L6
Maistr G11–G12
Mamhardtstr O8
Mariahilfplatz N12–O12
Marianhiltstr N12
Mariannenstr O4
Maria-Theresia-Str P8
Marienplatz B3, L8
Marienstr N8
Marstr F5
Marstallstr N6
Martin-Greif-Str D8
Mathildenstr H8
Matthias-Pschorr-Str C11
Maxburgstr J6
Maximilianbrücke P7
Maximiliansplatz J6–K6
Maximilianstr M11
Max-Joseph-Str M7–O7
Max-Joseph-Brücke R2
Max-Planck-Str Q7
Mazarastr A2
Metzgerstr S9
Metzstr S11
Milchstr R10
Mitterstr F7
Möhlstr S4–S6
Montgelasstr S2
Mozartstr E11–F11
Müllerstr J10
Münzstr D2, M7

N
Neuberghauser Str S3
Neuhauser Str J7
Neuturmstr N7
Nussbaumstr G9
Nymphenburger Str G6

O
Oberanger J9–K8
Odeonsplatz M5
Oettingenstr Q6–R2
Ohlmüllerstr M12
Orlandostr C11
Oskar-von-Miller-Ring L5
Ottostr K5

P
Pacellistr J6
Papa-Schmid-Str K10
Paradiesstr Q3
Parkstr B8
Paul-Heyse-Str E7

Penusstr L6
Pestalozzistr H12–J11
Pettenkoferstr Q4
Pfarrstr E9–H9
Pfeuferstr A12
Pfisterstr D1
Platenstr E11
Poccistr C12
Pralat-Miller-Weg C4
Pralat-Zistl-Str K9
Prannerstr K6
Praterwehrbrücke P7
Preysingplatz R9
Preysingstr QP–S9
Prielmayerstr Q6
Prinzregentenstr O5–S6
Pütrichstr R10

Q
Quellenstr P10

R
Rablstr P11–R12
Radlkoferstr B12
Radlsteg D4
Reichenbachbrücke M11
Reichenbachstr L10–L11
Reisingerstr H10
Reitmorstr Q5–Q6
Residenzstr M6
Rindermarkt A4, L8

Ringseistr G11
Robert-Koch-Str Q7
Rosenbuchstr O4
Rosenheimer Str P10–R11
Rosenstr A3, L8
Rosental A4, L8
Rottmannstr F3
Rückertstr E9
Rumfordstr M9–N9

S
Salvatorstr L6
Sandstr E3
Schäfflerstr A1, L7
Schellingstr J1–M2
Schiessstättstr B8
Schillerstr G7–G9
Schilbergstr Q7–Q9
Schleibingerstr Q11
Schleissheimer Str F2
Schlosserstr G7
Schmidstr J9
Schönfeldstr M4
Schrammerstr C1, L7
Schraudolphstr K1
Schubertstr E10
Schwanthalerstr G7
Schwanthalerstr M11
Schweigerstr N11
Schwindstr G1
Sckellstr R7
Seeaustr S11
Seeaust Q4
Seidlstr E5–F4

Seitzstr O6
Sendlinger Str J9–K8
Senefelderstr G7
Seybertstr S5
Siebolstr Q12
Sigmundstr N6
Sophienstr H7–H8
Sophienstr G5–H6
Sparkassenstr C3, M8
Sporerstr A2
Stainstr R9
St-Anna-Str O6–O7
Steinsdorfstr O9–P8
Steinstr R10–R11
Sternstr P7
Stielerstr C12–D12
Stollbergstr N8
St-Paul-Str E8

T
Tattenbachstr P6
Thalkirchner Str H10–H12
Theatinerstr B2–L6
Theklastr R7
Theodorparkstr R2
Theresienhöhe B11–C9
Theresienstr G2–L3
Thierschstr O9–P8
Thomas-Wimmer-Ring M9–O8
Tivolistr R2
Trifstr P6
Tulbeckstr A8

Tumblingerstr G12
Türkenstr K4–M1

U
Uhlandstr E9
Unsöldstr O5
Unterer Anger K10
Utzschneiderstr L9

V
Veterinärstr N2
Viktualienmarkt B4
Von-der-Tann-Str M4

W
Wagmüllerstr P5
Walter-Klingenbeck-Weg M3
Waltherstr G11
Weinstr B2, L7
Westendstr A7–B7
Westenriederstr C5, M8
Westermühlstr J11–K11
Widenmayerstr Q6–R5
Wilhelm-Hausenstein-Weg S4
Wittelsbacherstr K12
Wörthstr S9